ARISTOTLE'S *Politics*

ARISTOTLE'S *Politics*

◎ ◎

Second Edition

TRANSLATED AND WITH
AN INTRODUCTION,
NOTES, AND GLOSSARY BY
CARNES LORD

◎ ◎ ◎ ◎ ◎ ◎ ◎ ◎ ◎ ◎ ◎ ◎ ◎

The University of Chicago Press
CHICAGO AND LONDON

CARNES LORD is professor of military and naval strategy at the Naval War College. He is the author or editor of several books, including *The Modern Prince: What Leaders Need to Know Now*.

The University of Chicago Press, Chicago 60637
The University of Chicago Press, Ltd., London
© 1984, 2013 by The University of Chicago
All rights reserved. Published 2013.
Printed in the United States of America

23   12

ISBN-13: 978-0-226-92183-9 (cloth)
ISBN-13: 978-0-226-92184-6 (paper)
ISBN-13: 978-0-226-92185-3 (e-book)
ISBN-10: 0-226-92183-2 (cloth)
ISBN-10: 0-226-92184-0 (paper)
ISBN-10: 0-226-92185-9 (e-book)

Library of Congress Cataloging-in-Publication Data

Aristotle.
　　[Politics. English. 2013]
　　Aristotle's Politics / translated and with an introduction, notes, and glossary by Carnes Lord. — Second edition.
　　　　pages ; cm
　　Includes bibliographical references and index.
　　ISBN-13: 978-0-226-92183-9 (hardcover : alkaline paper)
　　　　ISBN-13: 978-0-226-92184-6 (paperback : alkaline paper)
　　　　ISBN-13: 978-0-226-92185-3 (e-book)
　　　　ISBN-10: 0-226-92183-2 (hardcover : alkaline paper)   1. Political science—Early works to 1800.   I. Lord, Carnes, translator, writer of added commentary.   II. Title.   III. Title: Politics.
　　JC71.A45L67 2013
　　320.1—dc23

                              2012030592

CONTENTS

INTRODUCTION

To say that Aristotle's *Politics* is a classic work of political thought is to under-state considerably the achievement and significance of this remarkable docu-ment. The *Politics* is a product of that singular moment in the history of the West when traditional modes of thinking in every area were being uprooted by the new mode of thinking that had made its appearance in the Greek world under the name of philosophy. It was in and through the elaboration of a philosophic-scientific approach to natural and human phenomena by the ancient Greeks—above all, by Plato and Aristotle—that the intellec-tual categories of the Western tradition took shape. The significance of Aris-totle's *Politics* lies in the first instance in the fact that it represents the earliest attempt to elaborate a systematic science of politics.

The subject matter of the *Politics* is "politics" in its original sense—the af-fairs of the polis, the classical city-state. The word *polis* cannot be translated by the English "state" or its modern equivalents because *polis* is a term of dis-tinction. It denotes a political form that is equally distant from the primitive tribe and from the civilized monarchic state of the ancient East. The polis, the form of political organization prevailing in the Greek world during its greatest period (roughly the eighth to the third century BC), was an inde-pendent state organized around an urban center and governed typically by formal laws and republican political institutions.[1] It is in important respects

1 · Of the classical city-states of the Greek world (see map, p. xlvii), Athens and Sparta are the best known to contemporary readers, yet in many ways, especially in popu-lation and extent of territory, they were exceptional. Kathleen Freeman, *Greek City-States* (New York, 1950), remains a useful introduction. See, more recently, Hansen 1991, 1993, 1998.

the forerunner, if not the direct ancestor, of the constitutional democracies of the contemporary West.[2]

Politics in its original sense is at once narrower and broader than politics in the contemporary sense. It is narrower in virtue of its association with an essentially republican political order, but broader by the fact that it encompasses aspects of life which are today regarded as both beyond and beneath politics. The *Politics* trespasses on ground that would today be claimed by the disciplines of economics, sociology, and urban planning, as well as by moral philosophy and the theory of education.

Yet the scope and range of the *Politics* represents more than a passive reflection of its historical moment. By exhibiting the complex unity of the elements of human life and the manner of their fulfillment in the polis and the way of life it makes possible, Aristotle provides at once an articulation of the phenomenon of politics in the fullness of its potential and a powerful defense of the dignity of politics and the political life. For this reason above all, the *Politics* is an original and fundamental book — one of those rare books that first defines a permanent human possibility and thereby irrevocably alters the way men understand themselves.

This much may be said at the outset regarding the general character and significance of the work before us. Before entering on a fuller consideration of the *Politics*, it is essential to present some account of Aristotle himself and the age in which he lived and wrote.

I

Aristotle's life is frequently presented as one of virtually uninterrupted devotion to study, with little connection to the great events of the age. To the extent that his well-attested relationship with the rulers of Macedon is acknowledged, it tends to be viewed as a sort of historical curiosity with few implications for Aristotle's own activity. Yet a good case can be made for quite a different interpretation. Although the evidence bearing on Aristotle's life is very incomplete and often conflicting and unreliable, it seems highly likely that he was more active politically on behalf of Macedon, and that his fortunes were more intimately bound up with those of its rulers, than is commonly supposed. At the same time, it appears that the traditional picture of Aristotle as a close associate and admirer of Alexander and his works is, at best, very overdrawn.[3]

2 · See, notably, Ober and Hendrick 1996.

3 · The case has been argued principally by Chroust (1979, 1:83–176). A comprehensive inventory of the evidence may be found in Düring 1957. On Aristotle and Alexander

Aristotle was born in 384 BC in the town of Stagira, in the Chalcidic peninsula of northern Greece. His father, Nicomachus, was court physician to Amyntas III of Macedon, and is said to have become the king's close friend and advisor; hence it would appear that Aristotle was brought up primarily in Macedonia itself. At the age of seventeen, Aristotle was sent to Athens to pursue his education. Most reports indicate that he immediately joined the Platonic Academy, though some evidence suggests that he may have enrolled initially in the rhetorical school of Isocrates, which was then better known throughout the Greek world.[4] He remained in Athens, in close association with Plato, for the next twenty years.

The circumstances of Aristotle's departure for Athens are of some interest. Amyntas III had died in 370/69. His eldest son and successor, Alexander, was murdered shortly thereafter by Amyntas's brother-in-law, Ptolemy of Alorus, thus initiating a dynastic struggle that was only resolved with the accession of Amyntas's younger son, Philip, in 359. It may well be that the dispatch of Aristotle to Athens in 367 had as much to do with the political turbulence at home as with the intrinsic attractions of that great center of culture and learning.

Similar considerations are likely to have played a role in Aristotle's departure from Athens in 348/47. It is usually assumed that Aristotle left the Academy after the death of Plato because of disappointment at the choice of Plato's nephew Speusippus as the new head of that institution rather than himself, and possibly because of sharpening philosophical disagreements with the followers of Plato generally. Another explanation is, however, at least equally plausible. Ten years of Philip's rule had brought internal stability to Macedon, and the beginnings of the aggrandizement of Macedonian power and influence that was shortly to make it the most formidable state in the Greek world. Athens, its traditional interests in the north of Greece menaced by these developments, found itself increasingly at odds with Philip. In the summer of 348, with the capture and sack of Olynthus, the capital of the Chalcidic Federation, Philip succeeded in bringing all of the neighboring Greek cities under his control, in spite of a belated Athenian intervention stimulated by the fiercely anti-Macedonian oratory of Demosthenes. Given

---

see Victor Ehrenberg, *Alexander and the Greeks*, trans. Ruth Fraenkel von Velsen (Oxford, 1938), ch. 3.

4 · See Chroust 1979, 1:96–102. Plato was not actually present in Athens at the time of Aristotle's arrival, returning from his Sicilian journey only in 365/64. The central place of rhetoric in the intellectual preoccupations of Aristotle's early years will be discussed below.

the atmosphere then prevailing in Athens, it would not be surprising if Aristotle had chosen to remove himself from the city. In fact, there is some evidence that Aristotle actually left Athens before the death of Plato; and one account explicitly states that the reason for his departure was that he was "frightened by the execution of Socrates"—that is, by the prospect of a revival of the politically motivated popular hostility to philosophy that had led to the trial and death of Plato's famous teacher at the hands of the Athenians a half century earlier.[5] Some forty years later, during another outburst of anti-Macedonian feeling in Athens, allegations of treasonous activity by Aristotle during the Olynthian crisis could still be used to support a motion to banish all alien philosophers from Athens.[6]

Aristotle's next five years were spent in Asia Minor. Two former members of the Platonic Academy had established a school at Assos in the Troad under the patronage of the local ruler, Hermias of Atarneus; it was here that Aristotle first settled. There is no direct evidence that Philip had begun to contemplate the possibility of an invasion of Asia Minor at this time, but the Atarnian state, which had been created at Persian expense during a period of imperial weakness, was a natural ally and staging area for any such undertaking. Philip soon received Persian exiles at his court in Pella, and when Hermias was captured in 341 thanks to the treachery of a Greek mercenary commander and brought to the Persian capital, the torture to which he was subjected appears to have had the purpose of laying bare the nature of Macedonian intentions in Asia. Given these circumstances, it seems quite possible that Aristotle had a role in forging an understanding of some sort between the two men. There is also evidence that Aristotle traveled to Macedonia prior to going to Assos in connection with the affairs of his native Stagira, which had been captured by Philip in the previous year. It may have been at this time that his relationship with the son of his father's patron was first firmly established.[7] In any event, Aristotle soon became an intimate of Hermias. This remarkable man—a eunuch, by report, who had risen from slavery to become a wealthy businessman before making himself "tyrant" of Atarneus—appears to have shared Aristotle's philosophical interests. The

5 · *II Vita Aristotelis Syriaca* 2–4 (Chroust 1979, 1:117–24).

6 · The orator Demochares, supporting the motion of a certain Sophocles, alleged among other things that letters Aristotle had sent to Macedonia at this juncture were intercepted by the Athenians (Chroust 1979, 1:121–22).

7 · Demetrius, *On Style* 29 = Aristotle, fr. 669 Rose. Aristotle's diplomatic role with respect to Hermias is accepted by J. R. Ellis, *Philip and Macedonian Imperialism* (London, 1976), 97–98. On Hermias's torture and death at Persian hands see further 172–73.

personal attachment of the two men is reflected in Aristotle's marriage to Hermias's niece and adopted daughter, Pythias.

Possibly because of the increasing precariousness of Hermias's position in the face of the revival of Persian power under Artaxerxes Ochus, Aristotle left Assos in 345/44 for nearby Mytilene on the island of Lesbos. Then, in 343/42, he was invited by Philip to take up residence in Macedonia and — according to tradition — undertake the education of his son Alexander, future conqueror of the Persian Empire.

At the time of Aristotle's arrival, Alexander was thirteen years old. Within two years he would be heavily engaged in the affairs of the kingdom as regent during Philip's prolonged absence on campaign in Thrace, and subsequently as one of his commanders in the campaign that culminated in the decisive battle of Chaeronea in central Greece in 338. In view of these circumstances, it is difficult to imagine that Aristotle's influence can have been as decisive in the formation of Alexander's outlook as is often assumed. Moreover, there is reason to wonder whether the traditional account of their relationship can actually be sustained on the basis of the evidence available. That Aristotle acted as Alexander's personal tutor by no means represents the consensus of his biographical tradition, and is not supported by any contemporary sources.[8] As regards philosophical affiliation, it has been persuasively argued that Alexander's political ideas were closer to Cynic cosmopolitanism than to the views of Plato or Aristotle.[9]

The most plausible explanation is that Aristotle was summoned by Philip to establish a school for the education of the sons of the Macedonian gentry, and only secondarily, if at all, for the sake of Alexander. Philip appears to have been concerned to inspire a spirit of unity and loyalty in the fractious nobles of his large and heterogeneous domains. One of his most significant measures to this end was the creation of a body known as the Royal Pages, adolescent sons of the nobility who were brought to Philip's court to prepare them for service to the monarchy and to Philip personally. Though evidence is lacking, it is plausible to imagine that Aristotle was charged with the education — an education in any case centered most probably on literary and rhetorical rather than philosophical subjects — of this select and important group. Among his students may have been the sons of Antipater, the re-

8 · Indeed, there is a competing tradition according to which Alexander's principal tutors were Leonidas, a relative of his mother Olympias, and a certain Lysimachus of Acarnania. See generally Chroust 1979, 1:125–32.

9 · See, for example, W. W. Tarn, *Alexander the Great* (Cambridge, 1948); Ernst Badian, "Alexander the Great and the Unity of Mankind," *Historia* 7 (1958): 425–44.

gent of Macedonia during Aristotle's first several years there as well as subsequently, and Ptolemy, the founder of the Lagid dynasty in Egypt, who was to be an important patron of the Peripatetic school after Aristotle's death. Aristotle evidently formed a close friendship with Antipater during these years, a friendship which seems to have been maintained through a regular correspondence after Aristotle's return to Athens.[10]

The extent of Aristotle's association with Philip himself is not known. Philip was absent from Pella during much of the period of Aristotle's stay. When the king again turned his attention to Greek affairs, however, Aristotle may well have played some advisory role, particularly with respect to Athens. [11] And we shall see that there is some evidence linking Aristotle to the political settlement imposed by Philip on the Greeks under the name of the League of Corinth. If Aristotle did have a hand in facilitating the reconciliation of the Athenians with Philip, it would help to explain his decision to return permanently to the city in 335. In spite of the renewed fighting that followed the assassination of Philip in 336 and Alexander's decidedly less gentle handling of the rebellious Greeks, Aristotle could still count on a store of popular good will sufficient to neutralize at least in part the resentment generated by his long-standing Macedonian associations. It may also be that Aristotle felt less welcome in a Macedonia now dominated by the partisans of Alexander.[12]

The next twelve years, during which Alexander destroyed the Persian Em-

10 · The location of the school appears to have been at a site near the city of Mieza (in the mountains southwest of the capital Pella) known as the Nymphaion (Ellis, 160–62).

11 · One of the Arabic biographies of Aristotle (*IV Vita Aristotelis Arabica* 17–19) records an inscription supposed to have been set up on the Acropolis honoring Aristotle's benefactions, and specifically his intervention with Philip on Athens's behalf. It makes sense to connect this with the circumstances of the Amphissan War of 338 and the aftermath of the battle of Chaeronea, when Philip behaved with great leniency toward defeated Athens (Chroust 1979, 1:133–44).

12 · A crisis in the relationship between Alexander and his father was created by Philip's decision in 337 to contract a new marriage with the Macedonian noblewoman Cleopatra. Although polygamy seems to have been an accepted royal practice, Alexander and his mother, Olympias, apparently saw this step as a threat to his succession. That Olympias was implicated in the assassination of Philip in the year following, as some sources claim, is unlikely, but it is not impossible that the later factional struggle between Olympias and the family of Antipater had its roots in this period, and that Aristotle's close identification with Philip and Antipater had placed him in an awkward position.

pire and extended Macedonian power as far as India and Central Asia, were relatively uneventful ones in Greece. Antipater presided effectively over the settlement of Greek affairs begun by Philip and Alexander. Athens continued as an independent state under a democratic regime, and even enjoyed something of a revival in consequence of the financial and military reforms of Lycurgus, its leading politician; but its foreign policy remained highly circumscribed. It was during this period that Aristotle founded his own school there, the Lyceum, established a program of systematic research and teaching in virtually every area of knowledge, and composed many if not most of the works currently extant under his name.[13]

The relative tranquility of this era was shattered by the death of Alexander in 323. News of this event led to a general anti-Macedonian uprising throughout Greece, in which Athens played a prominent role. A force under the Athenian general Leosthenes defeated Antipater and besieged his army in the town of Lamia; only the arrival of reinforcements from Asia permitted the Macedonians to recover their position. In this atmosphere, Aristotle was indicted on a charge of impiety in connection with the poem he had composed years before honoring Hermias of Atarneus. Remarking that he did not wish Athens to sin a second time against philosophy, Aristotle withdrew to the city of Chalcis on the nearby island of Euboea, where his mother's family owned property and a Macedonian garrison offered protection. He died there in 322. In the year following, Antipater brought the Lamian War to a close with the forced surrender of Athens, the suppression of its democratic regime, and the installation of Macedonian troops in the fort of Munychia.

The *Politics* itself is singularly uninformative concerning Aristotle's view of Macedon and the two men who were responsible for its rise to greatness. In spite of the wealth of detail he provides on the political events and circumstances of the Greece of his day, Aristotle refers explicitly only once to Philip, and never to Alexander, although the reference to Philip in book 5 as already dead indicates that Alexander must have attained considerable prominence by the time the *Politics* was written. There is one passage, however, which is of great interest in this connection. In the course of a discussion of the relative rarity of the regime based on the "middling" element in a city as distinct from the rich or poor, Aristotle notes that "those who have achieved leadership in Greece" (he appears to think of Athens and Sparta) have looked only

---

13 · For useful historical background relating to the Lyceum, see J. P. Lynch, *Aristotle's School* (Berkeley, 1972).

to their own regimes and established democracies or oligarchies, with the result that the middling regime has come into being infrequently if at all. He then adds: "For of those who have previously held leadership, one man alone was persuaded to provide for this sort of arrangement, whereas the custom is established now even among those in the cities not to want equality, but either to seek rule or endure domination." In spite of the absence of a learned consensus as to the identity of the individual in question, consideration of the context of the reference and the absence of plausible alternatives can leave little doubt, I believe, that Philip is meant. Philip was officially designated "leader" (*hēgemōn*) in his capacity as head of the League of Corinth, and the constitution of the League contained measures that were designed to moderate the struggle of rich and poor within member cities.[14]

If this interpretation is correct, the implications are considerable. It would appear that Aristotle looked with some sympathy on the quasi-federal League of Corinth, and regarded the Macedonian hegemony in Greece not as a necessary evil but as a potential instrument for remedying the historic defects of the domestic politics of the cities. Accordingly, there is reason to suppose that Aristotle would have welcomed in principle the restricted democracy imposed on Athens, first by Antipater in 321 and then by Demetrius of Phaleron—a politician schooled in Aristotle's Lyceum—in the name of Antipater's son Cassander in 317.[15]

Does Aristotle's apparent closeness to Philip and his views also mean that he approved the tendency of Philip's foreign policy, in particular his projects of conquest in the East? To what extent can he be supposed to have favored

14 · *Pol.* 4.11.1296a32–b2. The seemingly pointed use of the word "persuaded" in this context might be intended to suggest some involvement in the matter by Aristotle himself. Various figures prominent in the domestic politics of the Greek cities have been suggested (notably, the Athenian politician Theramenes; see for example Newman, 1:470–71), but the context almost certainly refers to interstate relations. Particularly revealing is the phrase "now even among those in the cities," the contrast apparently being between contemporary Greek politicians, their older counterparts, and leaders from outside the world of the polis, i.e. Philip. The identification has been made by Wilhelm Oncken, *Die Staatslehre des Aristoteles* (Leipzig, 1875, 2:267), and Maurice Defourny, *Aristote: Études sur la politique* (Paris, 1932, 534 ff.). The terms of the peace agreed to at the Congress of Corinth in 338/37 appear from [Demosthenes] 17.15; see the account of Ellis, 204–8. Cities were enjoined from actions such as unlawful executions or banishments, confiscation of property, dispersal of land, cancellation of debts, or emancipation of slaves, where these things might endanger the existing regime.
15 · For Demetrius see W. W. Fortenbaugh and Eckard Schütrumpf, eds., *Demetrius of Phalerum* (New Brunswick, NJ: 2000).

the growth of Macedonian imperialism? When Aristotle remarks, in book 7 of the *Politics*, that the Greek nation has the capacity to rule all men "if it should unite in a single regime,"[16] he has been frequently understood as endorsing both the political integration of Greece under Macedonian leadership and Alexander's war of conquest against the Persian Empire. A similar meaning is often found in the advice Aristotle is said to have given Alexander to treat the Greeks "after the fashion of a leader but the barbarians after the fashion of a master, demonstrating concern for the former as friends and kin, but behaving toward the latter as toward animals or plants."[17] Apart from the very questionable authenticity of this citation, the evidence of the *Politics* hardly bears out the notion that Aristotle supported the conquest and subjugation of foreign peoples as a principle of policy. Indeed, he is explicitly critical of such a view of international behavior, and is at pains to distinguish between the legitimate use of military force for the acquisition and maintenance of "hegemony" and its illegitimate use for unprovoked conquest.[18] As regards the "chauvinism" with which Aristotle is regularly taxed, it must be noted that he has high praise for the accomplishments of the Carthaginians, a conspicuous example of a non-Greek yet polis-dwelling people. That so-called barbarians and slaves were indistinguishable for him, as is sometimes asserted on the basis of several remarks in the *Politics*, cannot be seriously maintained.[19]

This is by no means to argue that Aristotle was indifferent to the Persian threat to Greece or unsympathetic to Philip's efforts to counter it. There is, however, a considerable difference between eliminating or diminishing the Persian presence in Asia Minor and overthrowing the entire Persian Empire. When Isocrates, in his exhortation to Philip to turn his energies against Persia, canvassed the strategic possibilities available to the king, he identified three: the conquest of the entire empire, the detachment of Asia Minor "from Cilicia to Sinope," and the liberation of the Greek cities of the coast.

---

16 · *Pol.* 7.7.1327b32–33.

17 · Plutarch, *On the Fortune of Alexander* 1.6 = Aristotle, fr. 658 Rose. See, for example, Oncken, 2.287 ff.; Defourny, 488, 494–95, 527–45; and Hans Kelsen, "The Philosophy of Aristotle and the Hellenic-Macedonian Policy," *Ethics* 48 (1937): 1 ff.

18 · *Pol.* 7.2–3, 14–15 (particularly 1338b38–34a2). For a full discussion of these passages, see Lord 1982, 189–96.

19 · Aristotle makes clear, for example, that at least certain barbarians are abundantly endowed with a psychological disposition that leads them to desire freedom from foreign domination and even rule over others (*Pol.* 7.2.1324b5–22, 7.1327b23–27). Carthage is discussed in 2.1.

After the battle of Issus in 333, the Persian king Darius twice offered Alexander a settlement essentially corresponding to the second of these options. Alexander was urged to accept the offer by his senior commander, Parmenion, who appears to have been intimately involved in Philip's planning of the enterprise, and this may well be reflective of his original intention.[20]

As regards the relationship between Macedon and Greece proper, there is good evidence that Philip was committed to a genuinely hegemonial rather than an imperial role with respect to the Greek cities, though it must be admitted that strategic considerations had somewhat eroded this distinction even in his own lifetime. By contrast, it is clear that Alexander became increasingly disinclined to treat Greece or Greeks on a privileged basis, whether out of a high-minded devotion to Cynic principles or a fascination with the trappings of oriental despotism. Alexander's execution of Aristotle's nephew Callisthenes in 328 for his refusal to do obeisance in Persian style, a pathological symptom of this development, permanently poisoned the relationship between Alexander and the Peripatetic school;[21] but it should not be assumed to have been the governing factor in Aristotle's view of Alexander. Unsatisfactory as the evidence is, it seems relatively safe to suppose that Aristotle was personally and politically closer to Philip from the beginning than to his extraordinary son.

II

Interpretation of the *Politics* is significantly complicated by a tangle of questions concerning the character and composition of this work and of Aristotle's writings generally. The interpretation of any work of political theory must depend importantly on one's view of the kind of work it is and the audience for which it was composed, or what may be called the literary character of the work in a broad sense. Is the *Politics* a finished book composed with at least ordinary care? Or is it an accretion of notes used by Aristotle as the basis of a course of lectures? Is the *Politics* a theoretical treatise addressed only to advanced students within Aristotle's school? Or is it addressed rather to a wider audience whose concerns are predominantly practical ones? These questions continue to elude easy resolution.

In the second place, the specific difficulties posed by the text of the *Politics* continue to be regarded by some as convincing evidence of a lack of unity

20 · I follow here the account of Ellis, 227–34.

21 · See Philip Merlan, "Isocrates, Aristotle and Alexander the Great," *Historia* 3 (1954–55), 78–81; Chroust 1979, 1:83–91.

or coherence in the work as a whole. According to the very influential view originated in the early decades of the twentieth century by Werner Jaeger, the *Politics* is essentially an amalgam of two separate treatises or collections of treatises written at different times and embodying different and conflicting approaches to the study of political phenomena. Jaeger's view, and the interpretation of Aristotle's intellectual development on which it rests, amounts in effect to a denial of the very existence of Aristotelian political theory as a single and self-consistent body of thought.[22]

The corpus of writings that has come down to us under the name of Aristotle represents only a portion of his original output. According to evidence supplied by various ancient sources and confirmed by references in the extant writings themselves, Aristotle's works fall into two broad categories: finished literary productions intended for circulation or use with a general audience, and a variety of more specialized works intended to support the research and teaching activities of the Lyceum. To the first category belong dialogues and treatises dealing primarily with moral, political, and literary subjects. Some or all of these writings are generally supposed to be identical with the so-called exoteric discourses (*hoi exōterikoi logoi*) cited on a number of occasions in the extant treatises. With the exception of a treatise in defense of philosophy—the *Protrepticus*—which has been reconstructed in substantial part from later ancient sources,[23] these works have been largely though not entirely lost. To the second category belong a series of "catalogues" or compilations of historical and other information, and a large number of more or less elaborate and finished treatises on all subjects. Apart from a study of Athenian constitutional history discovered in the late nineteenth century, and generally assumed to form part of the massive catalogue of "constitutions" (*politeiai*) put together by Aristotle and his students (whether Aristotle himself can be considered the author of this work is not certain), most of this material has also been lost. The Aristotelian corpus as it exists today consists overwhelmingly, then, of the specialized treatises. What is the character of these works?

It is generally agreed that the specialized treatises were not intended to be "books" in the contemporary meaning of that term, but rather were connected in some way with the educational activities of the Lyceum. The precise nature of this connection, however, remains uncertain. It is often as-

22 · Werner Jaeger, *Aristoteles: Grundlegung einer Geschichte seiner Entwicklung* (Berlin, 1921); see Jaeger 1948.
23 · Ingemar Düring, *Aristotle's Protrepticus: An Attempt at Reconstruction* (see bibliography).

sumed that the treatises are notes or outlines that were intended to serve as the basis for "lectures" given by Aristotle to students in the school. In the ancient library catalogues of the writings of Aristotle and other members of the Peripatos, there are a few entries which expressly mention "notes" (*hypomnēmata*) or "course of lectures" (*akroasis*), but for the most part only the title or subject matter of a work is given.[24] Of all the works appearing in the catalogues, only the *Politics* is invariably described as a "course of lectures," but it is not clear what inference is to be drawn from this. In any case, it makes sense to suppose that the treatises served also, or even primarily, as reference works which were treated to some extent as the common property of the school and were available for the use of students. The dense and carefully argued nature of these texts in any case makes it hard to believe that they were intended to be digested by students on an oral reading.

The fact that the specialized treatises appear to be distinguished by Aristotle from the "exoteric discourses" mentioned above has suggested to some interpreters that the former were intended only for the private use of students of the Lyceum. According to an extreme version of this view that acquired currency in late antiquity, the specialized treatises are deliberately written in a crabbed and obscure style in order to make them unintelligible to all but those who had been personally instructed by Aristotle or his associates.[25] Yet the term "esoteric" is never used by Aristotle or any early Peripatetic, and there is no contemporary evidence to support the notion that the specialized treatises contain a secret doctrine as such, or that there were significant differences between the doctrine of the specialized treatises and the more popular works.[26] Nor, for that matter, is there any real evidence that the lectures given by Aristotle based on the former were always restricted to members of the Lyceum. According to one account, Aristotle regularly lectured to students of the Lyceum in the morning, while in the afternoon he would give lectures for a public audience. But even if this story were true (the

24 · The lists also contain works that were probably not used for lecture purposes—in addition to the catalogue materials, collections of "theses" for training in dialectic and rhetoric and of "problems" reflecting the results of advanced research in various fields; it is sometimes difficult to distinguish these works as listed from the specialized treatises. The lists have been analyzed exhaustively by Paul Moraux, *Les listes anciennes des ouvrages d'Aristote* (Louvain, 1951), and Düring 1957; see also the extended discussion in Lord 1986. Texts of the catalogues may be found in Düring, 41–50, 83–89, 221–31, as well as in Rose's edition of the fragments of Aristotle (see bibliography), 1–22.

25 · Aulus Gellius 20.5, Plutarch, *Alexander* 7, Clement of Alexandria, *Stromata* 5.9.

26 · See George Boas, "Ancient Testimony to Secret Writing," *Philosophical Review* 62 (1953): 79–92; Düring 1957, 432–43.

source is in fact highly suspect),[27] it would not prove that Aristotle's "exoteric" lectures were based only on the "exoteric discourses" and not at all on the specialized treatises.

But whatever the situation with respect to the other specialized treatises, a good case can be made that the *Politics*, together with the closely linked ethical writings, was intended for an audience not limited to students of the Lyceum. That the *Politics* alone is consistently described in the ancient catalogues as a "course of lectures" may indicate that the work enjoyed a special and more public status. The assumption that the *Nicomachean Ethics* was intended for a wider audience is very helpful in explaining Aristotle's otherwise curious insistence that the subject of ethics is not one that can be profitably taught to the young. More importantly, the fact that Aristotle's ethical and political writings generally are expressly distinguished by a concern to benefit action or practice (*praxis*) rather than simply to advance knowledge strongly suggests that their intended effect was conceived as reaching beyond the confines of the school.[28] Generally speaking, the ethical and political writings appear to be addressed less to philosophers or students of philosophy than to educated and leisured men who are active in politics and actual or potential wielders of political power.

Such a view of the character of the *Politics* is supported by the evidence of Aristotle's own political involvement, and by what little is known of his early intellectual activity. One of the earliest of Aristotle's writings was a dialogue on rhetoric, and Aristotle is said to have given lectures on or instruction in rhetoric during the time of his association with Plato's Academy. According to one account, it seems that Aristotle undertook to teach rhetoric out of dissatisfaction with the education offered in the school of Isocrates, the most prominent rhetorician of the day, and that he did so in connection with an education in "political science" (*politikē*) designed to prepare students for a life of active participation if not a career in politics.[29] That Aristotle may

---

27 · Aulus Gellius 20.5.

28 · *Eth. Nic.* 1.2.1094a18–28, 9.1099b29–32, 10.9.1179a35–b4; *Eth. Eud.* 1.5.1216b11–25.

29 · Philodemus, *On Rhetoric* (*Volumina Rhetorica* 2.50–63 Sudhaus); see Düring 1957, 299–311; Chroust 1979, 1:105–16. According to Philodemus (an Epicurean philosopher hostile to the Peripatos), who seems to be paraphrasing a lost Aristotelian work either directly or as reported in an earlier polemical writing (perhaps the treatise *Against Aristotle* by Isocrates's student Cephisodorus), Aristotle taught that "political science is part of philosophy" and spoke of the differences between it and rhetoric (50–51), encouraging the study of political science on the grounds that too early an involvement in political activity would cut one off from "purer pursuits," while the pursuit of theoretical

actually have enrolled in the school of Isocrates on his arrival in Athens as a young man was mentioned earlier. But it may also be the case that Aristotle's early interest in rhetoric reflected dissatisfaction not only with Isocrates but with the school of Plato as well. If Isocrates's teaching was uninformed by genuine philosophy, Aristotle may have considered the Academy itself insufficiently concerned with the presentation of political skill or knowledge in a form capable of being assimilated and used by political men.[30]

The character and composition of the *Politics* cannot be adequately discussed without some consideration of the vexed question of the early history of the Aristotelian corpus. According to the famous tale recounted by Strabo and Plutarch,[31] Aristotle's library, following the death of Theophrastus, his successor as head of the Lyceum, was willed to a certain Neleus, who removed it from Athens to the town of Scepsis in Asia Minor. There it was hidden in a cellar by Neleus's heirs, then neglected and virtually forgotten until the beginning of the first century BC. After its rediscovery it found its way to Rome and was eventually acquired by a certain Andronicus, who undertook to bring order to the entire collection and produce definitive editions of Aristotle's surviving works. This story, at least in its main outlines, has been widely accepted as providing the most plausible explanation for the rapid eclipse of the Peripatetic school after the middle of the third century, and its later sudden revival. Other evidence seems to confirm that Andronicus's editorial interventions may have been fairly wide-ranging. Some scholars believe he may have been responsible for constituting some of the longer treatises of the corpus as we know it from a number of shorter and perhaps only loosely related works.

The implications of all this are potentially enormous. If the works of Aristotle existed in Roman times only in a disordered, unedited, and very likely physically damaged form, and were then subjected to substantial editing and reorganization on principles that today can only be guessed, the likelihood that the texts of the specialized treatises as we have them today are essentially

---

knowledge would not provide a basis for "engaging in politics, bringing an end to disorder and establishing a decent regime unless after a very long time" (60–61).

30 · For Aristotle's view of rhetoric and his relationship to the Platonic critique of rhetoric, see Lord 1981, 326–39. Even in the *Protrepticus*, an early work praising the philosophic life after the manner of Plato, Aristotle is at pains to show that "theoretical wisdom" is directly beneficial to human life and to political life in particular. *Protr.* frs. B46–B51 Düring.

31 · Strabo 13.1.54 and 4.2; Plutarch, *Sulla* 26.

as they were in Aristotle's own time seems small. But how credible is the story of the missing corpus? In fact, the consensus of recent research seems to be that in fundamental respects it is implausible and misleading.[32] The condition of most surviving Aristotelian texts does not support the hypothesis that they suffered substantial physical damage or drastic editing by later hands. Moreover, there is strong evidence that many of the specialized treatises were known and enjoyed some circulation outside the Peripatetic school during the period when they are supposed to have languished at Scepsis. Furthermore, a good case can be made that the definitive edition of the Aristotelian corpus was produced by Andronicus not at Rome in the years 40–20 BC, as implied in the traditional account, but at Athens perhaps some fifty years earlier. While very little is known with certainty of him, there is reason to believe that Andronicus was himself head of the Lyceum in that period, and hence might naturally have been occupied in assembling scattered writings of the founders of the school with a view to producing a new edition.

The chief evidence for the condition of the Aristotelian writings in antiquity is supplied by the library catalogues preserved in several biographies of Aristotle surviving from late Roman times. One of these clearly presupposes the edition of Andronicus, while the other two are now generally agreed to derive from an earlier source, probably from the last quarter of the third century BC.[33] Of all the major Aristotelian works, the *Metaphysics* and the *Politics* have been particularly singled out as evidence of Andronicus's editorial intervention. It is one of the oddities of the catalogues, however, that both works are cited under their present titles in at least one of the older lists. The case of the *Politics* is particularly striking. Almost alone among the major works, the *Politics* is cited by name and assigned the correct number of books in all of the ancient lists. There must be a strong presumption, therefore, that this work existed in something approaching its present form prior to the edition of Andronicus, if not during the lifetime of Aristotle himself. It is of considerable interest that our *Politics* is characterized in one of the older lists as "a course of lectures on politics like that of Theophrastus." Aristotle's successor was the author of a *Politics* (*politika*) in six books, now lost. The natural inference is that Aristotle's treatise was at this time less familiar

32 · See the authoritative account of Paul Moraux, *Der Aristotelismus bei den Griechen* (Berlin, 1973), 1:3–94.
33 · Moraux, *Listes*, 221–47. Moraux identified the source as Ariston, scholar of the Athenian Peripatos at the end of the third century, but other scholars continue to favor the Alexandrian librarian Hermippus (cf. Moraux, *Aristotelismus*, 4–5).

to the author of the catalogue than the similar work of Theophrastus, probably because it no longer had an active place in the school's teaching curriculum; at the same time, it was not an unknown quantity.

Discussion of the composition of the *Politics* and its early history was dominated throughout much of the twentieth century by the interpretation of Aristotle's intellectual development pioneered by Werner Jaeger. This interpretation rests largely on the view that the key to understanding Aristotle's thought lies in Aristotle's progressive estrangement from the doctrines and approach characteristic of the Platonic Academy in which he had been trained. As originally formulated by Jaeger, this view drew a considerable part of its power from the explanations it seemed to provide of the compositional problems connected with Aristotle's ethical and political writings. The *Eudemian Ethics*, formerly regarded by many as the work of Aristotle's student Eudemus of Rhodes, was now revealed as an early, "Platonizing" work of Aristotle himself. This could plausibly explain, among other things, the appearance of three books of the *Nicomachean Ethics* (5–7) in manuscripts of the *Eudemian Ethics*, as well as anomalies within the former work itself. As for the *Politics*, Jaeger was able to argue that the textual and interpretive difficulties which had caused a number of earlier editors to position books 7–8 before books 4–6 actually reflect the composite nature of the *Politics* as a collection of materials written at different periods of Aristotle's career for different purposes, and embodying very different approaches to the study of politics. According to Jaeger, books 7–8, reflecting the Platonic concern with a single ideal form of government, were composed during Aristotle's stay in Assos, when the influence of the Academy was still strong. Jaeger also assigns a relatively early date to books 2–3 (in spite of the extensive criticism of Plato's *Republic* in book 2), while placing books 4–6, with their detailed anatomy of existing regimes, toward the end of Aristotle's career, when his characteristically empirical or practical approach had most fully asserted itself.

This is not the place to address the general validity of Jaeger's approach. Suffice it to say that it has come under increasing challenge in recent years, especially (though not only) in Anglo-American scholarship.[34] Yet even if Jaeger

---

34 · Consider the following observations, by a leading contemporary British scholar: "Some have suggested that since Aristotle spent the first twenty years of his philosophical career in Plato's Academy, he is likely to have agreed with Plato, and likely to have moved away gradually from Platonic views. I will not discuss this view of Aristotle's development, since I think it has been refuted. There is no evidence that Aristotle was ever a disciple of Plato (in the sense of accepting all the main philosophical doctrines discoverable from Plato's dialogues), or that his later works are less Platonic than his

is right that Aristotle's rejection of the Platonic doctrine of ideas was the decisive event of his intellectual development, Jaeger assumed rather than proved that a rejection of Platonic metaphysics necessarily entails a rejection of Platonic politics, to say nothing of the fact that Jaeger's presentation of Platonic political philosophy can hardly be held to be satisfactory. To mention only one point, Jaeger fails completely to do justice to the place of the *Laws* in Plato's thought, or to acknowledge the close connection between that in many ways eminently practical work and the *Politics* as a whole. This is by no means to deny that there are important differences between Aristotle and Plato concerning politics or the study of politics. It is only to question whether those differences are well enough understood at present to permit their use as a benchmark for determining the relative dates of different portions of the *Politics*.[35]

Our *Politics* in its current form may be divided into six distinct units. These may be characterized briefly as follows: the city and the household (book 1); views concerning the best regime (book 2); the city and the regime (book 3);

---

earlier. A more plausible picture of Aristotle's development suggests that his earlier philosophical views are the product of his criticisms of Plato, resulting from actual debate in the Academy; further reflexion on Plato led him, in later works, to form a more sympathetic view of some of Plato's views and doctrines.... There are no Platonizing early works ..., but in works that are plausibly (on different grounds) regarded as earlier, Aristotle's position is further from Plato's on some important points than it is in some probably later works" (Irwin 1988, 11–12). See also G. E. L. Owen, "The Platonism of Aristotle," in *Logic, Science, and Dialectic* (Ithaca, NY, 1986), 200–20; and Pierre Pellegrin, "La *Politique* d'Aristote: Unité et fractures," in Aubenque 1993, 3–34, with the remarks of Aubenque, vii–ix. Jaeger's influence on *Politics* scholarship is comprehensively reviewed in Touloumakos 1993, 224ff. The recent, massive commentary of Eckard Schütrumpf embraces a modified form of Jaeger's approach, yet is also critical of some of his basic assumptions; see especially Schütrumpf 1991, 39–67.

35 · It is worthwhile considering briefly in this connection the cross-references within the *Politics*. Jaeger appeals to these references in order to establish the unity and early date of books 2–3 and 7–8, but he is able to do so only by arguing that explicit references to book 1 in 3 and 7 (*Pol.* 3.6.1278b17–19, 7.3.1325a27–31) are later additions by an editor. In both passages, Aristotle uses the phrase "the initial discourses" (*hoi prōtoi logoi*) to refer to book 1; there are also a number of unmistakable allusions to 1 in 3 (3.1276b1–2, 4.1277a5–12, 1277b18–25). Moreover, Jaeger overlooks a reference in book 2 that is almost certainly to 4 rather than 7. At the end of his account there of Plato's *Laws*, Aristotle refers to a later discussion of "this sort of regime" (2.6.1266a23–25). Although Jaeger among others takes this to be a reference to the best regime of book 7, the fact that Aristotle explicitly associates the regime of the *Laws* with polity rather than aristocracy (1265b26–31) indicates that he has in mind rather the account of polity in 4.7–9.

the varieties of regime and what destroys and preserves them (books 4–5); the varieties of democracy and of political institutions (book 6); education and the best regime (books 7–8). References throughout the *Politics* to an "inquiry" (*methodos*) are generally to one or another of these divisions of the work, which are also clearly marked by introductory and summary statements.

That there are differences of emphasis, style, and manner of argumentation in the various "inquiries" of the *Politics* will be denied by no one. Yet Jaeger never succeeded in showing that these differences could not be adequately accounted for by differences in subject matter. In particular, he never showed that there is a necessary incompatibility between Aristotle's concern with the best regime in books 7–8 and his concern in books 4–6 with the variety of existing regimes. That Aristotle himself was not aware of any such incompatibility seems quite clear from the introductory remarks to book 4, where the study of the regime that is best simply and the study of the regime that is best (or of regimes that are generally acceptable) for most societies are treated as equally necessary parts of political science. Jaeger's assumed disjunction between "idealistic" and "practical" elements of the *Politics* appears to rest finally on a failure to appreciate the extent to which the *Politics* is a fundamentally practical book, or the implications of Aristotle's assertion that political science is a practical science directed to action rather than a theoretical science pursued for the sake of knowledge.

In what sense the account of the simply best regime in the final books of the *Politics* may be considered necessary to a practical science of politics cannot be adequately discussed here.[36] Yet an excellent case can be made that the treatment there, with its emphasis on education and its striking neglect of political institutions, complements the account of inferior regimes in books 4–6 and is equally addressed to practical questions of political life. In large measure, it seems intended to provide practical guidance to leisured gentlemen or aristocrats, even—indeed, particularly—in regimes where they do not constitute a ruling class.[37] As regards the question of dating,

36 · Recent discussions: Stephen Salkever, "Whose Prayer? The Best Regime of Book 7 and the Lessons of Aristotle's *Politics*," *Political Theory* 35 (February 2007): 29–46; Robert C. Bartlett, "Aristotle's Science of the Best Regime," *American Political Science Review* 88 (1994): 143–55; Rowe and Schofield 2000, 366–89.

37 · See generally Lord 1982 and 1996. It is also important to see that the attention Aristotle gives in book 7 to questions relating to the physical setting of the city and the size and makeup of its population indicates that he is thinking in practical terms of the founding of new cities or colonies on the periphery of the Greek world. Aristotle himself is said to have written a work entitled *Alexander, or In Defense of Colonists*. This

there are no historical references in the *Politics* that require a date prior to Aristotle's Lyceum period. The supposedly "early" book 2 contains two allusions that are arguably (though not certainly) to events of the year 333 — which would make them the last datable references in the entire work.[38]

There remains the question of the textual condition of the *Politics*, particularly as regards the order of its books. The chief difficulties are that book 3 breaks off with a sentence that is repeated practically verbatim at the beginning of book 7, that the brief chapter concluding it (3.18) provides a problematic transition between books 3 and 4 but makes excellent sense as an introduction to book 7, and that book 4 appears in several places to refer *back* to the discussion of the best regime in books 7–8. In addition, it is obvious that the last book is incomplete as it stands, and the same seems to be true of book 6.

Prior to the twentieth century, a number of editors concluded that the order of books 4–6 and 7–8 should be reversed, and actually printed the text accordingly.[39] The main obstacle to doing so is that the final sentence of Aristotle's *Nicomachean Ethics* seems to refer to our *Politics* in a way that supports the order of these books as found in the manuscript tradition. There is no clear way to resolve this conundrum, and for that reason, I have seen fit to take the conservative approach of retaining the traditional order, even while I find the internal evidence for transposing the books difficult to dismiss.

Several types of explanation can be offered to account for the hypothetical alteration of the original order of the books and other anomalies in Aristotle's text. One is simply that the *Politics* as we have it was left unfinished. A second is that a (finished or unfinished) version of the work suffered physical damage or dislocation at some point after Aristotle's death, resulting in the loss of material originally written by Aristotle and in the reversal of the order of the books (Greek book manuscripts took the form of papyrus rolls whose correct order could readily be confused in this way). This could have happened if the *Politics* was among the Aristotelian treatises that found their way to the cellar in Scepsis. Alternatively, the damage might have occurred in the course of military events or political disturbances in Athens — for which we in fact have some evidence.[40] Finally, it is possible that a later hand or

---

point has recently been emphasized by Ober (1998, 327–28, 339–40, 346–50); cf. also Kraut 2002, 6–10.

38 · *Pol.* 2.9.1270b11–13, 10.1272b19–22. Cf. Newman ad loc.

39 · Thus most notably the edition of Newman. The recent translation of Simpson has reverted to this practice (see Simpson 1997, xvi–xx).

40 · As noted earlier, because of Aristotle's Macedonian connections, his relationship with the Athenians was not a comfortable one. The Lyceum was located outside the

hands made the alteration at some time during the early third century, along
with other changes intended to repair the apparent disorder of the work, fill
in missing pieces, or provide supplementary information.

Some remarks are in order at this point concerning the question of interpolation in the text of the *Politics* and in Aristotle's writings generally. Since
Jaeger, it has been fashionable to regard as misguided the attempts of phi-
lologists of the nineteenth century to identify passages of doubtful authenticity in the Aristotelian corpus. Jaeger's assumption that inconsistencies and
anomalies existing in a work composed over a period of time would have
been overlooked or permitted to stand by Aristotle is not, however, inher-
ently persuasive, at least so long as such a work was still in continuous use for
purposes of teaching and research. The fact that inconsistencies and anomalies do in fact exist is therefore a strong argument in favor of assuming non-
Aristotelian authorship in cases where interpretation is otherwise baffled. If
Aristotle's treatises indeed served not only as lecture notes but as reference
works for students, it is not difficult to understand how, once no longer con-
trolled and used by Aristotle himself, they could come to be annotated with
glosses and addenda of various sorts.

Although proof in such matters is difficult or impossible, the *Politics* almost certainly contains a number of passages of this kind. In general, the
endings of book rolls are likely places for interpolation, and there are lengthy
passages at the end of books 2 and 5 that arouse suspicion; the final paragraph
of book 8 is also dubious. Historical and schematic excursuses in the manner of the later Peripatos must also be questioned, particularly if they are not
clearly related to the main line of argument. The eleventh chapter of book 1
is perhaps the most important instance of such a passage, but there are others of varying length scattered throughout the work.

While it is necessary to recognize the existence of these and other textual problems in the *Politics*,[41] there would appear to be little basis for the
wholesale transpositions, reconstructions, and excisions routinely practiced

---

walls of the city proper, and was thus exposed to an invading military force; yet the action of an Athenian mob can certainly not be ruled out. Theophrastus's will set aside
money for the repair of the school's library and adjoining areas; this may well have reflected damage incurred during the anti-Macedonian rising of 288 (Diogenes Laertius
5.51–52). The vulnerability of the Lyceum may well be part of the explanation for the
subsequent removal of part of the library from the city, if there is anything to that story.
41 · See further the "Note on the Text and Translation." I have paid particular attention
to the possible existence of lacunae (dropped text) throughout the *Politics*, and have
provided notional supplements where it seemed appropriate.

on Aristotle's text by older generations of scholars. It is now largely accepted, for example, that cross-references in the text must be presumed to be Aristotle's own. Generally speaking, the text of the *Politics* is in good condition, the style and texture are very much of a piece, and the overall argument is consistent to a high degree, though the organization of the work as a whole, the various turns of the argument, apparent repetitions and minor inconsistencies, and the like, give rise to many questions. In this sense, at any rate, the *Politics* may for all practical purposes be considered and read as a book—a book composed by a single author over a continuous period and governed by a single conception of its subject matter.

III

It remains to clarify and elaborate what has been said concerning the character of Aristotle's "political science," and to consider the relationship between the *Politics* and Aristotle's ethical writings as well as the work of his predecessors. An understanding of the intention and scope of Aristotle's enterprise is essential if the *Politics* is to be appreciated in its own terms rather than on the basis of current preconceptions of the nature of its subject.

Aristotle distinguishes in several places between three fundamental types of science or knowledge (*epistēmē*): theoretical science, practical science, and productive science or "art" (*technē*).[42] This distinction is nowhere systematically developed, however, and Aristotle's conception of practical science in particular remains a matter of controversy. Generally speaking, practical science appears to differ from theoretical science in its objects, its method, its purpose, and the faculty it engages. The objects of theoretical science are things not subject to change, or things of which the principle of change lies in themselves; its method is analysis of the principles or causes of things and demonstration based on those principles or causes; its purpose is knowledge or understanding; its faculty is the scientific or theoretical portion of the rational part of the soul. Among the theoretical sciences recognized and pursued by Aristotle are metaphysics or theology, mathematics, physics, biology, and psychology (the "science of the soul"). Man is an object of several of these sciences under a variety of aspects. Man is uniquely the object of the practical sciences, but only insofar as he is a subject or cause of "action" (*praxis*). The objects of the practical sciences are the things acted upon or done (*ta prakta*)

42 · *Metaphysics* E. 1.1025b18–28, *Topics* 6.6. 145a15–18, *Eth. Nic.* 7.2. 1139a26–b4, 4.1140a1–23.

by man; because they depend on human volition, these things are essentially changeable. The purpose of practical science is not knowledge but the betterment of action; its characteristic faculty is the calculative or practical segment of the rational part of the soul, or what Aristotle terms "prudence" (*phronēsis*). As for the method of the practical sciences, while it is difficult to summarize with any confidence Aristotle's sparse and cryptic statements on this subject, he appears to conceive it as a mode of analysis leading not to an understanding of causes so much as to clarification of the phenomena of human action, through a dialectical examination and refinement of men's opinions concerning those phenomena.[43]

At all events, it is a mistake to expect Aristotle's practical or political writings to display the same degree of conceptual precision that can be found in his theoretical works. Aristotle expressly cautions against demanding such precision on account of the inherent uncertainty and variability of matters of action.[44] Accordingly, he does not proceed by deduction from immutable principles of human nature or laws of human behavior, and he retains the language and respects the manner of thinking of ordinary political men. Aristotle's frequent reliance on dialectical argumentation—that is, on a quasi-conversational mode of inquiry that begins from the probable premises embedded in common opinion—must be understood in relation to the purpose of practical science. Precisely because practical science is in the service of action, it must be centrally concerned with the presentation of its subject in a way that will engage and affect the opinions of its audience. This is not to say that practical science is in no way related to theoretical science as Aristotle conceives it. In several passages, he indicates that "theoretical philosophy" will have a place in his practical writings wherever it is proper to the inquiry, and his argument is informed throughout by assumptions deriving from theoretical psychology in particular.[45] Equally clear, however, is Aristotle's view that practical science cannot or should not depend directly on

43 · The key passages are *Eth. Nic.* 1.3. 1094b11–27, 4.1095a30–b13, 7.1098a26–b8, *Eth. Eud.* 1.5–6.1216b11–17a18. For discussion of these issues, see, for example, Bien 1973, 59–69, 103–37, and for Aristotle's dialectical method, Irwin 1988, chapters 1–2.

44 · *Eth. Nic.* 1.3. 1094b11–27, 7.1098a26–33.

45 · The term "political philosophy" occurs only once in the *Politics*, but the context is highly significant: *Pol.* 3.12.1282b14–21; compare also 3.8.1279b12–25, where it is indicated that the inquiry of the *Politics* is in some sense philosophical and "not merely looking toward action." Compare also *Eth. Eud.* 1.1.1214a9–14, where Aristotle indicates that "what involves theoretical philosophy alone" will be brought in only when proper to the inquiry, as well as 6.1216b35–39, where he suggests that "discourses philosophically argued" will have at best a restricted role.

theoretical science. At least part of the reason for this appears to lie in Aristotle's certainty that men of experience and practical ability are constitutionally vulnerable to the influence of philosophical arguments put forward by intellectuals lacking practical intelligence.[46] Anticipating, one might say, the invasion of politics by theory in modern times, Aristotle insists on preserving an area of autonomy for "prudence," the intellectual virtue proper to political men.[47]

The most extensive treatment of prudence and practical science occurs in book 6 of the *Nicomachean Ethics*. There Aristotle indicates that practical science is in a sense coextensive with both prudence and political science (*politikē*). Practical or political science has three main branches: ethics or the science of character, the science of household management, and political science in a more proper sense. It is of the utmost importance to bear in mind that the science of character is considered by Aristotle an integral part of political science in its broadest sense. For Aristotle, the good of the individual cannot be conceptually separated from the good of the community; political science is the "architectonic" or master science of practice because it establishes the framework within which all individual action takes place, or more precisely, because the city or the regime necessarily affects in fundamental ways the private behavior of individuals. By the same token, it must be remembered that politics in the narrower sense necessarily involves or presupposes a consideration of the characters and virtues of individuals. The *Politics* is incomplete, then, not only in the sense discussed earlier, but in the more important sense that it forms one part of a larger inquiry.

In the passage of the *Nicomachean Ethics* just referred to, Aristotle suggests a further articulation of the content of political science which is of particular importance for understanding the scope and character of the dis-

46 · "There are certain persons who, it being held to belong to a philosopher to say nothing randomly but rather to use reasoned argument, make arguments that are alien to the subject and empty (they do this sometimes out of ignorance and sometimes from charlatanry) and are not detected, thus taking in those who are experienced and capable of acting, though they themselves neither have nor are capable of architectonic or practical thinking" (*Eth. Eud.* 1217a1–6). Consider especially Aristotle's discussion of the views of Hippodamus of Miletus in *Pol.* 2.8.

47 · These considerations go some way toward refuting the notion that Aristotle's political science is invalidated by its association with an outmoded teleological or metaphysical natural science. Whether or to what extent Aristotle may be supposed to have recognized the possibility of a theoretical "anthropology" that would serve as the foundation for a practical science of politics is not easy to say. Cf. Lord 1991, Wolfgang Kullmann, "L'image de l'homme dans la pensée d'Aristote," in Aubenque 1993, 161–84.

cussion in the *Politics*. He distinguishes between an "architectonic" sort of prudence to which he gives the term "legislative" (*nomothetikē*), and a prudence concerned with particulars, of an "active and deliberative" sort, which he calls "political" in yet another sense of that term. In the narrowest sense, it seems, *politikē* is the "political expertise" men acquire and manifest in dealing with the deliberative issues that are the stuff of everyday politics.[48] Elsewhere, Aristotle repeats and elaborates this distinction. In a passage in the first book of the *Rhetoric*, he asserts that there are five important matters about which men particularly deliberate: revenues and expenditures, war and peace, defense of the territory, imports and exports, and legislation.[49] In regard to "legislation" (*nomothesia*), Aristotle makes the following remark: "the preservation of the city lies in its laws, so it is necessary to know how many kinds of regimes there are, which are advantageous to each sort of city, and through what things they are naturally apt to be destroyed—both of things proper to the regimes and of their opposites."[50]

It is clear from these passages that the inquiry contained in the *Politics* does not correspond to the full range of subjects belonging to political science or political expertise. Although there are scattered discussions throughout the *Politics* that touch on virtually all the deliberative issues mentioned in the *Rhetoric*, Aristotle makes no attempt to deal with any of them but the last in anything approaching a systematic fashion. Political science or political expertise in what may be called its operational sense must include some knowledge of (to substitute modern terminology for Aristotle's expressions) trade, finance, defense, and foreign policy; but it is not this knowledge that the *Politics* undertakes to provide. The science or expertise that Aristotle teaches in the *Politics* is limited to that category of political knowledge he calls legislation or legislative expertise.

It must be said at once that Aristotle's terminology is somewhat misleading. In the *Politics* itself, Aristotle makes clear that his primary interest is not laws or legislation as such, but only what one might call (again with a view to contemporary terminology) "constitutional law," or more generally, the legal and customary institutions and practices that define a city's politi-

---

48 · *Eth. Nic.* 6.8. 1141b23–33. For political science as the "architectonic" science and the subordination of ethics to it, see *Eth. Nic.* 1.2. 1094a26–b11, *Magna Moralia* 1.1. 1181a23–b28, *Rhet.* 1.2. 1356a25–28.

49 · *Rhet.* 1.4. 1359b19–23ff.

50 · *Rhet.* 1.4. 1360a19–23. Aristotle proceeds to recommend the study of works of geography or ethnography with a view to "legislation," and of works of history with a view to "political deliberations" (1360a30–37).

cal constitution or "regime" (*politeia*).[51] It is important to be clear on this point, as it is crucial to understanding the specific character and the original-ity of Aristotle's political teaching. Toward the end of the *Nicomachean Eth-ics*, Aristotle remarks on the absence in contemporary Greece of any genuine instruction in political or legislative expertise. As for those among the "soph-ists" who profess to offer it, "generally speaking," he says, "they do not even know what it is or what matters it concerns, for otherwise they would not have regarded it as the same as rhetoric or inferior to it, nor would they have supposed it is easy to legislate by collecting the most renowned laws."[52] The great defect of the sophistic approach to "legislation" is precisely its overcon-centration on laws as such—that is, laws abstracted from the context of the regime. Legislation is not easy because cities differ in fundamental ways and because they give rise to a variety of regimes with fundamentally different re-quirements. Just as Aristotle is at pains to argue that rhetoric should be min-isterial to a substantive science of politics from which its own effectiveness must in large measure derive,[53] so he insists that laws and institutions suit and support particular regimes. Not law but the regime is the fundamental political phenomenon.

The dissatisfaction Aristotle here expresses with the political science of his day would appear not to be limited to the sophists alone. When he goes on to remark that "since our predecessors [*hoi proteroi*] have left unexplored what concerns legislation, it is perhaps best if we investigate it ourselves, and in general therefore concerning the regime," Aristotle cannot be supposed to have forgotten that his predecessor and teacher had written a lengthy treatise on law. In his brief critique of Plato's *Laws* in the *Politics*, Aristotle notes that the *Laws* has little to say about the actual character of the regime it presents as the best practical political order.[54] Plato was by no means insensitive to the phenomenon of the regime and its central importance for political analysis: "regime" is the Greek title of Plato's *Republic*, and books 8 and 9 of that work contain a detailed account of the varieties of existing regimes and their social and psychological bases. But the preoccupation of the *Republic* is a best re-gime whose realization Plato admits to be highly unlikely if not impossible, while the *Laws*, which is more concerned with the possible and practicable, makes little attempt to analyze the varieties of cities or societies and the re-

51 · Consider particularly *Pol.* 3.15.1286a2–7, 4.1.1289a10–25; for the interpretation of the latter passage, see note 3 to book 4 below.

52 · *Eth. Nic.* 10.9. 1181a12–19. Isocrates is no doubt particularly meant.

53 · See the discussion in Lord 1981, 337–38.

54 · *Pol.* 2.6. 1265a1–2, b26–33.

gimes corresponding to them. In this sense, Aristotle can reasonably say that Plato left the subject of "legislation" unexplored, in spite of the fact that particular laws are elaborated and discussed in the *Laws* to an extent that the *Politics* does not begin to approach. Whatever Aristotle's final view of Plato's thinking on these questions, he is implicitly critical at least of its emphasis and manner of presentation. For Aristotle, the primary requirement of a practical science of politics is a knowledge of the varieties of regimes and of the things that create, support, preserve, and destroy them.

As indicated earlier, the final chapter of the *Nicomachean Ethics* concludes with what appears to be a transition to our *Politics*. It is worth quoting this passage in full:

> Now our predecessors have left the subject of legislation unexamined; it is perhaps best, therefore, that we should ourselves investigate it, and the question of the regime generally, in order to complete as best we can our philosophy of human things. First, then, if anything has been said well on any particular part of the subject by earlier thinkers, let us try to review it; then in the light of our collection of regimes let us study what sorts of things preserve and destroy cities, and what preserve or destroy particular types of regimes, and through what causes some are well governed and others not. For after these things have been investigated we will better grasp what sort of regime is best, how each type of regime is ordered, and what laws and customs each uses.

This brief forward glance at the contents of what is presumably our *Politics* is generally taken as support for the order of the books of the work as found in the manuscript tradition. In fact, this passage is problematic in several ways. To begin with, it seems to ignore the first book of our *Politics*. Nor does it clearly capture book 3. But what is most puzzling is that Aristotle's apparent reference to the discussion of the best regime in books 7–8 is then *followed* by a promise to discuss "how each type of regime is ordered, and what laws and customs each uses." This has the appearance of an extensive discussion corresponding to nothing in the extant *Politics*. How might it be explained?

It is necessary first of all to consider the chronological relationship of the *Politics* to Aristotle's ethical treatises generally. The most plausible and now generally accepted assumption is that the *Politics* is chronologically later than the *Eudemian Ethics*. All references in the *Politics* to the "discourses on ethics" are demonstrably or arguably to this work—including the three books common to both ethical treatises, which are now generally viewed as originating in the *Eudemian Ethics*.[55] The *Politics*, on the other hand, is evidently referred to in the *Nicomachean Ethics* but not the *Eudemian Ethics*. But if the *Politics* then predates the *Nicomachean Ethics*, the reference to the *Politics* at the end of the latter would have to be to an already completed and not just a projected text. This would seem to eliminate the possibility that Aristotle changed his mind about the organization of the *Politics* in the course of writing it.[56]

To account for the absence of books 1 and 3 from the passage in question is perhaps not an insuperable obstacle. Book 3 could be taken as a first or introductory part of the initial discussion of cities and regimes and what preserves or destroys them; book 1, on the other hand, might be taken as encompassed in the discussion of the views of Aristotle's predecessors.[57] What, though, of the section dealing with "how each regime is ordered, and what laws and customs it uses"? As mentioned earlier, there is considerable internal evidence in the *Politics* to support the hypothesis that an extensive portion of the original text has been lost. Book 6, which deals with political offices or institutions as they relate to regimes, is quite short and seems to break off prematurely; it could well be taken as just the beginning of what was once a more extended account of "how each regime is ordered."[58] Most importantly, however, there are a substantial number of unfulfilled forward references, particularly in books 7 and 8, that seem to point to a missing discussion centered on the household, property, and education in relation to the regimes—one which might possibly be described as relating to the "laws and customs" associated with different types of regimes.[59]

---

55 · See, for example, Vander Waerdt 1985a. This view has been challenged by Anthony Kenny, *The Aristotelian Ethics* (Oxford, 1978), who argues for an early date for the *Nicomachean Ethics*.

56 · As claimed, for example, by Newman, 1:3. Newman does, however, make this salient observation: "As much doubt has been thrown, not without good ground, on the authenticity of many of the references, backwards or forwards, to be found in the writings which bear the name of Aristotle, it may be as well to remark that this programme would hardly have been forged by any one who had the Politics before him either in its traditional order or perhaps in any conceivable order" (1:2, n. 3).

57 · Consider not only Aristotle's criticism of Plato in 1.1 but the implicit critique of sophistic political science that pervades the entire book, notably in the discussion of the naturalness of the city and natural slavery.

58 · Consider *Pol.* 6.1.1316b31–17a10. The second part of the program elaborated here is not carried out.

59 · The most important of these occurs at the end of book 1. As Aristotle says there, "Concerning husband and wife and children and father and the sort of virtue that is connected with each of these, and what is and what is not fine in their relations with

It is not possible here to pursue the implications of all this for the substance of Aristotle's thought, but they are potentially very significant. Recently, one scholar has used the concluding passage of the *Nicomachean Ethics* as part of a larger argument asserting the fundamental unity of Aristotle's
ethical and political writings, an issue of continuing contention. If his argument is correct, it would compel us to look at the *Politics* in quite a different
light than has been customary. In particular, it would suggest that themes
relating to education and culture loomed considerably larger in the original argument of the work than they do on the basis of the extant books 7
and 8 alone—and moreover, were more organically united with Aristotle's
"empirical" analysis of the types of regimes than one would have otherwise
supposed.[60]

The fact that the *Politics* is devoted almost entirely to regimes of the polis is frequently taken as indicative of a certain narrowness of outlook or lack
of imagination on Aristotle's part. It is surely a striking historical irony that
the *Politics* was composed precisely during the period when Philip and Alexander of Macedon were constructing the basis of a new political order in
the Greek world and beyond that would permanently eclipse the polis in its
classical form. In spite of the personal association between Aristotle and the
Macedonian royal house, there is little or no discussion in the *Politics* of the

one another and how one should pursue what is well and avoid the bad, these things
must necessarily be addressed in the discourses connected with regimes. For since the
household as a whole is a part of the city, and these things of the household, and one
should look at the virtue of the part in relation to the virtue of the whole, both children
and women must necessarily be educated looking to the regime, at least if it makes any
difference with a view to the city's being excellent that both its children and its women
are excellent. But it necessarily makes a difference: women are a part amounting to a
half of the free persons, and from the children come those who are partners in the regime" (1.13.1260b8–20). See further 1337a14–18.1335b2–5, 1336b24–27, 1338a32–36,
1339b10–11, 1341b38–40. "The [discourses] on the regimes" (*hoi [logoi] peri tas politeias*) referred to here are almost certainly internal to the *Politics* itself. If the "initial
discourses" refers to Book 1, the "discourses on the regimes" would seem to encompass
Books 2–8 and subsequent lost material, though it is also possible that Aristotle includes Book 2 under the former rubric as well.
60 · See Vander Waerdt 1985a and 1985b. Vander Waerdt's overall thesis is vigorously,
though in my view not effectively, contested by Schütrumpf 1991, 94–102. In particular,
Schütrumpf's assumption that moral or political education can have no public role for
Aristotle outside of the best regime is not sustainable. Consider Lord, "Politics and Education in Aristotle's *Politics*," in Patzig 1990, 203–15. There is a large literature on the
relationship of ethics and politics in Aristotle's thought; see Touloumakos 1997, 11–90.

political possibilities of a semihellenized territorial monarchy along the lines of Macedon or its successor states. Nor for that matter does Aristotle have anything to say about the political possibilities offered by federal arrangements linking groups of cities, a phenomenon already in evidence in his own day and one that would gain increasingly in prominence in the Greek world over the next several centuries.[61] Was Aristotle's preoccupation with the polis merely the expression of a blind nostalgia for a world already in the process of dissolution?

The evidence available to us in the *Politics* suggests that Aristotle's preference for the polis over other political forms rests on a thorough and carefully reasoned analysis of its advantages. While leaving open the theoretical possibility that monarchy might be the best form of government for an advanced society under certain conditions, Aristotle makes abundantly clear that monarchy is not naturally or normally suited to such a society. Why Aristotle did not devote more attention to monarchy and its various forms, or to states larger than the polis, is a different question, to which a number of answers are possible. It is not at all evident that Aristotle was convinced—or should have been convinced—that the extension of Macedonian imperialism represented an inexorable development or a permanent change in the political geography of the ancient world. It could also be that the subject was simply too sensitive politically given Aristotle's Macedonian ties and existing international realities.[62]

To assume that Aristotle only mirrors or defends the historical phenomenon of the Greek city is, in any event, to make a fundamental error.[63] In the first place, Aristotle makes quite plain that the polis is not an essentially Greek phenomenon: he treats the Phoenician colony of Carthage as superior in its form of government to virtually all existing Greek cities. Second, Aristotle maintains a resolute silence about many features of the Greek city that were of considerable historical importance. It suffices to refer to the matter of religion, which is almost entirely ignored in the *Politics* as we have it—in sharp contrast, it should be noted, to the extensive treatment it receives in the *Laws* of Plato. Finally, Aristotle is highly critical throughout the *Poli-*

---

61 · J. A. O. Larsen, *Greek Federal States* (Oxford, 1968).

62 · Cf. Kahn 1990, 372–75.

63 · This misconception is apparent even in the outlook of a contemporary philo-Aristotelian philosopher such as Alasdair MacIntyre. See Aristide Tessitore, "MacIntyre and Aristotle on the Foundation of Virtue," in Tessitore 2002, 133–61, esp. 147–49.

tics of both Athens and Sparta, the cities that had acted at various times as leaders and symbols of the two most powerful political tendencies in classical Greece. In the place of the narrow oligarchies and partisan democracies that dominated contemporary political practice, Aristotle holds up the alternative of the polity, the mixed regime that rests in the best case on a strong middle class.[64] In the place of the Spartan model, which continued to dominate contemporary theorizing about politics, he holds up the alternative of a best regime ruled by a cultured aristocracy dedicated to the pursuits of peace and leisure rather than to war.[65]

IV

While little is known of the place accorded to the study of politics in the Peripatetic school after Aristotle, it does not appear to have been a prominent one. As has been mentioned, from all indications, the *Politics* itself was unknown during the Hellenistic period, at least outside the confines of the Lyceum. The rapid development at this time of monarchic states and ideologies no doubt served to dampen whatever interest there may have been in analysis of the varieties of regimes of the polis.[66] The *Politics* surfaced again at Rome in the first century BC, but seems to have attracted little notice, perhaps in part for similar reasons. No commentary on it survives from later antiquity. The emperor Julian shows knowledge of it, and in the fifth century the Neoplatonic philosopher Proclus undertook a refutation of the critique of Plato in its second book.[67] But other commentators of this period refer to the work in a way that indicates it was not available to them, and no further mention of it occurs until the eleventh century, in the writings of the Byzantine scholar Michael of Ephesus. Unlike most other works of Aristotle and Plato, the *Politics* did not reach the Arabic world, and thus had no impact on the great flowering of Arabic and Jewish philosophic thought in the eleventh

64 · The best discussions of this key concept in historical perspective are Aalders 1968 and Nippel 1980.

65 · It is critical to appreciate Aristotle's reservations against traditional Greek cultural attitudes toward war and manliness. See Stephen G. Salkever, "Women, Soldiers, Citizens: Plato and Aristotle on the Politics of Virility," in Lord and O'Connor 1991, 165–90.

66 · See Rowe and Schofield 2000, chapter 19.

67 · Julian, *Letter to Themistius* 260d–61c, 263d; Proclus, *Commentary on Plato's Republic* 2:360–67 Kroll. See also Rowe and Schofield 2000, 661–65.

and twelfth centuries.[68] Manuscripts of the *Politics* first arrived in the West from Byzantium only in the thirteenth century.[69]

The first Latin translation of the *Politics* was produced around 1250 by William of Moerbeke as part of the larger project of Aristotelian translations initiated by Thomas Aquinas. St. Thomas's ambitious effort to fuse Aristotelian philosophy and Christian theology went some way toward making Aristotle's works intellectually respectable in Christian Europe. Yet the Thomistic synthesis had no real place for politics in the Aristotelian sense, beginning as it did from the notion of a natural law that prescribes universal standards of moral and political action; nor did Aquinas attempt to challenge the prevailing forces favoring monarchic and imperial forms of governance. Aristotelian arguments were extensively utilized, however, by champions of the independence of the Italian city-states from the Holy Roman Empire; and the *Politics* would play a significant role in the revival of republican political thought in Italy in the early Renaissance.[70] But the most faithful and influential adaptation of the *Politics* within the context of Christian Europe was the work of Marsilius of Padua, the principal political thinker of the philosophical movement often referred to as Latin Averroism. Marsilius's *Defender of the Peace*, in its bold attack on the political role of the Church and priesthood, anticipated by two centuries aspects of the Protestant Reformation, and developed a theory of political sovereignty that has strikingly popular overtones.[71] The *Politics* would continue to have resonance in Protestant Europe, especially Germany, well into the eighteenth century.[72]

Yet what the *Politics* gained in academic respectability during this period, it lost in real intellectual authority and influence. The displacement of Aristotle as the authoritative exponent of practical or political philosophy in the

---

68 · At the beginning of his commentary on Plato's *Republic*, for example, Averroes explains that he has chosen to write on this work because "Aristotle's book on governance has not yet fallen into our hands" (*Averroes on Plato's Republic*, ed. Ralph Lerner [Ithaca, 1974], 4).

69 · Discussion of the historical reception of the *Politics* may be found in Dreizehnter 1970, xv–xxi, and Günther Bien, "Die Wirkungsgeschichte der aristotelischen 'Politik,'" Patzig 1990, 325–56; see also the survey of the literature in Touloumakos 1998, 65–127.

70 · See particularly Quentin Skinner, *The Foundations of Modern Political Thought* (Cambridge, 1978), 1:3–12, 49–65.

71 · Alan Gewirth, *Marsilius of Padua: The Defender of the Peace* (New York, 1951).

72 · Cf. Bien, "Wirkungsgeschichte," 333–40.

West had begun in the early years of the sixteenth century, with Machiavelli's famous declaration that the "imagined republics and principalities" of the past could no longer be taken as a guide to political action, and his call for a new political science that would be firmly grounded in the "effectual truth" about man. The declining fortunes of republican government throughout the sixteenth and seventeenth centuries surely contributed to the eclipse of Aristotle's political teaching. The decisive factor, however, was the broad movement of thought inspired by Machiavelli and developed by such figures as Bacon, Hobbes, Locke, and Montesquieu, which would revolutionize men's understanding of politics and profoundly shape the character of modern societies. Under its impact, the *Politics* eventually ceased to be a work of living importance.

This is by no means to suggest that the *Politics* has lost all relevance for the study of politics today. To attempt a complete assessment of the enduring strengths of this work is obviously not possible here. What can be said, however, is that there has been a remarkable revival of interest in the *Politics* and in Aristotle's moral and political philosophy generally over the last three or four decades, in Europe as well as the United States. To some extent, this simply reflects the revival during this period of political philosophy itself as a discipline distinct from the history of political thought.[73] Arguably, though, it also reflects certain fundamental transformations in intellectual and political outlook in the West in the course of the twentieth century. Chief among these is what may be called the crisis of Enlightenment rationalism (seen most visibly in contemporary "postmodernism"), and associated with it, the manifest decay of Enlightenment liberalism as the philosophy or ideology undergirding liberal democracy in today's world. Classical rationalism, as exemplified in the writings of Plato and Aristotle, can be seen as a powerful alternative to the relativism and nihilism that so pervades the contemporary academy. And at the level of politics, dissatisfaction with the perceived thinness of the liberal account of the human good and the foundations of political community has led to renewed interest in the tradition of "classical republicanism" that originated in Greek and Roman antiquity and regained

---

73 · Consider especially John Rawls's use of Aristotle in his enormously influential *A Theory of Justice* (Cambridge, MA, 1971). The role of Leo Strauss in this development is critical; see Strauss 1953. In the field of moral philosophy, Aristotle has been central in the rediscovery of what is often called "virtue ethics" in contrast to characteristically modern approaches such as Kantianism and utilitarianism. See notably Alasdair MacIntyre, *After Virtue* (Notre Dame, 1981).

influence in the Renaissance and early modernity.[74] Aristotle in particular, a key figure in this tradition, is now widely seen to offer a model of "communitarian" republican or democratic governance that can mitigate the ills of modern liberal individualism.[75]

It can certainly be questioned whether those early modern thinkers who sought to ground political action in the self-interested passions of individuals succeeded as well as has often been assumed in disposing of the arguments of their older rivals. Of all the classical political thinkers, Aristotle is the least exposed to Machiavelli's charge of utopianism. In their haste to identify a formula for politics that would be applicable to all circumstances and all men, the modern thinkers tended to forget and obscure the lessons Aristotle taught concerning the essential diversity of human societies and the indispensability of prudent statesmanship. The moderns have not only proven unable to lay to rest the human impulses that stimulate utopian thinking, but have themselves fostered forms of utopianism more virulent and more destructive of sensible politics than anything known in the premodern world. From this point of view, Aristotle's "practical philosophy"—a political or social science that steers a deliberate course between "value-free" empiricism and value-driven advocacy—provides an alternative to current approaches that is of more than merely historical interest.[76]

74 · For an influential account, see J. G. A. Pocock, *The Machiavellian Moment* (Princeton, 1975). Pathbreaking in this regard was Hannah Arendt's *The Human Condition* (Chicago, 1958).

75 · See generally Tessitore 2002. This volume is particularly valuable in calling attention to the key role played by the German philosopher Martin Heidegger in preparing the way for what Tessitore calls the Aristotelian "renaissance" of the late twentieth century (see Tessitore's introductory comments, 1–6, as well as David K. O'Connor, "Leo Strauss' Aristotle and Martin Heidegger's Politics," 162–207). The German roots of this development are not widely appreciated; a useful account is Franco Volpi, "Rehabilitation de la Philosophie Practique et Néo-Aristotelianisme," in Aubenque 1993, 461–84. For Aristotle's (problematic) relationship to contemporary communitarianism, see Yack 1993.

76 · For Aristotle's relationship to contemporary social science, see further Salkever 1990, Lord and O'Connor 1991.

A NOTE ON THE TEXT AND TRANSLATION

The present translation has as its aim to produce as literal and faithful a rendering of this frequently difficult work as is compatible with contemporary English usage. It is hoped that the advantages of this procedure for serious study of Aristotle's text are sufficiently obvious not to require elaborate justification, and are not outweighed by the inevitable loss in readability. Except where a Greek word has more than one distinct meaning, I have translated key terms in the original by a single English word. In dealing with Aristotle's elliptical and compressed style, I have translated words not appearing in the text but clearly understood; in doubtful cases, and wherever it seemed desirable in order to improve the intelligibility of the translation, words or phrases elaborating the argument are added in square brackets. I have not always observed Aristotle's punctuation, and have not tried to reproduce in mechanical fashion the particles that contribute so much of the nuance in classical Greek. At the same time, I have made a serious effort to preserve the tone and style of the original, in the belief that the intention of Aristotle's work is not properly understood if it is made to sound like a ponderous academic treatise. Obviously, the requirements of literalness have imposed limits on this effort, and on occasion have no doubt produced jarring effects not intended by the author.

A glossary at the end of this volume is intended to provide the reader with working definitions of the key terms in Aristotle's philosophical-political vocabulary, as well as a guide to linguistic relationships that are not always reflected in equivalent English terms. Additional explanatory material is provided in the notes to the translation. I have generally resorted to annotation only to provide literary and historical references, to call attention to textual problems, and to supply such other information or interpretation as seems essential to the understanding of the argument. Scholarly commentaries and other secondary works are not regularly cited or discussed, though I have profited throughout from the labors of numerous learned predecessors.

The translation is based on the text of the *Politics* edited by Alois Drei-zehnter, *Aristoteles' Politik*, Studia et Testimonia Antiqua 7 (Munich, 1970). I have, however, given fresh consideration to all important textual problems and variant readings, and have not hesitated to deviate from Dreizehnter where this seemed appropriate; all such deviations are indicated in the notes. Generally speaking, I have been more conservative than Dreizehnter in re-taining the consensus reading of the manuscripts or of the best manuscripts (the family Π^2). At the same time, I have been readier to accept the existence of lacunae in the text (that is, dropped words, lines, or in some cases longer passages); in a number of places I believe I have identified lacunae not previ-ously noted by scholars. Supplements (conjectural language) are marked in the translation by square brackets.

For this second edition, I have reviewed the entire translation, with par-ticular attention to difficult or contested passages, in an effort to improve both its accuracy and its readability. These revisions have not been extensive, but neither are they insubstantial. In a number of cases, significant material has been added to the footnotes. In the course of this review, I have had the benefit of a number of outstanding scholarly commentaries that have ap-peared in the intervening years, notably those of Schütrumpf (1991–2005), Saunders (1995), Kraut (1997), Simpson (1998), and Keyt (1999). A compre-hensive overview and analysis of modern translations and commentaries on the *Politics* is now available in Touloumakos 1993, 182–224.

The division of the text of the *Politics* by numbered chapters and sections and by paragraphs has no authority. The numbers in the margins of the trans-lation refer to the pages, columns, and lines of the standard edition of Aris-totle's works prepared for the Prussian Academy by Immanuel Bekker and published in Berlin in 1831.

ANALYSIS OF THE ARGUMENT

The analysis of the *Politics* provided here is intended for the convenience of the reader; the divisions of the argument and the titles assigned them are wholly the responsibility of the translator. Book and chapter numbers of the *Politics* are given in parentheses. The analysis follows the order of the books as they are found in the manuscript tradition.

I. The City and the Household (book 1)
   A. The City and Man (1.1–2)
   B. The Household (1.3–13)
      1. The household in general (1.3)
      2. Slavery (1.4–7)
      3. Property and business (1.8–11)
      4. Household rule in general (1.12–13)

II. Views concerning the Best Regime (book 2)
   A. Best Regimes in Speech (2.1–8)
      1. The regime of Plato's *Republic* (2.1–5)
      2. The regime of Plato's *Laws* (2.6)
      3. The regime of Phaleas of Chalcedon (2.7)
      4. The regime of Hippodamus of Miletus (2.8)
   B. Regimes Held to Be Well Managed (2.9–11)
      1. The Spartan regime (2.9)
      2. The Cretan regime (2.10)
      3. The Carthaginian regime (2.11)
   C. Regimes and Legislators (2.12)

The GREEK WORLD

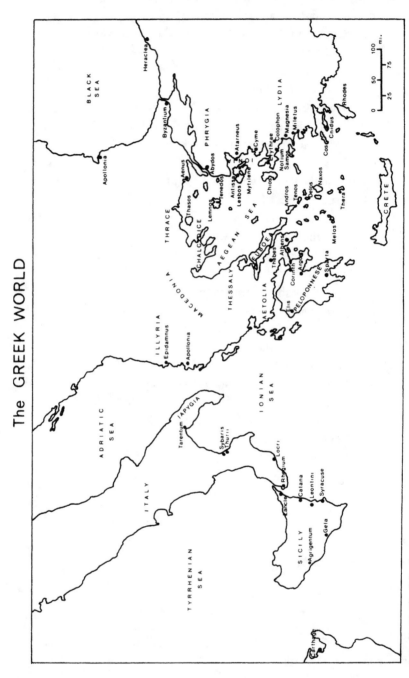

Map by Cecilia Schmitt.

GREECE circa 330 B.C.

ILLYRIA

THRACE

Abdera

MACEDONIA
Pella

Amphipolis

THASOS

ELIMEIA

Stagira

CHALCIDICE
Olynthus

Aphytis

MOLOSSIS

PERRHAEBIA

AEGEAN
SEA

CORCYRA

Larissa

MAGNESIA

THESSALY
Pharsalus

AMBRACIA

ACHAEA
PHTHIOTIS

LEUCAS

ACARNANIA

MALIS

HESTIAEA

AETOLIA

Thermopylae

LOCRIS
Opus

DORIS

PHOCIS

CHALCIS

Delphi

Chaeronea

ERETRIA

CEPHALLENIA

ACHAEA

BOEOTIA
Thebes

IONIAN
SEA

ELIS

SICYON

MEGARA

ATHENS

CORINTH

Salamis

Piraeus

CARYSTUS

Olympia

ARCADIA

MANTINEA

Aegina

Heraea

ARGOS

EPIDAURUS

Megalopolis

TROEZEN
HERMIONE

MESSENE

SPARTA

LACEDAEMON

0   20   40
     mi.
  10   30

Map by Cecilia Schmitt.

ARISTOTLE'S *Politics*

⊚ ⊚

Book 1

(1) Since we see that every city is some sort of community, and that every   1252a
community is constituted for the sake of some good (for everyone does
everything for the sake of what is held to be good), it is clear that all communities aim at some good, and that the community that is most authoritative   5
of all and embraces all the others does so particularly, and aims at the most
authoritative good of all. This is what is called the city or the political community.

(2) Those who suppose that the same person is expert in political rule,
kingly rule, managing the household, and being a master of slaves do not
argue finely.[1] For they consider that each of these differs in the number or
fewness of those ruled and not in kind—for example, the ruler of a few is a   10
master, of more a household manager, and of still more a political or kingly
ruler—the assumption being that there is no difference between a large
household and a small city; and as for the political and kingly rulers, they
consider a kingly ruler one who has charge himself, and a political ruler one
who, on the basis of the precepts of this sort of science, rules and is ruled in   15
turn.[2] But these things are not true. (3) This will be clear to those investigat-

---

1 · The reference appears to be particularly to Plato, *Statesman* 258e–59d; consider
also Xenophon, *Memorabilia* 3.4. 12 (cf. 6.14), *Oeconomicus* 13.5. "Expert in political
rule" (*politikos*) can equally be translated "statesman." *Kalōs* ("finely" or "nobly") often
means little more than "well" in Greek; but the nuance can sometimes be important,
suggesting conventional approbation rather than one's own considered view.
2 · That there is a single "science" of political and kingly rule is asserted in *Statesman*
259c. The "precepts" (*logoi*) in question would appear to be writings (i.e., laws) that con-
strain the political ruler but not the king (cf. *Statesman* 299c).

ing in accordance with our normal sort of inquiry.[3] For just as it is necessary
elsewhere to divide a compound into its uncompounded elements (for these
20   are the smallest parts of the whole), so too by investigating what the city is
composed of we shall gain a better view concerning these kinds of rulers as
well, both as to how they differ from one another and as to whether there is
some artful expertise[4] that can be acquired in connection with each of those
mentioned.

CHAPTER 2

(1) Now in these matters as elsewhere it is by looking at how things develop
25   naturally from the beginning that one may best study them. (2) First, then,
there must of necessity be a conjoining of persons who cannot exist without one another: on the one hand, male and female, for the sake of repro-
duction (which occurs not from intentional choice but—as is also the case
with the other animals and plants—from a natural striving to leave behind
30   another that is like oneself); on the other, the naturally ruling and ruled,
on account of preservation. For that which can foresee with the mind is the
naturally ruling and naturally mastering element, while that which can do
these things with the body is the naturally ruled and slave; hence the same
1252b   thing is advantageous for the master and slave. (3) Now the female is distinguished by nature from the slave. For nature makes nothing in an economiz-
ing spirit, as smiths make the Delphic knife,[5] but one thing with a view to
one thing; and each instrument would perform most finely if it served one
5   task rather than many. (4) The barbarians, though, have the same arrangement for female and slave. The reason for this is that they have no naturally
ruling element; with them, the community of man and woman is that of female slave and male slave. This is why the poets say "it is fitting for Greeks
to rule barbarians"[6]—the assumption being that barbarian and slave are by
nature the same thing.
10   (5) From these two communities, then, the household first arose, and
Hesiod's verse is rightly spoken: "first a house, and woman, and ox for

---

3 · The meaning of "our normal sort of inquiry" (hē hyphēgēmenē methodos) is not certain; the analytic approach alluded to here is by no means rigidly followed throughout
Aristotle's writings. Cf. 1.8. 1.
4 · Or "some technical skill" (ti technikon), from technē, art or skill.
5 · Probably a kind of knife used at the religious center of Delphi for a variety of sac-
rificial purposes, but the meaning is uncertain.
6 · Euripides, Iphigenia in Aulis 1400–1401.

ploughing"[7]—for poor persons have an ox instead of a servant. The household is the community constituted by nature for the needs of daily life; Charondas calls its members "mess-mates," Epimenides of Crete "stable-mates."[8] The first community arising from several households and for the sake of non-daily needs is the village. (6) By nature the village seems to be above all an extension of the household. Its members some call "milk-mates"; they are "the children and the children's children."[9] This is why cities were at first under kings, and nations are even now.[10] For those who joined together were already under kings: every household is under the eldest as king, and so also were the extensions [of the household making up the village] as a result of kinship. (7) This is what Homer meant when he says that "each acts as law to his children and wives"; for men were scattered and used to dwell in this manner in ancient times.[11] And it is for this reason that all assert that the gods are under a king—because they themselves are under kings now, or were in ancient times. For human beings assimilate not only the looks of the gods to themselves, but their ways of life as well.

(8) The complete community,[12] arising from several villages, is the city. It reaches a level of full self-sufficiency, so to speak; and while coming into being for the sake of living, it exists for the sake of living well. Every city, therefore, exists by nature, if such also are the first communities. For the city is their end, and nature is an end: what each thing is—for example, a human being, a horse, or a household—when its coming into being is complete is,

7 · Hesiod, *Works and Days* 405.

8 · The legislator Charondas of Catana is mentioned again in 3.12 and 4.11 and 13. Epimenides of Crete is said to have written poetry as well as a prose work on the Cretan regime (Diogenes Laertius 1.109–15).

9 · The latter phrase is Homeric in origin (*Iliad* 20.308; cf. Plato, *Laws* 681b); both expressions seem to have designated the extended family (*genos*). The word "extension" (*apoikia*) derives from a phrase meaning "away from the household"; it is the normal term for a colonial settlement. Precisely what Aristotle means by "village" (*kōmē*) is unclear. It is probably to be understood as a country district (canton) rather than a proto-commercial center or town; and Aristotle may be overstating the role of blood relationships in giving rise to it. Cf. Lord 1991, 64 n. 2, Saunders 1995, 66–67.

10 · "Nations" (*ethnē*) were communities organized on a tribal basis and lacking major urban centers—though often occupying more territory than an average polis.

11 · The reference is to the Homeric Cyclopes: "These have no assemblies to take counsel nor customary laws [*themistes*], but dwell in the heights of lofty mountains / in hollow caves: each acts as law to [*themisteuei*] his children and wives, and pays no attention to the others" (*Odyssey* 9.112–15). Cf. *Eth. Nic.* 1180a24–32, Plato, *Laws* 680b–e.

12 · That is, the community that is the perfect or final or fully realized (*teleios*) form of community.

we assert, the nature of that thing. (9) Again, that for the sake of which a thing exists, or the end, is what is best; and self-sufficiency is an end and what is best.[13]

1253a   From these things it is evident, then, that the city belongs among the things that exist by nature, and that man is by nature a political animal. He who is without a city through nature rather than chance is either a mean sort
5   or superior to man; he is "without clan, without law, without hearth," like the person reproved by Homer; (10) for the one who is such by nature has by this fact a desire for war, as if he were an isolated piece in a game of back-gammon.[14] That man is much more a political animal than any kind of bee or any herd animal is clear.[15] For, as we assert, nature does nothing in vain; and
10   man alone among the animals has speech. (11) The voice indeed indicates the painful or pleasant, and hence is present in other animals as well; for their nature has come this far, that they have a perception of the painful and pleasant and signal these things to each other. But speech serves to reveal the ad-
15   vantageous and the harmful, and hence also the just and the unjust. (12) For it is peculiar to man as compared to the other animals that he alone has a perception of good and bad and just and unjust and the other things of this sort; and community in these things is what makes a household and a city.[16]
20   The city is thus prior by nature to the household and to each of us. (13) For the whole must of necessity be prior to the part; for if the whole body is de-stroyed there will not be a foot or a hand, unless in the sense that the term is similar (as when one speaks of a hand made of stone), but the thing itself will

13 · The "end" (*telos*) of a thing is its complete or perfect form. Aristotle appeals here to the doctrine of final causes of his scientific writings (cf. *Physics* 194a27–33). It is far from clear, however, how far the analogy between the city and a living organism is meant to extend.

14 · Homer, *Iliad* 9.63–64: "Without clan, without law [*athemis*], without hearth is the man / who longs for chilling war among his people." (Note that Aristotle reverses the terms of this comparison.) It is not certain exactly what game is referred to, beyond one involving the use of dice; the piece is apparently given a technical name or descrip-tion, "unyoked" (*azyx*), suggesting an unprotected position.

15 · In *History of Animals* (1.1.487b34 ff.), Aristotle defines "political animal" as one that "has a single and common task [*ergon*]" or function, and indicates that the cate-gory includes bees, ants, and other animals of this sort in addition to man.

16 · The Greek word *logos* means both "speech" and "reason"; it is man's reasoning ability that enables him to distinguish between the just and unjust, and therefore to conduct himself morally in relation to others in a way that makes human community possible—whether in a household or a polis.

be defective. Everything is defined by its function and its capacity, and if it is no longer the same in these respects it should not be spoken of in the same way, but only as something similarly termed. (14) That the city is both by   25
nature and prior to each individual, then, is clear. For if the individual when separated from it is not self-sufficient, he will be in a condition similar to that of the other parts in relation to the whole. One who is incapable of sharing[17] or who is in need of nothing through being self-sufficient is no part of a city, and so is either a beast or a god.

(15) Accordingly, there is in everyone by nature an impulse toward this   30
sort of community. And yet he who first founded one is responsible for the greatest of goods. For just as man is the best of the animals when completed, when separated from law and adjudication he is the worst of all. (16) For injustice is harshest when it is furnished with arms; and man is born naturally possessing arms for [the use of] prudence and virtue which are nevertheless   35
very susceptible to being used for their opposites. This is why, without virtue, he is the most unholy and the most savage of the animals, and the worst with regard to sex and food.[18] Justice is a thing belonging to the city. For adjudication is an arrangement of the political community, and justice is judgment as to what is just.[19]

CHAPTER 3

(1) Since it is evident out of what parts the city is constituted, it is necessary   1253b
first to speak of household management; for every city is composed of households. The parts of household management correspond to the parts out of which the household itself is constituted. Now the complete household is made up of slaves and free persons. Since everything is to be sought for first   5
in its smallest elements, and the first and smallest parts of the household are master, slave, husband, wife, father, and children, three things must be investigated to determine what each is and what sort of thing it ought to be. (2) These are mastery, marital rule (there is no term for the union of man

17 · That is, sharing or being partner in (*koinōnein*) a community (*koinōnia*).
18 · Aristotle probably means to allude to incest, cannibalism, and similar phenomena; cf. *Eth. Nic.* 1145a15–33, 1148b15–49a20.
19 · Or "justice [*dikē*] is an ordering [*taxis*] of the political association," as it is usually understood. *Taxis* here appears to have the sense of "institution," while *dikē* refers to the process or administration of justice. "Justice" as used in the text here (*dikaiosynē*) connotes the virtue of justice. Cf. Saunders 1995.

10   and woman), and thirdly procreative rule[20] (this too has not been assigned a
term of its own). (3) So much, then, for the three we spoke of. There is a certain part of it, however, which some hold to be the same as household management, and others its greatest part; how the matter really stands has to be
studied. I am speaking of what is called the art of getting goods.

15   Let us speak first about master and slave, so that we may see at the same
time what relates to necessary needs and whether we cannot acquire something in the way of knowledge about these things that is better than current
conceptions. (4) For some hold that mastery is a kind of science, and that
managing the household, mastery, and political and kingly rule are the same,
20   as we said at the beginning. Others hold that exercising mastery is against
nature; for [as they believe] it is by law that one person is slave and another
free, there being no difference by nature, and hence it is not just, since it rests
on force.

CHAPTER 4

(1) Now property is a part of the household, and the art of acquiring it a part
of household management (for without the necessary things it is impossible
25   either to live or to live well); and just as the specialized arts must of necessity have their proper instruments if their function is to be performed, so
too must the household manager. (2) Now of instruments some are inanimate and others animate—the pilot's rudder, for example, is an inanimate
30   instrument, but his lookout an animate one; for the subordinate is a kind
of instrument whatever the art. A possession too, then, is an instrument for
the purposes of life, and one's property is the aggregate of such instruments;
and the slave is a possession of the animate sort.[21] Every subordinate, moreover, is an instrument that wields many instruments, (3) for if each of the in-
35   struments were able to perform its function on command or by anticipation,
as they assert those of Daedalus did, or the tripods of Hephaestus (which
the poet says "of their own accord came to the gods' gathering"),[22] so that
shuttles would weave themselves and picks play the lyre, master craftsmen
1254a   would no longer have a need for subordinates, or masters for slaves. (4) Now

20 · Reading *technopoiētikē* ("procreative rule") with the MSS rather than Dreizehnter's
conjectural *patrikē* ("paternal rule"), based on the use of that term in 12.1.
21 · The Greek words for "acquisitive art" (*ktētikē*), "possessions" (*ktēmata*), and
"property" (*ktēsis*) are closely related.
22 · Homer, *Iliad* 18.376. Daedalus was a legendary sculptor who was held to have the
power of creating animated statues.

the instruments mentioned are productive instruments, but a possession is an instrument of action. For from the shuttle comes something apart from the use of it, while from clothing or a bed the use alone. Further, since pro- 5 duction and action differ in kind and both require instruments, these must of necessity reflect the same difference. (5) Life is action, not production; the slave is therefore a subordinate in matters concerning action.

A possession is spoken of in the same way as a part. A part is not only 10 part of something else, but belongs wholly to something else; similarly with a possession. Accordingly, while the master is only master of the slave and does not belong to him, the slave is not only slave to the master but belongs wholly to him.

(6) What the nature of the slave is and what his capacity, then, is clear from these things. For one who does not belong to himself by nature but is 15 another's, though a human being, is by nature a slave; a human being is an-other's who, though a human being, is a possession; and a possession is an instrument of action and separate from its owner.

CHAPTER 5

(1) Whether anyone is of this sort by nature or not, and whether it is better and just for anyone to be a slave or not, but rather all slavery is against na-ture, must be investigated next. It is not difficult either to discern the answer 20 by reasoning or to learn it from what actually happens. (2) Ruling and being ruled belong among not only necessary but also advantageous things. And immediately from birth certain things diverge, some toward being ruled, others toward ruling. There are many kinds of things both ruling and ruled, and the rule is always better over ruled things that are better, for example 25 over a human being rather than a beast; (3) for the work performed by the better is better, and wherever something rules and something is ruled there is a certain work belonging to these together. For whatever is constituted out of a number of things—whether continuous or discrete—and becomes a single common thing always displays a ruling and a ruled element; (4) this 30 is something that animate things derive from all of nature, for even in things that do not partake in life there is a sort of rule, for example in a harmony.[23] But these matters perhaps belong to a more external sort of investigation.[24]

23 · In Greek musical language, the highest note in the tetrachord was known as the "leader"; cf. [Aristotle] *Problems* 920a22, with the comments of Schütrumpf.
24 · The phrase *exōterikōtera skepsis* appears to refer to a type of written composi-tion intended for circulation outside the Lyceum (the *exōterikoi logoi* or "external dis-

35   But an animal is the first thing constituted out of soul and body, of which the former is the ruling element by nature, the other the ruled. (5) It is in things whose condition is according to nature that one ought particularly to investigate what is by nature, not in things that are defective. Thus the human being to be studied is one whose state is best both in body and in soul—in him 1254b   this is clear; for in the case of the depraved, or those in a depraved condition, the body is often held to rule the soul on account of their being in a condition that is bad and unnatural.

(6) It is then in an animal, as we were saying, that one can first discern
5   both the sort of rule of a master and political rule. For the soul rules the body with the rule of a master, while intellect rules appetite with political and kingly rule; and this makes it evident that it is according to nature and advantageous for the body to be ruled by the soul, and the passionate part of the soul by intellect and the part having reason, while it is harmful to both
10   if the relation is equal or reversed. (7) The same holds with respect to man and the other animals: tame animals have a better nature than wild ones, and it is better for all of them to be ruled by man, since in this way their preservation is ensured. Further, the relation of male to female is by nature a relation
15   of superior to inferior and ruler to ruled. The same must of necessity hold in the case of human beings generally.

(8) Accordingly, those who are as different from other men as the soul from the body or man from beast—and they are in this state if their work is the use of the body, and if this is the best that can come from them—are
20   slaves by nature. For them it is better to be ruled in accordance with this sort of rule, if such is the case for the other things mentioned. (9) For he is a slave by nature who is capable of belonging to another—which is also why he belongs to another—and who participates in reason only to the extent of perceiving it, but does not have it. (The other animals, not perceiving reason, obey their passions.[25]) Moreover, the need for them differs only
25   slightly: bodily assistance in the necessary things is forthcoming from both, from slaves and from tame animals alike.

(10) Nature indeed wishes to make the bodies of free persons and slaves

------

courses"; see Introduction, p. xvii), but it is sometimes taken to mean merely "an investigation external to the subject."

25 · Reading *logou* with Π² instead of *logōi* with Π¹ and Dreizehnter. The latter reading produces the more usual translation: "The other animals do not obey reason, though perceiving it, but their passions." Aristotle appears to suggest that the slave differs from even a tame animal by perceiving and obeying reason as distinct from force or habit (cf. 13.2–3, 12–14).

different as well as their souls—those of the latter strong with a view to necessary needs, those of the former straight and useless for such tasks, but use-   30
ful with a view to a political way of life (which is itself divided between the
needs of war and those of peace); yet the opposite often results, some having the bodies of free persons while others have the souls. It is evident, at any
rate, that if they were to be born as different only[26] in body as the images of   35
the gods, everyone would assert that those not so favored merited being their
slaves. (11) But if this is true in the case of the body, it is much more justifiable to make this distinction in the case of the soul; yet it is not as easy to see
the beauty of the soul as it is that of the body. That some persons are free and   1255a
others slaves by nature, therefore, and that for these slavery is both advantageous and just, is evident.

CHAPTER 6

(1) That those who assert the opposite are in a certain manner correct, however, is not difficult to see. Slavery and the slave are spoken of in a double sense.
There is also a sort of slave or enslaved person according to convention,[27] the   5
convention being a certain agreement under which things conquered in war
are said to belong to the conquerors. (2) This [plea of] justice is challenged
by many of those conversant with the laws—as they would challenge an orator—on a motion of illegality,[28] on the grounds that it is a terrible thing if
what yields to force is to be enslaved and ruled by what is able to apply force   10
and is superior in power. And there are some of the wise as well who hold
this opinion, though some hold the other. (3) The cause of this dispute—and
what makes the arguments converge—is that virtue, once it obtains the necessary resources, is in a certain manner particularly able to apply force, and
what is dominant is always preeminent in some good, so it is held that there   15
is no force without virtue, and that the dispute concerns only [the plea of]
justice; (4) for on this account the ones hold that good will is [the measure
of] what is just, while the others hold that this very thing, the rule of the superior, is just. At any rate, if these arguments are set on one side, the other   20
arguments—which assume that what is better in virtue ought not to rule or

26 · Reading *monon* ("only") here with the MSS instead of at the end of the previous
sentence with Dreizehnter and most editors.
27 · Or "law" (*nomos*), as it is often translated elsewhere.
28 · "Motion of illegality" (*graphē paranomōn*) is a technical term of Athenian jurispru-
dence for a suit brought against anyone proposing in the public assembly a measure
contravening the fundamental laws of the city.

be master—have neither strength nor persuasiveness.²⁹ (5) Those who regard the slavery that results from war as just adhere wholly, as they suppose,
to a sort of justice (for law is just in a certain sense); yet at the same time they
deny [implicitly that it is in fact always just]. For the beginnings of wars are
not always just, and no one would assert that someone not meriting enslavement ought ever to be a slave. Otherwise, the result will be that those held
to be the best born will become slaves and the offspring of slaves if they happen to be captured and sold. (6) Accordingly, they do not want to speak of
these as slaves, but rather barbarians. When they say this, however, they are in
search of nothing other than the slave by nature of which we spoke at the beginning; for they must necessarily assert that there are some persons who are
everywhere slaves, and others who are so nowhere. (7) It is the same way with
good birth as well; for they consider themselves well born not only among
their own but everywhere, but barbarians only at home—the assumption
being that there is something well born and free simply, and something not
simply [but relatively], as Theodectes's Helen says:

  As offshoot of divine roots on either side
  Who would dare call me serving-maid?³⁰

(8) When they speak in this way, it is by nothing other than virtue or vice
that they define what is slave and what is free, who is well born and who is ill
born. For they claim that from the good should come someone good, just as
a human being comes from a human being and a beast from beasts. But while
nature wishes to do this, it is often unable to. (9) That there is some reason
in the dispute, therefore, and that it is not [simply] the case that the ones
are slaves by nature and the others free, is clear; and also that such a distinction does exist for some, where it is advantageous as well as just for the one
to be enslaved and the other to be master; and that the one ought to be ruled

29 · This difficult passage has been variously interpreted. Newman comments, "One
side argues from this, that, force being accompanied by virtue, and virtue attracting
good-will, slavery is just only where there is good-will between master and slave, and
that consequently the indiscriminate enslavement of those conquered in war is unjust;
the other side argues that as force implies virtue, wherever there is the force to enslave,
there is the right to enslave." The "good will" of the MSS (*eunoia*) has been questioned
by some editors; for the connection between good will and virtue, however, see *Eth.
Nic.* 1166b30–67a21. We have no other information about debates over slavery in ancient Greece, and it is quite uncertain to whom Aristotle is here referring. Cf. Saunders 1995.
30 · Theodectes, fr. 3 Nauck.

and the other to rule, and to rule by the sort of rule that is natural for them, which is mastery, (10) while bad rule is disadvantageous for both. For the   10 same thing is advantageous for the part and the whole and for body and soul, and the slave is a sort of part of the master—a part of his body, as it were, animate yet separate. There is thus a certain advantage—and even a friendship of slave and master for one another—for those slaves who merit being such by nature; but for those who do not merit it in this way but who are slaves according to convention and by force, the opposite is the case.[31]   15

CHAPTER 7

(1) It is evident from these things as well that mastery and political rule are not the same thing and that all the sorts of rule are not the same as one another, as some assert. For the one sort is over those free by nature, the other over slaves; and household management is monarchy (for every household is run by one alone), while political rule is over free and equal persons. (2) Now the master is so called not according to a science he possesses but through being a certain sort, and similarly with the slave and the free person. Still, there   20 could be a science of mastery and one of slavery. The science of slavery would be the sort of thing provided through the education offered by the fellow in Syracuse—for someone there used to receive pay for teaching slave boys their   25

31 · Aristotle's notorious defense here of "natural slavery" is problematic in a number of ways, and has given rise to very diverse interpretations. Some have argued that natural slaves are mentally deficient persons essentially incapable of taking care of themselves—which would imply that Aristotle was in fact a radical critic of slavery as it actually existed in his day (Athenians, for example, held some 100,000 slaves—twice the adult male population—at the outbreak of the Peloponnesian War). Others believe that natural slaves for him are deficient morally rather than mentally, and potentially represent a much larger group (consider Simpson 1998, 31–44). It is necessary to keep in mind the widespread sense of racial superiority among polis-dwelling Greeks over the "barbarians" of the Balkans and the Persian Empire, who made up a very large proportion of Greek slaves; this goes some way toward explaining the virtually universal acceptance among them of slavery as an institution—indeed, to the extent that slavery was controversial, it was relative to the enslavement of other Greeks (consider Plato, *Republic* 469b–c, 471a). In an important passage in *Pol.* 7 (7.1327b23–36), Aristotle appeals to differences in climate to account for the apparently innate differences between Greeks and those living to its north ("Europe") or east ("Asia"): Greeks possess both intelligence (*dianoia*) and "spiritedness" (*thymos*); conditions in Europe, on the other hand, favor the development of spiritedness without intelligence, while those in Asia favor intelligence but not spiritedness. This in turn explains why Greeks regularly best Asians in war—and why Asians make especially good slaves. See Kraut 2002, ch. 8.

regular serving chores; (3) and there might be additional learning in such matters, for example in cookery and other service of this type. For certain works are more honored or more necessary than others, and as the proverb has it, "slave before slave, master before master."[32] (4) All things of this sort, then, are sciences of slavery; but the science of mastery is expertise in using slaves, since the master is what he is not in the acquiring of slaves but in the use of them. This science has nothing great or dignified about it: the master must know how to command the things that the slave must know how to do. (5) Hence for those to whom it is open not to be bothered with such things, a steward assumes this prerogative, while they themselves engage in politics or philosophy. Expertise in acquiring slaves is different from both of these—that is, the just sort of acquiring, which is like a certain kind of war or hunting. Concerning slave and master, then, let the discussion stand thus.

30

35

40

CHAPTER 8

1256a   (1) But let us examine generally, in accordance with our normal sort of approach, possessions as such and the art of getting goods,[33] since the slave too turned out to be a part of one's possessions. In the first place, then, one might raise the question whether the art of getting goods is the same as household management, a part of it, or subordinate to it; and if subordinate, whether it is so in the way the art of making shuttles is to the art of weaving, or in the way the art of casting bronze is to the art of sculpture. For these are not subordinate in the same way, but the one provides instruments, the other the matter. (2) (By the matter I mean the substance out of which some work is performed—for example, wool for the weaver or bronze for the sculptor.) Now it is clear that household management is not the same as the art of getting goods, for it belongs to the latter to supply and the former to use. For what is the expertise that uses the things in the house if not expertise in

5

10

32 · Philemon, fr. 53 Kock.

33 · The term rendered "expertise in getting goods" is *chrēmatistikē*, from *chrēmata*, (material) "goods." Aristotle uses the term here in several distinct senses which it is critical to distinguish: as a neutral or general term (equivalent to "expertise in acquisition"), as a positive term for the activity of satisfying natural human needs, and in a negative sense, as the (unnatural) art of money-making; cf. Newman. At the risk of some confusion, I have translated the term as "the art of money-making" wherever it clearly bears the negative sense. *Pol.* 1.8–11 is the most important discussion of what we today call economics not only in Aristotle's works but in all of ancient literature. See generally Meikle 1995.

household management? But whether getting goods is a part of it or different in kind is a matter of dispute. (3) For if it belongs to the expert at getting   15
goods to discern how to get goods and property, and if property and wealth
encompass many parts, one must consider in the first place whether expertise in farming is part of expertise in getting goods[34] or different in kind,
and whether this is the case for the concern with sustenance generally and
the possessions connected with it. (4) There are indeed many kinds of sustenance, and therefore many ways of life both of animals and of human be-   20
ings. For it is impossible to live without sustenance, so that the differences
in sustenance have made the ways of life of animals differ. (5) For of beasts
some live in herds and others scattered—whichever is advantageous for their
sustenance, on account of some of them being carnivores, some herbivores,   25
and some omnivores; so that it is with a view to their convenience and their
predilections in these matters that nature has determined their ways of life.
And because the same thing is not pleasant to each kind of animal according
to nature but different things to different kinds, among the carnivores and
the herbivores themselves their ways of life differ from one another. (6) The
same is the case for human beings as well; for there are great differences in   30
their ways of life. The idlest are nomads: they derive sustenance from tame
animals without labor and amid leisure, though as it is necessary for their
herds to move about on account of their pastures, they are compelled to follow along with them, as if they were farming a living farm. (7) Others live   35
from hunting, and different sorts from different sorts of hunting. Some, for
example, live from brigandage;[35] others from fishing, if they dwell near lakes,
marshes, rivers, or a sea that is suitable; others from birds or wild beasts. But
the type of human being that is most numerous lives from the land and from
cultivated crops.   40

(8) The ways of life are, then, about this many, or at least those which involve self-generated work and do not supply sustenance through exchange
and commerce: the way of life of the nomad, the farmer, the brigand, the   1256b
fisher, and the hunter. There are also some who live pleasantly by combining
several of these in order to compensate for the shortcomings of one way of
life, where it happens to be lacking in sufficiency. For example, some combine
the nomad's with the brigand's, some the farmer's with the hunter's, and simi-   5
larly with others as well—they pass their time in the manner that need [to-

---

34 · Reading *chrēmatistikēs* with the MSS rather than the conjectural *oikonomikēs* ("of
expertise in household management") adopted by Dreizehnter.
35 · The term encompasses robbery on land as well as at sea, i.e. piracy. Cf. Plato,
Laws 823b.

gether with pleasure] compels them to.[36] (9) Now property of this sort is evidently given by nature itself to all animals, both immediately from birth and
10   when they have reached completion. (10) For at birth from the very beginning some animals provide at the same time as much sustenance as is adequate until the offspring can supply itself—for example, those that give birth to larvae or eggs; while those that give birth to live offspring have sustenance for these
15   in themselves for a certain period—the natural substance called milk. (11) It is clear in a similar way, therefore, that for grown things as well one must suppose both that plants exist for the sake of animals and that the other animals exist for the sake of human beings—the tame animals, both for use and sustenance, and most if not all of the wild animals, for sustenance and other assis-
20   tance, in order that clothing and other instruments may be got from them.[37] (12) If, then, nature makes nothing that is incomplete or purposeless, nature must necessarily have made all of these for the sake of human beings.

     Hence the art of war will also be in some sense a natural form of the acquisitive art; for one part of it is expertise in hunting, which should be
25   used with a view both to beasts and to those human beings who are naturally suited to be ruled but unwilling—this sort of war being by nature just. (13) One kind of the acquisitive art, then, is by nature a part of household management, and must either be available or be supplied by the latter so as to be available—the art of acquiring those goods a store of which is both nec-
30   essary for life and useful for the community of a city or household.[38] (14) At any rate, it would seem to be these things that make up genuine wealth. For sufficiency[39] in possessions of this sort with a view to a good life is not limitless, as Solon asserts it to be in his poem: "of wealth no boundary lies revealed to men."[40] (15) There is such a boundary, just as in the other arts; for there is
35   no art that has an instrument that is without limit either in number or in size, and wealth is the aggregate of instruments belonging to household managers and political rulers. That there is a natural art of acquisition for household managers and political rulers, then, and the cause of this, is clear.

36 · *Synanankazein*: cf. Newman.

37 · Reading this sentence with the MSS rather than as punctuated and supplemented by Dreizehnter.

38 · Reading *ho* with the MSS rather than *hōi* with Dreizehnter in b27. I understand *chrēmatōn* in 29 to depend on *ktētikēs* in 27.

39 · *To autarches einai*, often translated "self-sufficiency"; but the primary meaning here and throughout this discussion is "having enough," not "being independent of others." Cf. Meikle 1995, 44–45.

40 · Solon, fr. 1, 71 Diehl.

CHAPTER 9

(1) But there is another type of acquisitive art that they particularly call—   40
and justifiably so—the art of getting goods, on account of which there is
held to be no limit to wealth and property. This is considered by many to be   1257a
one and the same as the sort mentioned because of the resemblance between
them; and while it is not the same as the one spoken of, it is not far from it
either. The one is by nature, while the other is not by nature but arises rather
through a certain experience and art.   5

(2) Concerning this, let us take the following as our beginning. Every possession has a double use. Both of these uses belong to it as such, but not in the
same way, the one being proper and the other not proper to the thing. In the
case of shoes, for example, one can wear them or one can trade them.[41] Both   10
of these are uses of shoes; (3) for the one exchanging shoes with someone
who needs them in return for money or sustenance uses shoes as shoes, but
not in respect of their proper use; for they did not come to be for the sake of
exchange. The same is the case concerning other possessions as well. (4) For   15
trading can be applied to all things; it arises in the first place from something that is according to nature—the fact that human beings have either
more or fewer things than what is required. Thus it is also clear that commerce is not by nature part of the art of making money;[42] for it was necessary to make an exchange in order to obtain what they required. (5) In the
first community, then—that is, the household—it is evident that exchange   20
has no function, but only when the community has already become more
numerous. For those in the household shared all of the same things, while
persons separated into different households needed many other things as
well, and it was necessary to make transfers of these things according to their
needs, as many barbarian nations still do, through barter.[43] (6) For they ex-   25
change useful things for one another and nothing besides—giving, for example, wine and accepting grain, and similarly for other such things. This
sort of trading is not contrary to nature, nor is it any form of money-making,
for it existed in order to support natural sufficiency. (7) However, the latter   30
arose from it reasonably enough. For as the assistance of foreigners became

---

41 · Compare the general discussion of "exchange" in *Eth. Nic.* 5.5.

42 · That is, *chrēmatistikē* in the pejorative sense. Aristotle seems to use the terms
"trade" (*metablētikē*) and "commerce" (*kapelikē*) interchangeably; in normal Greek usage, the latter term tends to be limited to local or retail as distinct from long-distance
trade.

43 · Rendering *kapelikē* "barter," with Newman.

greater in importing what they were in need of and exporting what was in surplus, the use of money was necessarily devised. (8) For the things necessary by nature are not in each case easily portable; hence with a view to exchanges they made a compact with one another to give and accept something which was itself one of the useful things and could be used flexibly to suit the needs of life, such as iron and silver and whatever else might be of this sort. At first this was something with its value determined simply by size and weight, but eventually they impressed a mark on it in order to be relieved of having to measure it, the mark being put on as an indication of the amount. (9) Once a supply of money came into being as a result of such necessary exchange, then, the other kind of goods-getting arose—that is, commerce. At first this probably existed in a simple fashion, while later through experience it became more a matter of art—the art of discerning what and how to trade in order to make the greatest profit. (10) It is on this account that the art of goods-getting is held to be particularly connected with money, and to have as its function the ability to discern what will provide a given amount of it; for it is held to be productive of wealth and goods. Indeed, they often define wealth as a given amount of money, since this is what money-making or commerce is connected with. (11) At other times, however, money seems to be something nonsensical and to exist altogether by convention,[44] and in no way by nature, because when changed by its users it is worth nothing and is not useful with a view to any of the necessary things; and it will often happen that one who is wealthy in money will go in want of necessary sustenance. Yet it would be absurd if wealth were something one could have in abundance and die of starvation—like the Midas of the fable, when everything set before him turned into gold on account of the greediness of his prayer.[45] (12) Hence they seek another definition of wealth and the getting of goods, and correctly so. For the getting of goods and the wealth that is according to nature is something different: this is the art of household management, while the other is commerce, which is productive of wealth not in every way but through trafficking in goods, and is held to be connected with money, since money is the medium and goal of exchange. (13) And the wealth deriving from this sort of getting of goods is indeed without limit. For just as the art of medicine has no limit with respect to being healthy, or any of the other arts with respect to its end (for this is what they particularly wish to

44 · There is a play here on the words for "money" (*nomisma*) and "convention" (*nomos*).
45 · Midas was the legendary founder of the Phrygian kingdom.

accomplish), while there is a limit with respect to what exists for the sake of
the end (since the end is a limit in the case of all of them), so with this sort of
goods-getting there is no limit with respect to the end, and the end is wealth   30
of this sort and property in money. (14) But of household management as
distinguished from money-making there is a limit; for that is not the function of household management. Thus in one way it appears necessary that
there be a limit to all wealth; yet if we look at what actually occurs we see
that the opposite happens—all who engage in money-making increase their
money without limit. (15) The cause of this is the nearness to one another   35
of these [forms of goods-getting]. For they converge in the matter of use,
the same thing being used in the case of either sort of goods-getting. For the
same property is being used,[46] though not in the same respect, but in the one
case the end is increase, in the other something else. So some hold that this
is the function of household management, and they proceed on the supposition that they should either preserve or increase without limit their holdings   40
of money. (16) The cause of this condition is that they are serious about living, but not about living well; and since that desire of theirs is without limit,   1258a
they also desire what is productive of unlimited things. Even those who also
aim at living well seek what conduces to bodily gratifications, and since this
too appears to be available in and through property, their pursuits are wholly   5
connected with making money, and this is why the other form of the art of
getting goods has arisen. (17) For as gratification consists in excess, they seek
the sort of art that produces the excess characteristic of gratification; and if
they are unable to supply it through getting goods, they attempt this in some
other fashion, using each sort of capacity in a way not according to nature.   10
For it belongs to courage to produce not goods but confidence; nor does
this belong to the military or medical arts, but it belongs to the former to
produce victory, to the latter, health. (18) But all of these they make forms
of money-making, as if this were the end and everything else had to march
toward it.

Concerning the unnecessary sort of getting goods, then, both as regards   15
what it is and why we are in need of it, enough has been said; and also concerning the necessary sort—that it is different from the other, being household management according to nature (the sort connected with sustenance),
and is not without limit like the other, but has a defining principle.

---

46 · Reading *chrēseōs ktēsis* in b37 with the MSS rather than the conjectural *ktēseōs
chrēsis* ("use is of the same property") adopted by Dreizehnter.

CHAPTER 10

(1) It is also clear what the answer is to the question raised at the beginning
20   whether the art of getting goods belongs to the expert household manager
or political ruler or not, but should rather be available to him. For just as
political expertise does not create human beings but makes use of them after receiving them from nature, so also should nature provide land or sea or
something else for sustenance, while it befits the household manager to have
25   what comes from those things in the state it should be in. (2) For it does not
belong to the art of weaving to make wool, but to make use of it, and to know
what sort is usable and suitable or poor and unsuitable. Otherwise one might
raise the question why the art of getting goods should be a part of household
30   management but not the medical art, since those in the household ought to
be healthy, just as they must live or do any other necessary thing. (3) But just
as seeing about health does indeed belong to the household manager and the
ruler in a sense, but in another sense not but rather to the doctor, so in the
case of goods it belongs to the household manager in a sense, but in another
35   sense not but rather to the subordinate art. This should be available above
all, as was said before, by nature. For it is a work of nature to provide sustenance to the newly born, everything deriving sustenance from what remains
of that from which it is born. (4) The art of getting goods relative to crops
40   and animals is thus natural for all. But since it is twofold, as we said, part of
it being commerce and part the art of household management, the latter nec-
1258b   essary and praised, while the art of exchange is justly blamed since it is not
according to nature but involves taking from others, usury is most reasonably hated, because one's possessions derive from money itself and not from
that for which it was supplied. (5) For it came into being for the sake of ex-
5   change, but interest actually creates more of it. And it is from this that it gets
its name: offspring are similar to those who give birth to them, and interest
is money born of money.[47] So of the sorts of goods-getting this is the most
contrary to nature.

CHAPTER 11

(1) Since we have discussed adequately what relates to knowledge, what re-
10   lates to utility must be treated. All things of this sort have room for a free

47 · The word for "interest" (*tokos*) also means "offspring."

sort of study, but experience in them is a necessity. The useful parts of the art of getting goods are: to be experienced regarding livestock—what sorts are most profitable in which places and under what conditions (for example, what sort of horses or cattle or sheep ought to be kept, and similarly with the other animals, (2) for one needs to be experienced as regards those that are most profitable both compared with one another and in particular places, since different kinds thrive in different areas); next, regarding farming, both of grain and fruit; and finally, regarding beekeeping and the raising of other animals, whether fish or fowl, from which it is possible to derive benefit. (3) Of the art of getting goods in its most proper sense, then, these are the parts and primary elements. Of the art of exchange the greatest part is trade, of which there are three parts: provisioning the ship, transport, and marketing (these differ from each other by the fact that some are safer while others provide greater remuneration); the second is moneylending; and the third is wage labor, (4) of which one sort involves workers' arts,[48] while the other is performed by those who lack any art but are useful only for their bodies. There is a third kind of art of getting goods between this and the first, since it has some part both of the sort that is according to nature and of the art of exchange: this deals with things from the earth and unfruitful but useful things that grow from the earth, and includes activities such as lumbering and every sort of mining (5) (this now encompasses many different types, as there are many kinds of things mined from the earth).

A general account has now been given of each of these things; a detailed and exact discussion would be useful in undertaking the works themselves, but to spend much time on such things is crude. (6) The most artful of these works are those which involve chance the least; the most vulgar, those in which the body is most damaged; the most slavish, those in which the body is most used; the most ignoble, those which are least in need of virtue.

(7) Since some have written on these matters—as Chares of Paros and Apollodoros of Lemnos on farming both of grain and fruit, for example, and others on other things—they may be studied there by anyone concerned

15

20

25

30

35

40

1259a

---

48 · This is perhaps the least misleading English equivalent to the untranslatable *banausos*, usually rendered by "vulgar" or "mechanical." The reference is to a class of artisans who work indoors and with their hands at repetitive tasks, as in modern factory work. There was a powerful prejudice against such persons in the contemporary Greek world, and they were often excluded from full citizenship. Strikingly, Aristotle suggests that they have less virtue even than slaves, whose work was also mostly menial (1.13.13); see further especially 3.5.

with them; but, in addition, what has been said in various places concerning
5   the ways some have succeeded in getting goods should be collected.⁴⁹ (8) For
all these things are useful for those who honor the art of getting goods. There
is, for example, the scheme of Thales of Miletus.⁵⁰ This is a money-making⁵¹
scheme that is attributed to him on account of his wisdom, yet it happens to
be general in application. (9) For they say that when some on account of his
10   poverty reproached him with the uselessness of philosophy, Thales, observ-
ing through his knowledge of astronomy that there would be a good harvest
of olives, was able during the winter to raise a small sum of money to place
in deposit on all the olive presses in both Miletus and Chios, which he could
hire at a low rate because no one was competing with him; then, when the
15   season came, and many of them were suddenly in demand at the same time,
he hired them out on what terms he pleased and collected a great deal of
money,⁵² thus showing how easy it is for philosophers to become wealthy
if they so wish, but it is not this they are serious about. (10) Thales, then, is
20   said to have made a display of his wisdom in this manner, though, as we said,
this piece of the art of money-making is universal, if someone is able to establish a monopoly for himself. Thus even some cities raise revenue in this way
when they are short of money; they establish a monopoly on things being
sold. (11) In Sicily, a man used some money⁵³ deposited with him to buy all
25   the iron from the iron foundries, and when traders came from their trading
places he alone had it to sell; and though he did not greatly increase the price,
he made a hundred talents' profit out of an original fifty. (12) When Diony-
30   sius heard of this, he ordered him to take his money⁵⁴ and leave Syracuse, on
the grounds that he had discovered a way of raising revenue that was harmful
to Dionysius's own affairs.⁵⁵ Yet the insight was the same as that of Thales, for
both artfully arranged a monopoly for themselves. (13) It is useful for political rulers also to be familiar with these things. For many cities stand in need

49 · The work of Apollodorus is cited and used in the agricultural writings of Varro
and Pliny; Chares is otherwise unknown. The suggestion concerning collecting accounts of success in money-making appears to be taken up in the second book of the
pseudo-Aristotelian *Economics*.
50 · Thales, the founder of Greek philosophy, lived in the late sixth and early fifth
centuries.
51 · *Chrēmatistikon*.
52 · *Chrēmata*.
53 · The Greek here is *nomisma*, the normal term for "money," rather than *chrēmata*.
54 · *Chrēmata*.
55 · It is not clear whether Dionysius I (405–367 BC) or Dionysius II (367–44 BC) of
Syracuse is meant.

of money-making and revenues of this sort, just as households do, yet more   35
so. Thus there are some even among those engaged in politics who are concerned only with these matters.[56]

CHAPTER 12

(1) Since there are three parts of the art of household management—mastery, which was spoken of earlier, paternal rule, and marital rule—[the latter two must now be taken up. These differ fundamentally from the former,
since one ought][57] to rule a wife and children as free persons, though it is not   40
the same manner of rule in each case, the wife being ruled in political, the   1259b
children in kingly fashion. For the male, unless constituted in some respect
contrary to nature, is by nature more expert at leading than the female, and
the elder and complete than the younger and incomplete. (2) In most political offices, it is true, there is an alternation of ruler and ruled, since they tend   5
by their nature to be on an equal footing and to differ in nothing; all the
same, when one rules and the other is ruled, the ruler seeks to establish differences in external appearance, forms of address, and prerogatives, as in the
story Amasis told about his footpan.[58] The male always stands thus in rela-   10
tion to the female. (3) But rule over the children is kingly. For the begetter is
ruler on the basis of both affection and age, which is the very mark of kingly
rule. Homer thus spoke finely of Zeus when he addressed as "father of men
and gods" the king of them all. For by nature the king should be different, but   115
he should be of the same stock; and this is the case of the elder in relation to
the younger and the begetter to the child.

CHAPTER 13

(1) It is evident, then, that household management gives more serious attention to human beings than to inanimate property, to the virtue of these rather   20
than to that of property (which we call wealth), and to the virtue of free per-

---

56 · Aristotle may be thinking particularly of the contemporary Athenian politician
Eubulus. Some have suspected this chapter of being a later interpolation; cf. Newman.
The chief difficulty is that it seems to undercut the critique of "money-making" in the
preceding chapters.

57 · Dreizehnter marks a lacuna at this point in the text; I have supplied what I take
to be the sense.

58 · Amasis, an Egyptian king of lowly origin, had his subjects worship a statue of a
god fashioned from a golden footpan. Cf. Herodotus 2.172.

sons rather than to that of slaves. (2) First, then, one might raise a question concerning slaves: whether there is a certain virtue belonging to a slave beside the virtues of an instrument and a servant and more honorable than these,
25   such as moderation and courage and justice and the other dispositions of this sort, or whether there is none beside the bodily services. (3) Questions arise either way, for if there is such a virtue, how will they differ from free persons? But if there is not, though they are human beings and share in reason, it is
30   odd. Nearly the same question arises concerning woman and child, whether there are virtues belonging to these as well—whether the woman should be moderate and courageous and just, and whether a child is [capable of being] licentious and moderate or not. (4) And in general, then, this must be investigated concerning the ruled by nature and the ruler, whether virtue is
35   the same or different. For if both should partake in gentlemanliness,[59] why should the one rule and the other be ruled once and for all? For it is not possible for them to differ by greater and less, since being ruled and ruling differ in kind, not by greater and less; (5) but that one should have such virtue and the other not would be surprising. For unless the ruler is moderate and just,
40   how will he rule finely? And unless the ruled is, how will he be ruled finely?
1260a   For if he is licentious and cowardly he will perform none of his duties. It is evident, then, that both must of necessity partake in virtue, but that there are differences in their virtue, as there are in the virtue of those who are by nature ruled. (6) Consideration of the soul guides us straightway to this con
5   clusion. For in this there is by nature a ruling and a ruled element, and we assert there is a different virtue of each—that is, of the element having reason and of the irrational element. It is clear, then, that the same thing holds in the other cases as well. Thus by nature most things are ruling and ruled. (7) For
10   the free person rules the slave, the male the female, and the man the child in different ways. The parts of the soul are present in all, but they are present in a different way. The slave is wholly lacking the deliberative element; the female has it but it lacks authority;[60] the child has it but it is incomplete. (8) It
15   is to be supposed that the same necessarily holds concerning the virtues of

59 · "Gentlemanliness" (*kalokagathia*), the exemplary virtue of a "noble and good man" (*kaloskagathos*). As Newman notes, "the question is put as paradoxically as possible, for *kalokagathia* is precisely the type of virtue from which slaves and women and children are furthest removed." Cf. *Eth. Nic.* 4.7.1124a1–4, 10.10.1179b4–16.

60 · Or "is not sovereign" (*akyron*). Some have taken this simply as referring to a woman's subordination to her husband, but it seems more likely that Aristotle means to suggest that the deliberative element in women is weaker relative to their own passions.

character: all must share in them, but not in the same way, but to each in relation to his own function. Hence the ruler must have complete virtue of character (for his function is in an absolute sense that of a master craftsman, and
reason is a master craftsman); while each of the others must have as much as
falls to him. (9) It is thus evident that there is a virtue of character that be-   20
longs to all these mentioned, and that the moderation of a woman and a man
is not the same, nor their courage or justice, as Socrates supposed, but that
there is a ruling and a serving courage, and similarly with the other virtues.
(10) This is clear further if we investigate the matter in more detail. For those   25
who say in a general way that virtue is a good condition of the soul or acting
correctly or something of this sort deceive themselves. Those who enumerate the virtues, like Gorgias, do much better than those who define it in this
way.[61] (11) One should thus consider that matters stand with everyone as the
poet said of woman: "to a woman silence is an ornament,"[62] though this is   30
not the case for a man. Since the child is incomplete, it is clear that its virtue
too is not its own as relating to itself, but as relating to its end and the person
leading it. (12) The same is true of that of the slave in relation to a master.
We laid it down that the slave is useful with respect to the necessary things,
so that he clearly needs only a small amount of virtue—as much as will pre-   35
vent him from falling short in his work through licentiousness or cowardice.
One might raise the question whether, if what has just been said is true, artisans too will need virtue, since they often fall short in their work through licentiousness. (13) Or is the case very different? For the slave is a sharer in the   40
master's life, while the other is more remote, and has virtue only so far as he
is also a slave. For the manufacturing artisan is under a special sort of slavery,   1260b
and while the slave belongs among those persons or things that are by nature,
no shoemaker does, nor any of the other artisans. (14) It is evident, therefore,
that the master should be responsible for instilling this sort of virtue in the
slave; he is not merely someone possessing an art of mastery that instructs the
slave in his work. Those who deny reason to slaves and assert that commands   5
only should be used with them do not argue finely: admonition is to be used
with slaves more than with children. (15) But concerning these matters let
our discussion stand thus. Concerning husband and wife and children and
father and the sort of virtue that is connected with each of these, and what is   10
and what is not fine in their relations with one another and how one should

61 · The reference is to Plato, *Meno* 71d ff.
62 · Sophocles, *Ajax* 293.

pursue what is well and avoid the bad, these things must necessarily be addressed in the discourses on the regimes.[63] For since the household as a whole is a part of the city, and these things of the household, and one should look at the virtue of the part in relation to the virtue of the whole, both children and women must necessarily be educated looking to the regime, at least if it makes any difference with a view to the city's being excellent that both its children and its women are excellent. (16) But it necessarily makes a difference: women are a part amounting to a half of free persons, and from the children come those who are sharers in the regime. So since there has been discussion of these matters, and we must speak elsewhere of those remaining, let us leave off the present discourses as having reached an end and make another beginning to the argument. Let us investigate in the first instance the views that have been put forward about the best regime.

63 · There is no discussion of this sort in the remainder of the *Politics* as we have it. What is meant by "the [discourses] on the regimes" is not certain; the reference would seem to be to books 2–8 or 3–8 of the *Politics*. See Introduction, n. 63.

Book 2

(1) Since it is our intention to study the sort of political community that is superior to all for those capable of living as far as possible in the manner one would pray for,[1] we should also investigate other regimes, both those in use in some of the cities that are said to be well managed and any others spoken about by certain persons that are held to be in a fine condition, in order that both what is correct in their condition and what is useful may be seen—and further, that to seek something apart from them may not be held wholly to belong to those wishing to act the sophist,[2] but that we may be held to enter into this inquiry because those regimes now available are in fact not in a fine condition. (2) We must make a beginning that is the natural beginning for this investigation. It is necessary that all the citizens either share in everything, or in nothing, or in some things but not in others. Now it is evident that to share in nothing is impossible; for the regime is a certain sort of community,[3] and it is necessary in the first instance to share in a location: a single city occupies a single location, and the citizens are sharers in a single city. (3) But, of the things in which there can be sharing, is it better for the city that is going to be finely administered to share in all of them, or is it better to share in some but not in others? For it is possible for the citizens to share with one another in respect to children and women and possessions, as in the *Republic* of Plato; for there Socrates asserts that children and women

30

35

40

1261a

5

1 · Or literally "according to prayer" (*kat' euchēn*), an expression Aristotle uses in a quasi-technical way to characterize the best or (as it is often translated) "ideal" regime.
2 · Probably a reference to Isocrates (*Antidosis* 83); cf. *Eth. Nic.* 10.9.1181a12–19.
3 · It is important to keep in mind throughout the link between "sharing" (*koinōnein*) and "community" (*koinōnia*).

and property should be common.⁴ Which is better, then, the condition that
exists now or one based on the law that is described in the *Republic*?

CHAPTER 2

10   (1) Having women common to all involves many difficulties; but a particular
difficulty is that the reason Socrates gives as to why there should be legislation of this sort evidently does not result from his arguments. Further, with
respect to the end which he asserts the city should have, it is, as has just been
said, impossible; but how one should distinguish a sense in which it is pos-
15   sible is not discussed. (2) I mean, that it is best for the city to be as far as
possible entirely one; for this is the basic premise Socrates adopts. And yet it
is evident that as it becomes increasingly one it will no longer be a city. For
the city is in its nature a sort of aggregation, and as it becomes more a unity
it will be a household instead of a city, and a human being instead of a house-
20   hold; for we would surely say that the household is more a unity than the city,
and the individual than the household. So even if one were able to do this,
one ought not do it, as it would destroy the city. (3) Now the city is made up
not only of a number of human beings, but also of those differing in kind: a
city does not arise from persons who are similar. A city differs from an alli-
25   ance. The latter is useful by its quantity, even if its parts are the same in kind
(since an alliance exists by nature for mutual assistance), as when a greater
weight is added to the scale. In this sort of way, too, a city differs from a nation, when the multitude is not scattered in villages but rather is like the Ar-
30   cadians.⁵ Those from whom a unity should arise differ in kind. (4) It is thus
reciprocal equality that preserves cities, as was said earlier in the [discourses
on] ethics.⁶ This is necessarily the case even among persons who are free and
equal, for all cannot rule at the same time, but each rules for a year or ac-
35   cording to some other arrangement or period of time. (5) In this way, then,
it results that all rule, just as if shoemakers and carpenters were to exchange

4 · Plato, *Republic* 449a ff. "Common" translates the adjective *koinos*.
5 · The meaning of this sentence has been much disputed (cf. Newman). Aristotle's argument seems to presuppose a distinction between nations (*ethnē*) consisting simply
of autonomous villages and nations consisting of villages subject to some central authority: the relatively primitive Arcadians had been organized in a kind of federal state
since the founding of the fortified center of Megalopolis in 362 BC. Aristotle suggests
that a state of this sort differs from a city by being merely an alliance of elements (villages) not differing in kind.
6 · *Eth. Nic.* 1132b33–34 and ff.

places rather than the same persons always being shoemakers and carpenters. (6) But since that condition is better also with respect to the political community, it is clear that it is better if the same always rule, where this is possible; but in cases where it is not possible because all are equal in their nature, and it is at the same time just for all to have a share in ruling (regardless of whether ruling is something good or something mean), there is at least an imitation of this.[7] (7) For some rule and some are ruled in turn, as if becoming other persons. And, in the same way, among the rulers different persons hold different offices. It is evident from these things, then, that the city is not naturally one in this sense as some argue, and what was said to be the greatest good for cities actually destroys them; yet the good of each thing is surely what preserves it. (8) It is evident in another way as well that to seek to unify the city excessively is not good. For a household is more self-sufficient than one person, and a city than a household; and a city tends to come into being at the point when the community formed by a multitude is self-sufficient. If, therefore, the more self-sufficient is more choiceworthy, what is less a unity is more choiceworthy than what is more a unity.

CHAPTER 3

(1) But even if it is best for the community to be as far as possible a unity, even this does not appear to be proved by the argument that it will follow if all say "mine" and "not mine" at the same time; for Socrates supposes this is an indication of the city being completely one. (2) For "all" has a double sense. If it means "each individually," perhaps this would be closer to what Socrates wants to do, for each will then speak of the same boy as his own son and the same woman as his own wife, and similarly with regard to property and indeed to everything that comes his way. But those who have wives and children in common will not speak of them in this way, but as all collectively and not individually; (3) and similarly with respect to property, as all collectively but not individually. It is evident, then, that a certain fallacy is involved in the

---

7 · The text is uncertain at this point. Dreizehnter brackets the sentence following as a gloss; none of its variant forms yields a satisfactory sense, but the general idea appears merely to elaborate the remark that alternation of rule among equals imitates the permanent differentiation of rulers and ruled in a society of unequals. Saunders translates: "But among those among whom this is not possible, since they are all by nature equal, and among whom it is also at the same time just that all should share in the benefit or chore of ruling, then the principles (a) that equals should yield place in turn, and (b) that out of office they should be similar, approximate to that practice."

phrase "all say"—indeed, the double sense of "all," "both," "odd," and "even"
30   produces contentious syllogisms in arguments as well.[8] Therefore that "all
say the same thing" is in one way fine, though impossible, while in another
way it is not even productive of concord.

(4) Furthermore, the formula is harmful in another way. What belongs in
common to the most people is accorded the least care: they take thought for
35   their own things above all, and less about things common, or only so much
as falls to each individually. For, apart from other things, they slight them on
the grounds that someone else is taking thought for them—just as in household service many attendants sometimes do a worse job than fewer. (5) Each
of the citizens comes to have a thousand sons, though not as an individual,
40   but each is in similar fashion the son of any of them; hence all will slight
them in similar fashion.

1262a   Further, each says "mine" of a citizen who is acting well or ill only in this
sense, that he is one of a certain number: each really says "mine or his," meaning by this every individual of the thousand or however many the city has.
5   And even then he is in doubt, for it is unclear who has happened to have offspring, or whether any have survived. (6) Yet which is superior—for each of
two thousand (or ten thousand) individuals to say "mine" and address the
same thing, or rather the way they say "mine" in cities now? (7) For now the
10   same person is addressed as a son by one, by another as a brother, by another
as a cousin, or according to some other sort of kinship, whether of blood or of
relation and connection by marriage—in the first instance of himself, then
of his own; and further, another describes him as clansman or tribesman. It is
better, indeed, to have a cousin of one's own than a son in the sense indicated.

15   (8) Actually, though, it is impossible to avoid having some suspect who
their brothers and sons or fathers and mothers really are; for they will of necessity find proofs of this in the similarities that occur between children and
their parents. (9) Indeed, some of those who have written accounts of travels[9]
20   assert that this in fact happens; for they say that some inhabitants of upper
Libya have women in common, yet the children they bear are distinguishable
according to their similarities. There are some women, and some females of
other animals such as horses and cattle, that are particularly inclined by nature to produce offspring similar to the parents, like the mare at Pharsalus
called the Just.

8 · See Aristotle, *Sophistic Refutations* 166a33 ff.
9 · An apparent reference to the geographer Eudoxus of Cnidos (cf. frs. 322, 323, and
360 Lasserre); see also Herodotus 4.180.

CHAPTER 4

(1) Further, it is not easy for those establishing this sort of partnership to   25
avoid such difficulties as outrages or involuntary homicides, for example, or
voluntary homicides, assaults, or verbal abuse. None of these things is holy
when it involves fathers, mothers, or those not distant in kinship, as distinct
from outsiders; yet they must necessarily occur more frequently among those   30
who are ignorant of their relatives than among those familiar with them, and
when they do occur, only those who are familiar with their relatives can perform the lawful expiations, while the others cannot. (2) It is also odd that
while sons are made common, only sexual intercourse between lovers is eliminated, but love[10] is not forbidden, or other practices which are improper   35
particularly for a father in relation to his son or a brother in relation to his
brother, as indeed is love by itself. (3) It is also odd that sexual intercourse is
eliminated for no other reason than that the pleasure involved is too strong,
it being supposed that it makes no difference whether this occurs between a   40
father and a son or between brothers.[11]

(4) It would seem to be more useful for the farmers to have women and
children in common than for the guardians.[12] For there will be less affection   1262b
where children and women are common; but the ruled should be of this sort
if they are to obey their rulers and not engage in subversion. (5) In general,
there must necessarily result from a law of this sort the very opposite of what   5
correctly enacted laws ought properly to cause, and of what caused Socrates
to suppose that the matter of children and women should be arranged in
this way. (6) For we suppose affection to be the greatest of good things for
cities, for in this way they would least of all engage in factional conflict; and
Socrates praises above all the city's being one, which is held to be, and which   10
he asserts to be, the work of affection—just as in the discourses on love[13]
we know that Aristophanes speaks of lovers who from an excess of affection
"desire to grow together," the two of them becoming one. (7) Now here it
must necessarily happen that both, or one of them, disappear in the union;
in the city, however, affection necessarily becomes diluted through this sort   15

10 · That is, erotic love (*ēros*), as opposed to friendship or affection (*philia*).
11 · Plato, *Republic* 403b.
12 · The best regime of the early books of the *Republic* consists fundamentally of two
classes, a producing class (farmers and artisans) and a ruling and military class (called
by Plato "guardians"). It is left unclear in the *Republic* whether communism is meant to
be extended to the lower class.
13 · In Plato's *Symposium* (191a ff.).

of community, and the fact that a father least of all says "mine" of his son, or the son of his father. (8) Just as adding much water to a small amount of wine makes the mixture imperceptible, so too does this result with respect to the
20   kinship with one another based on these terms, it being least of all necessary in a regime of this sort for a father to take thought[14] for his sons as sons, or a son for his father as a father, or brothers for one another as brothers. (9) For there are two things above all which make human beings cherish and feel affection—what is one's own and what is dear; and neither of these can be available to those who govern themselves in this way.

25   There is also considerable uncertainty concerning the manner in which children are to be transferred from the farmers and artisans to the guardians as well as from the latter to the former; at any rate, those who transfer and assign them necessarily know who has been assigned to whom. (10) Further,
30   what was mentioned before must necessarily result above all in these cases— that is, assaults, love affairs, murders; for those who have been assigned to the other class of citizens will no longer address the guardians as brothers, children, fathers, or mothers, nor will those among the guardians so address the other class of citizens, so that they avoid doing any of these things on account
35   of their kinship. Concerning the community in children and women, then, let our discussion stand thus.

CHAPTER 5

(1) Next after this it remains to investigate property and how it should be instituted for those who are going to govern themselves under the best regime—whether property should be common or not. (2) This may be investigated
1263a   even apart from the legislation concerning children and women. I mean, as regards what is connected with property, even if the former are held separately, which is the way all do it now, one may investigate in particular whether it is better for both property and uses to be common[, or whether one should be common and the other separate].[15] For example, farmland could be held separately while the crops are brought into a common store
5   and consumed in common, as some nations do; or the opposite could happen, land being held and farmed in common and the crops divided for private use (some barbarians are said to have this approach to sharing as well); or

14 · Accepting the reading of the MSS here rather than the conjectural alterations adopted by Dreizehnter.
15 · I follow many editors in marking a lacuna here, and supply what I take to be the sense.

both farmland and crops could be common. (3) Now if the farmers were of a different class, the approach would be different and easier, but if the citizens undertake the labor for themselves, the arrangements concerning property would give rise to many resentments. For if they turn out to be unequal rather than equal in the work and in the gratifications deriving from it, accusations against those who can gratify themselves or take much while laboring little must necessarily arise on the part of those who take less and labor more. (4) In general, to live together and share in any human matter is difficult, and particularly things of this sort. This is clear in communities of fellow travelers, most of whom are always quarreling as a result of friction with one another over everyday and small matters. Again, friction particularly arises with the servants we use most frequently for regular tasks. (5) Having property in common involves, then, these and other similar difficulties, and the approach that prevails now—if reinforced with good character[16] and an arrangement of correct laws—would be more than a little better. For it would have what is good in both—by both I mean what comes from having property in common and what from having it privately. For it should be common in some sense, yet private generally speaking. (6) Dividing the care of property will cause them not to raise these accusations against one another, and will actually result in improvement, as each applies himself to his own; and it will be through virtue that "the things of friends are common," as the proverb has it, with a view to use. Even now this approach can be found in outline in some cities, so it is not impossible; in finely administered cities especially some of these things already exist, while others could be brought into being. (7) In these cities everyone has his own property, but he makes some of it useful to his friends, and some he uses as common things. In Sparta, for example, they use each other's slaves, as well as their horses and dogs, as practically their own, and anything they need by way of provisions from the fields when they travel in their territory. (8) It is evident, then, that it is better for property to be private, but to make it common in use. That the citizens become such as to use it in common—this is a task proper to the legislator.

Further, it makes an immense difference with respect to pleasure to consider a thing one's own. It is surely not to no purpose that everyone has affection for himself; this is something natural. (9) Selfishness is justly blamed; but this is not having affection for oneself simply, but rather having more affection than one should—just as in the case of the greedy person; for prac-

---

16 · Reading *ēthesin* with Π² and Dreizehnter rather than *ethesin* ("habits") with Π¹, Ross, and others.

5 tically everyone has affection for things of this sort. Moreover, it is a very
pleasant thing to help or do favors for friends, guests, or club-mates; and this
requires that property be private. (10) Those who make the city too much of
a unity not only forfeit these things; in addition, they manifestly eliminate

10 the functions of two of the virtues, moderation concerning women (it being a fine deed to abstain through moderation from a woman who belongs
to another) and liberality concerning property. For it will not be possible to
show oneself as liberal or to perform any liberal action, since the function of
liberality lies in the use of property.

15   (11) This sort of legislation has an attractive face and might be held hu-
mane; he who hears of it accepts it gladly, thinking it will produce a mar-
velous affection in all for each other, especially when it is charged that the

20 ills that now exist in regimes come about through property not being common—I am speaking of lawsuits against one another concerning contracts,
trials involving perjury, and flattery of the rich. (12) Yet none of these things
comes about because of the lack of sharing, but through depravity. For it is
precisely those who possess things in common and share whom we see most

25 at odds,[17] not those who hold their property separately (though those at odds
as a result of sharing are few to observe in comparison with the many who
own property privately). (13) Further, it is only just to speak not only of the
number of ills they will be deprived of by sharing, but also the number of
good things. Indeed, it is a way of life that appears to be altogether impossible.

30   The cause of Socrates's going astray one should consider to be the incor-
rectness of his basic premise. (14) Both the household and the city should be
one in a sense, but not in every sense. On the one hand, as the city proceeds
in this direction, it will at some point cease to be a city; on the other hand,
while remaining a city, it will be a worse city the closer it comes to not being

35 a city—just as if one were to reduce a consonance to unison, or a meter to a
single foot.[18] (15) Rather, as was said before, the city, being a multitude, must
be made one and common through education. It is odd that one who plans
to introduce education[19] and who holds that it is through this that the city
will be excellent should suppose it can be corrected by things of that sort,

17 · The holding of property in common by brothers was an accepted practice in
Athens and elsewhere, and the reference is probably to this.

18 · Greek meters typically admit of much variation in the feet or units that make up
a line of poetry.

19 · This seems to refer specifically to the discussion of the education of philosophers
in *Republic* 6–7.

and not by habits, philosophy, and laws, just as the legislator in Sparta and   40
Crete made common what is connected with property by means of common
messes.[20] (16) Nor should one ignore the fact that it is necessary to pay atten-   1264a
tion to the length of time and the many years during which it would not have
escaped notice if this condition were a fine one; for nearly everything has
been discovered, though some things have not been brought together, while
others are known but not practiced. (17)That it is not fine would become   5
evident above all if one could see such a regime actually being instituted; for
it will not be possible to create a city without introducing parts and dividing
it, on the one hand into common messes, on the other into clans and tribes.
So nothing else will result from the legislation except that the guardians will   10
not farm; yet the Spartans attempt to do this even now.[21]

(18) Neither, for that matter, has Socrates told us what the manner of organization of the regime as a whole will be for those sharing in it; nor is it easy
to say. At all events, the bulk of the city is the multitude of the other citizens,
and yet there is no discussion of whether the farmers too should have prop-   15
erty in common or each individual should have private property as well, or
further, whether women and children should be private or common. (19) If
everything is to be common to all in the same manner, how will these differ
from the guardians? What more will they get by submitting to their rule? Or
how will they be forced to submit[22] to it, unless the guardians act the soph-   20
ist and devise something like the Cretans have? For these allow their slaves
to have the same things as themselves, except that they forbid them exercises
and the possession of arms. (20) But if the farmers have those things, as they
do in other cities, what manner of community will it be? For there must nec-   25
essarily be two cities in one, and these opposed to one another. For he makes
the guardians into a sort of garrison, while the farmers and artisans and the
others are the citizens.[23] (21) Accusations and lawsuits and whatever other ills
he asserts exist in cities—all will exist among these as well. And yet Socrates
speaks[24] as if they will have little need for ordinances—urban or market ordi-   30
nances, for example, or others of this sort—on account of their education, al-

20 · These "common messes" (*syssitia*), which also served as a form of social organization, are discussed further below.

21 · The Spartan ruling class was supported by the labor of agricultural serfs, the so-
called helots.

22 · Literally, "suffering what will they submit," reading *pathontes* with some MSS and
Susemihl instead of the *mathontes* ("learning") accepted by Dreizehnter.

23 · Cf. *Republic* 415d–17b, 419a–20a, 543b–c.

24 · *Republic* 425c–d.

though he assigns education only to the guardians. (22) Further, he gives the
farmers control over their possessions and has them pay a tax;[25] but then they
35   are much more likely to be difficult and filled with high thoughts than the
helots or serfs that some hold today,[26] or than slaves. (23) Whether the same
things are necessary in a similar way for this class or not is in fact nowhere
discussed, nor matters connected with this—what regime and education
they have, and what laws. It is not easy to discover what sort of people these
40   are, yet it makes no little difference with a view to the preservation of the
1264b   community of guardians. (24) But if he is going to make women common
and property private, who will manage the household while the men work
in the fields? (Or, for that matter, if property and the wives of the farmers are
5   both common?) Moreover, it is odd that in order to show that women should
have the same pursuits as men he makes a comparison with the animals,[27]
among which household management is nonexistent.

(25) Also, the way Socrates selects the rulers is hazardous; for he has the
same persons always ruling. This can become a cause of factional conflict
even in the case of those possessing no particular claim to merit, not to speak
10   of spirited and warlike men. (26) That it was necessary for him to make the
same persons rulers is evident; for the gold from god is not mixed in the souls
of some at one time and others at another, but always in the same—he says
that directly at birth gold is mixed with some, silver with others, and bronze
15   and iron with those who are going to be artisans and farmers.[28] (27) Further, he even destroys the guardians' happiness, asserting that the legislator should make the city as a whole happy.[29] But it is impossible for it to be
happy as a whole unless most people, or all or some of its parts, are happy.
20   For happiness is not the same kind of thing as evenness: this can exist in the
whole but in neither of its parts, but happiness cannot. (28) But if the guardians are not happy, which others are? For the artisans and the multitude
of the vulgar surely are not, at any rate. The regime which Socrates spoke
25   about raises, then, these questions, as well as others no less considerable than
these.

25 · *Apophora*: the term used at Sparta to designate the tax or rent in kind provided by
the helots to their masters. Cf. *Republic* 416e.
26 · The term "serf" (*penestēs*) was usually applied specifically to the agricultural serfs
of Thessaly, as the term "helot" was to the serfs of Laconia and Messenia.
27 · *Republic* 451d ff.
28 · *Republic* 415a ff.
29 · *Republic* 420b ff.

CHAPTER 6

(1) Very similar is the case of the *Laws*, which was written later, so it is best to investigate briefly the regime there as well. In the *Republic*, after all, Socrates has discussed very few matters—how things should stand concerning the community in women and children, property, and the arrangement of the   30
regime; (2) for he divides the mass of inhabitants into two parts, the farmers and the military part, and from these a third that is the deliberative and authoritative part of the city. (3) As for the farmers and artisans, whether they   35
partake in rule to some extent or not at all, or whether they should possess arms and join in warfare themselves, is nowhere discussed by Socrates; yet he supposes that the women should join in warfare and share in the same education as the guardians.[30] Otherwise, he has filled out the argument with ex-   40
traneous issues, particularly concerning the sort of education the guardians should have.

(4) The *Laws* deals for the most part with laws, and little is said about   1265a
the regime. As to this, although he wishes to make it more attainable by cities, he gradually brings it around again toward the other regime [of the *Republic*]. (5) For apart from the community in women and property, the other   5
things he assigns it are the same for both regimes: education is the same, as is the life of abstention from necessary work and of common messes; only here he asserts that there should be common messes for women as well, and that the number of those possessing arms should be five thousand, whereas it is a   10
thousand there.[31] (6) All the discourses of Socrates are extraordinary: they are sophisticated, original, and searching. But it is perhaps difficult to do everything finely. With regard to the multitude just mentioned, it should not be overlooked that so many will need the territory of Babylon[32] or some other   15
that is unlimited in extent to sustain in idleness five thousand of them and a crowd of women and attendants about them many times as large. (7) Now one's basic premises should indeed accord with what one would pray for; yet nothing should be impossible. It is said that the legislator should look to two things in enacting laws, the territory and the human beings who inhabit it.[33]   20

30 · *Republic* 451e–52a.
31 · In the *Republic* (458c–d) women are included in the common messes of the male guardians; in the *Laws* (780d–81d, 806d) they are assigned separate messes. On the size of the citizen body see *Republic* 423a and *Laws* 737e, 740a–41a.
32 · Cf. 3.3. 5.
33 · This is not clearly stated in the *Laws*, but see 704a ff.

But, further, one would do finely to add that he should look to the neighboring regions, in the first place if the city is to lead a political way of life and not
one of isolation;[34] for it is necessary that it use for war the arms that are use-
25   ful not only on its own territory but in foreign regions as well. (8) But if one
does not accept this way of life either as one's own or as the common way of
life of the city, still men should be formidable to their enemies not only when
these enter their territory but also when they leave it.

As regards the aggregate of property, too, one should see whether it would
30   not be better to determine this differently and more clearly. For he asserts
that there should be as much as is needed to live with moderation,[35] which is
as if one were to say "to live well": (9) it is too general. Moreover, it is possible
to live with moderation but wretchedly. A better defining principle would
be "with moderation and liberally" (for when separated the one will tend
35   toward luxury, the other toward a life of hardship), since these alone are the
choiceworthy dispositions concerning the use of property: it is not possible
to use property gently or courageously, but it is possible to use it with moderation and liberally, so the dispositions connected with it must be these.

(10) It is also odd that while property is equalized, nothing is instituted
40   regarding the number of the citizens, but procreation is left unrestricted, on
the grounds that it will remain sufficiently close to the same number through
childlessness on the part of some no matter how many births there may be,[36]
1265b because this is held to be the result in cities now. (11) But the precision this
requires is not the same there and in cities now; for now no one becomes
poor, on account of the splitting of properties to accommodate any number of heirs, but there, as properties are indivisible, persons who are in sur-
5   plus must necessarily have nothing, whether they are more or fewer in number. (12) One would suppose that procreation should be restricted sooner
than property, so that there would not be births beyond a certain figure, and
that the whole number would be fixed by looking to the chances of some of
10   those born dying and of childlessness on the part of others. (13) To leave it
alone, as in most cities, must necessarily cause poverty among the citizens,
and poverty produces factional conflict and crime. Pheidon of Corinth, one
of the very ancient legislators, in fact supposed that the households and the
15   number of citizens should be kept equal, even if the allotments of all were
originally unequal in size; in the *Laws* it is just the opposite of this. (14) But

34 · Cf. *Pol.* 7.1–3.
35 · *Laws* 737d ff.
36 · *Laws* 740d–e.

about these matters and how we suppose they could be better handled we
will speak later.[37]

Also omitted in the *Laws* is the matter of the rulers, and how they will
differ from the ruled. For he asserts that just as the warp is made of a differ-   20
ent kind of wool from the woof, so the rulers should stand with respect to
the ruled.[38] (15) And since he permits the whole of one's property to increase
as much as fivefold,[39] why should this not be allowed up to a certain point
with respect to land? It needs also to be investigated whether the separation
of housing sites is not disadvantageous for household management; for he   25
assigned two housing sites to each individual and made them separate and
distinct,[40] yet it is difficult to administer two houses.

(16) The organization of the regime as a whole is intended to be neither
democracy nor oligarchy, but the one midway between them which is called
a polity; for it is based on those who bear heavy arms.[41] Now if he institutes this as being the most attainable of all the regimes for cities, he has per-   30
haps argued finely; but if as being the best after the first sort of regime, not
so.[42] For one might well praise that of the Spartans more, or some other that
is more aristocratic. (17) Now there are certain people[43] who say that the
best regime should be a mixture of all the regimes, and who therefore praise   35
that of the Spartans. Some of them assert it is a mixture of oligarchy, monarchy, and democracy, calling the kingship monarchy, the rule of the senators oligarchy, and saying it is democratically run by virtue of the rule of the
overseers,[44] on account of the overseers' being drawn from the people; but   40
others call the board of overseers a tyranny, and find it democratically run
by virtue of the common messes and the rest of their everyday way of life.
(18) In the *Laws*, on the other hand, it is said that the best regime should   1266a
be composed out of democracy and tyranny[45]—which one might regard either as not being regimes at all or as the worst of them all. More nearly right,

37 · 7.10.9–13.
38 · *Laws* 734e–35a.
39 · *Laws* 744d–e.
40 · *Laws* 745e. The second house is evidently intended for the use of a married son
(776a).
41 · That is, so-called "hoplites." *Laws* 753b.
42 · See *Laws* 739a–e.
43 · It is not known to whom this refers.
44 · The Spartan "Overseers" (*ephoroi*) were a board of five men with powers comparable to Roman tribunes. See on them and the Spartan system generally 2.9 below.
45 · *Laws* 693d. Actually, Plato speaks here of "monarchy," not tyranny.

5   then, are those who mix more of the regimes, for the regime that is composed out of more is better. Actually, though, the regime of the *Laws* manifestly lacks a monarchic element; its characteristics are oligarchic and democratic, although its tendency is to incline more toward oligarchy. (19) This
is clear from the system of selecting officials.[46] Selection by lot from among
persons previously elected is common to both oligarchy and democracy; but
10   for those who are better off to be compelled to attend the assembly, vote for
officials, and perform other political [tasks], while the others are let off, is
oligarchic, as is the attempt to have the majority of officials from among the
well off, and the greatest officials from among those with the greatest assess-
15   ments. (20) He also makes election of the council oligarchic. It is compulsory for all to elect—from the first assessment, and then from the second in
equal number, and then from the third; except it is not compulsory for those
from the first and second to elect from the fourth; (21) and he then says that
20   from among those elected in this way they should designate an equal number from each assessment. Hence those who are from the highest assessments
and better will be more numerous,[47] since some from the popular classes will
not elect because it is not compulsory.

     (22) That a regime of this sort should not be constituted out of democ-
racy and monarchy, then, is evident from these things and from what will be
25   said later, when the investigation turns to this sort of regime.[48] Also, with regard to the election of officials, it is dangerous to have them elected from persons previously elected; for if even a relatively few are willing to combine, the
election will always take place in accordance with their wishes. This, then, is
30   the way matters stand concerning the regime in the *Laws*.

CHAPTER 7

     (1) There are certain other regimes as well, some of private individuals, oth-
ers of philosophers and political rulers; but all of them are closer than either of those just discussed to established regimes under which men are now
35   governed. For no one else has shown originality regarding community of
women and children or regarding common messes for women; they begin
rather from the necessary things. (2) For some of them hold that a fine arrangement concerning property is the greatest thing: it is about this, they as-

---

46 · *Laws* 756b–e, 763d ff., 765b ff.

47 · Or "those who are from the highest assessments will be more numerous and better."

48 · The reference would appear to be to 4.7–9. Cf. Introduction, n. 35.

sert, that all factional conflicts arise. The first to introduce this was Phaleas   40
of Chalcedon,[49] who asserts that the property of the citizens should be equal.
(3) He supposed this would not be difficult to do in cities just being settled;   1266b
in those already settled he supposed it would be troublesome, but that a leveling could be most quickly brought about by having the wealthy give dowries
but not receive them, and the poor receive but not give them. (4) Plato, when   5
writing the *Laws*, supposed increase in properties should be allowed up to a
certain point, no citizen being permitted to possess a property more than five
times the size of the smallest one, as was said earlier.[50] (5) But those who legislate in this fashion should not overlook—what they overlook now—that
an arrangement concerning the extent of property should properly include   10
an arrangement concerning the number of children as well. If the number of
children outstrips the size of the property, the law will surely be abrogated;
and, abrogation aside, it is a bad thing to have many of the wealthy become
poor, for such persons are apt to become subversives. (6) Thus the leveling of   15
property does indeed have a certain power to affect the political community.
This was plainly recognized by some of former times, as in the legislation of
Solon,[51] and others have a law which forbids the acquisition of land in whatever amount one wishes. Similarly, some laws forbid the sale of property, for
example among the Locrians, where there is a law against sale unless one can   20
show he has suffered manifest misfortune; (7) and some attempt to preserve
original allotments [of land in colonies]. It was the abrogation of this sort of
law at Leucas that led to their regime becoming overly popular; for the result was that offices were no longer filled from the designated assessments.[52]
Yet it is possible to have equality of property, but for the amount to be either   25
too great (so that luxury results) or too little (so that they live in penury). It is
clear, then, that it is not enough for the legislator to make property equal; he
must also aim at a mean. (8) Yet even if one were to arrange a moderate level
of property for all, it would not help. For one ought to level desires sooner   30
than property; but this is impossible for those not adequately educated by
the laws. Phaleas would perhaps object that this is what he himself is saying;
for he supposes that cities must have equality in these two things, property

49 · Nothing else is known of Phaleas. Cf. Schütrumpf.
50 · 2.6. 8–9.
51 · The Athenian legislator who abolished the debts of the poor and established a
moderate democracy; see 2.12.1–6.
52 · What evidently happened was that permitting division of the original allotments
created a shortage of individuals with the requisite property qualification for office,
and the qualification was then reduced to allow poorer men to serve. Cf. 6.4. 10.

35 and education. (9) But one ought to say what the education is to be. Having
it one and the same is no help, for it is possible for it to be one and the same,
and yet of such a sort that they intentionally choose to aggrandize themselves
with respect to material goods or honor or both. (10) Further, factional conflict occurs not only because of inequality of property, but also because of
40 inequality of honors, though in an opposite way in each case; for the many
1267a engage in factional conflict because possessions are unequal, but the refined
do so if honors are equal—hence the verse "in single honor whether vile or
worthy."[53] (11) Nor do human beings commit injustice only on account of the
necessary things—for which Phaleas considers equality of property a rem-
5 edy, so that no one will steal through being cold or hungry; they also do it
for enjoyment and the satisfaction of desire. For if they have a desire beyond
the necessary things, they will commit injustice in order to cure it—(12) and
not only for this reason, for they might desire merely the enjoyment[54] that
comes with pleasures unaccompanied by pains.

10   What remedy is there, then, for these three things? For the one, a minimum of property and work; for the other, moderation. As for the third,
if certain persons should want enjoyment through themselves alone, they
should not seek a remedy except in connection with philosophy; for the
other [pleasures] require human beings. (13) The greatest injustices are committed out of excess, then, not because of the necessary things—no one be-
15 comes a tyrant in order to get in out of the cold (hence the honors too are
great if one kills a tyrant rather than a thief). So it is only with a view to minor injustices that the approach of Phaleas's regime is of assistance.

       (14) Further, most of what Phaleas wants to institute is designed to enable
them to engage in politics finely among themselves; but they should do so
120 also with a view to their neighbors and all foreigners. Therefore it is necessary that the regime be organized with a view to military strength, and he has
said nothing about this. (15) And similarly concerning property: it should be
adequate not only for political uses but also for foreign dangers. Hence the
25 extent of it should neither be so much that those near at hand and stronger
will desire it and those having it will be unable to ward off the attackers, nor
so little that they will be unable to sustain a war even against those who are
equal and similar. (16) Although he has not discussed this, then, one should
not overlook the extent of property that is advantageous.[55] Perhaps the best

53 · Homer, *Iliad* 9.319.
54 · Reading *an epithymoien* with the MSS rather than bracketing the phrase with
Dreizehnter.
55 · Or perhaps "that some amount of property is advantageous."

defining principle is that there should be just so much that those who are stronger will not gain if they go to war because of the excess, but will go to war only under such circumstances as they would even if their property were not so great. (17) For example, when Autophradates was about to beseige Atarneus, Euboulus bid him examine how much time would be required to take the place and calculate what the expense for this time would be, as he was willing to abandon Atarneus at once for less than this; and by saying this he caused Autophradates to have second thoughts and give up the seige.[56]

(18) For the property of the citizens to be equal, then, is indeed an advantage with a view to avoiding factional conflict between them, but it is by no means a great one. For the refined[57] may well become disaffected, on the grounds that they do not merit [mere] equality, and for this reason they are frequently seen to attack the people and engage in factional conflict. (19) Further, the wickedness of human beings is insatiable: at first the two obol allowance was adequate, but now that this is something traditional, they always ask for more, and go on doing so without limit.[58] For the nature of desire is without limit, and it is with a view to satisfying this that the many live. (20) To rule such persons, then, [requires[59]] not so much leveling property as providing that those who are respectable by nature will be the sort who have no wish to aggrandize themselves, while the mean will not be able to, which will be the case if they are kept inferior but are done no injustice.[60]

(21) But not even what he has said about equality of property is right. For he equalizes only the possession of land; but there may also be wealth in slaves, livestock, or money, and there is a great supply of it in movables, so-called. Either, then, equality is to be sought in all these things, or some moderate arrangement, or all are to be left alone. (22) It is also evident from this legislation that he is instituting a small city; at any rate, all the artisans will be public slaves and will not contribute to the full complement of the city. (23) But if there should be public slaves at all, it is those who work at com-

30

35

40

1267b

5

10

15

---

56 · Atarneus, a strongly fortified town on the coast of Asia Minor, together with other territory in the area, formed an independent state under Euboulus—originally a wealthy moneychanger—and his successor Hermias; the incident involving the Persian general Autophradates probably occurred during the 350s.

57 · *Hoi charientes*, a common euphemism for the upper class.

58 · The "two obol allowance" (*diōbolia*) was a subsidy paid Athenian citizens out of a special fund for attendance at the theater, and later at all public festivals.

59 · Or "A beginning point in such matters is ..." I read *archē* with the MSS instead of Dreizehnter's conjecture.

60 · "Respectable" (*epieikeis*) and "mean" (*phauloi*) are also terms referring primarily to social class.

mon tasks who should be in this condition, as at Epidamnus, or as Diophantus once tried to institute at Athens.[61] Concerning the regime of Phaleas,
20 then, whether he happens to have argued finely in some respect or not may
be discerned from what has been said.

CHAPTER 8

(1) Hippodamus, the son of Euryphon, of Miletus, who invented the division
of cities and laid out Piraeus—and who was extraordinary in other aspects
25 of his life through ambition, so that he seemed to some to live in a rather
overdone manner, with long hair and expensive ornaments, and furthermore
with cheap and warm clothing which he wore not only in winter but also in
summer weather, and who wished to be learned with regard to nature as a
whole—was the first of those not engaged in politics to undertake to give an
30 account of the best regime.[62] (2) He wanted to institute a city of ten thousand
men, divided into three parts, and to make one part artisans, one farmers,
and the third the military part and that possessing arms. (3) He also divided
the territory into three parts, one sacred, one public and one private:[63] the
35 sacred to provide what custom requires to be rendered to the gods, the public
for the warriors to live off of, and the private that belonging to the farmers.
(4) He supposed that there are three kinds of laws as well, since the things
concerning which cases arise are three in number—arrogant behavior, in-
40 jury, and death.[64] He also wished to legislate a single authoritative court, to
which all cases that are held not to have been rightly judged should be ap-

---

61 · Text and meaning are somewhat uncertain; I read *eiper dei dēmosious einai, tous ta
koina ergazomenous dei, kathaper ...*, *touton echein ton tropon* with Welldon. We have
no other information about the arrangement at Epidamnus or the scheme (or identity)
of Diophantus.

62 · Hippodamus seems to have gone around the middle of the fifth century as a colo-
nist to Italy, where he planned the city of Thurii (Diodorus Siculus 12.10.7); nothing is
known of his activity in Piraeus, the port of Athens. He apparently introduced the division of cities into regular quarters and straight streets, which Aristotle will later criticize (7.11.6–7). Hippodamus's interest in natural philosophy seems to be reflected in
his predilection for threefold divisions; this suggests the influence of Pythagoreanism
(cf. Aristotle, *On the Heavens* 268a10–20). Aristotle's personal comments on him are
extraordinary and indeed unique in his writings.

63 · This division was a relatively common one in Greek cities.

64 · This division is roughly congruent with the categories of Greek private law, but
it omits all offenses relating to the city or to religion (cf. Plato, *Laws* 853b–64e). "Arrogant behavior" (*hybris*) encompassed sexual as well as physical assault.

pealed; this he wanted to institute out of a certain number of elected elders.
(5) He supposed that decisions in the courts should not be rendered by a bal-   1268a
lot, but that each should deposit a tablet on which, if he condemned simply,
he should write the verdict, or if he acquitted simply, leave it blank, but if
neither, he should make distinctions. For he supposed current legislation is   5
not fine in this regard, as it compels men to perjure themselves if they judge
one way or the other. (6) He also wanted to enact a law concerning those
who discover something useful to the city, so that they might obtain honor,
and one providing that the children of those who die in war should receive
sustenance from public funds (he supposed this had never been legislated by   10
others, although such a law exists now both in Athens and in other cities).
(7) The rulers were all to be elected by the people, the people being the three
parts of the city; those elected were to take care of common matters, matters
affecting aliens, and matters affecting orphans.

These are most of the elements of Hippodamus's arrangement and those   15
most deserving mention. The first question one might raise concerns the division of the multitude of the citizens. (8) The artisans and the farmers and
those possessing arms all share in the regime, although the farmers have no
arms and the artisans neither land nor arms—so that they become virtually   20
slaves of those possessing arms. (9) It is impossible, then, for them to partake
of all the prerogatives,[65] since the generals and regime guardians[66] and practically all the authoritative offices will necessarily be selected from among
those possessing arms; yet if they do not take part in the regime, how will
they feel any affection toward it? Those possessing arms would then have   25
to be superior to both of the other parts; but this would not be easy unless
there were many of them. (10) Yet if that is to be the case, why should the others take part in the regime and have authority with respect to the selection
of rulers? Furthermore, what use are the farmers to the city? It is necessary   30
that there be artisans, for every city needs artisans, and they can subsist, as
they do in other cities, from their arts. It would have been reasonable to make
the farmers a part of the city if they provided sustenance to those possessing
arms; as it is, however, they have private land and are to farm this privately.
(11) As for the common land, from which the warriors are to have their suste-   35
nance, if they are to farm it themselves there would be no difference between
the fighting and the farming element, contrary to the wish of the legislator;
but if there are to be others different from both those farming privately and

65 · Or "honors" (*timai*).
66 · *Politophylakes:* the term is probably Hippodamus's own; it is uncertain what kind
of officials are meant.

40 from the fighters, this will be an additional fourth part of the city which shares in nothing and is foreign to the regime. (12) On the other hand, if one makes the same persons farm both the private and the public land, will not

1268b the amount of crops from each one's farming be insufficient for two households? Or why is it they do not simply take sustenance for themselves from the land and their own allotments and also provide it to the fighters? In all of these things there is much confusion.

5 (13) Nor is the law concerning judging a fine one—to require the one judging to make distinctions when the indictment in a case is simple, thus making the juror an arbitrator. This can be done in an arbitration, even by many persons, since they may confer together over the judgment; but it is not possible in courts where most legislators have made provision for the oppo-

10 site of this—that the jurors do not confer together. (14) But further, how will the judgment be other than confused, when the juror finds something owed, but not as much as claimed by the plaintiff? He claims twenty minas, but a juror judges ten minas (or the one more and the other less), another judges

15 five, another four—it is clear they will split in this way; but others will condemn for all, and others for nothing. (15) How then will they calculate the votes? Moreover, no one compels the one who simply acquits or condemns

20 to perjure himself, at least if the indictment is simple (and justly so). For the one acquitting does not judge that he owes nothing, but that he does not owe the twenty minas, though the one indeed perjures himself who condemns without believing he owes the twenty minas.

(16) Concerning the matter of those who discover something advantageous for the city, to legislate that they receive some honor is not safe, though

25 it sounds appealing: it would involve harassments[67] and, it might well happen, changes of regime. But this leads into another problem and a different investigation. For some raise the question whether it is harmful or advantageous for cities to change traditional laws, if some other one should be better. (17) If indeed it is not advantageous, it would not be easy to agree

30 readily with what has been said; but it is not impossible that some might propose the dissolution of the laws or the regime as something in the common good. Since we have made mention of this, it will be best to expand a bit further on it. (18) For it involves, as we said, a question, and change might seem to be better. This has been advantageous, at any rate, in the other sci-

67 · Aristotle suggests that the legislation would provide opportunities for judicial "harassment" or blackmail (*sykophantia*) of the wealthy or politically powerful—a common phenomenon in democratic Athens—through pretended "discovery" of various kinds of malfeasance.

ences—medicine, for example, has changed from its traditional ways, and   35
gymnastic, and the arts and capacities generally, so that as political expertise too is to be regarded as one of these, it is clear that the same must necessarily hold concerning this as well. (19) One might assert that evidence
is provided by the facts themselves: the laws of ancient times were overly
simple and barbaric. For the Greeks used to carry weapons and purchase   40
their wives from one another, (20) and whatever other ancient ordinances
still remain somewhere are altogether silly. At Cyme, for example, there is   1269a
a law concerning cases of homicide, to the effect that the accused shall be
guilty of murder if the plaintiff can provide a certain number of witnesses
from among his own relatives. (21) In general, all seek not the traditional
but the good. The first human beings, whether they were earthborn or pre-   5
served from a cataclysm, are likely to have been similar to any chance person
or even the simpleminded today, as indeed is said of the earthborn;[68] so it
would be odd to abide by the opinions they hold. In addition to this, it is not
best to leave written laws unchanged. (22) For just as in the case of the other
arts, so with respect to political arrangements it is impossible for everything   10
to be written down precisely; for it is necessary to write them in universal
fashion, while actions concern particulars. From these things it is evident,
then, that some laws must be changed at some times; yet to those investigating it in another manner this would seem to require much caution. (23)
For when the improvement is small, and since it is a bad thing to habituate   15
people to the reckless dissolution of laws, it is evident that some errors both
of the legislators and of the rulers should be let go; for the city will not be
benefited as much from changing them as it will be harmed through being
habituated to disobey the rulers. (24) And the argument from the example
of the arts is false. Change in an art is not like change in law; for law has no   20
strength with respect to obedience apart from habit, and this is not created
except over a period of time. Hence the easy alteration of existing laws in
favor of new and different ones weakens the power of law itself. (25) Further, if they are indeed to be changeable, are all to be, and in every regime?   25
And by anyone, or by whom? For these things make a great difference. Let
us therefore set aside this investigation for the present; it belongs to other
occasions.[69]

68 · This perhaps alludes to Plato, *Statesman* 272b–d. For the traditional view of the
earliest men as "earthborn," see Plato, *Statesman* 271a ff., *Menexenus* 237d–38b; for the
view that they were survivors of a universal cataclysm, *Laws* 676a ff.
69 · This subject does not appear to be dealt with further in the remainder of the *Politics* as we have it.

CHAPTER 9

30   (1) Concerning the regime of the Spartans[70] and the Cretan regime, and indeed virtually all other regimes, there are two investigations: one, whether
some aspect of the legislation is fine or not with respect to the best arrangement; the other, whether it is opposed to the basic premise and the manner
[of organization][71] of the regime they actually have. (2) Now it is agreed that
35   any city that is going to be finely governed must have leisure from the necessary things; but in what manner it should have this is not easy to grasp. For
the serfs of Thessaly have often attacked the Thessalians, and similarly with
the Spartans' helots, who are constantly awaiting their misfortunes as if in
40   ambush.[72] In the case of the Cretans, however, nothing of this sort has hap-
1269b   pened. The cause of this is perhaps that neighboring cities there, even when
at war with one another, never ally themselves with those in revolt, since as
possessors of subjects[73] themselves it would not be to their advantage; but all
the neighbors of the Spartans—the Argives, Messenians, and Arcadians—
5   have been their enemies. In the case of the Thessalians, too, they revolted in
the beginning when there was still war with those in adjacent territories—
Achaeans, Perrhaebeans, and Magnesians.[74] (4) But it would appear that,

70 · *Lakedaimonioi.* Aristotle follows general Greek practice in using "Lacedaemonian" to refer to the Spartan state as a whole and "Spartan" (*Lakōn*) or "Spartiate" to
refer to the Spartan citizen class. There were several categories of free persons—freed
helots and the semiautonomous "subjects" (*perioikoi*) primarily—who did not enjoy
political rights or share the way of life of full citizens, yet played some role in the state,
particularly militarily.

71 · The Greek terms here are *hypothesis* and *tropos.*

72 · The reference here is to the "Spartans" (*tois Lakosi*) proper. Thessaly, Sparta, and
Crete (and probably a number of other Greek cities) had systems of agricultural serfdom for which there were different names, the Thessalian name (*penestēs*) being closest
to a generic term "serf." These serfs probably consisted largely of pre- or proto-Greek
peoples who had been brought into subjection at the time of the Dorian invasions. In
the case of Sparta, however, a considerable proportion of the helots were neighboring
Messenians of Greek stock who had been conquered in the recent past and remained
extremely restive. They sustained a revolt for ten years following a severe earthquake
in 464, and were a constant preoccupation of the Spartans during the Peloponnesian
War (see Thucydides 1.101, 4.41, 80, 5.14, 23). After their decisive defeat at Leuctra and
a Theban invasion of the Peloponnese in 370, the Spartans were forced to restore to
Messenia its independence.

73 · "Subjects" (*perioikoi*) was the specific term for the serfs of Crete.

74 · These territories were subsequently reduced to subjection by the Thessalians. Thessalian serfdom is alleged to have originated in mutual agreement (Athenaeus 264a).

apart from anything else, supervision of them is troublesome in itself—what the manner of one's relations with them should be; for if it is lax, they become arrogant and claim to merit equality with those in authority, and yet if harshly treated they come to hate and conspire against them. It is clear, then, that those who have this happen to them in connection with helotry have not discovered the manner that is best.

(5) Furthermore, their laxness concerning women is harmful with a view both to the intention[75] of the regime and to the happiness of the city. For just as man and woman are a part of the household, it is clear that the city should be held to be very nearly divided in two—into a multitude of men and a multitude of women; so in regimes where what is connected with women is poorly handled, one must consider that legislation is lacking for half of the city. (6) This very thing has happened there; for the legislator[76] wished the city as a whole to be hardy, and this is manifest in terms of the men; but he thoroughly neglected it in the case of the women, who live licentiously in every respect and in luxury. (7) Wealth will necessarily be honored in a regime of this sort, particularly if they are dominated by the women, as is the case with most stocks that are fond of soldiering and war (excluding the Celts and any others that openly honor sexual relations among males). (8) For the one who first told the fable was not unreasonable in pairing Ares and Aphrodite:[77] all those of this sort are possessed, as it were, when it comes to relations with either men or women. This was the case with the Spartans, and many matters were administered by the women during the period of their [imperial] rule.[78] (9) And yet what difference is there between women ruling and rulers who are ruled by women? For the result is the same. Bold-

75 · Or "deliberate choice" (*proairesis*); this quasi-technical term in Aristotle's moral philosophy (Saunders renders it here "chosen aim") is apparently used synonymously with "basic premise" (*hypothesis*) immediately above.

76 · Lycurgus was traditionally regarded as the founder of Sparta's characteristic institutions and way of life, and Aristotle appears elsewhere to have accepted this tradition (10.2; cf. Plutarch, *Lycurgus* 1). However, it should not be assumed that Aristotle's references to "the legislator" are in all cases to Lycurgus (cf. n. 86). There remains considerable uncertainty as to the historicity of Lycurgus and the date and character of the Lycurgan reforms; these are most commonly connected with the circumstances of the Second Messenian War (probably mid-seventh century).

77 · The story is told by Hesiod (*Theogony* 933–37), but it is uncertain whether the reference is intended to be a precise one.

78 · The term is *archē*, meaning both rule in general and empire. The apparent reference is to the period of Spartan hegemony in Greece following its defeat of Athens in the Peloponnesian War.

ness is something useful in war (if then) rather than in everyday matters; but the Spartan women have been very harmful even in this respect. (10) This became clear during the Theban invasion: they were not only wholly useless, like women in other cities, but they created more of an uproar than the enemy.[79]

40
1270a
Now this laxness concerning women appears to have arisen among the Spartans in a way that is quite reasonable. (11) They spent much time away from their own land when they were at war with the Argives, and later with the Arcadians and Messenians; and thus once they had leisure they could
5 place themselves in the hands of the legislator having been well prepared by the soldiering life—for it involves many of the parts of virtue. As for the women, they say Lycurgus attempted to lead them toward the laws, but they were resistant, and he gave it up.[80] (12) The causes of what has happened, then, and of this error of theirs, are these; but we are not investigating whom
10 to excuse in this matter, but what is correct or incorrect. (13) That what is connected with the women is not finely handled would seem not only to create an unseemliness in the regime in its own terms, as was said earlier,
15 but to contribute to their greed. For after what has just been said, one might censure what pertains to the disparity in property. (14) For it has happened that some of them possess much too much property, and others very little; hence the land has come into the hands of a few. This too was poorly ar-
20 ranged in the laws. For the legislator made the buying or selling of existing property in land something not noble, and correctly so; but he left it open to them to give or bequeath it if they wished, although the result must be the same in this case as in that. (15) Indeed, nearly two-fifths of the entire territory belongs to women, both because many have become heiresses and
25 because large dowries are given. It would have been better to have none, or to arrange for a dowry to be small or even moderate. As it is now, [not only is there no limit on its size, but everyone] is permitted to give an heiress in marriage to whomever he wishes, and if he dies intestate, his heir can give her to anyone he pleases.[81] (16) Accordingly, although the territory was capable

79 · For these events see Xenophon, *Hellenica* 6.5. 28, Plutarch, *Agesilaus* 31.

80 · This account appears to place the Lycurgan reforms at the end of the First Messenian War (late eighth century). Cf. Plutarch, *Lycurgus* 14.

81 · The nature of the Spartan system of land tenure and inheritance is controversial. Generally speaking, land was not owned by the citizens but held under a system of entail based on an original distribution (on what basis is highly uncertain) of "allotments." Aristotle seems to suggest that alienation of the allotments was not strictly il-

of sustaining fifteen hundred cavalrymen and thirty thousand heavy-armed   30
troops, they were reduced to less than a thousand in number. But it became
clear through the facts themselves how poor their condition was as a result
of this arrangement; for the city could not bear up under a single blow, but
was ruined through its lack of manpower.[82] (17) It is said that at the time of
the earlier kings they gave others a place in the regime, and so had no lack of   35
manpower then even though they were at war for a long time; indeed, they
say there were once ten thousand Spartiates. But regardless of whether these
things are true or not, it is better for the city to have an abundance of men
through the leveling of property. (18) The law concerning procreation is also   40
an obstacle to correcting this. For the legislator, wishing there to be as many   1270b
Spartiates as possible, encourages the citizens to have as many children as
possible; for there is a law that one who has fathered three sons is exempted
from garrison duty,[83] and one with four is exempted from all taxes. (19) Yet
it is evident that if many are born and the land remains divided as it is, many   5
of them will be poor.

Also poorly handled is the matter of the overseers. This office has authority by itself over the greatest matters among them, yet it is filled entirely from
the people,[84] so that very poor men often join the board who because of their   10
poverty can be bought. (20) They have often made this clear both in the past

legal but only carried disgrace. There is (disputed) evidence concerning a change in
the law effected earlier in the fourth century: the overseer Epitadeus is said to have
introduced a bill that would "permit a man during his lifetime to give his estate and
allotment to anyone he wished or to leave it so in his will" (Plutarch, *Agis* 5). It is possible that Aristotle is here alluding to this change, which would appear to have involved
merely a liberalization of restrictions on the persons permitted to receive gifts or inheritances in land (cf. 5.8. 20). Also involved may have been the disposition of heiresses
in cases where no will existed: previously, it would seem, this had been a prerogative of
the kings (Herodotus 6.57).

82 · The blow in question is the defeat at Leuctra in 371. The figures given by Aristotle appear to apply to Spartan territory prior to the loss of Messenia in 370, and seem
related to Plutarch's claim (*Lycurgus* 8) that Lycurgus distributed thirty thousand allotments to the Spartan "subjects" and nine (or perhaps six) thousand to the citizens.
Prior to Leuctra, the Lacedaemonian army (which included an unknown number of
"subjects" serving as regular heavy-armed troops) seems to have amounted to about
six thousand men.

83 · Or perhaps "exempt from normal military service" (*aphrouron*)—*phroura* being
a Spartan word for a military levy or expedition.

84 · Reading *pantes* with the MSS rather than *pantos* with Dreizehnter ("from the entire people").

and now in the Andros matter, where some of them, having been corrupted
by silver, did all that was in them to ruin the city as a whole.[85] Also, because
15   the office is overly great—like a tyranny, in fact—even the kings were compelled to try to become popular with them; this has done added harm to the
regime, for from an aristocracy it has become a democracy. (21) It is indeed
the case that this board holds the regime together: the people keep quiet because they share in the greatest office, and so whether it was through the leg-
20   islator or by chance that this came about, it is advantageous for their affairs.[86]
(22) If a regime is going to be preserved, all the parts of the city must wish it
to exist and continue on the same basis. Now the kings are in this condition
because of the honor accorded them, the gentlemen on account of the Senate
25   (for this office is a prize of virtue), and the people on account of the overseers,
who are selected from all. (23) This office should have been elected from all,
to be sure, but not in the way it is now, which is overly childish.[87] Further, although they are of an average sort, they have authority in the most important
[judicial] decisions.[88] Hence it would be better if they judged not at discre-
30   tion but in accordance with written rules and the laws. (24) Also, the com-
portment of the overseers does not agree with the inclination of the city: it is
overly lax, though in other respects the city goes to excess in the direction of
35   harshness—with the result that they cannot endure it, but secretly run away
from the law and seek gratification in bodily pleasures.

85 · The reference is uncertain, but probably concerns Spartan intrigues with Persia
just prior to the victory of Alexander at Issus in 333. A Persian fleet active in the Aegean
at this time appears to have put in at Andros and may have been met there by certain
Spartan overseers; King Agis is supposed to have met the Persians at the island of Siph-
nos and entered into negotiations concerning a subsidy and military aid against Macedon (Arrian 2.13.4 ff., Quintus Curtius 4.1. 37).

86 · It seems to have been widely believed that the board of "overseers" (*ephoroi*) was
not part of the original Lycurgan regime; Aristotle himself later (5.11.2–3) ascribes its
institution to the early Spartan king Theopompus, as does Plutarch (*Lycurgus* 7; cf.
Cleomenes 7). Other explanations (none are mutually exclusive) are that the overseers
evolved from a college of priests or a council of headmen of the five Spartan tribes; the
facts of the matter remain quite uncertain.

87 · This is our only information on the mode of selection of the overseers, and its
meaning is uncertain. It is often assumed that the overseers were elected by a vote of
the popular assembly in the same manner as the senators (cf. n. 89); in a later remark
(4.9. 9), however, Aristotle seems to imply this was not the case. It has been suggested
(on the basis of Plato, *Laws* 692a; cf. 690c) that their selection somehow involved the
taking of auspices.

88 · Cf. 3.1. 10.

The matter of the office of senator is also not finely handled by them. (25) Now if these were respectable persons adequately educated with a view to the qualities of a good man, one would probably say it is advantageous to the city, though doubts could be raised about their having authority in important [judicial] decisions throughout their lifetime (since old age affects   40
the mind as well as the body). Yet when their education is such that even the   1271a
legislator himself lacks trust in them as not being good men, it is not safe. (26) It is evident that those who have shared in this office have been thoroughly affected by bribery and favoritism in handling many common matters. Hence it is better that they not go unaudited; now they do. The office   5
of overseer might be held to be the proper one to audit all the offices; but this is too great a gift to the overseers, and it is not in this way that we say the auditing ought to be carried out. (27) Further, the election they hold of senators is childish in its manner of decision,[89] and to have one who claims   10
to merit the office ask for it himself is not correct; for one who merits the office should rule whether he wishes to or not. (28) As it is, the legislator is evidently doing what he has done with respect to the rest of the regime; it is with a view to making the citizens ambitious that he has used this [device] in   15
the election of the senators—for no one would ask for office unless he were ambitious. And yet most voluntary acts of injustice among human beings result from ambition or greed.[90]

(29) Concerning kingship and whether it is better for it to exist in cities or not, there will be discussion later;[91] but it is surely better in any event not to   20
have it as at present, [a hereditary office,] but to judge each king on the basis of his own manner of life. (30) Now it is clear that the legislator did not himself suppose it possible to make them gentlemen. At any rate, he lacks trust in them as not being sufficiently good men; and it is on this account that they repeatedly send them on embassies accompanied by their enemies, and hold   25
that factional conflict between the kings means preservation for the city.[92]

---

89 · Senators were chosen in the popular assembly by an archaic process of acclamation (Plutarch, *Lycurgus* 26).

90 · Literally, "love of honor" (*philotimia*) and "love of money" (*philochrēmatia*).

91 · 3.14–18.

92 · Sparta had a system of dual kingship, each king being drawn from a separate hereditary line; factional conflict between the kings and their partisans was thus a natural development. The kings were regularly accompanied by several overseers when on military expeditions, but kings did not as a rule undertake diplomatic missions. Aristotle perhaps has in mind "the Andros matter" (see n. 84).

The legislation concerning common messes—the so-called friends' messes[93]—was also not finely handled by the one who first established it. (31) The support for this should have come primarily from the treasury,[94] as in Crete; but among the Spartans everyone must contribute, even though some of them are very poor and unable to afford the expense. Hence the result is the opposite of the legislator's intention; (32) for he wants the institution of common messes to be a democratic one, but it is least of all democratic as a result of the legislation being handled this way. For it is not easy for the very poor to take part in it, and yet this is the traditional defining principle of the regime among them—that whoever is unable to contribute this fee does not take part in the regime.[95]

(33) The law concerning admirals has been criticized by others, and correctly so. It is a cause of factional conflict: the position of admiral has been established almost as another kingship over against the kings, who are generals in perpetuity.[96]

(34) Moreover, one may criticize the basic premise of the legislator, in the way Plato criticizes it in the *Laws*:[97] the entire organization of the laws is with a view to a part of virtue—warlike virtue; for this is useful with a view to domination. Yet while they preserved themselves as long as they were at war, they came to ruin when they were ruling an empire through not knowing how to be at leisure, and because there is no training among them that has more authority than the training for war. (35) This error is no slight one. They consider that the good things men generally fight over are won by virtue rather than vice, and finely so; but they conceive these things to be better than virtue, which is not fine. (36) Also poorly handled among the Spartiates is the matter of common funds. For there is nothing in the treasury of the city in spite of their being compelled to carry on great wars, and they are very

93 · *Phiditia:* the etymology of the term is uncertain, but it may derive from a dialect form of the word "friend" (*philos*).

94 · Literally, "the common thing" (*to koinon*).

95 · This suggests that a certain number of Spartan citizens were excluded from full political rights on account of their failure to support the expense of the common messes; this may be the class of "inferiors" (*hypomeiones*) referred to by Xenophon (*Hellenica* 3.3. 6), which figured in the conspiracy of Cinadon early in the fourth century.

96 · Originally occupied periodically by the kings themselves, the office of admiral (*nauarchos*) had come under the control of the overseers by the late fifth century. Though subject to renewal every year, the office accumulated considerable power, particularly in the field of foreign policy, during the tenure of Lysander late in and after the Peloponnesian War.

97 · Plato, *Laws* 625c–38b and passim.

backward in paying [special war] taxes. For because most of the land belongs
to the Spartiates, they do not scrutinize each other's payments of such taxes.   15
(37) The consequence for the legislator has been the opposite of advantageous: he has created a city lacking in funds, and individuals greedy for them.

Concerning the regime of the Spartans, then, let this much be said; for
these are the things one might particularly criticize.

CHAPTER 10

(1) The Cretan regime[98] is very close to this one, and while it has a few features   20
that are not worse, most of it is less fully finished. It appears, and it is said,
that the regime of the Spartans is an imitation of the Cretan in most respects;
but most ancient things are less fully articulated than newer things. (2) They
say that Lycurgus, when he gave up his stewardship of King Charilaus and left   25
home, spent most of his time in Crete on account of kinship; for the Lyctians
were colonists of the Spartans, (3) and those who had gone to the colony had
adopted the arrangement of laws that existed among those who dwelt there   30
then. Thus even now the subjects use them in the same manner, and assume
that Minos was the first to institute this arrangement of laws.[99]

The island seems naturally situated for rule in Greece. It lies across the
entire sea, and most of the Greeks are settled around the sea: it is not far dis-   35
tant from the Peloponnese on the one side, and on the other from the part of
Asia around Cape Triopium and Rhodes. (4) Hence Minos established rule
over the sea, subduing some of the islands and settling others; and finally he
attacked Sicily, and ended his life there near Camicus.[100]   40

The Cretan arrangement corresponds to the Spartan. (5) For the hel-

98 · This expression refers to a type of regime that was evidently common to most
or all of the (independent) Cretan cities. Crete was not politically unified in historical Greek times.

99 · For the derivation of the Spartan regime from the Cretan, see Herodotus 1.65 and
Ephorus, *FGH* 70F148 ff. (an account which Aristotle here seems to draw on in other
respects as well). Aristotle's argument is that the Spartan colonists in Crete adopted the
institutions of the original inhabitants—the people who subsequently became their
"subjects" or serfs; that the "subjects" still retained most of these ancestral institutions
was indicated at an earlier point (2.5. 19).

100 · This paragraph is detached from the main argument, and probably represents an
annotation by a later reader. Newman suggests it may actually be an extract from the
historian Ephorus. Crete had been the seat of the maritime empire established by
the semi-mythical Minos (cf. Thucydides 1.15), but played little role in the politics
of the Greek world during the classical period.

1272a   ots farm for the latter, while the subjects do it for the Cretans; and both
have common messes, which the Spartans called "men's messes" rather than
"friends' messes" in ancient times, just as the Cretans do now, from which it
is clear that they came from there. The same holds for the arrangement of the
5   regime. (6) For the overseers have the same powers as the so-called orderers
in Crete, except that the former are five in number and the latter ten. The
senators are the equals of their senators, whom the Cretans call the council. As for kingship, there was one in earlier times, but the Cretans later over-
10   threw it, and the orderers now have leadership in war. (7) All take part in
an assembly, but it has authority to do nothing other than ratify proposals of
the senators and orderers.

The matter of common messes is better handled by the Cretans than the
15   Spartans. In Sparta, each contributes a set amount; otherwise, the law pro-
hibits him from taking part in the regime, as was said earlier. (8) In Crete,
it is handled instead in more common fashion: from all the crops and livestock derived from the public land and from the contributions of the sub-
20   jects, one portion is set aside for the gods and for common sorts of public
service, and another for the common messes, so that everyone—women,
children, and men—receives sustenance from the treasury. (9) The legislator has been clever[101] in devising many things with a view to ensuring a beneficial scantiness of food; and with a view to segregating the women, so as to
prevent them having many children, he has provided for relations between
25   men (whether this was poorly done or not will be investigated on another
occasion).[102] That the matter of common messes is better arranged among
the Cretans than the Spartans, then, is evident.

The matter of the orderers,[103] however, is even worse than that of the
overseers. (10) For whatever is bad in the board of overseers exists in theirs
30   as well (for it consists of average persons); but whereas here it is advantageous
for the regime, there it is not. Here, since the election is from all, the people
share in the greatest office and hence wish the regime to continue. There,
however, they do not elect the orderers from all, but from certain families,
35   and the senators from those who have been orderers. (11) And one might
make the same arguments about these as about those who become overseers
in Sparta: it is not safe that they should go unaudited, that they should have

101 · Literally, "has philosophized" (*pephilosophēken*).

102 · There is no discussion of this question in the remainder of the *Politics* as we
have it.

103 · The Greek term is *kosmoi*.

throughout their lifetime a privilege which is greater than their merit, and
that they should rule not by written rules but at discretion. (12) Nor is it a
sign of a fine arrangement that the people keep quiet, though not taking part.   40
For the orderers have no source of gain, as the overseers do, since they dwell   1272b
on an island far away from those who might corrupt them. (13) The cure they
have found for this error is an odd one, characteristic not of political rule but
rule of the powerful.[104] For often the orderers are expelled by a combination
either of their own colleagues or of private individuals; and it is also open to
the orderers to resign the office in the middle of a term. But it is better if all   5
these things are done in accordance with law rather than in accordance with
human wish, as the latter is not a safe standard. (14) But the worst thing of
all is the [condition termed] "lack of order," which the powerful frequently
establish when they do not wish to submit to punishment[105]—by which it is
clear that their arrangement has elements of a regime but is not so much a re-   10
gime as it is rule of the powerful. It is habitual with them to have followings
among the people and their friends, create [petty] monarchies, and engage in
factional conflict and fighting against one another.[106] (15) Yet how does this
sort of thing differ from the city actually ceasing to be such for a certain period, and the political community dissolving?   15

A city in this condition is also in great danger from those who wish and
are able to attack it. But, as was said, Crete is preserved by its location: distance has acted as the equivalent of a law expelling foreigners.[107] (16) On this
account too the subjects put up with the Cretans, while the helots frequently
revolt. For the Cretans do not share in external rule, and only recently has   20
foreign war come to the island and made evident the weakness of the laws
there.[108] Concerning this regime, then, let us say this much.

104 · "Rule of the powerful" (*dynasteia*) is a term Aristotle will use of a narrow, kin-
based oligarchy that rules in a personalistic manner rather than under law.
105 · Apparently the entire office could be declared to be in abeyance, though how this
was done is not known. It would seem that the orderers acted as public prosecutors in
the Senate for certain types of crimes involving "the powerful."
106 · What Aristotle describes here is in effect something akin to the feudal system of
medieval Europe.
107 · The Spartans were well known for their strict control and periodic expulsion
of aliens present in Spartan territory. See, for example, Xenophon, *Constitution of the
Lacedaemonians* 14.4.
108 · This could refer to either or both of the following events: the operations conducted in Crete by the Phocian adventurer Phalaecus in 345–43 BC; the subjugation
of the island by Agesilaus, brother of the Spartan king Agis, in 333.

CHAPTER 11

(1) The Carthaginians are also held to govern themselves in a way that is
25   fine and in many respects extraordinary compared to others; but in certain
respects they are particularly similar to the Spartans.[109] For these three regimes—the Cretan, the Spartan, and, thirdly, that of the Carthaginians—
are very close to one another in a sense, and at the same time very different
30   from the others. Many of their arrangements are finely handled. (2) It is a
sign of a well-organized regime if the people voluntarily acquiesce in the arrangement of the regime, and if there has never been factional conflict worth
mentioning, or a tyrant. (3) The common messes of their clubs are similar
35   to the friends' messes of the Spartan regime, and their office of the hundred
and four to the overseers. And it is by no means worse: the latter are drawn
from average persons, but they elect the former on the basis of desert. The
kings and the senate are comparable to the kings and senators there; (4) yet
it is better [handled in Carthage] insofar as the kings do not derive from
40   the same family, nor an average one, but if any is outstanding whether [in
birth or virtue, it is from such families that they are chosen, and the senators
too] are elected from these rather than [occupying the office] on the basis
of age.[110] For as they have authority in great matters, if they are insignificant
1273a   persons they do great harm; and they have already done harm to the city of
the Spartans.

(5) Now most of what may be criticized as deviations from the best regime
happens to be common to all the regimes mentioned. As regards what may
5   be criticized with a view to the basic premise of aristocracy and polity, some
features incline toward rule of the people, others toward oligarchy. The kings
and the senators together have authority to submit or not submit a proposal
to the people if all are agreed on it, but if not, the people have authority
over these things as well. (6) And when the former propose something, it is
10   granted to the people not only to hear out [and approve] the opinions of the
rulers, but they have authority to come to a decision of their own, and whoever wishes is permitted to speak against the proposals—something which
does not exist in the other regimes. (7) But to have the committees of five,
which have authority in many great matters, elected by their own, to have

109 · Almost nothing is known of the political institutions of early Carthage apart from
the information Aristotle provides.
110 · Text and meaning are uncertain here. I assume a lacuna with Conring and others
rather than accepting the conjectural reconstruction of Dreizehnter, and supply what
I take to be the sense.

them elect to the greatest office, the hundred [and four],[111] and further, to   15
have them rule for a longer period than the others (for they rule [in effect]
even after they have left office and before they enter it)—all this is oligarchic.
On the other hand, that officials are unpaid and not chosen by lot must be
regarded as aristocratic, as well as other things of this sort; and also having all   20
cases tried by boards and not some by other [bodies] as in Sparta.[112]

(8) But the Carthaginian arrangement deviates from aristocracy toward
oligarchy particularly as regards a certain thought which is held jointly [by
the few and] by the many:[113] they suppose that the rulers ought not to be
elected on the basis of desert alone but also on the basis of wealth, it being   25
impossible for a poor person to rule finely and be at leisure. (9) If, therefore,
election on the basis of wealth is oligarchic and election in accordance with
virtue aristocratic, the arrangement by which the Carthaginians and others
have organized matters pertaining to the regime would be of a third sort. For
they look to both of these things when they elect—particularly in the case of
the greatest offices, kings and generals. (10) One should consider this devia-   30
tion from aristocracy an error of the legislator. It is among the most necessary things at the beginning to see how the best persons can be at leisure and
avoid disgraceful conduct not only when they are ruling but even as private   35
individuals. But if for the sake of leisure one should indeed look to what is
needed for being well off, it is a poor thing that the greatest offices—those of
both king and general—can be bought. (11) For this law makes wealth something more honored than virtue, and the city as a whole greedy. For whatever the authoritative element conceives to be honorable will necessarily be   40
followed by the opinion of the other citizens. Where virtue is not honored
above all, there cannot be a securely aristocratic regime. (12) And it is reason-   1273b
able that those who have bought an office will become habituated to profiting from it, since they spent so much in order to rule.[114] For it would be odd
if, when even a respectable person who is poor will want to profit from office,

---

111 · It is not completely certain that this is the same body referred to earlier.

112 · Or "all cases tried by all official bodies [*archeia*] and not some by some and some
by others [*allas hyp' allōn*]," as it is sometimes understood. But it is difficult to see how
the arrangement could be aristocratic unless a distinction is being drawn between trials by select "boards" and trials by larger bodies such as a senate or popular assembly.
The Spartan assembly appears to have functioned as a court at least in cases involving
disputed royal succession. Cf. 3.1.10–11.

113 · Or "by many": it is not clear whether the expression refers to the Carthaginian
lower class or to non-Carthaginians generally.

114 · The Greek word *archē* can mean either "rule" or (ruling) "office."

5 a worse one will not want to when he has already spent so much. Therefore, those capable of ruling best should rule. It would be better, if not for the legislator to enable the respectable to be well off, at least to take care that they will have leisure while they are ruling.

(13) It would also seem a poor thing to have the same person hold several offices—something that is held in high repute among the Carthaginians. 10 For one task is best accomplished by one person. The legislator should try to see that this happens, and not command the same person to play the flute and make shoes. (14) Except where the city is small, it is more political to have more persons take part in offices, and also more popular; for it is more 15 common, as we said, and each of these things[115] is accomplished more finely and more quickly. This is clear in military and maritime matters, for in both cases ruling and being ruled extends through practically everything.

(15) Although the regime is oligarchic, they escape the consequences of this in the best way by the fact that a part of the people is always becoming 20 wealthy through being sent out to the cities;[116] for by doing this they heal the ills of the regime and make it lasting. But this is really the work of chance, whereas they ought to be free of factional conflict through the legislator. (16) As it is, should some mischance occur and the multitude of the ruled revolt, there is no medicine that will restore quiet through the laws.

25 This, then, is the way matters stand concerning the regime of the Spartans, the Cretan regime, and that of the Carthaginians, which are justly held in high repute.

CHAPTER 12

(1) Of those who have put forward some view concerning the regime, some did not share in political actions of any sort, but led entirely private lives; 30 concerning them, if there is anything that merits mention, it has been spoken about for the most part in the case of all of them. But others became legislators—some for their own cities, others for certain foreigners as well—and engaged in politics themselves; and of these some were craftsmen of laws only, but others of a regime as well—for example, Lycurgus and Solon, who 35 established both laws and regimes. (2) Now the regime of the Spartans has

115 · Or "each of the same things." I read *tōn autōn* with the MSS rather than *tōn archōn* ("of the offices") with Dreizehnter. The reference would seem to be to 2.4–7.
116 · Cf. 6.5. 9. Carthage was an imperial city, and Aristotle evidently refers to "cities" that were subject to it. Whether the people were sent out as officials or colonists or for trading purposes of some sort is unclear.

been spoken of. As for Solon, there are some who suppose him to have been an excellent legislator.[117] For [they say] he dismantled an oligarchy that was too unmixed, put an end to the slavery of the people, and established the traditional democracy, under which the regime was finely mixed—the council of the Areopagus being oligarchic, the element of elective offices being aristocratic, and the courts being popular. (3) It would seem, though, that Solon found these things existing previously—the council and election to offices—and did not dismantle them, but established rule of the people by making the courts open to all. Thus there are also some who blame him for dissolving the other elements of the existing regime by giving authority to the court, which was to be chosen from all by lot. (4) For once this had become strong, they tried to gratify the people as if it were a tyrant, and altering the regime established the current democracy. Ephialtes and Pericles cut back the council of the Areopagus, Pericles established pay for the courts,[118] and in this manner each of the popular leaders proceeded by increasing [the power of the people] in the direction of the current democracy. (5) Yet this appears to have happened coincidentally rather than in accordance with the intention of Solon. For because the people were the cause of [Athens's] naval supremacy during the Persian wars, they began to have high thoughts and to obtain mean persons as popular leaders when they were opposed politically by the respectable.[119] Solon seems, at any rate, to have granted only the most necessary power to the people, that of electing to office and auditing; for if the people did not even have authority over this, they would be enslaved and an enemy to the regime. (6) But all the offices established by him were to be chosen from among notable and well-off persons—from the five-hundred-bushel-men, the team-men, and the third rating, the so-called cavalrymen; but the fourth, the laborers, had no part in any office.[120]

Other legislators were Zaleucus for the Epizephyrian Locrians, and Charondas of Catana for both his own citizens and the other Chalcidic cities in

---

117 · Solon was traditionally regarded as the founder of the democratic regime in Athens in the early sixth century. The identity of the proponents of the views described here is not certain; Aristotle himself later (3.11.8–9, 4.11.15) indicates approval of the Solonian legislation.

118 · These reforms were effected around 460 BC.

119 · The aristocratic party in Athens following the Persian Wars was headed by Cimon; Ephialtes and Pericles were the chief popular leaders. For the significance of Athenian naval power for the internal political struggle see 5.4. 8.

120 · A key element of the Solonian reforms was the establishment of a system of four assessment classes based on landed wealth as distinct from birth. See *Ath. Pol.* 7.

25   Italy and Sicily. (7) Some persons attempt to connect them, their view being that Onomacritus, a Locrian, was the first to become skilled in legislation, having been trained in Crete when he visited there in connection with
his practice of the divining art, that Thales became a companion of his, and
30   that Lycurgus and Zaleucus became students of Thales, and Charondas of
Zaleucus. (8) But they say these things without much of an investigation of
chronology.[121] But Philolaus of Corinth was a legislator for the Thebans.
Philolaus was of the Bacchiad family; he became a lover of Diocles the Olym-
35   pic victor, and when the latter left the city in disgust at his mother Alcyone's
love for himself, he went to Thebes, and there both of them ended their lives.
(9) And even now they show their tombs, which are in full view of one another, but one has a view toward Corinthian territory and the other does not,
40   the tale being told that they arranged the burial this way—Diocles, out of
hatred for the passion of his mother, so that the territory of Corinth would
1274b   not be visible from his mound, Philolaus, so that it would be from his. (10) So
they settled among the Thebans for this reason, and Philolaus became a legislator for them concerning childbearing among other matters—what they
5   call "adoptive laws"; this is something peculiar to his legislation, its purpose
being that the number of allotments should be preserved.[122] (11) Nothing is
peculiar to Charondas except trials in cases of perjury, for he was the first to
introduce denunciation for this; but in the precision of his laws he is more
polished even than current legislators. (12) Peculiar to Phaleas is the level-
10   ing of property; to Plato, having in common women and children as well as
property; and further, the law concerning drinking—that the sober must act
as rulers of drinking parties; and also that aspect of military training which
has them develop ambidexterity, the assumption being that they should not
15   have one useful and one useless hand.[123] (13) There are laws of Draco, but he
laid them down for an existing regime; there is nothing peculiar to these laws
that is worth recalling, except the harshness deriving from the size of the penalties.[124] Pittacus too was a craftsman of laws and not of a regime; peculiar to
20   him is a law that those who are drunk should pay a greater penalty than the

121 · Charondas and Zaleucus (seventh century BC) were sometimes connected with
the circle of Pythagoras. Onomacritus is probably the Orphic soothsayer who was influential in Athens at the time of the Pisistratid tyranny; the Thales in question is the
poet Thales (or Thaletas) of Gortyn in Crete.
122 · Nothing else is known of Philolaus.
123 · Plato, *Laws* 671d–72a, 794d–95d.
124 · Draco was considered the author of the first Athenian legal code (late seventh
century BC).

sober if they commit an offense. For on account of the fact that more persons commit outrages when drunk than when sober, he did not have regard for an indulgence that should be shown toward those who are drunk, but rather for what is advantageous.[125] (14) Androdamas of Rhegium also was a legislator for the Chalcidians of Thrace in matters concerning homicides and heiresses; but there is nothing peculiar to him that one might mention.[126] What concerns regimes—both those that have authority and those spoken about by certain persons—may be considered to have been studied, then, in this manner.[127]

125 · Pittacus was elected dictator of Mytilene during a period of civil strife there in the early sixth century; he was later enrolled (together with Solon) among the "seven wise men" of Greece.

126 · Nothing else is known of Androdamas.

127 · Much or all of this chapter is regarded by many scholars as of doubtful authenticity. For a detailed discussion see Schütrumpf.

Book 3

(1) For one investigating the regime—what each sort is and what its quality—virtually the first investigation concerns the city, to see what the city actually
35 is. For as it is, there are disputes, some arguing that the city performed an action, others that it was not the city but the oligarchy or the tyrant. We see that the entire activity of the political ruler and the legislator is concerned with the city, and the regime is a certain arrangement of those who inhabit the city. (2) But since the city belongs among composite things, and like other com-
40 posite wholes is made up of many parts, it is clear that the first thing that must
1275a be sought is the citizen; for the city is a certain multitude of citizens. Thus who ought to be called a citizen and what the citizen is must be investigated.

There is often much dispute about the citizen, for not everyone agrees that the same person is a citizen. Someone who is a citizen in a democracy is
5 often not one in an oligarchy. (3) Those who happen to be so designated but in some other sense—for example, honorary citizens—must be disregarded; nor is the citizen a citizen by inhabiting a place, for aliens and slaves share in the habitation; (4) nor are those partaking in matters of justice to the extent
10 of being subject to lawsuits and adjudication, for this exists even for those who share as a result of contractual agreements, since these things exist for them as well. For that matter, in many places not even aliens partake completely in these things, but they must necessarily find a patron, so that they take part in this sort of community in an incomplete sense. (5) Like children
15 who are not yet enrolled because of age and elderly persons who have been relieved,[1] they must be admitted to be citizens in a sense, but not unquali-

---

1 · Those beyond a certain age were apparently relieved of political as well as military duties; cf. Plato, *Republic* 498c.

fiedly, but rather with the addition of "incomplete" or "superannuated" or something else of this sort—it makes no difference, as what has been said is clear. We are seeking the citizen in an unqualified sense, one who has no de- 20 fect of this sort requiring correction, since questions may be raised and re-solved concerning such things in the case of those who have been deprived of their prerogatives or exiled as well.[2] (6) The citizen in an unqualified sense is defined by no other thing so much as by partaking in decision and office. Now some offices are differentiated by time, so that in some cases the same person is not permitted to hold them twice, or only after some definite pe- 25 riod of time has passed; but other offices are indefinite, such as that of juror or assemblyman. (7) Perhaps someone might say that the latter are not rul-ers and do not take part in office on account of these things; yet it would be ridiculous to deprive those with greatest authority of the title of office. But it should make no difference: the argument is over a term, for what is common 30 to juror and assemblyman lacks a name that could apply to both. For the sake of definition, then, let it be "indefinite office." (8) We set it down, then, that citizens are those who take part in this way.

The definition of citizen that fits best with all those who are called citi-zens is, therefore, something of this sort. But it should not be overlooked 35 that of things where the constituent elements differ in kind—one of them being primary, one secondary, another derivative—the common element ei-ther is not present at all insofar as they are such, or only slightly. (9) We see that regimes differ from one another in kind, and that some are prior and some posterior; for those that are errant and deviant must necessarily be pos- 1275b terior to those that are without error. (In what sense we are speaking of devi-ant regimes will be evident later.[3]) Hence the citizen must necessarily differ in the case of each sort of regime. (10) Accordingly, the citizen that was spo- 5 ken of is a citizen above all in a democracy; he may, but will not necessarily, be a citizen in the others. In some regimes there is no people, nor is an as-sembly recognized in law, but [only a consultative meeting of specially] sum-moned persons,[4] and cases are adjudicated by groups of officials. In Sparta, for example, different overseers try different cases involving agreements, the 10 senators those involving murder, and another office perhaps others; (11) and

2 · "Deprived of prerogatives" (*atimos*) was a technical term for persons formally stripped of citizenship.
3 · 3.6. 11.
4 · Aristotle appears to be thinking of consultative bodies such as the council of five thousand, which formed part of the moderate oligarchic regime established in Athens in 411 BC (Thucydides 8.67.3).

it is the same in the case of Carthage, where certain offices try all cases.[5] But our definition of the citizen [can stand, as it] admits of correction. In the other regimes, it is not the indefinite ruler who is assemblyman or juror, but one whose office is definite. For of these either all or some are assigned to deliberate and adjudicate, either concerning all matters or concerning some.

(12) Who the citizen is, then, is evident from these things. Whoever is entitled to share in an office involving deliberation or decision is, we can now say, a citizen in this city; and the city is the multitude of such persons that is adequate with a view to a self-sufficient life, to speak simply.

CHAPTER 2

(1) As a matter of usage, however, a citizen is defined as a person from parents who are both citizens, and not just one, whether the father or the mother; and some go even further back, seeking two or three or more generations of citizen forebears. But these being political and offhand definitions, some raise the question of how that third or fourth generation ancestor will have been a citizen. (2) Gorgias of Leontini therefore, perhaps partly by way of raising a question and partly in irony, said that just as mortars are made by mortar makers, so Larisaeans are made by craftsmen, since some of them are "Larisa makers."[6] (3) The matter is simple. If they took part in the regime according to the definition that has been given, they were citizens; for, at any rate, it is impossible that the definition from citizen father or mother should fit in the case of the first inhabitants or founders.

But perhaps more of a question is involved in the case of those who came to take part in the regime after a revolution—for example, the citizens created in Athens by Cleisthenes after the expulsion of the tyrants; for he enrolled in the tribes many foreigners and alien slaves.[7] The dispute about these

5 · Cf. 2.11.7. Aristotle's argument is that regimes like those of Sparta and Carthage handle judicial business primarily through tribunals of officials rather than large popular juries, as was the case in democracies like Athens; he had previously indicated that Carthage is even more restrictive in this respect than Sparta.

6 · Gorgias puns on the word *dēmiourgos*, which means both "craftsman" and "magistrate." Larisa was a town in Thessaly; the occasion of the remark is unknown, but would appear to have involved a wholesale enfranchisement of noncitizens.

7 · The democratic reforms effected by Cleisthenes after the overthrow of the Pisistratid tyranny (510 BC) involved abolishing the original four tribes of Athens and creating

is not over who is a citizen, but whether they are so justly or unjustly. (4) And yet a further question might be raised as to whether one who is not justly a citizen is a citizen at all, the assumption being that "unjust" and "false" amount to the same thing. (5) But since we also see certain unjust rulers, whom we assert do rule but unjustly, and since the citizen is defined by a kind of office (for someone who shares in that sort of office is a citizen, as we said), it is clear that these too must be admitted to be citizens.

1276a

5

CHAPTER 3

(1) The question of whether some are citizens justly or unjustly touches on the dispute mentioned previously. For some raise the question of when the city performed an action and when it did not—for example, at the time when a democracy replaces an oligarchy or a tyranny. (2) At these times, some do not want to fulfill contractual agreements on the grounds that it was not the city but the tyrant who entered into them, or many other things of this sort, the assumption being that some regimes exist through domination and not because they are to the common advantage. However, if some are run democratically in this same fashion, the actions of this regime must then be admitted to belong to the city in just the same way as the actions of the oligarchy or the tyranny.

10

15

(3) This argument seems related to the question of the sense in which the city ought to be spoken of as the same, or as not the same but different. Now the most superficial way of examining this question concerns the location and the human beings constituting it; for the location and the human beings can be disjoined, with some inhabiting one location and others another, and it will still be a city. (4) The question in this form is to be regarded as a slight one, for the fact that the city is spoken of in several senses makes the examination of such cases easy.[8] And similarly in the case of human beings inhabiting the same location, if one asks when the city should be considered one. (5) For it is surely not by the fact of its walls—it would be possible to

20

25

---

ten new ones in order to accommodate the new citizens. The text and the exact meaning of Aristotle's description of these citizens is controversial.

8 · "City" (*polis*) has both a physical and a political sense: two cities "disjoined" in place or geography might nevertheless form part of a single city in the political sense. Aristotle may have in mind island cities that possessed territory and towns on the mainland (such as Lesbos or Samos) or cities with substantial dependent ports (such as Athens or Megara).

build a single wall around the Peloponnese. Babylon is perhaps a city of this
sort, or any that has the dimensions of a nation rather than a city; at any rate,

30   they say that its capture was not noticed in a certain part of the city for three
days.[9] (6) But the investigation of this question will be useful on another occasion.[10] For the size of the city—as regards both quantity and whether it
is advantageous to have one or several [locations][11]—should not be overlooked by the political ruler. But where the same persons inhabit the same

35   location, must it be asserted that the city is the same as long as the stock of
inhabitants remains the same, even though some are always passing away and
some being born (as we are accustomed to speaking of rivers and springs as
the same even though more water is always coming and flowing away)? Or

40   must it be asserted that the human beings are the same for this sort of reason,
1276b but that the city differs? (7) For if the city is a type of community, and if it is a
community of citizens in a regime, if the regime becomes and remains different in kind, it might be held that the city as well is necessarily not the same.

5   At any rate, just as we assert that a chorus which is at one time comic and at
another tragic is different even though the human beings in it are often the
same, (8) it is similar with any other community and any compound, when
the compound takes a different form—for example, we would say that the
mode is different even when the notes are the same, if it is at one time Dorian

10   and at another Phrygian.[12] (9) If this is indeed the case, it is evident that it is
looking to the regime above all that the city must be said to be the same; the
name[13] one calls it can be different or the same no matter whether the same
human beings inhabit it or altogether different ones. As to whether it is just
to fulfill or not to fulfill contractual agreements when the city undergoes rev-

15   olution into another regime, that is another argument.

9 · Babylon was captured by the Persians under Cyrus in the sixth century. Cf. Herodotus 1.191.

10 · 7.4. ff.

11 · The text is uncertain here. I follow Dreizehnter in considering the accepted reading *ethnos* a conjectural addition, but prefer the version of Π² (*hen ē pleiō*) to his own
conjecture (*genē pleiō*); possibly the original text was *ton topon hen ē pleiō*, though this
would not seem necessary for the sense. Aristotle seems to have in mind the advantages
of a separate port city (cf. 7.6. 5).

12 · Reading *legoimen* with the MSS ("we would say") rather than *legomen* ("we say")
with Dreizehnter. The point of the comparison seems to depend on the considerable
overlap between the notes utilized for the Dorian and Phrygian modes as well as the
very different spirit of these modes (cf. 8.5. 22, 7.9–12).

13 · For evidence for changes in the names of cities, see Newman's note.

CHAPTER 4

(1) Connected with what has been said is the investigation of whether the virtue of the good man and the excellent citizen[14] is to be regarded as the same or as not the same. If we are indeed to examine this, however, the virtue of the citizen must first be grasped in some sort of outline. Now just as a sailor is one of a number of sharers, so, we assert, is the citizen. (2) Although sailors are dissimilar in their capacities (one is a rower, another a pilot, another a lookout, and others have similar sorts of designations), it is clear that the most precise account of their virtue will be that peculiar to each sort individually, but that a common account will in a similar way fit all. For the safety of the ship in its voyage is the task of all of them, and each of the sailors strives for this. (3) Similarly, although citizens are dissimilar, preservation of the community is their task, and the regime is this community; hence the virtue of the citizen must necessarily be with a view to the regime. If, then, there are indeed several forms of regime, it is clear that it is not possible for the virtue of the excellent citizen to be single, or complete virtue. (4) But the good man we assert is so in accordance with a single kind—complete virtue.[15] That it is possible for a citizen to be excellent yet not possess the virtue in accordance with which he is an excellent man, therefore, is evident.

By raising questions in a different manner, the same argument can be made concerning the best regime. (5) For if it is impossible for a city to consist entirely of excellent persons, yet if each should perform his own task well, and this [means] out of virtue, since it is impossible for all the citizens to be similar, there would still not be a single virtue of the citizen and the good man. The virtue of the excellent citizen must exist in all, for it is necessarily in this way that the city is excellent, but this is impossible in the case of the virtue of the good man, unless all the citizens of an excellent city are necessarily good men. (6) Further, since the city is made up of dissimilar persons—as an animal is made up of soul and body, for instance, soul of reason and appetite, and a household of man and woman and master and slave,[16] in the same

14 · The terms translated "good" and "excellent" are *agathos* and *spoudaios* (literally, "serious"), respectively; Aristotle seems to use them interchangeably (that is, "excellent" should not be taken as a superlative). Both words connote moral virtue rather than any sort of instrumental excellence.
15 · This sentence is omitted in most MSS.
16 · I follow Bernays in bracketing *ktēsis* in a8. Translating the text of the MSS: "and a household of man and woman, and possessions of master and slave...."

way a city is made up of all of these, and in addition to these it consists of
10   other dissimilar kinds of persons—the virtue of all the citizens is necessarily not single, just as that of a head and a file leader in a chorus is not single.
(7) That it is not the same in an unqualified sense, therefore, is evident from
these things. But will there be some case, then, in which the virtue of the ex-
15   cellent citizen and the excellent man is the same? We assert that the excellent
ruler is good and prudent, while the excellent citizen is not necessarily prudent.[17] (8) Indeed, some say that the very education of a ruler is different, as
is manifestly the case with the sons of kings who are educated to be expert in
riding and in war; and when Euripides says "no subtleties for me, but what is
20   needed for the city,"[18] the assumption is that there is a certain education of a
ruler. (9) If the virtue of the good ruler and the good man is the same, and if
one who is ruled is also a citizen, the virtue of citizen and man would not be
the same unqualifiedly, but only in the case of a certain sort of citizen. For the
virtue of ruler and citizen is not the same, and it was perhaps for this reason
25   that Jason said he was hungry except when he was tyrant, as one who did not
know how to be a private individual.[19]

(10) At the same time, the capacity to rule and be ruled is praised, and
the virtue of a citizen of reputation is held[20] to be the capacity to rule and be
ruled finely. Now if we regard the virtue of the good man as being of a ruling
sort, while that of the citizen is both of a ruling and a ruled sort, they would
30   not be praiseworthy to a similar extent. (11) Since both views are sometimes
held—that the ruler and the ruled ought to learn different things and not
the same, and that the citizen must know both sorts of things and partake
in both—the next step becomes visible. There is rule of a master, by which
we mean that connected with the necessary things. It is not necessary for
35   the ruler to know how to perform these, but only to use those who do; the
other [sort of knowledge] is servile (by the other I mean the capacity to perform the subordinate tasks of a servant). (12) Now we speak of several forms
of slave; for the sorts of work are several. One sort is that done by menials:
1277b   as the term itself indicates, these are persons who live by their hands; the

17 · On "prudence" (*phronēsis*), a key concept in Aristotle's thought, see *Eth. Nic.*
6.13.1144a28 ff.
18 · Euripides, fr. 16. Nauck. The lines are from the *Aeolus*, and were apparently spoken by the king about his sons.
19 · Jason of Pherae, in Thessaly, was a notorious tyrant of the early fourth century.
20 · The text is somewhat uncertain: I read *dokimou <dokei>* with Bernays and Newman instead of *dokei pou* ("the virtue of a citizen is surely held") with Jackson and
Dreizehnter.

manufacturing artisan belongs among them. Hence among some peoples the craftsmen did not partake in offices in former times, prior to the emergence of rule of the people in its extreme form.[21] (13) Now the tasks of those ruled in this way should not be learned by the good man or the political ruler or the good citizen, unless he does it for himself out of some need of his own (for then it does not result in one person becoming master and another slave).

But there is also a sort of rule in accordance with which one rules those who are similar in stock and free. (14) For this is what we speak of as political rule, and the ruler learns it by being ruled—just as the cavalry commander learns by being commanded, the general by being led, and similarly in the case of the leader of a regiment or company. Hence this too has been finely said—that it is not possible to rule well without having been ruled.[22] (15) Virtue in each of these cases is different, but the good citizen should know and have the capacity both to be ruled and to rule, and this very thing is the virtue of a citizen—knowledge of rule over free persons from both points of view. (16) Both belong to the good man too, as well as whatever kind of moderation and justice is characteristic of ruling. For it is clear that a virtue— of justice, for example—would not be a single thing for [a ruler and for[23]] a ruled but free person who is good, but has different kinds in accordance with which one will rule or be ruled, just as moderation and courage differ in a man and a woman. (17) For a man would be held a coward if he were as courageous as a courageous woman, and a woman talkative if she were as modest as the good man; and household management differs for a man and a woman as well, for it is the work of the man to acquire and of the woman to guard. But prudence is the only virtue peculiar to the ruler. The others, it would seem, must necessarily be common to both rulers and ruled, (18) but prudence is not a virtue of one ruled, but rather true opinion; for the one ruled is like a flute maker, while the ruler is like a flute player, the user [of what the other makes].[24] Whether the virtue of the good man and the excellent citizen is the same or different, then, and in what sense it is the same and in what sense different, is evident from these things.

21 · Aristotle seems to allude in particular to Athens, where the exclusion of laborers (the assessment class of *thētes*) from office (Plutarch *Solon* 18) seems to have persisted through much of the fifth century.
22 · A saying of this sort was ascribed to Solon (Diogenes Laertius 1.60).
23 · Accepting Bernays's supplement *archontos kai* in 18.
24 · For the relationship of "making" and "using" arts see 1.8. 1–2; for the example, see Plato, *Republic* 601d.

CHAPTER 5

(1) One of the questions concerning the citizen still remains. Is he only truly a
35   citizen to whom it is open to share in office, or are workers also to be regarded
as citizens?[25] For if those too are to be so regarded who have no part in offices, then the virtue we have discussed cannot belong to every citizen, as this
sort is then a citizen. On the other hand, if none of these sorts is a citizen, in
which class is each sort to be placed?[26] For he is neither a resident alien nor a
1278a   foreigner. (2) Or shall we assert that there is nothing odd about this, at least
on the basis of this argument? Neither slaves nor freedmen belong to those
just mentioned. And this is true: not all those are to be regarded as citizens
without whom there would not be a city, since children are not citizens in the
5   same sense that men are; the latter are unqualifiedly, but the former only by
way of a presupposition—they are citizens, but incomplete ones. (3) Now in
ancient times among some peoples the working element was slave or foreign,
and for this reason many are such even now; but the best city will not make a
worker a citizen. But if this sort is a citizen, the virtue of a citizen, as we have
10   been discussing it at any rate, cannot be spoken of as belonging to everyone
or even to every free person, but only to those who have been relieved of necessary sorts of work. (4) Those who perform necessary services for one person are slaves; those who do so for the community are workers and laborers.[27]

If we investigate a bit further from this point it will be evident how matters stand concerning them. What has already been said will itself make this
15   clear, once it is recalled.[28] (5) Since there are several regimes, there must necessarily be several kinds of citizen, and particularly of the citizen who is ruled.
Thus in one sort of regime the worker and the laborer must necessarily be
citizens, while in others this is impossible—for example, in any of the sort
20   they call aristocratic, in which prerogatives are granted in accordance with
virtue and merit; for it is impossible to pursue the things of virtue when one
lives the life of a worker or a laborer. (6) In oligarchies, on the other hand, it
is not possible for a laborer to be a citizen, for taking part in offices is on the
basis of large assessments, but it is possible for a worker, since many artisans

---

25 · Cf. 1.11, note 48.

26 · Aristotle seems to anticipate the subsequent introduction (5.4) of "laborers" as a
distinct "sort" of persons excluded from office.

27 · The term "laborers"(*thētes*) was the formal designation of the lowest of the four
Athenian assessment classes (cf. 2.12); the word itself connotes unskilled or semi-
skilled wage laborers.

28 · This appears to be a reference to 1.8–9, but the exact sense is uncertain.

become wealthy. (7) In Thebes there used to be a law that one who had not   25
abstained from the market for ten years could not take part in office. But in
many regimes the law pulls in even some foreigners; for one descended from
a citizen mother is a citizen in some democracies, and it is the same way with
bastards in many regimes. (8) Nevertheless, since it is because of a lack of   30
genuine citizens that they make for themselves citizens of this sort (for they
use such laws on account of a shortage of manpower), when they are well off
as regards numbers they gradually disqualify first those with a slave as father
or mother, then those with citizen mothers [but foreign fathers], and finally
they make citizens only those with two native parents.

(9) That there are several kinds of citizens, therefore, is evident from these   35
things, as is the fact that one who takes part in prerogatives is particularly
spoken of as a citizen—thus, for example, Homer's line "like some vagabond
without honor."²⁹ For one who does not take part in prerogatives is like an
alien. But wherever this sort of thing is kept concealed, it is for the sake of
deceiving the [excluded] inhabitants.   40

(10) As to whether the virtue that constitutes the good man and the excellent citizen is to be regarded as the same or different, then, it is clear from   1278b
what has been said that in one sort of city this person is the same and in another different, and that even in the former sort it is not everyone but the
political ruler and the one having authority or capable of having authority,
either by himself or together with others, over the superintendence of com-   5
mon matters.

CHAPTER 6

(1) Since these things have been discussed, what comes after them must be investigated—whether we are to regard there as being one regime or many, and
if many, which and how many there are and what the differences are between
them. The regime is an arrangement of a city with respect to its offices, particularly the one that has authority over all matters.³⁰ For what has authority   10
in the city is everywhere the governing body, and the governing body *is* the
regime.³¹ (2) I mean, for example, that in democratic regimes the people have

29 · Homer, *Iliad* 9.648, 16.59. "Prerogatives" and "honor" both translate the word
timē.
30 · The term rendered throughout as "authority" or "authoritative" (*kyrios*) can and
often has been translated "sovereign," but this is misleading to the extent that it suggests
a legally recognized status in the modern sense.
31 · "Governing body" translates the term *politeuma.*

authority, while by contrast it is the few in oligarchies. The regime too, we say, is different in these cases; and we shall speak in the same way concerning
15   the others as well.

First, then, we must lay down by way of a basic premise what it is for the sake of which the city is established, and how many kinds of rule are connected with man and the community in life. (3) It was said in our initial discourses, where household management and mastery were discussed, that
20   man is by nature a political animal. Hence even when they have no need of assistance from one another, they no less yearn to live together—not but that the common advantage too brings them together, to the extent that it falls to each to live finely. It is this above all, then, which is the end for all both in
25   common and separately; but they also join together, and maintain the political community, for the sake of living itself. For there is perhaps something fine in living just by itself, provided there is no great excess of hardships. It is clear that most men will endure much harsh treatment in their longing for life, the assumption being that there is a kind of joy inherent in it and a natural sweetness.

30   As for the modes of rule that are spoken of, it is easy to distinguish them, and we discuss them frequently in the external discourses.[32] Mastery, in spite of the same thing being in truth advantageous both to the slave by nature and
35   to the master by nature, is still rule with a view to the advantage of the master primarily, and with a view to that of the slave accidentally (for mastery cannot be preserved if the slave is destroyed). Rule over children and wife and the household as a whole, which we call household management, is either for the sake of the ruled or for the sake of something common to both—
40   in itself it is for the sake of the ruled, as we see in the case of the other arts
1279a   such as medicine and gymnastic, but accidentally it may be for the sake of the rulers themselves. For nothing prevents the trainer from being on occasion one of those engaging in gymnastic, just as the pilot is always one of the
5   sailors: the trainer or pilot looks out for the good of the ruled, and when he becomes one of them himself, he shares accidentally in the benefit; for the one is a sailor, and the other becomes one of those engaging in gymnastic, though still a trainer. Hence with respect to political offices too, when the
10   regime is established in accordance with equality and similarity among the citizens, they claim to merit ruling in turn. Previously, as accords with nature, they claimed to merit doing public service by turns and having someone look to their good, just as when ruling previously they looked to his advantage.

32 · For Aristotle's "external discourses" see Introduction, pp. xvii–xix above.

Now, however, because of the benefits to be derived from common things
and from office, they wish to rule continuously, as if they were sick persons   15
who were always made healthy by ruling; at any rate, these would perhaps
pursue office in a similar fashion.[33]

It is evident, then, that those regimes which look to the common advantage are correct regimes according to what is unqualifiedly just, while those
which look only to the advantage of the rulers are errant, and are all devia-   20
tions from the correct regimes; for they involve mastery, but the city is a community of free persons.

CHAPTER 7

(1) These things having been determined, the next thing is to investigate regimes—how many in number and which sorts there are, and first of all the
correct ones; for the deviations will be evident once these have been deter-   25
mined. (2) Since "regime" and "governing body" signify the same thing,[34]
since the governing body is the authoritative element in cities, and since it is
necessary that the authoritative element be either one or a few or the many,
when the one or the few or the many rule with a view to the common advantage, these regimes are necessarily correct, while those with a view to the   30
private advantage of the one or the few or the multitude are deviations. For
either it must be denied that persons taking part in the regime are citizens,
or they must share in its advantages. (3) Now of monarchies, that form which
looks toward the common advantage we are accustomed to call kingship;
rule of the few (but of more than one person) we are accustomed to call ar-   35
istocracy—either because the best persons are ruling, or because they are
ruling with a view to what is best for the city and for those sharing in it;
and when the multitude governs with a view to the common advantage, it
is called by the term common to all regimes, polity.[35] (4) This happens reasonably. It is possible for one or a few to be outstanding in virtue, but where   40
more are concerned it is difficult for them to be proficient with a view to vir-   1279b
tue as a whole, but some level of proficiency is possible particularly regarding
military virtue, as this arises in a multitude; hence in this regime the warrior

33 · These remarks seem to be directed at Athens in particular.
34 · The term "governing body" (*politeuma*) derives from *politeia*. A more colloquial
rendering might be "the political class."
35 · Wherever Aristotle uses the term *politeia* to refer to this particular type of regime,
it will be translated "polity." There are some passages, however, where the distinction
is not completely clear.

element is the most authoritative, and it is those possessing heavy arms who
5   take part in it. (5) Deviations from those mentioned are tyranny from kingship, oligarchy from aristocracy, democracy from polity. Tyranny is monarchy with a view to the advantage of the monarch, oligarchy rule with a view
to the advantage of the well off, democracy rule with a view to the advantage
10   of those who are poor; none of them is with a view to the common gain.

CHAPTER 8

(1) It is necessary to speak at somewhat greater length of what each of these
regimes is. For certain questions[36] are involved, and it belongs to one philosophizing in connection with each sort of inquiry and not merely looking
15   toward action not to overlook or omit anything, but to make clear the truth
concerning each thing. (2) Tyranny, as was said, is monarchic rule of a master over the political community; oligarchy is when those with property have
authority in the regime; and democracy is the opposite, when those have au-
20   thority who do not possess a great amount of property but are poor. (3) The
first question has to do with the definition. If a well-off majority has authority, and similarly in the other case, if it somewhere happened that the poor
were a minority with respect to the well off but were superior and had au-
25   thority in the regime, although when a small number has authority it is called
oligarchy, this definition of the regimes would not be held to be a fine one.
(4) But even if one were to combine fewness with being well off and number
with being poor and described the regimes accordingly (oligarchy being that
in which those who are well off and few in number have the offices, and de-
30   mocracy that in which those who are poor and many in number have them),
another question is involved. (5) What shall we say of the regimes that were
just mentioned—those in which the majority is well off and the poor are
few and each has authority in the regime—if there is no other regime be-
35   side those we spoke of? (6) The argument seems to make clear, therefore,
that it is accidental that few or many have authority in oligarchies on the one
hand and democracies on the other, and that this is because the well off are
everywhere few and the poor many. Hence it also turns out that the causes
40   of the differences are not what was mentioned. (7) What makes democracy
1280a   and oligarchy differ is poverty and wealth: wherever some rule on account of
wealth, whether a minority or a majority, this is necessarily an oligarchy, and

36 · This term (*aporia*), characteristic of Aristotle's more theoretical writings, might
be more precisely rendered "philosophical puzzle" or "conundrum."

wherever those who are poor, a democracy. (8) But it turns out, as we said, that the former are few and the latter many; for few are well off, but all share   5 in freedom—which are the causes of both disputing over the regime.

CHAPTER 9

(1) It is necessary first to grasp what they speak of as the defining principles of oligarchy and democracy and what justice[37] is [from] both oligarchic and democratic [points of view]. For all fasten on a certain sort of justice, but proceed only to a certain point, and do not speak of the whole of justice in   10 its authoritative sense. For example, justice is held to be equality, and it is, but for equals and not for all; (2) and inequality is held to be just and is indeed, but for unequals and not for all; but they disregard this element of persons and judge badly. The cause of this is that the judgment concerns them-   15 selves, and most people are bad judges concerning their own things. (3) And so since justice is for certain persons, and is distinguished in the same manner with respect to objects and for persons, as was said previously in the discourses on ethics,[38] they agree as to the equality of the object, but dispute about it for persons. They do this particularly because of what was just spo-   20 ken of, that they judge badly with respect to what concerns themselves, but also because both, by speaking to a point of a kind of justice, consider themselves to be speaking of justice simply. (4) For the ones, if they are unequal in a certain thing, such as goods, suppose they are unequal generally, while the others suppose that if they are equal in a certain thing, such as freedom, they are equal generally. (5) But of the most authoritative thing they say noth-   25 ing. For if it were for the sake of possessions that they shared and joined together, they would take part in the city just to the extent that they did in property, so that the argument of the oligarchs might be held a strong one; for [they would say] it is not just for one who has contributed one mina to share equally in a hundred minas with the one giving all the rest, whether he   30 comes from those who were there originally or the later arrivals.[39] (6) But if

37 · That is, "the just" (*to dikaion*) or "right" as distinct from the virtue of justice (*dikaiosynē*). Fundamental for this entire discussion is the more theoretical analysis of "distributive justice" in *Eth. Nic.* 5.6.

38 · *Eth. Nic.* 1131a14–24.

39 · Or, as the phrase is generally translated, "whether of the original sum or of the accruing profits." Following Bernays, I take the remark rather to be the oligarchic response to a (democratic or aristocratic) argument for special treatment in consequence of descent from the original settlers.

the city exists not only for the sake of living but rather primarily for the sake
of living well (for otherwise there could be a city of slaves or of animals—
as things are, there is not, since they do not partake in happiness or in living
in accordance with intentional choice), and if it does not exist for the sake
of an alliance to prevent their suffering injustice from anyone, nor for purposes of exchanges and use of one another—for otherwise the Tyrrhenians
and Carthaginians, and all who have agreements with one another, would
be as citizens of one city—(7) at any rate, there are compacts between them
concerning imports, agreements to abstain from injustice, and treaties of alliance. But no offices common to all have been established to deal with these
things, but different ones in each city; nor do those of one city take thought
that the others should be of a certain quality [in their character], or that none
of those coming under the compacts should be unjust or depraved in any way,
but only that they should not act unjustly toward one another. (8) Whoever
takes thought for good governance,[40] however, gives careful attention to political virtue and vice. It is thus evident that virtue must be a care for every
city, or at least every one to which the term applies truly and not merely in
a manner of speaking. For otherwise the community becomes an alliance
which differs from others—from alliances of remote allies—only by location, and law becomes a compact and, as the sophist Lycophron said, a guar-
antor among one another of the just things, but not the sort of thing to make
the citizens good and just.[41] (9) But that the matter stands thus is evident. For
even if one were to bring the locations together into one, so that the city of
the Megarians were fastened to that of the Corinthians by walls,[42] it would
still not be a single city. (10) Nor would it be if they practiced intermarriage
with one another, although this is one of the shared things that are peculiar
to cities. Nor, similarly, if certain persons dwelled in separate places, yet were
not so distant as to have nothing in common, but had laws not to commit injustice toward one another in their transactions—for example, if one were a
carpenter, one a farmer, one a shoemaker, one something else of this sort, and
they were ten thousand in number, yet had nothing in common except things
of this sort, exchange and alliance; not even in this way would there be a city.
(11) What, then, is the reason for this? It is surely not on account of a lack

40 · This term (*eunomia*), connoting orderly government under law, had a conservative flavor in contemporary political discourse. Cf. *Eth. Nic.* 3.5.1112b11–14.

41 · Nothing else is known of Lycophron, whose dictum strikingly anticipates early
modern social contract theory.

42 · The territory of Megara bordered that of Corinth, though the cities themselves
were relatively distant.

of proximity of the community. For even if they joined together while shar-   25
ing in this way, but each nevertheless treated his own household as a city and
each other as if there were a defensive alliance merely for assistance against
those committing injustice, it would not by this fact be held a city by those
studying the matter precisely—if, that is, they shared in a similar way when
joined together as they had when separated. (12) It is evident, therefore, that   30
the city is not a community sharing a location and for the sake of not committing injustice against each other and conducting trade. These things must
necessarily be present if there is to be a city, but not even when all of them
are present is it yet a city, but the city is the community in living well both of
households and families[43] for the sake of a complete and self-sufficient life.
(13) This will not be possible, however, unless they inhabit one and the same   35
location and make use of intermarriage. It was on this account that marriage
connections arose in cities, as well as clans, festivals, and the pastimes of living together.[44] This sort of thing is the work of affection; for affection is the
intentional choice of living together. Living well, then, is the end of the city,
and these things are for the sake of this end. (14) A city is the community of   40
families and villages in a complete and self-sufficient life. This, we assert, is   1281a
living happily and finely. The political community must be regarded, therefore, as being for the sake of noble actions, not for the sake of living together.
(15) Hence those who contribute most to a community of this sort have a   5
greater part in the city than those who are equal or greater in freedom and
descent[45] but unequal in political virtue, or those who outdo them in wealth
but are outdone in virtue.

That all who dispute about regimes speak of some part of justice, then, is   10
evident from what has been said.

CHAPTER 10

(1) There is a question as to what the authoritative element of the city should
be. It is either the multitude, the wealthy, the respectable, the one who is
best of all, or the tyrant; but all of these appear to involve difficulties. How

---

43 · More precisely, a *genos* denotes an extended family, clan or (noble) "house," and in
a broader sense, birth or descent; cf. 1281a6. It will sometimes also be translated "stock."
44 · "Clans" or "brotherhoods" (*phratriai*) were bodies of citizens linked by (largely
mythical) blood ties. "Pastime" (*diagōgē*) will emerge as a major theme of Aristotle's
discussion of education and culture in books 7–8.
45 · *Genos.* The occurrence of the word here would appear to confirm the interpretation given above of 1280a30–31; see note 39.

15   could they not? If the poor by the fact of being the majority distribute among
themselves the things of the wealthy, is this not unjust? "By Zeus, it was resolved in just fashion by those in authority!" (2) What, then, ought one to
say is the extreme of injustice? Again, taking all [the citizens] into consideration, if the majority distributes among itself the things of a minority, it is
20   evident that it will destroy the city. Yet it is certainly not virtue that destroys
the element possessing it, nor is justice destructive of a city; so it is clear that
this law cannot be just. (3) Further, [on such an assumption] any actions carried out by a tyrant are necessarily just: he is superior and uses force, like the
multitude with respect to the wealthy.

25   But is it just, therefore, for the minority and the wealthy to rule? If they
act in the same way and rob and plunder the possessions of the multitude,
is this just? If so, the other is as well. (4) That all of these things are bad and
unjust, then, is evident. But should the respectable[46] rule and have authority
30   over all matters? In this case, all the others are necessarily deprived of prerogatives, since they are not honored by attaining political offices. For we say
that offices are honors, and when the same persons always rule the others are
necessarily deprived of [these honors or] prerogatives.[47] (5) But is it better
for the one who is most excellent of all to rule? But this is still more oligarchic, as more are deprived of prerogatives. One might perhaps assert, how-
35   ever, that it is bad for the authoritative element generally to be man instead
of law, at any rate if he has the passions that result [from being human] in his
soul. But if law may be oligarchic or democratic, what difference will it make
with regard to the questions that have been raised? For what was said before
will result all the same.

CHAPTER 11

40   (1) Concerning the other matters let there be another argument.[48] That the
multitude should be the authoritative element rather than those who are best
but few, though, [is a position involving difficulties which] could be held to
be [in need of being] resolved,[49] and while questionable, it perhaps also in-

---

46 · *Epieikeis*, that is, gentlemen or aristocrats.

47 · The argument depends on the technical use of the word *atimoi* (literally, "those
without honor") to designate persons judicially deprived of certain prerogatives of
citizenship.

48 · See 3.12–13.

49 · Or, as it is most generally understood, "[is a position giving rise to objections
which] could be held to be refutable." The meaning and syntax of the phrase *doxeien*

volves some truth. (2) The many, of whom none is individually an excellent   1281b
man, nevertheless can when joined together be better—not as individuals but
all together—than those [who are best], just as dinners contributed by many
can be better than those equipped from a single expenditure. For because
they are many, each can have a part of virtue and prudence, and on their join-   5
ing together, the multitude, with its many feet and hands and having many
senses, becomes like a single human being, and so also with respect to character and mind. (3) Thus the many are also better judges of the works of music
and of the poets; some [appreciate] a certain part, and all of them all the parts.
(4) But it is in this that the excellent men differ from each of the many indi-   10
vidually, just as some assert beautiful persons differ from those who are not
beautiful, and things painted by art from genuine things, by bringing together
things scattered and separated into one; for taken separately, at any rate, this
person's eye will be more beautiful than the painted one, as will another part   15
of another person. (5) Whether this difference between the many and the few
excellent can exist in the case of every people and every multitude is not clear.
Or rather, [it might be objected,] "by Zeus, it is clear that in some cases it is
impossible: the same argument would apply to beasts—for what difference   20
is there between some multitudes and beasts, so to speak?" But nothing prevents what was said from being true of a certain kind of multitude.

(6) Through these things, accordingly, one might resolve both the question spoken of earlier [concerning who should rule] and one connected with
it—over what matters free persons or the multitude of the citizens (these being whoever is neither wealthy nor has any claim at all deriving from virtue)   25
should have authority. (7) For having them take part in the greatest offices is
not safe: through injustice and imprudence they would act unjustly in some
respects and err in others. On the other hand, to give them no part and for
them to have no part in the offices is a matter for alarm, for when there exist many who are deprived of prerogatives and poor, that city is necessarily   30
filled with enemies. (8) What is left, then, is for them to take part in deliberating and judging. Hence Solon and certain other legislators arrange to have
them both choose officials and audit them, but do not allow them to rule
alone.[50] (9) For all of them when joined together have an adequate percep-   35

---

an luesthai are uncertain, and the soundness of the MSS here has been questioned. I
share Newman's suspicion that something has dropped out of the text—at least the
word *dei* ("in need of being"), and perhaps an entire line; I have supplied what I take
to be the overall sense.

50 · Cf. 2.12.2–3, 5–6. An "audit" (*euthynē*) was a formal review of the performance of
officials conducted on an annual basis at Athens and other Greek cities.

tion and, once mixed with those who are better, bring benefit to cities, just as impure sustenance[51] mixed with the pure makes the whole more useful than the small amount of the latter, but each separately is incomplete with respect to judging.

(10) But this arrangement of the regime involves questions. In the first place, it might be held that it belongs to the same person to judge whether someone has healed in correct fashion and to heal and make healthy one who is suffering from a particular disease, this being the doctor; and similarly also with respect to other kinds of experience and art. Just as a doctor must submit to audit by doctors, then, so must the others submit to audit by those similar to them. (11) But "doctor" [is a term that can be applied to] the [ordinary] craftsman, the master craftsman, and thirdly, the person who is educated with respect to the art; for there are some of this sort in the case of nearly all the arts, and we assign the task of judging to the educated no less than to those who know the art. (12) And it might be held that the case is the same with respect to the choice of officials. Choosing correctly is indeed also the work of those who know—for example, choosing a geometer is the work of experts in geometry, and a pilot that of experts in piloting. If certain non-professionals share in some of these works and arts, however, they do not do so to a greater extent than those who know. (13) So according to this argument the multitude ought not to be given authority either over the choice of officials or over their auditing. (14) But perhaps not all of these things have been finely argued, both because of the previous argument, provided the multitude is not overly slavish (for each individually will be a worse judge than those who know, but all when joined together will be either better or no worse), and because there are some arts concerning which the maker might not be the only or the best judge, but where those who do not possess the art also have some knowledge of its works. The maker of a house, for example, is not the only one to have some knowledge of it, but the one who uses it judges better than he does, and the one who uses it is the household manager; and a pilot judges rudders better than a carpenter, and the diner, not the cook, is the better judge of a banquet.

(15) This question, then, may perhaps be held to be adequately resolved in this fashion. But there is another connected with it. It is held to be absurd for mean persons to have authority over greater matters than the respectable; but auditing and the choice of officials are a very great thing, and in some regimes, as was said, these are given to the people, for the assembly

---

51 · Food in a raw or crude state; cf. *Generation of Animals* 728a26 ff.

has authority over everything of this sort. (16) Hence, persons from the lowest assessments and of whatever age share in the assembly and deliberate and   30
adjudicate, while those from the greatest assessments are the treasurers and
generals and hold the greatest offices. Now one might resolve this question
as well in a similar way. (17) For perhaps these things too are handled correctly: neither the juror nor the councilman nor the assemblyman acts as
ruler, but the court, the council and the people, and each individual is only   35
a part of these things just mentioned—I mean by "part" the councilman,
the assemblyman, and the juror. (18) So the multitude justly has authority
over greater things, for the people, the council, and the court are made up
of many persons. Also, the assessment of all of them together is more than   40
that of those who hold great offices, whether taken singly or as a [group
of a] few.

(19) Let the discussion of these things stand thus, then. As regards the first   1282b
question, it makes nothing more evident than that it is laws—correctly enacted—that should be authoritative and that the ruler, whether one person
or more, should be authoritative with respect to those things about which
the laws are completely unable to speak precisely on account of the difficulty   5
of making clear general declarations about everything. (20) But as to what
the quality of the laws should be if they are to be correctly enacted, it is not at
all clear, and the question that was raised previously remains. Laws are necessarily poor or excellent and just or unjust in a manner similar to the regimes
to which they belong: (21) if nothing else, it is evident that laws should be   10
enacted with a view to the regime. But if this is the case, it is clear that those
enacted in accordance with the correct regimes are necessarily just, and those
in accordance with the deviant ones, not just.

CHAPTER 12

(1) Since in all the sciences and arts the end is some good, it is the greatest   15
and primary good in that which is the most authoritative of all; this is the
political capacity. The political good is justice, and this is the common advantage. Justice is held by all to be a certain equality, and up to a certain point
they agree with the discourses based on philosophy in which ethics has been   20
discussed;[52] for they assert that justice is a certain thing for certain persons,
and should be equal for equal persons. (2) But equality in what sort of things
and inequality in what sort of things—this should not be overlooked. For

52 · Apparently a reference to *Eth. Nic.* 5.6113 ᵃ9 ff.

this involves a question, and political philosophy.[53] One might perhaps assert that offices should be unequally distributed in accordance with a preeminence in any good even among persons who do not differ in any other respect but happen to be similar, on the grounds that justice and what accords with merit is different for those who differ. (3) But if this is true, it will mean some aggrandizement in claims to political justice[54] for those who are preeminent in complexion, height, or any other good. (4) Is this not plainly false? That it is false is evident in the case of the other sciences and capacities: where flute players are similar with respect to the art, aggrandizement in flutes is not granted to those who are better born.[55] They will not play the flute better on this account; but it is to one who is preeminent in the work that preeminence in the instruments should be granted. If what has been said is in some way not clear, it will be still more evident if we take it further. (5) If someone were preeminent in flute playing, but very deficient in good birth or fine looks, even if each of those goods is greater than flute playing (I mean good birth and fine looks), and even if they are proportionately more preeminent with respect to flute playing than he is preeminent in flute playing, the outstanding flutes nevertheless ought to be given to him. For preeminence in wealth and good birth should contribute something to the work; but they contribute nothing. (6) Further, according to this argument every good would have to be commensurable with every other. For if being of a certain height [provided] more [in the way of a claim],[56] then height generally would be in rivalry with both wealth and freedom. So if this person is more outstanding in height than that one in virtue, and is more preeminent generally in respect to height than virtue,[57] everything would be commensurable. For if some amount of height is superior to some amount of virtue, it

25

30

35

40

1283a

5

---

53 · This is the only occurrence of the phrase "political philosophy" (*philosophia politikē*) in the *Politics*.

54 · Here and frequently, justice or the just (*to dikaion*) means more precisely a claim to justice, that is, something approaching a "right" in the modern sense. "Aggrandizement" (*pleonexia*), literally, "having more," has the strongly negative connotation of taking something unjustly.

55 · The term is *eugenia*, from *genos*, "family." Again, it is important to keep in mind that good birth throughout this discussion is a claim that can be made by the people as well as the ("well-born") gentlemen.

56 · Reading *ei gar mallon to ti megethos* with the MSS rather than the conjectural *ei gar symballoito ti megethos* ("if height contributed something") adopted by Dreizehnter. The phrase, which is awkward in any event, has been variously understood.

57 · Or "and height generally is more preeminent than virtue," as it is usually understood.

is clear that some amount is equal. (7) Since this is impossible, it is clear that   10
in political matters too it is reasonable for them not to dispute over offices
on the basis of every inequality. If some are fast and others slow, they should
not have more or less on this account; it is in gymnastic contests that being
outstanding in these things wins honor. (8) The dispute necessarily occurs in   15
respect to those things that constitute a city. It is reasonable, therefore, that
the well born, the free, and the wealthy lay claim to honor. For there must be
both free persons and those paying an assessment, since a city cannot consist
wholly of those who are poor, any more than of slaves; (9) yet if these things
are needed, so also, it is clear, are the virtue of justice and military[58] virtue. It   20
is not possible for a city to be administered without these things. But whereas
without the former elements there cannot be a city, without the latter one
cannot be finely administered.

CHAPTER 13

(1) Now with a view to the existence of a city, all or at least some of these
things might be held to have a correct claim in the dispute; but with a view to
a good life it is education and virtue above all that would have a just claim in   25
the dispute, as was also said earlier. But since those who are equal in one thing
alone should not have equality in everything, nor those who are unequal in
a single thing inequality, all regimes of this sort are necessarily deviations.
(2) It was also said previously that all dispute justly in a certain way, but not   30
justly in an unqualified sense. The wealthy have a claim because they have the
greater part of the territory, and the territory is something common; further,
for the most part they are more trustworthy regarding agreements. The free
and well born have a claim as being close to one another; for the higher born   35
are more particularly citizens than the ignoble, and good birth is honorable
at home among everyone. (3) Further, the well born have a claim because it
is likely that better persons come from those who are better, for good birth is
virtue of a family. In a similar way, then, we shall assert that virtue has a just
claim in the dispute, for we assert that justice is a virtue characteristic of communities, and that all the other virtues necessarily follow on it.[59] (4) Finally,   40
the majority has a just claim in relation to a minority, for they are superior
and wealthier and better [born] when the majority is taken together in relation to the minority.

58 · Some MSS have "political" instead of "military" virtue, accepted by Ross.
59 · An apparent allusion to *Eth. Nic.* 1129b25–30a5.

1283b   If, therefore, all should exist in a single city—I mean, both the good and
the wealthy and well born,[60] as well as a political multitude[61] apart from
them—will there be a dispute as to which should rule, or will there not?
5   (5) Now the judgment as to who should rule is not disputed under each of
the regimes that have been mentioned, for they differ from one another by
their authoritative elements: for one the authoritative element is the wealthy,
for another the excellent men, and in the same manner for each of the others. Still, we are investigating how the matter is to be determined when these
10   things are present simultaneously. (6) Now if those possessing virtue were
very few in number, in what way should one decide it? Or should the fact
that they are few be investigated with a view to the work involved—whether
they are capable of administering the city, or whether there is a multitude of
them large enough to form a city? But there is a question affecting all of those
15   who dispute over political honors. (7) Those who claim to merit rule on account of wealth could be held to have no argument of justice at all, and similarly with those claiming to merit rule on the basis of family; for it is clear
that if there is one person wealthier than all of them, this one person should
rule all of them in accordance with the same claims of justice, and similarly,
20   that one who is outstanding in good birth should rule those who dispute on
the basis of freedom.[62] (8) And this same thing will perhaps result with respect to aristocracies in the case of virtue; for if one man should be better
than the others in the governing body, even though they are excellent, this
one should have authority in accordance with the same claims of justice, and
if it is because they are superior to the few that the multitude should have au-
25   thority, if one or more persons—though fewer than the many—should be
superior to the rest, these should have authority rather than the multitude.
      (9) All of these things seem to make it evident, then, that none of the de-
fining principles on the basis of which they claim they merit rule, and all the
30   others merit being ruled by them, is correct. (10) For, indeed, multitudes
have an argument of some justice to make against those claiming to merit
authority over the governing body on the basis of virtue, and similarly also
against those claiming it on the basis of wealth: nothing prevents the multitude from being at some point better than the few and wealthier—not as
35   individuals but taken together. (11) Hence also it is possible to confront in

60 · Aristotle appears here to distinguish three types of claims by the few or upper
classes: (genuine) virtue, wealth, and good birth.
61 · That is, that part of the "multitude" who are actual citizens.
62 · In other words, that the aristocrat of most distinguished birth could contest the
claims of the many freeborn (in Athens's case, "earthborn").

this manner a question which certain persons pursue and put forward.[63] For some raise the question whether the legislator who wants to enact the most correct laws should legislate with a view to the advantage of the better persons or that of the majority, when what was spoken of turns out to be the case. (12) But correctness must be taken to mean "in an equal spirit": what is [enacted] in an equal spirit is correct with a view both to the advantage of the city as a whole and to the common [advantage] of the citizens. A citizen in the common sense is one who shares in ruling and being ruled; but he differs in accordance with each regime. In the case of the best regime, he is one who is capable of and intentionally chooses being ruled and ruling with a view to the life in accordance with virtue.

(13) If there is one person so outstanding by his excess of virtue — or a number of persons, though not enough to provide a full complement for the city — that the virtue of all the others and their political capacity is not commensurable with their own (if there are a number) or his alone (if there is one), such persons can no longer be regarded as a part of the city. For they will be done injustice if it is claimed they merit equal things in spite of being so unequal in virtue and political capacity; for such a person would likely be like a god among human beings. (14) From this it is clear that legislation must necessarily have to do with those who are equal both in family and capacity, and that for the other sort of person there is no law — they themselves are law. It would be ridiculous, then, if one attempted to legislate for them. They would perhaps say what Antisthenes says the lions say when the hares are making their harangue and claiming that everyone merits equality.[64] (15) Hence democratically run cities enact ostracism for this sort of reason. For these are surely held to pursue equality above all others, and so they used to ostracize and banish for fixed periods from the city those who were held to be preeminent in power on account of wealth or abundance of friends or some other kind of political strength.[65] (16) The tale is told that the Argonauts left Heracles behind for this sort of reason: the Argo was unwilling to have him on board because he so exceeded the other sailors.[66] Hence also

40

1284a

5

10

15

20

25

---

63 · It is not known to whom Aristotle is here referring.

64 · "Where are your claws and teeth?" (Aesop, *Fables* 241). It is not known to what work of Antisthenes Aristotle here refers.

65 · Ostracism was particularly employed in Athens in the fifth century, but appears to have fallen into disuse by Aristotle's time; see the account in *Ath. Pol.* 22. The fixed period seems to have been ten years originally, later five.

66 · In the version of the myth to which Aristotle seems to be alluding, the ship Argo refused (through its speaking mast) to accept Heracles on account of his great weight.

those who criticize tyranny and the advice Periander gave to Thrasyboulus must not be supposed to be simply correct in their censure. (17) It is reported that Periander said nothing by way of advice to the messenger who had been
30   sent to him, but merely lopped off the preeminent ears of corn and so leveled the field. When the messenger, who was in ignorance of the reason behind what had happened, reported the incident, Thrasyboulus understood that he was to eliminate the preeminent men.[67] (18) This is something that is ad-
35   vantageous not only to tyrants, nor are tyrants the only ones who do it, but the matter stands similarly with respect both to oligarchies and to democracies; for ostracism has the same power in a certain way as pulling down and exiling the preeminent. (19) And the same thing is done in the case of cities and nations alike by those with control of [military] power—for ex-
40   ample, the Athenians in the case of the Samians, Chians, and Lesbians, for no sooner was their [imperial] rule firm than they humbled these cities, con-
1284b   trary to the compacts they had with them.[68] And the king of the Persians frequently pruned back the Medes and Babylonians and others who harbored high thoughts on account of once exercising [imperial] rule themselves.

(20) The issue is one that concerns all regimes generally, including correct
5   ones. For the deviant ones do this looking to the private advantage of the rulers, yet even in the case of those that look to the common good the matter stands in the same way. (21) This is clear as well in the case of the other arts and sciences. For a painter would not allow himself to paint an animal with
10   a foot that exceeded proportion, not even if it were outstandingly beautiful, nor would a shipbuilder permit himself to build a stern or any of the other parts of a ship that exceeded proportion, nor indeed would a chorus master allow someone with a voice louder and more beautiful than the entire chorus to be a member of it. (22) So on this account there is nothing that prevents
15   monarchs from being in consonance with their cities when they do this, provided their own rule is beneficial to their cities. Thus in connection with the generally agreed forms of preeminence the argument concerning ostracism

67 · The story is recounted at greater length in Herodotus 5.92, though there it is Thrasyboulus (tyrant of Miletus) who gives the advice to Periander (tyrant of Corinth). Cf. 5.11.4–5.
68 · It is not certain to what events Aristotle is referring. As the most powerful of the island states in the alliance formed by Athens after the Persian wars, Lesbos, Chios, and Samos were treated more favorably than the others (cf. *Ath. Pol.* 24). Samos was crushed by Athens in 439 BC after it revolted in protest against an Athenian prohibition of its prosecution of a local war; the humiliations in question were most probably similar attempts by Athens prior to this time to limit the autonomy of these allies.

involves a certain political justice. (23) Now it is better if the legislator constitutes the regime from the beginning in such a way that it does not need this
sort of healing; but the "second voyage,"[69] if the contingency should arise, is
to try to correct the regime with some corrective of this sort. But this is not   20
what used to happen in the case of the cities that used it: they did not look to
the advantage of their own regime but used ostracisms for purposes of factional conflict.

(24) In the deviant regimes it is evident that ostracism is advantageous
[for the rulers] privately[70] and is just; and perhaps that it is not simply just   25
is also evident. In the case of the best regime, however, there is considerable
question as to what ought to be done if there happens to be someone who
is outstanding not on the basis of preeminence in the other goods such as
strength, wealth, or abundance of friends, but on the basis of virtue. (25) For
surely no one would assert that such a person should be expelled and banished. But neither would they assert that there should be rule over such a   30
person: this is almost as if they should claim to merit ruling over Zeus by
splitting the offices.[71] What remains—and it seems the natural course—is
for everyone to obey such a person gladly, so that persons of this sort will be
permanent kings in their cities.

CHAPTER 14

(1) Perhaps it is the right thing after these arguments to make a transition   35
and investigate kingship; for we assert that this is one of the correct regimes.
What must be investigated is whether it is advantageous for the city or the
territory that is to be well administered to be under a kingship or not, or
some other regime instead, or whether it is advantageous for some but not
others. (2) First, it should be determined whether there is one single type or   40
whether it has several varieties.

This, at any rate, is surely easy to discern—that it encompasses several   1285a
types, and that the manner of rule is not the same in all. (3) For that of the
Spartan regime is held to be particularly representative of kingships based on
law; it does not have authority over all matters, but when the king goes out-   5

69 · A proverbial expression meaning "second best."
70 · Or "is advantageous [for each regime] individually," as it is generally understood;
but the phrase in question (*idiai sympherei*) seems to look back to 13.20.
71 · The meaning is somewhat uncertain. The phrase "splitting the offices" (*merizōn
tas archas*) seems to refer to rotation in office (cf. 6.5. 11); "this is almost as if they should
claim to merit ruling over Zeus" is sometimes taken as a parenthetical remark.

side their territory he has leadership in matters related to war, and matters related to the gods are further assigned to the kings. (4) This kind of kingship, then, is a sort of permanent generalship of plenipotentiaries. The king does not have authority in matters of life and death, except in certain kingships such as those in ancient times, [where he could put men to death] on military expeditions by the law of might. Homer makes this clear: Agamemnon endured being spoken ill of in assemblies, but when they went out to fight he had authority even in matters of life and death. (5) At any rate, he says: "Anyone I find apart from the battle, he shall have no hope of escaping the dogs and birds; for death is in my power."[72] This, then, is one kind of kingship, generalship for life; and some of these are constituted on the basis of family, while others are elective.

(6) Beside this there is another form of monarchy—the kingships that exist among some of the barbarians. All of these are very near to tyrannies in their power, but are based on law and hereditary. It is because barbarians are more slavish in their characters than Greeks (those in Asia being more so than those in Europe) that they put up with a master's rule without making any difficulties. (7) They are tyrannical, then, through being of this sort; but they are stable because they are hereditary and based on law. For the same reason, their bodyguard is of a kingly rather than a tyrannical sort. For the citizens guard kings with their own arms, while a foreign element guards the tyrant, since the former rule willing persons in accordance with law, while the latter rule unwilling persons. So the ones have a bodyguard provided by the citizens, the others one that is directed against them.

(8) These, then, are two kinds of monarchy, but there is another that existed among the ancient Greeks—rule by those they call dictators.[73] This is, to speak simply, an elective tyranny, and differs from barbarian kingship not by not being based on law but only by not being hereditary. (9) Some ruled in this office for life, others for certain fixed periods of time or for [the purpose of performing] certain actions. For example, the Mytilenaeans once elected Pittacus to defend them against the exiles headed by Antimenides and the poet Alcaeus. (10) Alcaeus makes clear in one of his drinking songs

72 · Homer, *Iliad* 2.391–93. The last phrase of the quotation is not found in our texts of Homer.

73 · The term is *aisymnētai* (which probably derives from an expression meaning "those mindful of the auspices"), a magistracy that was generally (though not invariably) comparable to the "dictatorship" in Rome. It was usually created under unusual circumstances of civil disorder or external threat.

that they elected Pittacus tyrant; for he censures them because "they set up
Pittacus, base of lineage, as tyrant of a city lacking bile and heavy with doom, 1285b
with great praise from the crowd."[74] (11) These are and were like rule of a
master on account of their being tyrannical, but like kingship on account
of their being elective and over willing persons. But there is another kind
of kingly monarchy, those belonging to the times of the heroes, which were 5
willing, hereditary, and arose in accordance with law.[75] (12) For because the
first kings had been benefactors of the multitude in connection with the arts
or with war or by bringing them together [in a city] or providing them land,
these came to be kings over willing persons, and their descendants took over
from them. They had authority regarding leadership in war and those sacri- 10
fices that did not require priests; in addition to this, they were judges in legal
cases. Some of them did this under oath and others not; the oath was a lift-
ing up of the scepter.[76] (13) In ancient times they ruled continuously, dealing
with city matters, rural matters, and matters beyond the borders. Later, how- 15
ever, some of these things were relinquished by the kings, some were taken
away by the mob, and in most cities the kings were left only with the sacrifices. Wherever there was a kingship worth speaking of, they only held the
leadership in military matters beyond the borders.

(14) These, then, are the kinds of kingship, being four in number: one, 20
that of the times of the heroes, which was over willing persons but for certain
fixed purposes, the king being general and juror and having authority over
matters related to the gods; second, the barbaric, which is rule of a master in
accordance with law, and deriving from family; third, what they call dictator- 25
ship, which is elective tyranny; and fourth among them, the Spartan, which
to speak simply is permanent generalship based on family. (15) These differ
from one another, then, in this manner. But there is also a fifth kind of kingship, when one person has authority over all matters, just as each nation and 30
each city has authority over common matters, with an arrangement that re-
sembles household management. For just as rule of the household manager
is a kind of kingship over the house, so this kind of kingship is household
management for a city or a nation (or several nations).

74 · Alcaeus, fr. 87 Diehl.
75 · Kingship of the "times of the heroes" (the period of the Trojan War as described
in the poetry of Homer) was limited monarchy of a feudal type reflecting a predominantly rural and tribal society.
76 · In later times all adjudication was done under oath; the remark seems intended
to point to kingly prerogatives which had since disappeared.

CHAPTER 15

(1) There are, then, fundamentally two kinds of kingship which must be in-
35   vestigated, this and the Spartan. For most of the others are between these:
they have authority over fewer matters than absolute kingship does, but more
than Spartan kingship. (2) So the investigation is fundamentally about two
things: one, whether it is advantageous for cities to have a permanent general
1286a   (whether chosen on the basis of family or by turns) or not; the other, whether
it is advantageous for one person to have authority over all matters or not.
Now to investigate this sort of generalship has the look of an investigation
of laws rather than the regime, since this is something that can arise in all re-
5   gimes; so the first may be dismissed. (3) The remaining mode of kingship,
however, is a kind of regime, so this should be studied and the questions it
involves gone over.

The beginning point of the inquiry is this: whether it is more advanta-
10   geous to be ruled by the best man or by the best laws. (4) Those who consider
it advantageous to be under a kingship hold that laws only speak of the universal and do not command with a view to circumstances. So to rule in accordance with written rules is foolish in any art; and in Egypt it is permissible for
doctors to alter the treatment after the fourth day, though before then they
15   may do so at their own risk. It is evident, therefore, for the same reason that
the best regime is not one based on written rules and laws. (5) And yet that
same argument concerning the universal applies also to rulers;[77] and what
is unaccompanied by the passionate element generally is superior to that in
which it is innate. Now this is not present in law, but every human soul nec-
20   essarily has it. But one might perhaps assert that this is made up for by the
fact that he will deliberate in finer fashion concerning particulars. (6) That
the ruler must necessarily be a legislator, then, and that laws must exist, is
clear; but they must not be authoritative insofar as they deviate [from what is
right], though in other matters they should be authoritative.[78] But as regards
25   the things that law is unable to judge either generally or well, should the one
best person rule, or all? (7) As it is, [citizens] come together to adjudicate and
deliberate and judge, and the judgments themselves all concern particulars.
Any one of them taken singly is perhaps inferior in comparison [to the best
man]; but the city is made up of many persons, just as a feast to which many
30   contribute is finer than a single and simple one, and on this account a crowd

77 · That is, even rulers necessarily make decisions in accordance with general principles at some level. Cf. Newman.
78 · That is, the king should retain the authority to overrule deviant laws.

also judges many matters better than any single person. (8) Further, what is many is more incorruptible: like a greater amount of water, the multitude is more incorruptible than the few. The judgment of a single person is necessarily corrupted when he is dominated by anger or some other passion of this sort, whereas it is hard for all to become angry and err at the same time. (9) But the multitude must be free persons acting in no way against the law, except in those cases where it necessarily falls short. This is certainly not easy for many, but if there were a number who were both good men and good citizens, is the one ruler more incorruptible, or rather the larger number who are all good? Is it not clear that it is the larger number? "Yet the latter will have factional conflict, while the former will be without it." (10) But against this should perhaps be set down that they may be excellent in soul, just like the single person. If, then, the rule of a number of persons who are all good men is to be regarded as aristocracy, and the rule of a single person as kingship, aristocracy would be more choiceworthy for cities than kingship (whether the office brings power with it or not), provided it is possible to find a number of persons who are similar.

(11) And this is perhaps why peoples were under kingships originally—because it was rare to discover men who were very outstanding in virtue, especially since the cities they inhabited then were so small. Also, they selected kings on account of their benefactions, something that is the work of good men. But when it happened that many arose who were similar with respect to virtue, they no longer tolerated kingship but sought something common and established a polity. (12) As they became worse and gained at the expense of common funds, it was reasonable that oligarchies should arise as a result, for they made wealth a thing of honor. After this there was a change first into tyrannies, then from tyrannies into democracy. For by bringing things into fewer hands through a base longing for profit, they made the multitude stronger, and so it attacked them and democracies arose. (13) Now that it has happened that cities have become even larger, it is perhaps no longer easy for any regime to arise other than a democracy.

But if one were to regard kingship as the best thing for cities, how should one handle what pertains to the offspring? Must the family rule as kings also? But if those born into it are persons of average quality, it would be harmful. (14) Perhaps he will not turn it over to his children in spite of having authority to do so? But it is not easy to believe this either; it would be difficult, and require greater virtue than accords with human nature. There is a question also concerning his power—whether one who is going to rule as king should have about himself some force by which he will be able to compel those who do not want to obey, or how otherwise the office can be administered. (15) For even if he had authority in accordance with law and acted in nothing on the basis of his own will contrary to the law, still there must necessarily be available to him some power by which to safeguard the laws. (16) In the case of a king of this sort it is perhaps not difficult to determine

35 this: he himself should have a certain force, but the force should be such that it is superior to individuals both by themselves and taking many of them together, but inferior to the multitude. It was thus that the ancients gave a bodyguard whenever they selected someone to be what they called dictator

40 or tyrant of the city; and when Dionysius requested a bodyguard, someone advised the Syracusans to give him a bodyguard of this size.[79]

CHAPTER 16

1287a (1) The argument has now come around to the king who acts in all things according to his own will, and this must be investigated. Now the king, so-called, who rules according to law is not, as we said, a kind of kingship.[80]

5 There can be a permanent general in all regimes—in democracy or aristocracy, for example; and many give one person authority over administration—there is an office of this sort at Epidamnus, for instance, and one of somewhat lesser extent at Opus as well. (2) Concerning so-called absolute

10 kingship, on the other hand (this is where the king rules in all matters[81] according to his own will),[82] some hold that it is not even in accordance with nature for one person among all the citizens to have authority,[83] where the city is constituted out of similar persons. For in the case of persons similar by nature, justice and merit must necessarily be the same according to nature;

15 and so if it is harmful for their bodies if unequal persons have equal sustenance and clothing, it is so also [for their souls if they are equal] in what pertains to honors, and similarly therefore if equal persons have what is unequal.

79 · For an account of the origins of the tyranny of Dionysius at Syracuse, see Diodorus Siculus 13.85–94.

80 · Reading *basileias* with the MSS rather than the conjectural *politeias* ("of regime") adopted by Dreizehnter. This was strongly implied, if not precisely said, in 15.2–3.

81 · Reading *panta* with the MSS rather than *pantōn* ("over all persons") with Dreizehnter (on the basis of a citation by Julian).

82 · I follow Susemihl in suspecting a lacuna at this point in the text.

83 · Or "for one person to have authority over all the citizens," as it is generally understood. But the phrase *kyrios pantōn* seems regularly used elsewhere (consider 14.3) in the sense "have authority over all matters," and a limitation of kingly sovereignty over persons is nowhere discussed by Aristotle.

(3) Hence it is no more just for equal persons to rule than to be ruled, and it is therefore just that they rule and be ruled by turns. But this is already law; for the arrangement of ruling and being ruled is law. Accordingly, to have law rule is to be chosen in preference to having one of the citizens do so, ac-   20
cording to this same argument, (4) and if it should be better to have some of them rule, these must be established as law-guardians and as servants of the laws; for there must necessarily exist certain offices [by which persons rule and not law], but they deny that it is just that this one person rule, at least when all are similar. For that matter, as regards those things which law is held not to be capable of determining, a human being could not decide   25
them either. (5) Rather, the law educates especially for this, and hands over what remains [undetermined by law itself] to be judged and administered "by the most just decision" of the rulers.[84] Further, it allows them to make corrections in cases where they hold something to be better than the existing laws on the basis of their experience. One who asks law to rule, therefore, seems to be asking god and intellect alone to rule, while one who asks man   30
adds the beast. Desire is a thing of this sort; and spiritedness perverts rul-ers and the best men. Hence law is intellect without appetite. (6) And the argument from the example of the arts may be held to be false—that it is a poor thing, for example, to heal in accordance with written rules, and one should choose instead to use those who possess the arts. (7) For these do not   35
act against reason on account of affection, but earn their pay by making the sick healthy; but those in political offices are accustomed to acting in many matters with a view to spite or favor. In any case, if doctors were suspected of being persuaded by a person's enemies to do away with him for profit, he   40
would be more inclined to seek treatment from written rules. (8) Moreover, doctors bring in other doctors for themselves when they are sick, and train-   1287b
ers other trainers when they are exercising, the assumption being that they are unable to judge what is true on account of judging both in their own case and while they are in a state of suffering. So it is clear that in seeking justice they are seeking impartiality; for law is impartiality. (9) Further, laws based   5
on [unwritten] customs are more authoritative, and deal with more authori-tative matters, than those based on written rules; so if it is safer for a human being to rule than laws based on written rules, this is not the case for laws based on custom. Moreover, it is not easy for one person to survey many things. Accordingly, there will be a need for a number of persons to be se-lected as rulers under him—but then what difference is there between hav-   10

---

84 · An allusion to the oath sworn by jurors at Athens.

ing them present right from the beginning and having one person select them
in this manner? (10) Further, there is what was said earlier: if it is just for the
excellent man to rule because he is better, two good persons are better than
the one. Thus the saying "two going together," and Agamemnon's prayer for
15   "ten such counselors for myself."[85] Even now there are offices (that of juror,
for example) which have authority to judge concerning some matters that
the law is unable to determine; for in the case of those it is able to determine,
at any rate, no one would dispute that the law would be the best ruler and
judge concerning them. (11) But because some things can be encompassed
20   by the laws and others cannot, the latter cause the question to be raised and
pursued whether the rule of the best law is more choiceworthy than that of
the best man. For to legislate concerning matters of deliberation is impossible. Now their counterargument is not that it is not necessary for a human
being to judge in such matters, but rather that there should be many persons
25   instead of one only. (12) For every ruler judges finely if he has been educated
by the law; and it would perhaps be held to be odd if someone should see
better with two eyes, judge better with two ears, and act better with two feet
and hands than many persons would with many. For as it is, monarchs cre-
30   ate many eyes for themselves, and ears, feet, and hands as well; for those who
are friendly to their rule and themselves they make co-rulers. (13) If they are
not friends, they will not behave in accordance with the monarch's intention,
but if they are friends to him and his rule, the friend is someone similar and
equal, so if he supposes these should rule, he necessarily supposes that those
35   who are similar and equal should rule similarly. The arguments of those who
dispute against kingship are, then, essentially these.

CHAPTER 17

(1) And yet while these arguments hold in some cases, in others perhaps they
do not. For by nature there is a certain people apt for mastery, another apt
for kingship, and another that is political, and this is both just and advanta-
40   geous. (Nothing, however, is naturally apt for tyranny, or for the other regimes that are deviations: these cases are contrary to nature.) (2) From what
1288a   has been said, at any rate, it is evident that among similar and equal persons
it is neither advantageous nor just for one person to have authority over all
matters, regardless of whether there are laws or not and he acts as law himself,

85 · Homer, *Iliad* 10.224, 2.372.

whether he and they are good or not, and even whether he is better in respect   5
to virtue—unless it is in a certain manner.

(3) What that manner is must now be spoken of, though in a sense it was
spoken of previously as well. We must first determine what it is that is apt for
kingship, what is aristocratic, and what is political. (4) What is apt for kingship, then, is a multitude of such a sort that it accords with its nature to support a family that is preeminent in virtue relative to political leadership; an
aristocratic multitude is one of such a sort that it accords with its nature to   10
support a multitude capable of being ruled in accordance with the rule that
belongs to free persons by those whose virtue makes them expert leaders relative to political rule; and a political multitude is one in which there arises
in accordance with its nature a military multitude capable of ruling and being ruled in accordance with a law distributing offices on the basis of merit
to those who are well off.[86] (5) Now when it happens that a whole family, or   15
even some one person among the rest, is so outstanding in virtue that this virtue is more preeminent than that of all the rest, it is just in that case that the
family be a kingly one and have authority over all matters, or that this one
person be a king. (6) For as was said earlier, the matter stands thus not only   20
on the basis of the sort of justice that is customarily alleged by those who establish aristocracies and oligarchies, or for that matter democracies—they
all[87] claim to merit rule on the basis of some preeminence, though not the
same preeminence—but also in accordance with that sort of justice mentioned earlier.[88] (7) For it is surely not proper to execute or exile or ostracize   25
a person of this sort, or claim that he merits to be ruled in turn. It does not
accord with nature for the part[89] to be preeminent over the whole, but this
is the result in the case of someone having such superiority. (8) So all that remains is for a person of this sort to be obeyed, and to have authority simply
and not by turns. Concerning kingship, then, the varieties that it has, and   30

86 · Reading this passage (a10–15) with the MSS rather than as rearranged by
Dreizehnter. Aristotle's argument is intelligible as it stands if the word "multitude"
(plēthos) is understood in a narrower as well as a wider sense—as the equivalent of the
"governing body" in a polity or aristocracy (consider 13.6, 15.9, 18.1). The term "well
off" (euporos) connotes not great but moderate wealth of the kind sustaining those capable of affording heavy arms.
87 · Reading pantes with Π² rather than pantēi ("entirely") with Π¹ and Dreizehnter.
88 · 3.13.24–25.
89 · The comparison seems to be suggested by the fact that the same word (meros)
means both "turn" and "part."

whether it is advantageous for cities or not, and if so, which and in what fashion, let our discussion stand thus.

CHAPTER 18

(1) Since we assert that there are three correct regimes, that of these that one is necessarily best which is managed by the best persons, and that this is the
35   sort of regime in which there happens to be one certain person or a whole family or a multitude that is preeminent in virtue with respect to all the rest, of persons capable of being ruled and of ruling with a view to the most choiceworthy way of life, and since in our earlier discourses it was shown that the virtue of man and citizen is necessarily the same in the best city,[90] it is ev-
40   ident that it is in the same manner and through the same things that a man becomes excellent and that one might constitute a city under an aristocracy
1288b   or a kingship. So the education and the habits that make a man excellent are essentially the same as those that make him a political or kingly ruler.

(2) These things having been determined, we must now attempt to speak about the best regime—in what manner it accords with its nature to arise
5   and to be established. It is necessary, then, for one who is going to undertake the investigation appropriate to it....[91]

90 · 3.4–5.
91 · This sentence, which is incomplete in the MSS, is repeated verbatim at the beginning of book 7. See Introduction, pp. xxv–xxvi above.

Book 4

(1) In all arts and sciences which have not arisen on a partial basis but are   10
complete with respect to some one type of thing, it belongs to a single one to
study what is fitting in the case of each type of thing. In the case of training
for the body, for example, it belongs to it to study what sort is advantageous
for what sort of body; which is best (for the best is necessarily fitting for the
body that is naturally the finest and is most finely equipped); which is best—   15
a single one for all—for most bodies (for this too is a task of gymnastic expertise); (2) and further, if someone should desire neither the disposition nor
the knowledge befitting those connected with competitions, it belongs no
less to the sports trainer and the gymnastic expert to provide this capacity as
well. We see a similar thing occurring in the case of medicine, shipbuilding,   20
the making of clothing, and every other art.

(3) So it is clear that, with regard to the regime, it belongs to the same
science to study what the best regime is, and what quality it should have to
be what one would pray for above all, with external things providing no impediment; which regime is fitting for which cities—for it is perhaps impos-   25
sible for many to obtain the best, so neither the one that is superior simply
nor the one that is the best that circumstances allow should be overlooked
by the good legislator and the political ruler in the true sense; (4) further,
thirdly, the regime based on a presupposition—for any given regime should
be studied with a view to determining both how it might arise initially and   30
in what manner it might be preserved for the longest time once in existence
(I am speaking of the case where a city happens neither to be governed by
the best regime—and is not equipped even with the things necessary for
it—nor to be governed by the regime that is the best possible among existing ones, but one that is poorer); (5) and besides all these things, the regime

35   that is most fitting for all cities should be recognized. Thus most of those
who have expressed views concerning the regime, even if what they say is
fine in other respects, are in error when it comes to what is useful. (6) For
one should study not only the best regime but also the regime that is the best
possible, and similarly also the regime that is easier and more attainable for
all. As it is, however, some seek only the one that is at the peak and requires
40   much equipment, while others, though speaking of an attainable sort of re-
1289a gime, disregard those that exist and instead praise the Spartan or some other
single one. (7) But one ought to introduce an arrangement of such a sort
that they will easily be persuaded and be able to share in it by the fact that it
arises directly out of those that exist, since to reform a regime is no less a task
5   than to institute one from the beginning, just as unlearning something is no
less a task than learning it from the beginning. Hence in addition to what
has been said the political expert should be able to assist existing regimes as
well, as was also said earlier.[1] (8) But this is impossible if he does not know
how many kinds of regime there are. As it is, some suppose there is one sort
10   of democracy and one sort of oligarchy; but this is not true. So the varieties
of the regimes—how many there are and in how many ways they are combined—should not be overlooked. (9) And it belongs to this same practical
science[2] to see both what laws are best and what are fitting for each of the regimes. For laws should be enacted—and all are in fact enacted—with a view
15   to the regimes, and not regimes with a view to the laws. (10) For a regime is
an arrangement in cities connected with the offices, establishing the manner
in which they have been distributed, what the authoritative element of the
regime is, and what the end of the community is in each case;[3] and among the
things that are revealing of the regime, some laws stand out—those in accor-
20   dance with which the rulers must rule and guard against those transgressing
them.[4] (11) So it is clear that it is necessary to have a grasp of the varieties of

1 · Possibly a reference to 2.1. 1, though it is generally taken to be to the immediate
context.

2 · Literally, "prudence" (*phronēsis*).

3 · Reading *hekastēs* with Dreizehnter; but *hekastois* ("for each individually") has
some manuscript authority, and is perhaps right.

4 · Or, as this clause is generally understood, "but laws are distinct from the things
that are revealing of the regime [*nomoi de kechōrismenoi tōn dēlountōn tēn politeian*],
and it is in accordance with them that the rulers must rule and guard against those
transgressing them." But the general argument is concerned to establish the *connection*
between laws and the regime; and Aristotle seems to be thinking specifically here of
"constitutional" laws regulating the tenure of officials (cf. 3.16.3) and protecting against
legislative subversion of the regime (cf. 1.6. 2).

each regime and their number with a view to the enactment of laws as well.
For it is impossible for the same laws to be advantageous for all oligarchies or
for all democracies, at least if there are several kinds of them and not merely
a single sort of democracy or of oligarchy.   25

CHAPTER 2

(1) Since in our first inquiry concerning regimes we distinguished three correct regimes—kingship, aristocracy, and polity—and three deviations from
these—tyranny from kingship, oligarchy from aristocracy, and democracy   30
from polity;[5] and since aristocracy and kingship have been spoken of—for
to study the best regime is the same as to speak about the regimes designated
by these terms as well, as each of them wishes to be established on the basis
of virtue that is furnished with equipment;[6] and further, since the difference between aristocracy and kingship and when a regime should be con-   35
sidered kingship[7] were discussed earlier;[8] what remains is to treat polity—
that which is called by the name common to all regimes—and the other
regimes—oligarchy and democracy, and tyranny.
　　(2) Now it is evident also which of the deviations is the worst and which
second worst. For the deviation from the first and most divine regime must   40
necessarily be the worst, but kingship must necessarily either have the name
alone without being such, or rest on the great superiority of the person rul-   1289b
ing as king. So tyranny is the worst, and the farthest removed from a regime;[9]
oligarchy is second worst, for aristocracy stands far from this regime; and
democracy is the most moderate. (3) Now an earlier [thinker] has expressed   5
this view as well, though without looking to the same thing we do.[10] For he
judged them all to be respectable (there being a good sort of oligarchy, for example, as well as of the others), with democracy as the worst, but the best of
the bad sorts; but we assert that these are generally thoroughly in error, and

---

5 · 3.6–8.

6 · This is often referred to 3.15–16, but the only real discussion of aristocracy as the
best regime occurs in 7. See Introduction, p. xxv above.

7 · Or, as it is generally understood, "when kingship should be established." The rendering here gives the normal meaning of *nomizein*.

8 · The reference would seem to be particularly to 3.15–16.

9 · Or "from polity," as it is sometimes taken; but both alternatives pose difficulties.
What is wanted instead is a reference to kingship, and it is possible that something of
this kind has dropped out of the text here.

10 · Plato, *Statesman* 302e–03a.

10   that it is not right to speak of one sort of oligarchy as better than another,
but rather as less bad.

(4) As regards this sort of judgment, let us dismiss the matter for the
present. Instead, we must distinguish, first, the number of varieties of regimes, if indeed there are several kinds both of democracy and of oligarchy;
15   next, which is the most attainable and which the most choiceworthy after
the best regime, and if there is some other that is aristocratic and finely constituted but fitting for most cities, which it is; (5) next, which of the others
is choiceworthy for which cities—for perhaps democracy is more necessary
20   for some than oligarchy, and for others the latter more than the former; after these things, in what manner the one wishing to do so should establish
these regimes—I mean, democracy in each of its kinds and likewise oligarchy; (6) and finally, when we have provided as far as possible a concise treatment of all these matters, we must attempt to describe the sources of destruc-
25   tion and preservation for regimes both in general and in the case of each
separately, and the reasons for which these things particularly come about in
accordance with the nature of the matter.[11]

CHAPTER 3

(1) Now the reason for there being a number of regimes is that there are a
number of parts in any city. For, in the first place, we see that all cities are
30   composed of households, and next that of this aggregation some are necessarily well off, others poor, and others middling, and that of the well off
and the poor there is an armed and an unarmed element. (2) And we see
that the people has a farming, a marketing, and a working element. In the
case of the notables too there are differences based on wealth and the ex-
35   tent of their property—for example, in the matter of horse breeding, which
is not easy to do for those who are not wealthy. (3) Hence in ancient times
those cities whose power lay in horses had oligarchies, for they used horses
in wars against their neighbors—for example, the Eretrians and Chalcidians,
40   the Magnesians on the Maeander, and many others in Asia. (4) Further, in
addition to the differences based on wealth, there is that based on family
1290a   and that based on virtue, and indeed whatever else was said to be a part of
the city in the [discourses] on aristocracy (for there we distinguished how

11 · These topics appear to correspond respectively to 4.3–6, 4.7–11, 4.12–13, 4.14–
16, and 5.

many necessary parts there are in every city);[12] for of these parts all take part
in the regime in some cases, and in others more or fewer. (5) It is evident,   5
therefore, that there must necessarily be a number of regimes differing from
one another in kind, since these parts differ from one another in kind. Now
a regime is the arrangement of offices, and all distribute these either on the
basis of the power of those taking part in the regime or on the basis of some
equality common to them—I mean, [the power of] the poor or the well off,   10
or some [equality] common to both.[13] (6) There are necessarily, therefore, as
many regimes as there are arrangements based on the sorts of preeminence
and the differences of the parts.

But there are held to be two sorts of regimes particularly: just as in the case
of winds some are called northern and others southern and the others devi-   15
ations from these, so many hold there are two sorts of regimes, rule by the
people and oligarchy. (7) They regard aristocracy as a kind of oligarchy on
the grounds that it is a sort of rule by the few, and so-called polity as a kind
of democracy, just as among the winds the western is regarded as belonging
to the northern, the eastern to the southern. It is similar also in the case of   20
harmonies, so some assert: they regard there as being two kinds of these as
well, Dorian and Phrygian, while the other modal arrangements they call
either "Doric" or "Phrygic."[14] (8) Men are accustomed particularly, then, to
conceive of regimes in this way. But it is truer and better to distinguish as we
have, and say that one or two are finely constituted and the others deviations   25
from them—deviations from the well-blended harmony as well as from the
best regime, the more taut [of the harmonies] being oligarchic and more like
rule of a master, the relaxed and soft being popular.[15]

12 · This is often referred to 3.12.8–9, but the reference would seem rather to be to
7.7–9.
13 · This clause, sometimes bracketed as an interpolation, is usually understood to
mean "[some equality common to] the badly off or the well off, or some [equality] common to both"; it has also been explained as "[the power of] the badly off or the well off,
or [the power] common to both."
14 · This view seems to underlie Plato's treatment of the modes or harmonies (*Republic* 399a–c), which is generally taken as reflecting the musical doctrines of the school
of Damon.
15 · The interpretation of this passage has been much disputed. I retain *harmonias* in
a26 instead of bracketing the word with Immisch and Dreizehnter ("from the well-
blended regime as well as from the best regime"); and I understand the final clause as
referring to harmonies instead of regimes, as it is generally assumed to do, and take
the word *despotikōteras* ("closer to rule of a master") as predicate rather than subject.

CHAPTER 4

30   (1) One should not regard democracy, as some are accustomed to do now,
as existing simply wherever the multitude has authority, since in oligarchies
and indeed everywhere the major part has authority, nor oligarchy as existing wherever the few have authority over the regime. (2) For if the male inhabitants of a city were one thousand three hundred in all, and a thousand

35   of these were wealthy and gave no share in ruling to the three hundred poor,
though these were free persons and similar in other respects, no one would
assert that they are under a democracy. (3) Similarly, if the poor were few, but
superior to a majority of well-off persons, no one would describe this sort of

40   thing as an oligarchy, if the others had no part in the prerogatives although
1290b they were wealthy. It must rather be said, therefore, that rule of the people
exists when free persons have authority, and oligarchy when the wealthy have
it; (4) but it turns out that the former are many and the latter few, for many
are free but few wealthy. Otherwise, there would be an oligarchy where they

5   distributed offices on the basis of size, as some assert happens in Ethiopia,[16]
or on the basis of good looks; for the number of both good-looking and tall
persons is few. (5) Yet neither is it adequate to define these regimes by these
things alone. But since there are a number of parts both in the case of rule

10   of the people and of oligarchy, it must be grasped further that rule of the
people does not exist even where a few free persons rule over a majority who
are not free, as at Apollonia on the Ionian Sea, for example, or Thera (in
each of these cities those who were outstanding in good birth on account of
descent from the first settlers of the colony—a few among many—held the
prerogatives); nor is there rule of the people where the wealthy rule through

15   being preeminent in number, as was formerly the case at Colophon (there the
majority possessed large properties prior to the war against the Lydians).[17]
(6) Democracy exists when the free and poor, being a majority, have author-

---

The "well-blended harmony" would seem to be Mixed Lydian, which forms a mean between the extremes of "taut" Lydian (*syntonolydisti*) and Phrygian on the one hand and
the "relaxed" Lydian and Ionian harmonies on the other; and the second of the "one or
two" well-constituted harmonies would seem to be Dorian (see 8.5. 22). The implicit
comparison, then, would appear to be between Mixed Lydian and polity—a "mixture"
of oligarchy and democracy (4.8. 3); and the "one or two" well-constituted regimes
would seem to be (at least if the parallel is meant to be exact) polity and aristocracy.
16 · Herodotus 3.20.
17 · The war between Colophon and the kingdom of Lydia occurred in the first half
of the seventh century. Cf. Herodotus 1.14.

ity to rule; oligarchy, when the wealthy and better born have authority and   20
are few.

(7) That there are a number of regimes, then, and the reason for this, has
been spoken of. As to why there are more than the ones spoken of, which
these are, and how they come to exist, let us speak of this, taking as our beginning point what was mentioned earlier. We agree that every city has not one
part but several. (8) Now if we chose to acquire a grasp of kinds of animals,   25
we would first enumerate separately what it is that every animal must necessarily have—for example, certain of the sense organs and something that can
work on and receive sustenance, such as a mouth and a stomach, and in addition to these, parts by which each of them moves; and if there were then
only so many kinds,[18] and there were varieties of these (I mean, for example,   30
a certain number of types of mouth and stomach and sense organs, and further of the locomotive parts), the number of combinations of these things
will necessarily make a number of types of animals, since it is impossible for
the same animal to have a number of varieties of mouth or of ears; so when   35
taken together all the possible pairings of them will make kinds of an animal,
and as many kinds of the animal as there are combinations of the necessary
parts. (9) One may proceed in the same manner in the case of the regimes
spoken of. For cities are composed not of one but of many parts, as we have
often said.[19] Now one of these is the multitude that is concerned with suste-   40
nance, those called farmers. A second is what is called the working element.   1291a
This is the one that is concerned with the arts without which a city cannot be
inhabited (though of these arts only some must exist of necessity, while others are directed toward luxury or living finely). (10) A third is the marketing
element, by which I mean that which spends its time concerned with buy-   5
ing and selling and trade and commerce. A fourth is the laboring element; a
fifth type is the warrior element—which is no less necessary than the others
if they are not to be the slaves of whomever marches against them. (11) For it
is impossible that a city that is by nature slavish merits being called such: the   10
city is self-sufficient, but what is slavish is not self-sufficient.

Hence what is said in the *Republic*, though sophisticated, is not adequate.[20] (12) For Socrates asserts that a city is composed of the four most
necessary persons, and he says these are a weaver, a farmer, a shoemaker, and
a builder; and then, on the grounds that these are not self-sufficient, he adds a   15
smith and persons in charge of the necessary herds, and further both a trader

18 · Reading *eidē* with the MSS rather than the conjectural *eiē* adopted by Dreizehnter.
19 · Cf. 2.2. 3, 3.1. 2, 7.8. 7–9.
20 · Cf. Plato, *Republic* 369d–71e.

and one engaged in commerce. All of these make up the complement of the first city, as if every city were constituted for the sake of the necessary things and not rather for the sake of what is noble, and as if it were equally in need

20   of shoemakers and farmers. (13) But he does not assign it a warrior part until, with the increase in their territory and its encroaching on that of their neighbors, they become involved in war. Moreover, even among four persons, or however many sharers there are, there must necessarily be someone who assigns and judges what is just. (14) If, then, one were to regard soul as more a

25   part of an animal than body, things of this sort—the military element and the element sharing in justice as it relates to adjudication, and in addition the deliberative element, which is the work of political understanding—must be regarded as more a part of cities than things relating to necessary needs. (15) (Whether these belong to certain persons separately or to the same ones

30   makes no difference to the argument; indeed, it often happens that the same persons bear arms and farm.) So if both the former and the latter are to be regarded as parts of the city, it is evident that the heavy-armed element, at any rate, is a necessary part of the city.[21]

A seventh is the element that performs public service by means of its property[22]—what we call the well off. (16) An eighth is the magisterial, or that

35   performing public service with respect to offices, since a city cannot exist without officials. There must, then, of necessity be certain persons who are capable of ruling and who perform public service for the city in this connection either continuously or in turn. (17) There remain the things we just happened to discuss, the element that deliberates and the element that judges

40   concerning the just things for disputants. If these things must exist in cities,

1291b   then, and exist in a way that is fine and just, there must necessarily be certain persons who partake of the virtue of political rulers.[23] (18) Now the other capacities are held by many to be susceptible of belonging to the same persons. For example, the warriors, farmers, and artisans could be the same persons,

21 · The omission of a sixth element in the enumeration suggests a lacuna in the text at this point; the parallel account in 7.8. 7–9 points to the priesthood as the missing element. Another possibility is that the deliberative and judicial functions are implicitly considered a single element, as they seem to be in 4.17 (and in 7.8. 7 and 9).

22 · Wealthier persons at Athens were expected as a "public service" (*leitourgia*) to underwrite expenses for civic events such as dramatic performances, religious sacrifices, and the like.

23 · Or "certain political men who share in virtue," or possibly "certain persons who share in virtue as it relates to political things."

and all lay claim even to virtue, and suppose themselves capable of ruling in   5
most offices. But it is impossible for the same persons to be poor and wealthy.
(19) Hence these are particularly held to be parts of the city, the well off and
the poor. Further, on account of the fact that the former are for the most part
few and the latter many, these parts of the city are seen as opposed to one   10
another. Accordingly, regimes are instituted on the basis of the sorts of preeminence associated with these, and there are held to be two sorts of regimes,
democracy and oligarchy.

(20) That there are several sorts of regimes, then, and what the reasons are
for this, was stated earlier; we may now say that there are also several kinds   15
of democracy and of oligarchy. This is evident from what has been said as
well. (21) For there are several kinds both of the people and of the so-called
notables.[24] In the case of the people, for example, there are the farmers, the
element engaged in the arts, the marketing element, whose pursuits are buy-   20
ing and selling, and the element connected with the sea. Of the latter, there
is a military, merchant,[25] ferrying, and fishing element. (In many places one
of these can amount to a considerable crowd—for example, the fishermen
in Tarentum and Byzantium, the warship crews at Athens, the trading element in Aegina and Chios, and the ferrying in Tenedos.) In addition, there   25
is the menial element and that having little property, so as to be incapable
of being at leisure; and further, the free element that is not descended from
citizen parents on both sides, and whatever other similar kind of multitude
there may be. (22) In the case of the notables, there are kinds distinguished
by wealth, good birth, virtue, education, and whatever is spoken of as based   30
on the same sort of difference as these.

The first sort of democracy, then, is that which is particularly said to be
based on equality. The law in this sort of democracy asserts that there is equality when the poor are no more preeminent than the well off, and neither have
authority, but both are similar. (23) For if freedom indeed exists particularly in a democracy, as some conceive to be the case, as well as equality, this   35
would particularly happen where all share in the regime as far as possible in
similar fashion. But since the people are a majority, and what is resolved by
the majority is authoritative, this will necessarily be a democracy. (24) This
is one kind of democracy; another is the kind where offices are filled on the
basis of assessments, but these are low, and it is open to anyone possessing the   40

24 · The term is *gnōrimoi*, another euphemism for the upper classes.
25 · Literally, the "goods-getting element" (*to chrēmatistikon*).

1292a amount to take part, while anyone losing it does not take part. Another kind of democracy is where all citizens of unquestioned descent take part, but law rules. (25) Another kind of democracy is where all have a part in the offices provided only they are citizens, but law rules. Another kind of democracy is
5 the same in other respects, but the multitude has authority and not the law. This comes about when decrees rather than law are authoritative, and this happens on account of the popular leaders.[26] (26) For in cities under a democracy that is based on law a popular leader does not arise, but the best of
10 the citizens preside; but where the laws are without authority, there popular leaders arise. For the people become a monarch, from many combining into one—for the many have authority not as individuals but all together. (27) What Homer means when he says "many-headed rule is not good"[27] is not clear—whether it is this sort of rule, or the sort when there are a num-
15 ber of rulers acting as individuals. At any rate, such a people, being a sort of monarch, seek to rule monarchically on account of their not being ruled by law, and become like a master: flatterers are held in honor, and this sort of rule of the people bears comparison with tyranny among the forms of monarchy. (28) Hence their character is the same as well: both are like masters
20 with respect to the better persons; the decrees of the one are like the edicts of the other; and the popular leader and the flatterer are the same or comparable. These are particularly influential in each case, flatterers with tyrants and popular leaders with peoples of this sort. (29) These are responsible for
25 decrees having authority rather than the laws because they bring everything before the people. For they become great through the people's having authority in all matters, and through having authority themselves over the opinion of the people, since the multitude is persuaded by them. (30) Moreover, some bring accusations against certain persons holding offices and assert that the
30 people should judge; the invitation is gladly accepted, and all the offices are thus overthrown. One may hold it a reasonable criticism to argue that a democracy of this sort is not a regime.[28] For where the laws do not rule there is no regime. (31) The law should rule in all matters, while the offices and the
35 regime[29] should judge in particular cases. So if democracy is one of the sorts

26 · That is, "demagogues" (*hoi dēmagōgoi*).

27 · Homer, *Iliad* 2.204.

28 · Probably a reference to Plato, *Republic* 557c–58c.

29 · Something may be wrong with the text here. *Politeia* is often explained as meaning "citizen body," but it is doubtful whether Aristotle elsewhere uses the word in this sense.

of regime, it is evident that such a system, in which everything is administered through decrees, is not even democracy in the authoritative sense, since no decree can be general. This may stand, then, as our discussion of the kinds of democracy.

CHAPTER 5

(1) Of the kinds of oligarchy, one is where the offices are filled on the basis of assessments of such a size that the poor do not share, though they are a majority, while it is open to anyone possessing the amount to take part in the regime. Another is when the offices are filled on the basis of large assessments, and they themselves elect in filling vacancies (if they do this out of all of these it is held to be more aristocratic, but if from certain special ones, oligarchic).[30] (2) Another form of oligarchy is when son succeeds father. A fourth is when what was just spoken of occurs, and not law but the officials rule. This is the counterpart among oligarchies to tyranny among monarchies, and to the sort of democracy we spoke of last among democracies; they call such an oligarchy "rule of the powerful."[31]

(3) There are, then, this many kinds of oligarchy and democracy. But it should not be overlooked that it has happened in many places that, although the regime insofar as it is based on the laws is not a popular one, it is governed in popular fashion as a result of the character and regimen[32] of the citizens. Similarly, it has happened elsewhere that the regime insofar as it is based on the laws tends toward the popular, but through the citizens' regimen and habits tends to be oligarchically run. (4) This happens particularly after revolution in regimes. For the transition is not immediate: they are content at first to aggrandize themselves at the expense of the others only in small ways, so that the laws that existed before remain, although those who have made the revolution in the regime are dominant.

40
1292b

5

10

15

20

---

30 · This sentence has been differently understood. The words *autoi hairontai* ("they themselves elect") appear to refer to a process of cooptation by which the officials themselves would choose their successors (in contrast to the first variety, where election to office is by the entire citizen body). But they have sometimes been taken to refer to the entire citizen body, and the process interpreted (in the light of 6.9) as involving the admission of noncitizens to citizenship.

31 · *Dynasteia*; cf. 2.10.13–14.

32 · *Agōgē*, a term commonly used of Spartan civic education or training.

CHAPTER 6

(1) That there are this many kinds of democracy and oligarchy is evident
from what has been said. For, necessarily, either all the parts of the people
that have been spoken of share in the regime, or some do and some do not.
(2) Now when the farming element and that possessing a moderate amount
of property have authority over the regime, they govern themselves in accordance with laws. For they have enough to live on as long as they work,
but are unable to be at leisure, so they put the law in charge and assemble
only for necessary assemblies. As for others, it is open to them to take part as
soon as they are in possession of the assessment defined by the laws; hence
it is open to all who possess the amount to take part. (3) In general, it is oligarchic when it is not open to all [actually to take part in office in spite of
being full citizens,] but that it should be open to them to be at leisure is impossible unless there are revenues.[33] For these reasons, then, this is one kind
of democracy. Another kind arises through the next sort of distinction. For
it is possible for it to be open to all of unquestioned descent with respect to
family to take part in the regime, but for those [only actually] to share who
are able to be at leisure; (4) hence in a democracy of this sort the laws rule
on account of there not being a revenue. A third kind is when it is open to
all who are free persons to take part in the regime, but they do not [actually]
take part for the reason just mentioned, so in this as well the law necessarily
rules. (5) A fourth kind of democracy is the one that was the last to arise in
cities. For on account of cities' having become much larger than they originally were and having available abundant sources of revenues, all take part in
the regime on account of the preeminence of the multitude, and all share and
engage in politics, as even the poor are able to be at leisure through receiving
pay. (6) A multitude of this sort is indeed particularly at leisure: the care of
their private affairs is in no way an obstacle for them, while it is an obstacle
for the wealthy, so that the latter frequently do not share in the assembly or in
adjudicating. Hence the multitude of the poor comes to have authority over
the regime, and not the laws.

(7) The kinds of democracy, then, are such and so many on account of
these necessities. As for the kinds of oligarchy, when a larger number of per-

33 · Text and meaning are uncertain. I follow the text of Dreizehnter (apart from his
unnecessary supplement) rather than the reconstruction of Rassow, but suspect a lacuna following *to men* at the end of b31; I have supplied what I take to be the sense.
There would seem to be little question that the term *prosodoi* refers to state revenues.

sons owns property, but in lesser amounts and not overly much, this is the first kind of oligarchy. Taking part in the regime they make open to who- 15 ever possesses the amount of the assessment; (8) and as there is a multitude of persons taking part in the governing body, not human beings but the law necessarily has authority. For the further removed they are from monarchy, and have neither so much property that they can be at leisure without con- cerning themselves with it, nor so little that they must be sustained by the city, they will necessarily claim to merit having the law rule for them rather 20 than ruling themselves. (9) Now when those who own property are fewer than those mentioned earlier, and the properties greater, the second kind of oligarchy arises. Being more influential, they claim to merit aggrandizement for themselves; hence they themselves elect from the others those who are to enter the governing body. But as they are not yet strong enough to rule with- 25 out law, they make a law of this sort.[34] (10) If they tighten it by being fewer and having larger properties, the third advance in oligarchy occurs—that where the offices are in their own hands, in accordance with a law requiring that the deceased be succeeded by their sons. (11) When they tighten it exces- 30 sively with respect to their properties and in the extent of their friendships, this sort of rule of the powerful is close to monarchy, and human beings rule rather than the law. This is the fourth kind of oligarchy, the counterpart to the final kind of democracy.

CHAPTER 7

(1) There are, further, two sorts of regimes besides democracy and oligar- 35 chy, one of which is spoken of by all—and we spoke of earlier—as one of the four kinds of regimes (the four they speak of are monarchy, oligarchy, democracy, and fourthly, so-called aristocracy). There is a fifth sort, which is referred to by the term common to all—they call it polity; but because it 40 has not often existed, it is overlooked by those who undertake to enumerate the kinds of regimes, and they use only the four (as Plato does) in the [works 1293b of theirs treating] regimes.[35] (2) Now it is right to call aristocracy the regime

34 · Or possibly "they make the law a thing of this sort," i.e., the ruling authority.
35 · Or perhaps "they use only the four, as Plato does in the [section of his work treat- ing] regimes," i.e., *Republic* 8–9. Plato's enumeration includes, beside an aristocracy of philosophers, timocracy (or "so-called aristocracy" on the model of Sparta), oligarchy, democracy, and tyranny. It is not known to what other authorities Aristotle might be referring.

we treated in our first discourses.[36] Only the regime that is made up of those
who are best simply on the basis of virtue, and not of men who are good in
relation to some presupposition, is justly referred to as an aristocracy; for
only here is it simply the case that the same person is a good man and a good
citizen, while those who are good in others are so in relation to their regime.
(3) Nevertheless, there are certain regimes which differ both from those that
are oligarchically run and from so-called polity, and are called aristocracies.
For wherever they elect to offices not only on the basis of wealth but also
on the basis of desert, the regime itself is different from both of these and is
called aristocratic. (4) For, indeed, in cities that do not make virtue a common concern there are still certain persons who are of good reputation and
held to be respectable. Wherever, therefore, the regime looks both to wealth
and to virtue as well as the people, as in Carthage, it is aristocratic; and so
also those which, like the Spartan regime, look to two alone, virtue and the
people, and where there is a mixture of these two things, democracy and virtue. (5) There are, therefore, these two kinds of aristocracy besides the first
or the best regime. And there is a third: those forms of so-called polity which
incline more toward oligarchy.

CHAPTER 8

(1) It remains for us to speak of what is termed polity as well as of tyranny. We
have arranged it thus, although polity is not a deviation, nor are those sorts
of aristocracies just spoken of, because in truth all fall short of the most correct regime, and because [usually] enumerated with them are those which are
themselves deviations from them, as we said in our initial discourses.[37] (2) It
is reasonable to make mention of tyranny last since of all of them this is least
a regime, while our inquiry concerns the regime. The reason it has been arranged in this manner, then, has been spoken of; now we must set out [our
view of] polity. Its capacity should be more evident now that we have discussed what pertains to oligarchy and democracy.

(3) Simply speaking, polity is a mixture of oligarchy and democracy. It
is customary, however, to call polities those sorts that tend toward democ-

36 · The reference appears to be to the discussion of the best regime in 7–8, rather
than to the various allusions to aristocracy in 3 (consider particularly 7.3, where the definition given of aristocracy seems clearly intended to be a generic one).

37 · This is usually referred to 3.7. 5, but the reference seems to be rather to 4.2, if the
translation given here (which accepts the interpretation though not the supplement of
Thurot) is correct.

racy, and those tending more toward oligarchy, aristocracies, on account of the fact that education and good birth particularly accompany those who are better off. (4) Further, those who are well off are held to possess already the things for the sake of which the unjust commit injustice; this is why they are referred to as gentlemen and notables. Since aristocracy tries to assign preeminence to the best of the citizens, it is asserted that oligarchies too are made up particularly of gentlemen. (5) Also, it is held to be impossible for a city to have good governance if it is run not aristocratically but by the base, and similarly, for one that does not have good governance to be aristocratically run. For good governance does not exist where the laws have been well enacted yet are not obeyed. (6) Hence one should conceive it to be one sort of good governance when the laws are obeyed as enacted, and another sort when the laws being upheld have been finely enacted (for it is possible that even badly enacted ones will be obeyed). This may be done in two ways: they may obey either the laws that are the best of those possible for them, or those that are the best simply.

(7) Aristocracy is held to be most particularly the distribution of prerogatives on the basis of virtue; for the defining principle of aristocracy is virtue, as that of oligarchy is wealth, and of rule of the people freedom. (The [principle of] what the major part resolves is present in all: in an oligarchy, an aristocracy, or in regimes ruled by the people, what is resolved by the greater part of those taking part in the regime is authoritative.) (8) Now in most cities the kind of regime [that is commonly called aristocracy is not correctly so] called.[38] For the mixture aims only at the well off and the poor, at wealth and freedom, since in most places the well off are held to occupy the place of gentlemen. (9) Since there are three things disputing over equality in the regime,[39] freedom, wealth, and virtue (for the fourth—what they call good birth—accompanies the latter two, good birth being old wealth and virtue together), it is evident that a mixture of the two—of the well off and the poor—is to be spoken of as polity, while a mixture of the three should (apart from the genuine and first form) be spoken of most particularly as aristoc-

40

1294a

5

10

15

20

---

38 · Text and meaning are uncertain. The expression *to tēs politeias eidos kaleitai* is explained by Newman as "the form which is called polity exists," but it is hardly clear how this allegedly idiomatic sense of *kalein* helps to make sense of the larger context; others have suggested a variety of emendations, none very satisfying. I believe something has dropped out of the text, and supply what I take to be the sense.

39 · Or "disputing for equal treatment in the regime," as it is usually translated; but the reference appears to be to the fundamental discussion of democratic and oligarchic views of the *meaning* of equality in 3.9.

25   racy. (10) That there are other kinds of regimes apart from monarchy, de-
     mocracy, and oligarchy, then, has been stated, and it is evident which sorts
     these are, in what ways aristocracies differ among themselves and polities
     from aristocracy, and that they are not far from one another.

CHAPTER 9

30   (1) In what manner so-called polity comes into being beside democracy and
     oligarchy, and how it should be established, we shall speak of now in confor-
     mity with what has been said. At the same time, it will be clear also what it
     is that defines democracy and oligarchy; for the distinction between these
35   must be grasped, and a combination then made out of these, taking from
     each a tally, as it were.[40] (2) There are three defining principles of this com-
     bination or mixture. One is to take elements of the legislation of each, as for
     example concerning adjudication. In oligarchies they arrange to fine the well
40   off if they do not take part in adjudicating, and provide no pay for the poor,
     while in democracies they provide pay for the poor and do not fine the well
     off. (3) What is common to and a mean between these is to have both [ar-
1294b   rangements], and hence this is characteristic of polity, which is a mixture
     formed from both. This, then, is one mode of conjoining them. Another is
     to take the mean between the arrangements of each. For example, in the one
     case they attend the assembly on the basis of no assessment at all or a very
     small one, and in the other on the basis of a large assessment: what is com-
5   mon here is neither of these, but the mean between the assessments. (4) A
     third is a selection from both arrangements, taking some from the oligar-
     chic law and some from the democratic. I mean, for example, it is held to be
     democratic for offices to be chosen by lot, oligarchic to have them elected,
10   and democratic not to do it on the basis of an assessment, oligarchic to do it
     on the basis of an assessment. (5) It is characteristic of aristocracy and pol-
     ity, therefore, to take an element from each—from oligarchy making offices
     elected, from democracy not doing it on the basis of an assessment.
        (6) The manner of mixing them, then, is this. The defining principle of a
15   good mixture of democracy and oligarchy is that it should be possible for the
     same polity to be spoken of as either a democracy or an oligarchy, and it is
     clear that it is because the mixture is a fine one that those who speak of it do
     so in this way. The mean too is of this sort: each of the extremes is revealed

---

40 · A "tally" (*symbolon*) was one of two halves of a token which two contracting parties broke between them for purposes of identification.

in it. (7) Just this happens in the case of the Spartan regime. Many attempt to   20
speak of it as if it were a democracy on account of the fact that the arrangement has many democratic elements. In the first place, for example, as far as
the rearing of children is concerned, those of the wealthy are reared in similar fashion to those of the poor, and they are educated in a manner such that
the children of the poor can also afford it. (8) It is similar as well in the age   25
following; and when they become men the same approach is followed. For
a wealthy person is in no way marked off from a poor one: the sustenance
they get in the common messes is the same for all, and the dress of the rich is
of a sort that any of the poor could also provide himself with. (9) Further, it
seems democratic by the fact that, of the two greatest offices, one is elected
by the people, while they take part in the other—for they elect the senators   30
and take part in the board of overseers. On the other hand, others call it oligarchy on account of its having many oligarchic elements. For example, all
the offices are chosen by election and none by lot, a few have authority over
cases with penalties of death and exile, and many other such things. (10) In a   35
polity that is finely mixed, the regime should be held to be both—and neither. And it should be preserved through itself, not from outside—through
itself not because those wishing its preservation are a majority[41] (since this
might be the case even in a base regime), but because none of the parts of the
city generally would wish to have another regime.

In what manner polity should be established, and similarly the regimes   40
termed aristocracies, has now been spoken of.

CHAPTER 10

(1) It remains for us to speak about tyranny; not that there is room for much   1295a
argument about it, but that it may have its part in the inquiry, since we
placed it too among the regimes. Now we discussed kingship in our first discourses, where we made an investigation of what is most particularly spo-   5
ken of as kingship—whether it is disadvantageous or advantageous for cities,
who should be king, where he should be drawn from, and how the kingship
should be established.[42] (2) We distinguished two kinds of tyranny while investigating kingship, as their power in a sense overlaps with kingship as well   10
on account of the fact that both of these sorts of rule are based on law. For
among some of the barbarians they choose plenipotentiary monarchs, and

41 · Bracketing *exothen* with Thurot.
42 · 3.14–17.

formerly among the ancient Greeks there arose in this manner certain mon-
15   archs who were called dictators. (3) There are certain differences between
these; but both were kingly by the fact of being based on law and a monarchic rule over willing persons, and at the same time tyrannical by the rule being characteristic of a master and in accordance with their own will. There is
also a third kind of tyranny, the one that is most particularly held to be tyranny, being a sort of counterpart to absolute kingship. (4) Any monarchy
20   must necessarily be a tyranny of this sort if it rules in unchallenged fashion
over persons who are all similar or better, and with a view to its own advantage and not that of the ruled. Hence it is rule over persons who are unwilling; for no free person would willingly tolerate this sort of rule. The kinds of
tyranny, then, are these and this many for the reasons spoken of.

CHAPTER 11

25   (1) What regime is best and what way of life is best for most cities and most
human beings, judging with a view neither to virtue of the sort that is beyond private persons, nor to education, in respect to those things requiring
[special advantages provided by] nature and an equipment dependent on
chance, nor to the regime that one would pray for, but a way of life which it is
30   possible for most to share in, and a regime of which most cities can partake?
(2) For those that are called aristocracies—the ones we were just speaking
of—either fall outside [the range] of most cities, or border on so-called polity; hence we may speak of both as one.
35   Judgment in all these matters rests on the same elements. (3) If it was correctly said in the discourses on ethics[43] that the happy life is one in accordance
with virtue and unimpeded, and that virtue is a mean, then the middling sort
of life is best—the mean that is capable of being attained by each sort of indi-
40   vidual. These same defining principles must also define virtue and vice in the
1295b   case of a city and a regime; for the regime is the way of life of a city. (4) Now
in all cities there are three parts of the city, the very well off, the very poor,
and third, those in the middle between these. Since, however, it is agreed
that what is moderate and middling is best, it is evident that in the case of the
5   goods of fortune as well a middling possession is the best of all. (5) For it is
readiest to obey reason, while for one who is overly handsome, overly strong,
overly well born, or overly wealthy—or the reverse of these things, overly in-
digent, overly weak, or very lacking in honor—it is difficult to follow reason.

43 · E.g., *Eth. Nic.* 1101a14–16.

The former sort tend to become arrogant and base on a grand scale, the latter   10
malicious and base in petty ways; and acts of injustice are committed either
through arrogance or through malice. Moreover, these are least inclined either to avoid ruling or to wish to rule, both of which things are injurious to
cities.[44] (6) In addition, those who are preeminent in the goods of fortune—
strength, wealth, friends, and the other things of this sort—neither wish to   15
be ruled nor know how to be. This is something that marks them from the
time they are children at home, for the effect of living in luxury is that they
do not become habituated to being ruled even at school; but those who are
excessively needy with respect to these things are too humble. (7) So the ones
do not know how to rule but only how to be ruled, and then only to be ruled
like a slave, and the others do not know how to be ruled by any sort of rule,   20
but only to rule like a master. What comes into being, then, is a city not of
free persons but of slaves and masters, the ones consumed by envy, the others
by contempt. Nothing is further removed from affection and from a political
community; for community involves the element of affection—enemies do
not wish to have even a journey in common. (8) The city wishes, at any rate,   25
to be made up of equal and similar persons to the extent possible, and this is
most particularly the case with the middling elements. So this city must necessarily be governed in the best fashion if it is made up of the elements out
of which we assert the city is by nature constituted. Also, of citizens in cities
these most particularly preserve themselves. (9) For neither do they desire the   30
things of others, as the poor do, nor others their things, as the poor desire
those of the wealthy; and as a result of not being plotted against or plotting
against others they pass their time free from danger. On this account, the
prayer of Phocylides was a fine one: "Many things are best for the middling;
I would be of the middling sort in the city."[45]

(10) It is clear, therefore, that the political community that depends on the   35
middling sort is best as well, and that those cities are capable of being well
governed in which the middling element is numerous—most particularly if

---

44 · Text and meaning are uncertain. I accept Bernays's conjectural *phygarchousi*
("avoid ruling") for the *phylarchousi* or *philarchousi* of the MSS; but the verbs *phyg-
archein* and *boularchein* (in the sense of "wish to rule") are found nowhere else, and the
entire clause may be corrupt or out of place (it is bracketed by Dreizehnter as a gloss).
It is perhaps possible to take it to mean that both rich and poor (and not the middle
class, the apparent antecedent of "these") shun public service as cavalry commander
(*phylarchos*) or head of council (*boularchos*), but this is not very satisfactory in its immediate context.

45 · Phocylides, fr. 12 Diehl.

it is superior to both of the other parts, but if not, superior to either of them; for when added to one it will tip the scale and prevent the opposing excesses

40   from arising. (11) Thus it is the greatest good fortune for those who are en-

1296a gaged in politics to have a middling and sufficient property, because where some possess very many things and others nothing, either rule of the people in its extreme form must come into being, or unmixed oligarchy, or—as a result of both of these excesses—tyranny. For tyranny arises from the most

5   headstrong sort of democracy and from oligarchy, but much less often from the middling sorts of regime and those close to them. (12) We will speak of the reason for this later in the discourses on revolutions in regimes.[46] But that the middling sort is best is evident. It alone is without factional conflict, for where the middling element is numerous, factional conflicts and splits over the regimes occur least of all. (13) And large cities are freer of factional con-

10   flict for the same reason—that the middling element is numerous. In small cities it is easier for all to be separated into two factions and have no one left in the middle, and nearly everyone is either poor or well off. (14) And democracies are more stable than oligarchies and more durable on account of those

15   of the middling sort, who are more numerous and have a greater part in the prerogatives in democracies than in oligarchies. When the poor predominate numerically in the absence of these, they fare badly and are quickly ruined. (15) It should be considered an indication of this that the best legislators are

20   from the middling citizens. Solon was one of these, as is clear from his poems, and Lycurgus (for he was not king), Charondas, and most of the others.[47]

(16) It is also evident from these things why most regimes are either democratic or oligarchic. For as a result of the fact that the middling element is of-

25   ten few in them, whichever is preeminent, whether those owning property or the people, oversteps the middle [path] and conducts the regime to suit itself, so that either rule of the people comes into being or an oligarchy. (17) In addition to this, on account of the factional conflicts and fights that arise between the people and the well off, whichever of the two succeeds in dominat-

30   ing its opponents does not establish a regime that is common or equal, but they grasp for preeminence in the regime as the prize of victory. (18) Further, those who have achieved leadership in Greece have in either case looked to their own regime in establishing either democracies or oligarchies in cities,[48]

46 · The reference appears to be to 5.8. 7.

47 · For Solon see *Ath. Pol.* 5 and Plutarch, *Solon* 1 and 14; the view that Lycurgus was king at Sparta and therefore a wealthy man appears, for example, in Plutarch, *Lycurgus* 3 and *Solon* 16 (but cf. *Cleomenes* 10).

48 · The reference is to the Athenians and the Spartans respectively.

having in view not what is advantageous for the cities but rather what is ad- 35
vantageous for themselves. (19) So for these reasons the middling regime
has either never arisen or has done so infrequently and in a few cities. For
of those who have previously held leadership, one man alone was persuaded
to provide for this sort of arrangement;[49] and the custom is now established 40
that those in the cities do not even want equality, but either seek to rule or 1296b
endure being dominated.

(20) What the best regime is, then, and for what reason, is evident from
these things. As for the other regimes (since we assert that there are several
sorts of democracies and several of oligarchies), once the best is defined it is
not difficult to see which is to be regarded as first, which second, and so on 5
in the same manner according to whether it is better or worse. (21) The one
that is closest to this must of necessity always be better, the one that is more
removed from the middle, worse, provided one is not judging with a view to 10
a presupposition. I say "with a view to a presupposition" because while one
sort of regime is more choiceworthy, there is often nothing to prevent another regime being more advantageous for certain cities.

CHAPTER 12

(1) What regime is advantageous for which cities, and what sort for which
sort of persons, is to be treated next after what has been spoken of. Now the
same thing must first be grasped about all of them generally: the part of the 15
city that wants the regime to continue must be superior to the part not wanting this. Every city is made up of both quality and quantity. By quality I mean
freedom, wealth, education, and good birth; by quantity, the preeminence
belonging to the multitude. (2) It is possible that, while quality belongs to 20
one part of the city among all those of which a city is constituted, and quantity to another part (for example, the ignoble may be more in number than
those of good family, or the poor than the wealthy), the larger part is nevertheless not preeminent in quantity to the same extent that it falls short in
quality. Hence these [two factors] must be judged in relation to one another.
(3) Where the multitude of the poor is preeminent, therefore, with respect to 25
the proportion mentioned, there a democracy is what accords with nature —
and each kind of democracy according to the preeminence belonging to each

---

49 · The identity of this individual has been much disputed. Solon and Theramenes
are commonly cited as possibilities, but what seems wanted is the leader of a hegemonial state; the most plausible candidate would appear to be Philip of Macedon. Cf. Introduction, pp. xiii–xiv above.

sort of people. If, for example, the multitude of farmers predominates, it will
30   be the first sort of democracy; if that of workers and wage earners, the last
sort, and similarly for the others between these. But where the element of the
well off and the notables predominates in quality to a greater extent than it
falls short in quantity, there it is oligarchy that accords with nature, and in a
similar manner each of its kinds according to the preeminence belonging to
the oligarchic multitude.

35   (4) The legislator should always add those of the middling sort to the
dominant element in the regime. If he enacts oligarchic laws, he ought to aim
at the middling sort; if democratic ones, he ought to attach these to them.
Where the multitude of middling persons predominates either over both of
40   the extremities together or over one alone, there a lasting polity[50] is capable
1297a   of existing. (5) For there is no reason to fear that the wealthy and the poor
will come to an agreement against them: neither will want to be the slaves
of the other, and if they seek a regime in which they will have more in common, they will find none other than this. They would not put up with ruling
5   in turn on account of their distrust toward one another. The most trustworthy person everywhere is the arbitrator; but the middling person is a sort of
arbitrator. (6) The better the mixture in the polity, the more lasting it will
be. Many of those who want to set up aristocratic regimes as well [as polities]
thoroughly err not only by the fact that they distribute more to the well off,
10   but also by deceiving the people. For in time from things falsely good there
must result a true evil, and the aggrandizements of the wealthy are more ru-
inous to the polity than those of the people.

CHAPTER 13

15   (1) The devices used in polities[51] as pretexts against the people are five in
number, being connected with the assembly, the offices, the courts, armament, and exercise. As regards the assembly, the device is that it is open to
all to attend assemblies, but either a fine is imposed on the well off alone for

50 · Here and in the rest of this chapter, *politeia* is frequently taken to be used in its
generic sense of "regime" rather than in its specific sense of "polity," though I think
wrongly (consider particularly the reference to polities which seems implicit in the
text in a6–7).

51 · *Politeia* is here frequently taken in its generic sense. But the reference back to this
passage in 5.8. 2–4 confirms what is indicated at the end of 4.12, that the use of such
devices is characteristic of "well-blended" regimes—polities and aristocracies that approach polities.

not attending, or a much larger one on them; (2) as regards the offices, that   20
it should not be open to those who are assessed to abjure,[52] but it should be
to the poor; as regards the courts, that there should be a fine against the well
off if they do not attend, but impunity for the poor, or else a large fine for the
ones and a small fine for the others, as in the laws of Charondas. (3) In some
places it is open to all to enroll themselves for the assembly and courts, but if   25
they do not attend the assembly or adjudicate once they are enrolled they are
fined heavily—in order that they avoid enrolling, and through not being enrolled do not adjudicate or attend the assembly. (4) They legislate in a similar
manner concerning the possession of heavy arms and exercising. It is open to   30
those who are poor not to possess them, but the well off are fined if they do
not, while if they do not exercise there is no fine for the former, but the well
off are fined, so that the ones take part in these things on account of the fine,
and the others do not take part through not being afraid of it.

(5) Now these devices of legislation are oligarchic. In democracies, how-   35
ever, there are counterdevices to them. To the poor they give pay for attending the assembly and adjudicating, and arrange not to have the well off fined
for not attending. (6) So it is evident that if one wishes to have a just mixture,
elements from both must be brought together—for example, the ones being   40
provided pay, the others fined; in this way all would participate, while in the
other way the regime comes to belong to one side alone.   1297b

(7) A polity should be made up only of those possessing heavy arms. But it
is not possible to define the amount of assessment in simple fashion and say
that so much must be available; rather, one should investigate what sort of
amount is the largest that would let those taking part in the regime be more   5
numerous than those not taking part, and arrange for it to be this. (8) For the
poor are willing to remain tranquil even when they take no part in the prerogatives, provided no one acts arrogantly toward them nor deprives them of
any of their property. Yet this is not easy; for it does not always turn out that
those taking part in the governing body are the refined sort. (9) And when   10
war comes, they are in the habit of shirking if they are poor, unless they receive sustenance; if someone provides them sustenance, however, they are
willing to go to war.

In some cases, the regime [of a polity] is made up not only of those bearing
heavy arms, but of those who had once done so. Among the Malians the regime was made up of both of these, though they elected to offices from those   15

52 · That is, to decline office with an oath supporting the claim that it would be un-
duly burdensome for financial or other reasons.

who were actually soldiers. (10) And the first sort of regime that arose among the Greeks after kingships was made up of the warrior elements, and initially of cavalrymen. For strength and preeminence in war then belonged to the 20 cavalrymen: without organization the heavy-armed element is useless, but experience in such matters and tactical arrangements were lacking among the ancients, so that their strength lay in the cavalrymen. But as cities increased in size and those with heavy arms provided relatively more strength, more persons took part in the regime. (11) Hence the regimes we now call polities 25 used to be called democracies. That the ancient regimes were oligarchic and kingly is reasonable: on account of a lack of manpower cities did not have much of a middling element, so being relatively both few in number and weak in organization, the people put up with being ruled.

(12) For what reason there are several sorts of regimes, then; why there are 30 other sorts beyond those [generally] spoken of (for democracy is not one in number, and similarly with the others); further, what the varieties are and for what reason it happens that they are different; in addition, which is the best of the regimes for the majority of cases, and of the other regimes which sort suits which sort of city—this has been spoken of.

CHAPTER 14

35 (1) Let us speak of what comes next again both generally and separately for each regime, taking the beginning point that is appropriate to it. There are, then, three parts in all regimes with respect to which the excellent lawgiver must attempt to discern what is advantageous for each. As long as these are in a fine condition, the regime is necessarily in a fine condition; and regimes 40 necessarily differ from one another as a result of differing in each of these parts. (2) Of these three things, one is the part that is to deliberate about 1298a common matters; the second, the part connected with offices—that is, which offices there should be, over what matters they should have authority, and in what fashion the choice of persons to fill them should occur; and the third, the adjudicative part.

(3) The deliberative element has authority concerning war and peace, 5 alliances and their dissolution, laws, [judicial cases carrying penalties of] death or exile or confiscation, and the choosing and auditing of officials. It is necessary either that all these sorts of decision be assigned to all the citizens, that all be assigned to some of the citizens (for example, by assigning all to one particular office or several, or some to some and some to others), or that some of them be assigned to all of the citizens and others to some.

(4) Now that all decide concerning all is characteristically popular; for the   10
people seek this sort of equality. But there are several modes in which all decide. One is by turns rather than all together, as in the regime of Telecles of
Miletus; and there are other regimes in which deliberation is carried out by
officials meeting jointly, with all entering office by turns from the tribes and   15
the smallest parts of the city until all have been gone through, and they meet
[all together] only concerning legislation or matters affecting the regime, or
to listen to announcements by the officials.[53] (5) Another mode is when all   20
decide together, but meet only with a view to the choosing of officials, legislation, what concerns war and peace, and audits, while in other matters deliberation is carried out through offices arranged to deal with each sort of
thing, and the offices are chosen from all by election or by lot. (6) Another
mode is when the citizens get together in connection with offices and audits   25
and to deliberate about war and alliance, while other matters are administered by offices that are chosen by election to the extent possible [rather than
by lot]—those in which it is necessary to have knowledgeable persons ruling. (7) A fourth mode is when all meet to deliberate on all matters, while   30
the offices decide on nothing but merely make preliminary decisions. This is
the mode in which the final sort of democracy—the sort that we assert bears
comparison with dynastic oligarchy and tyrannical monarchy—administers
itself now.

All these modes, then, are democratic, while having some decide in all
matters is oligarchic. (8) This too has several varieties. Where they are   35
elected on the basis of moderate assessments and are numerous because of
the moderateness of the assessment, where they do not attempt change in
matters where the laws forbid it but instead follow the laws, and where it is
open to anyone possessing the assessment to take part in deliberation, such
a regime is indeed an oligarchy, but by the fact of its moderateness, polity-   40
like. When all do not take part in deliberation but only those elected to do   1298b
so, and they rule in accordance with law, it is oligarchic as before. (9) When
those who have authority over deliberation elect themselves, and when son
succeeds father in office and they have authority over the laws, this arrangement is necessarily very oligarchic. (10) But when some have authority in   5
some matters [and all in some]—for example, when all have it concerning
war and peace and audits, and officials in other matters, these being chosen

---

53 · The practice of governing through joint official boards (*synarchiai*) seems to have
become fairly common by Aristotle's day. The "smallest parts" referred to here would
seem to be political subdivisions of the type of the "quarters" (*dēmoi*) of Athens. Nothing else is known of Telecles of Miletus.

either by election or by lot—it is aristocracy or polity. If persons chosen by
election have authority in some matters and persons chosen by lot in others,
with those chosen by lot being chosen either simply [from all] or from a pre-
10   selected group, or if persons chosen by election and by lot have authority in
common, these are features on the one hand of an aristocratic regime, and on
the other of a polity. (11) The deliberative element is distinguished in relation
to the regimes in this manner, then, and each regime administers matters in
accordance with the definition mentioned.

(12) In the sort of democracy which is now most particularly held to be
15   democracy (I mean, the sort in which the people has authority even over the
laws), it is advantageous with a view to deliberating better to do the same
thing that is done in regard to the courts in oligarchies. For they arrange to
fine for nonattendance those they want to have adjudicate to ensure that
they do adjudicate, while the popular sort provide pay for the poor. This
20   should be done in regard to assemblies as well. For all will deliberate better
when they do so in common—the people with the notables and these with
the multitude. (13) It is also advantageous if those who deliberate are chosen
by election or by lot in equal numbers from the parts of the city; and where
the popular sort among the citizens greatly exceed the notables in number, it
25   is advantageous too either not to provide pay for all but only for as many as
will balance the multitude of notables, or else to exclude the excess by lot
[from participating].[54]

(14) In oligarchies it is advantageous either to elect additionally certain
persons from the multitude to serve as officials, or to establish an official
board of the sort that exists in some regimes, made up of those they call "preliminary councillors" or "law guardians," and to [have a popular assembly
30   that will] take up only that business which is considered in the preliminary
council; for in this way the people will share in deliberating but will not be
able to overturn anything connected to the regime. (15) Further, it is advantageous to have the people vote on measures which are either the same as those
brought before them [by a preliminary council] or not contrary to them, or

54 · Text and meaning are somewhat uncertain. I read *politōn* ("among the citizens") with one MSS rather than *politikōn* with most MSS and Dreizehnter. Retaining
politikōn, the meaning could be either "where the popular sort greatly exceed the political sort in number," or "where the popular sort among political [men] greatly exceed
[the notables] in number." The parts of the city referred to here would seem to be administrative divisions such as tribes or quarters rather than social classes. All of these
devices are intended to increase the participation of the upper classes in decision making in democracies.

to allow all to advise but the officials to deliberate. Here the opposite of what   35
occurs in polities should be done: the multitude should be given authority
to veto measures but not to pass their own, these being referred to the officials. (16) The converse is done in polities, where the few have authority to
veto measures but not to pass them; measures of the latter sort are always re-   40
ferred to the many.

Concerning the deliberative and authoritative element of the regime,   1299a
then, let our discussion stand in this manner.

CHAPTER 15

(1) Next after these things is the distinction among offices. For this part of
the regime also involves many differences: how many offices there are, in   5
what matters they have authority, and in regard to time, how long each office
lasts (for some make them for a year, others for a shorter period, others for
a longer one), and whether offices should be perpetual or of long duration
or neither, but the same persons should be permitted to hold them several
times or the same person not even twice but only once, and further in regard   10
to the selection of officials, from which persons they should come, by which
persons they should be selected, and how they should be selected. (2) With
regard to all of these one should be able to distinguish how many modes can
exist, and then fit the sorts of offices to the sorts of regimes for which they
are advantageous.

Even to determine which should be called offices, however, is not easy.   15
The political community requires many functionaries, so that not all of those
chosen by election or lot can be regarded as officials. Priests, for example, in
the first place (for this must be regarded as something apart from the political offices), (3) and further, equippers and heralds, and also envoys, are chosen by election but are not officials. Of the sorts of superintendence some   20
are political, and are either over all of the citizens with a view to a certain action (as, for example, a general is over them when they are campaigning) or
over a part (for example, the manager of women or the manager of children);
some are related to management of the household (for they often elect grain
measurers[55]); and some are subordinate, and of such a sort that cities that are
well off arrange to have slaves do them. (4) Simply speaking, those should   25
be most particularly spoken of as offices to which are assigned both deliberation and judgment concerning certain matters and command, but most par-

---

55 · Probably an office created on an occasional basis for rationing purposes.

ticularly the latter, for command is more characteristic of ruling. But these things make almost no difference with a view to use, as no judgment has ever

30   been handed down to anyone disputing over the term, though there is room for some further treatment of them in thought.

(5) Which sort and how many offices are necessary for a city to exist, and what sort are not necessary but rather useful with a view to an excellent regime, are questions one can raise in relation to every regime, but especially

35   in the case of small cities. (6) In large cities one can and should arrange to have a single office to handle a single task: because there are many citizens, many persons can take up office, the offices being held after a long interval or only once, and each sort of task is better done when the superintendence of it is handled as a single matter rather than together with many other mat-

1299b   ters. (7) In small cities, however, many offices are necessarily brought under a few persons. Because of the lack of manpower it is not easy to have many persons in the offices, for if this were the case, who will be those who suc-

5   ceed them? Sometimes small cities need the same offices and laws as large ones; but the latter need them often, while the former do only at long intervals. (8) Hence, there is nothing to prevent small cities from mandating that they supervise many things at once. They will not interfere with one another; and on account of the lack of manpower it is necessary for them to

10   make their boards of officials like spit-lamps.[56] If, then, we are able to say how many offices necessarily belong to every city and how many offices should[57] but need not necessarily belong, one who knew this could more easily bring under one office the sorts of offices it is fitting to bring under a single one.

15   (9) It is also fitting not to neglect this—what sort of matters should be supervised by many boards[58] on a local basis and over what sort a single office should everywhere have authority. (In regard to orderliness, for example, should the market-manager have authority over this in the market and another official in another place, or should the same one have it everywhere?) Also, whether one should distinguish offices on the basis of their activity or of the human beings they supervise. (I mean, for example, whether there

20   should be a single office for orderliness, or one for children and another for women). (10) Also, in connection with the kinds of regimes, whether the types of offices too differ for each sort—whether the same offices have authority in, for example, a democracy, an oligarchy, an aristocracy, and a mon-

56 · Apparently, a spit that could also serve as a lamp holder, i.e., with a dual purpose.
57 · Reading *dei* with the MSS rather than the conjecture adopted by Dreizehnter.
58 · Reading *poiōn* and *polla* with Thurot and Dreizehnter rather than *poia* and *pollōn* with the MSS ("what sort of boards should supervise many matters").

archy, but are not made up of equal [numbers of] nor similar sorts of persons, but rather of different sorts in different regimes (in aristocracies, for 25 example, of the educated, in oligarchies of the wealthy, and in democracies of the free), or whether it happens that certain of the offices exist as a result of these very differences, and that in some cases the same offices are advantageous, while in others they differ (for it is fitting for the same to be 30 large here, small there). (11) Some offices are indeed peculiar to particular regimes, such as that of preliminary councillors; this is not democratic, whereas a council is popular. For there should be something of this latter sort which takes care of preliminary deliberation for the people, so that they can pursue their occupations; this is oligarchic [only] when they are few in number. But the number of preliminary councillors is necessarily few, and so this is necessarily oligarchic. (12) But where both these offices exist, the 35 preliminary councillors have been established as a counter to the councillors; for the councillor is popular, the preliminary councillor oligarchic. Yet even the power of the council is overturned in those sorts of democracies in 1300a which the people themselves meet and transact all business. (13) This is usually the result when those coming to the assembly are either well off or get pay;[59] for as they have leisure they can collect together frequently and decide all things themselves. The manager of children, the manager of women, and 5 any other office that has authority for this sort of superintendence is aristocratic, and not democratic. For how is it possible to prevent the wives of the poor from going out? Nor is it oligarchic, for the wives of oligarchs live luxuriously.

(14) Concerning these matters let this much be said for now, and let us make an attempt to treat the selection of officials, beginning from the begin- 10 ning. The varieties of selection depend on three defining principles, which when combined necessarily embrace all the modes. Of these three the first is who selects the officials, the second, from whom they are selected, and finally, in what manner. (15) In the case of each of these three there are three[60] varieties. For either all of the citizens select or some; they select either from 15 all or from certain special persons, [distinguished] by assessment, for example, or family, or virtue, or some other such thing (as in Megara it is from those who returned from exile together and fought in alliance against the

59 · Reading *euporia tis ēi ē misthos* with the MSS rather than *euporia tis ēi misthou* ("are well off through pay") with Spengel and Dreizehnter.

60 · Reading *treis* with the MSS rather than *duo* ("two") with Schneider and Dreizehnter. In each case there are two simple varieties and a third formed by combining them.

people[61]); and selection is made either by election or by lot. (16) And these
20 may again be conjoined, by which I mean that some offices may be selected
by some and others by all, some may be selected from all and others from
some, and some may be selected by election and others by lot. In the case
of each of these varieties there will be four modes. (17) For either all select
from all by election or all from all by lot (and from all[62] either by turn, for ex-
25 ample on the basis of tribes, quarters, or clans, until all the citizens have been
gone through, or from all each time), [or all select from some by election or
all from some by lot];[63] and[64] offices can be selected partly in one way, partly
in another. (18) Again, if some are selecting, they may do so either from all
by election or from all by lot, or from some by election or from some by lot;
30 or offices can be selected partly in one way, partly in another—I mean, [for
example,] they can be selected from all partly by election, partly by lot. So
twelve modes arise, apart from the [other] two conjunctions.[65]

(19) Of these systems of selection two are popular: for all to select from
all by election or by lot[66] (or by both, some of the offices being selected by
lot, others by election). When all select but not at the same time, and select
35 either from all or from some, either by lot or by election or both, or select
from all and some from some [either by lot or by election or][67] by both (by
"both" I mean some offices by lot and others by election), it is characteristic of polity. (20) When some select from all by election or by lot or by both
40 (some offices by election and others by lot), it is characteristic of an oligarchic [polity], though by both is more oligarchic; when some offices are selected [by all] from all and others from some, this is characteristic of a polity
1300b [run] in aristocratic fashion, [or offices are selected by election], or some by

---

61 · Possibly a reference to the overthrow of the democracy at Megara in 424 BC
(Thucydides 4.66–74), but this is not certain.

62 · Bracketing *ē* with Newman. Throughout this much-disputed passage I adhere
to the order of the MSS rather than to the reconstructions offered by Dreizehnter or
others.

63 · Accepting the supplement of Dreizehnter.

64 · Reading *kai* with Π² rather than *kai ē* with Π¹ and Dreizehnter.

65 · The twelve modes are as follows: all selecting from all by election or lot or both,
all selecting from some by election or lot or both, some selecting from all by election
or lot or both, some selecting from some by election or lot or both. The other two conjunctions are when selection is done by both some and all, and when it is done from
both some and all.

66 · Bracketing *ginesthai* with Dreizehnter. It seems possible that a line has dropped
out of the text at this point.

67 · Accepting the supplement of Newman.

election and others by lot.[68] (21) It is oligarchic when some select from some [by election],[69] and similarly when some select from some by lot (though this does not occur), and when some select from some by both. It is aristocratic when some select from all, and on occasion all from some, by election.

(22) The modes concerning offices are, then, so many in number, and are distinguished in this manner in accordance with the regimes. Which are advantageous for which regimes, and how their selection should occur, will become evident together with the powers of the offices and which these are.[70] By power of an office I mean, for example, having authority over revenues or having authority over defense. For a different kind of power is involved in generalship and in having authority over agreements in the market.

CHAPTER 16

(1) Of the three parts it remains to speak of the adjudicative. The modes of these [bodies] too must be grasped in accordance with the same presupposition. There is a distinction among courts deriving from three defining principles: from whom they are selected, on what matters they decide, and in what manner they are selected. By "from whom" I mean whether they are selected from all or some; by "on what," how many kinds of courts there are; by "in what manner," whether by lot or election.

(2) Let us first distinguish, then, how many kinds of courts there are. They are eight in number. One is concerned with audits; another is for anyone committing a crime with respect to common matters; another is concerned with what bears on the regime; a fourth is for both officials and private individuals and concerns disputes over fines; a fifth is that concerned with private transactions of a certain magnitude. Besides these there is one concerned with homicide and one with aliens. (3) (The kinds of homicide court, whether having the same persons as jurors or others, are: one concerned with premeditated homicides; one with involuntary homicides; one with cases where there is agreement [on the fact of homicide] but a dispute over what is just; and a fourth with cases involving those who had been exiled for homicide after their return, as is said to be the case, for example, with the court of

---

68 · The text and meaning of this sentence (all of which is bracketed by Dreizehnter) are uncertain and much disputed. But the basic argument seems clear: what is being discussed are the nondemocratic variants of polity. The minimum supplement would appear to be *ē pantas hairesei* ("or offices are selected by election") in b1.

69 · Accepting the supplement of Lambinus.

70 · 6.8.

30   Phreatto in Athens, although such cases are few over the whole of time even
      in large cities.[71]) (4) Of the court for aliens, one kind is for aliens disputing
      against aliens, one for aliens against townspeople. Further, besides all these
      there is one concerned with small transactions—those involving a drachma,
      five drachmas, or slightly more. For a decision has to be given in such cases as
35   well, but it does not require a multitude of jurors.

         (5) But these courts—both those concerned with homicide and those
      concerned with aliens—may be dismissed; let us speak of the political ones.
      It is in connection with these that factional conflicts arise when matters are
      not finely handled, and revolutions in regimes. Now necessarily either all de-
      cide on all the matters which have been distinguished having been selected
40   by election or by lot, or all decide on all having been selected in part by lot
      and in part by election, or all decide on some of the same matters, these being
1301a selected on the one hand by lot, on the other by election. (6) These modes
      are, then, four in number; and there are as many again based on a part [of the
      citizens rather than all]. For those adjudicating may also[72] be selected from
      some and decide on all matters by election, or be selected from some and de-
      cide on all matters by lot, or in part by lot and in part by election, or some
5   courts that decide on the same matters may be made up of persons selected
      both by lot and election. As was said, these modes [are counterparts[73]] to the
      ones spoken of. (7) Further, these same ones may be conjoined—I mean, for
      example, some courts may be selected from all, some from some, and some
      from both (in which case the same court would have some selected from all
10   and some from some), and either by lot or election or both.

         (8) How many modes there are for courts has, then, been spoken of. Of
      these the first—those selected from all[74] that decide on all matters—are
      popular. The second—those selected from some to decide on all matters—
15   are oligarchic. The third are characteristic of aristocracy and polity—those
      selected in part from all and in part from some.

---

71 · These four courts closely correspond to Athenian practice. All unpremeditated
murders (as well as killings of slaves and foreigners) fell under the jurisdiction of the
second court; the third dealt with cases where the killing could be argued to be accidental or otherwise "just" or justified. In the court at Phreatto the defendant argued
his case from a boat anchored off shore. See *Ath. Pol.* 57.3–4.

72 · Retaining *kai* rather than bracketing it with Spengel and Dreizehnter; the reference would seem to be to the earlier discussion of officials.

73 · Something appears to have dropped out of the text here; I translate the supplement of Newman.

74 · Bracketing *ē* ("or") with Susemihl and Dreizehnter.

Book 5

(1) Nearly everything else that we intended to speak of has been treated. What things bring about revolutions in regimes and how many and of what 20 sort they are; what are the sources of destruction for each sort of regime and into which sort of regime a regime is most particularly transformed; further, what are the sources of preservation both for regimes in common and for each sort of regime separately; and further, by what things each sort of regime might most particularly be preserved—these matters must be investi- 25 gated in conformity with what has been spoken of.

(2) It is necessary first to take as a beginning point the fact that many sorts of regimes have arisen because, while all agree regarding justice and proportionate equality, they err about this, as was also said earlier.[1] (3) Rule of the people arose as a result of those who are equal in any respect supposing they are equal simply, for because all alike are free persons, they consider them- 30 selves to be equal simply; and oligarchy arose as a result of those who are unequal in some one respect conceiving themselves to be wholly unequal, for as they are unequal in regard to property they conceive themselves to be unequal simply. (4) Then the former claim to merit taking part in all things equally on the grounds that they are equal, while the latter seek to aggrandize 35 themselves on the grounds that they are unequal, since "greater" is something unequal.[2] (5) All regimes of this kind have, then, a certain sort of justice, but in an unqualified sense they are in error. And it is for this reason that, when either group does not take part in the regime on the basis of the conception it happens to have, they engage in factional conflict. (6) Those who are out- 40

1 · 3. 9.1–4, 12.1–2.
2 · Aristotle alludes to the etymology of *pleonektein* ("to aggrandize themselves"), which literally means "to seek to have more," or "to take a greater share."

standing in virtue would engage in factional conflict most justifiably, yet they
1301b   do it the least of all; for it is most reasonable for these only to be unequal in
an unqualified sense. (7) There are also certain persons who are preeminent
on the basis of family and claim not to merit equal things on account of this
inequality: they are held to be well-born persons, to whom belong the virtue
and wealth of their ancestors.

5   These, then, are in a manner of speaking the beginning points and springs
of factional conflicts. (8) Hence revolutions also occur in two ways.[3] Sometimes factional conflict is with a view to the regime, so that it will be transformed from the established one into another sort, for example from democracy into oligarchy or from oligarchy into democracy, or from these into a
10   polity or aristocracy, or from the latter into the former; sometimes it is not
with a view to the established regime, and they intend that the system remain
the same, but want to have it in their own hands, as in the case of oligarchy
or monarchy. (9) Further, there may be factional conflict concerning more
and less—for example, where there is an oligarchy, to make it more oligarchi-
15   cally run or less, or where there is a democracy, to make it more democratically run or less, and similarly in the case of the remaining regimes, either to
tighten or to loosen them. (10) Further, there may be factional conflict with
a view to changing a part of the regime—for example, to establish or abol-
20   ish a certain office. Some assert that Lysander tried to eliminate the kingship
at Sparta, and King Pausanias the board of overseers;[4] in Epidamnus too the
regime was altered partially—a council replaced the tribal officials, (11) but it
is still compulsory [only] for those of the governing body who hold offices to
25   come to the hall when there is voting for an office, and the single [supreme]
official was also an oligarchic feature of that regime.[5] Factional conflict is everywhere the result of inequality, at any rate where there is no proportion
among those who are unequal (a permanent kingship is unequal if it exists

3 · "Factional conflict" (stasis) is a key term in Aristotle's analysis throughout book 5;
it encompasses a range of phenomena from factional political infighting to subversion,
rebellion, and civil war. "Revolution" is a conventional but not altogether satisfactory
translation of metabolē, which, as Aristotle makes clear, encompasses other forms of
what may be called constitutional change less drastic than the violent overthrow of a
regime. Cf. Keyt 1999, 64–66.

4 · It is not clear whether Lycurgus sought to abolish the monarchy simply or only
the hereditary rule of the Heracleidae. The Pausanias in question is apparently the victor of the battle of Plataea during the Persian Wars (cf. 7.4, 7.14.20).

5 · The change described, of which nothing further is known, appears to have been
from a restricted oligarchy to a moderate oligarchy or polity.

among equal persons); in general it is equality they seek when they engage
in factional conflict.

(12) Equality is twofold: one sort is numerical, the other according to   30
merit. By numerical I mean being the same and equal in number or size; by
according to merit, being equal in respect to a ratio. For example, three exceeds two and two one by an equal amount numerically, whereas four exceeds
two and two one by an equal amount with respect to a ratio, both being   35
halves. (13) Now while there is agreement that justice in an unqualified sense
is according to merit, there are differences, as was said before: some consider
themselves to be equal generally if they are equal in some respect, while others claim to merit all things unequally if they are unequal in some respect.

(14) Hence two sorts of regimes particularly arise — rule of the people   40
and oligarchy. Good birth and virtue exist among few persons, these things   1302a
among more: nowhere are there a hundred well-born and good persons, but
in many places the well off are many. Yet to have everywhere an arrangement
that is based simply on one or the other of these sorts of equality is a poor
thing. This is evident from the result: none of these sorts of regimes is lasting.   5
(15) The reason for this is that, once the first and initial error is committed,
it is impossible not to encounter some ill in the end. Hence numerical equality should be used in some cases, and in others equality according to merit.
Nevertheless, democracy is more stable and freer from factional conflict than
oligarchy. (16) In oligarchies two sorts of factional conflict arise, one against   10
each other, the other against the people; in democracies, though, there is
only that against the oligarchy, there being none that arises among the people
against itself that is worth mentioning. Moreover, the regime made up of the
middling elements is closer to rule of the people than to rule of the few, and   15
this is the most stable of regimes of this sort.

CHAPTER 2

(1) Since we are investigating the things from which both factional conflicts
and revolutions affecting regimes arise, one must first grasp their beginning
points and causes in a general way. These are, roughly speaking, three in
number, and must be discussed first by themselves in outline. One should   20
grasp what condition men are in when they engage in factional conflict; for
the sake of what they do so; and thirdly, what the beginning points are of political disturbances and of factional conflicts among one another.

(2) The general cause of men being in a certain condition with respect to

25 revolution should be regarded as the one we have spoken of already. Some
engage in factional conflict because they aim at equality, if they consider that
they have less in spite of being equal to those who are aggrandizing themselves; others, because they aim at inequality and preeminence, if they conceive themselves to be unequal but not to take a greater part, but an equal or
lesser one. (3) To strive for these things may be justified; it may also be unjus-
30 tified. The lesser engage in factional conflict in order to be equal; those who
are equal, in order to be greater.

What their condition is when they engage in factional conflict, then, has
been spoken of. As for the things over which they engage in factional conflict, these are profit and honor and their opposites (for they may engage in
factional conflict in cities in order to avoid dishonor or punishment either
for themselves or for their friends).

35 (4) The causes and beginning points of the changes through which they
come to be in a state of the sort spoken of and concerning the things mentioned are in one sense seven in number, but in another sense more. (5) Of
these, two are the same as the ones spoken of, though not in the same way.
For men are stirred up against one another by profit and by honor—not in
40 order to acquire them for themselves, as was said earlier, but because they
1302b see others aggrandizing themselves (whether justly or unjustly) with respect
to these things. They are stirred up further by arrogance, by fear, by preeminence, by contempt, by disproportionate growth, and further, though in another manner, by electioneering, by underestimation, by [neglect of] small
things, and by dissimilarity.

CHAPTER 3

5 (1) Of these, the power that arrogance[6] and profit have, and the sense in
which they are causes, is fairly evident. For it is when those who are in office
behave arrogantly and aggrandize themselves that men engage in factional

6 · The Greeks had a highly developed aversion to "arrogance" (*hybris*) that needs to
be kept in mind throughout the discussion here. Elsewhere, Aristotle has this to say
about it: "And the man who is arrogant belittles his victim. For arrogance is doing and
saying things which bring shame to the victim, not in order that something may come
out of it for the doer other than the mere fact that it happened, but so that he may get
pleasure.... The cause of the pleasure enjoyed by those who are arrogant is that they
think that in doing ill they are themselves much superior. That is why the young and
the wealthy are arrogant. For they think that in being arrogant they are superior" (*Rhet.*
1378b23–29).

conflict—both against one another and against the regimes which provide
them license to do so. (Aggrandizement occurs sometimes at the expense of   10
private, sometimes at the expense of common funds.) (2) It is also clear what
the power of honor is, and in what sense it is a cause of factional conflict. Men
engage in factional conflict both when they themselves are dishonored and
when they see others honored. This occurs unjustifiably in cases where certain persons are either honored or dishonored contrary to their merit, and
justifiably in cases where it happens in accordance with their merit.

(3) There is factional conflict through preeminence when a certain person   15
or persons are greater in power than accords with the city and the power of
the governing body; from such persons there customarily arises a monarchy
or rule of the powerful. Hence in some places they have the custom of ostracism—at Argos and Athens, for example. It is better to see to it from the
beginning that no one is preeminent to such an extent, however, than to let   20
them arise and to heal the ill afterwards.

(4) Men engage in factional conflict through fear, both when they have
committed injustice and are frightened of paying the penalty, and when they
are about to suffer injustice and wish to forestall it—as at Rhodes, where the
notables joined together against the people on account of the suits being
brought against them.[7]

(5) Through contempt as well men engage in factional conflict and at-   25
tack one another—in oligarchies, for example, when those not taking part
in the regime are a majority (for they suppose themselves superior), and in
democracies, when the well off are contemptuous of the disorder and anarchy. In Thebes, for example, the democracy collapsed as a result of their be-   30
ing badly governed following the battle of Oenophyta, the one at Megara
through disorder and anarchy when they were defeated; and [contempt was
similarly aroused] in Syracuse prior to the tyranny of Gelo and by the people
in Rhodes prior to the revolt [of the notables].[8]

(6) Revolutions in regimes also occur through disproportionate growth
of a part. A body is composed of parts which must increase in proportion if   35
a balance is to be maintained, and if this does not happen it perishes—for
example, when a foot is four yards long and the rest of the body two feet

7 · The reference is probably to an oligarchical revolution in 390 BC (cf. Diodorus
Siculus 14.97).
8 · The battle of Oenophyta occurred in 457 BC; it is not known when the democracy
at Thebes was replaced by the oligarchy that governed there during the Peloponnesian
War. Gelon seized power at Syracuse in 491 BC. It is not known to what events the allusion to Megara refers.

high; and sometimes too it may be altered to the shape of another animal, if
40   the increase is not only quantitative but qualitative and contrary to propor-
1303a   tion. So too is a city composed of parts; and frequently an increase in one of
them is overlooked—for example, the multitude of the poor in democracies
and polities. (7) Sometimes this happens also through chance occurrences.
At Tarentum, for example, a democracy replaced a polity when many of the
5   notables were defeated and killed by the Iapygians shortly after the Persian
War.[9] At Argos, when those of the seventh[10] were killed by Cleomenes of
Sparta, they were compelled to accept in the regime some of their subjects;
and at Athens the notables became fewer as a result of their misfortunes on
10   land, because they campaigned during the Spartan War on the basis of an en-
rollment list of citizens.[11] (8) This happens in democracies as well, though
to a lesser extent. When there come to be more persons who are well off, or
when properties increase, they undergo revolution and become oligarchies
and regimes ruled by the powerful.

(9) Regimes undergo revolutions without factional conflict too, both
15   through electioneering—as at Heraea, where they had the officials chosen by
lot instead of by election because those engaging in electioneering were getting elected[12]—and through underestimation, when they allow persons who
are not friends of the regime to occupy the authoritative offices. In Oreus,
for example, the oligarchy was overthrown when Heracleodorus became one
20   of the officials: he instituted in place of the oligarchy a polity, or rather a democracy.[13]

(10) Further, regimes undergo revolution through [neglect of] small differences. I mean that a great shift in usages often occurs unnoticed when
a small thing is overlooked. In Ambracia, for example, the assessment was

9 · This occurred in 473 BC; see Diodorus Siculus 11.52, Herodotus 7.70.

10 · Probably a reference to the day of the month on which the battle was fought (cf.
Plutarch, *On the Virtues of Women* 4), but the meaning is uncertain. For the wars of
Cleomenes against Argos (early fifth century) see Herodotus 6.76–83.

11 · During the Peloponnesian War, members of the Athenian army were drawn from
a list of citizens of the wealthier classes, while the navy was manned by the poorer citizens. In Aristotle's time the army consisted primarily of mercenaries.

12 · It is important to keep in mind that selection to office by lot, not election, was regarded by the Greeks as characteristic of democracies. The term translated "electioneering" (*eritheia*) is rare and of uncertain meaning.

13 · Accepting the standard view of *kai* as epexegetic; but something may be wrong
with the text here. Oreus (also known by its older name Hestiaea; cf. 4.4), a town in
Euboea, revolted from Sparta and joined the Second Athenian League in 377 BC; the
change in regime may have been connected with this event.

small, and eventually they came to hold office with none at all, the assumption being that there was little or no difference between none and a small one.[14]

(11) Dissimilarity of stock is also conducive to factional conflict, until a   25
cooperative spirit develops.[15] For just as a city does not arise from any chance multitude, so it does not arise in any chance period of time. Hence those who have admitted joint settlers or later settlers [of different stock] have for the most part split into factions. For example, the Achaeans settled Sybaris   30
jointly with the Troezenians, but when the Achaeans came to be more numerous they expelled the Troezenians; this is what gave rise to the curse of the Sybarites.[16] (12) At Thurii, too, the Sybarites [became involved in factional conflict] with those who had settled it jointly with them: they claimed to merit aggrandizement on the grounds that the territory was theirs, and were driven out.[17] The later settlers were discovered conspiring against the Byzantines and were driven out after a battle; the Antissaeans expelled af-   35
ter a battle the Chian exiles they had admitted; the Zanclaeans were themselves driven out by the Samians they had admitted.[18] (13) The Apolloniates (those on the Black Sea) fell into factional conflict after bringing in later settlers; the Syracusans fell into factional conflict and battled one another   1303b
when they made citizens of foreigners and mercenaries after the period of the tyrants; and the Amphipolitans, after admitting later settlers from among the Chalcidians, were almost all driven out by them.[19]

(14) In oligarchies, as was said earlier, the many engage in factional conflict on the grounds that they are done an injustice because they do not par-   5
take of equal things in spite of being equal. In democracies the notables en-

14 · Nothing else is known of this revolution at Ambracia.

15 · Literally, "until they draw breath together," like horses in harness; cf. Plato, Laws 708d.

16 · Nothing else is known of these events, or of the curse (presumably connected with the destruction of Sybaris in 510 BC).

17 · For this incident see Diodorus Siculus 12.11.1, Strabo 6.1. 13.

18 · Nothing is known of the events at Byzantium or Antissa. The factional struggle at Zancle (Messina) was the result of the influx of refugees there following the suppression of the revolt of the Ionians against Persian rule in 494 BC; see Herodotus 6.22–24.

19 · Nothing is known of the events at Apollonia; the reference to Syracuse is to the period following the fall of the tyrant Thrasyboulus in 467 BC (cf. Diodorus Siculus 11.72.3); the expulsion of the original Athenian colonists of Amphipolis and the incorporation of the city into the Chalcidian Confederation probably occurred around 370 BC.

gage in factional conflict because they partake of equal things although they
are not equal.[20]

(15) Cities sometimes fall into factional conflict on account of location,
when the territory is not naturally apt for there being a single city. At Clazomenae, for example, those in Chytrus engaged in factional conflict against
10   those on the island; so also the Colophonians and Notians.[21] At Athens too
there is dissimilarity: those living in Peiraeus are more of the popular sort
than those living in town. (16) For just as in war the crossing of ditches, even
if they are very small, splits apart the ranks, so every difference, it appears,
15   makes a factional split. The greatest factional split is perhaps that between
virtue and depravity; then there is that between wealth and poverty, and so
on with others in varying degree, one of these being that just spoken of.

CHAPTER 4

(1) Factional conflicts arise, then, not over small things but from small
things—it is over great things that men engage in factional conflict. And
20   even small ones acquire great strength when they arise among those in authority, as happened in Syracuse, for example, in ancient times, when the
regime underwent a revolution because two young men who were holding
office came into conflict in connection with a love affair. (2) For when one
was away, the other, in spite of being his club mate, seduced his lover; the
25   first, enraged at him, induced his wife to commit adultery; afterwards they
attached to themselves the entire governing body and created a factional
split.[22] (3) Hence one should take precautions when such things are beginning so as to head off factional conflicts among leading and powerful persons. The error arises at the beginning, and the beginning is said to be "half
of the whole," so that even a small error there is comparable to any made
30   throughout the other parts.[23] (4) In general, the factional conflicts of the

20 · This paragraph seems out of place here; Newman has suggested transposing it to
follow 1.5 (1301a39).

21 · Chytrus was evidently a mainland dependency of the island city of Clazomenae;
Notium was the port of Colophon. Nothing is known of the events referred to.

22 · The episode is usually referred to the period of the oligarchy of the Gamori at Syracuse shortly before its overthrow by the people and the subsequent seizure of power by
the tyrant Gelon in 485 BC. Cf. Plutarch, *Precepts for Governing a Republic* 32.

23 · This sentence turns on an untranslatable pun on the word *archē*, which means
both "beginning" and "rule" or "government." "The beginning is half of the whole"
was a common Greek proverb.

notables are felt jointly by the entire city as well. In Hestiaea after the Persian Wars, for example, it happened that two brothers quarreled over the distribution of their inheritance: the one who was less well off, claiming the other had not declared the full extent of the property or the treasure their father had found, enlisted the popular element, while the other, who had much property, enlisted the well off.[24] (5) At Delphi, too, it was a quarrel arising from a marriage that was the beginning of all the later factional conflicts. The bridegroom, having come for the bride, took some accident as a bad omen and went away without her; the bride's relatives, considering this an act of arrogance, subsequently introduced some sacred objects among those he was sacrificing and then killed him for committing sacrilege.[25] (6) At Mytilene as well a factional conflict arising concerning heiresses was the beginning of many of their ills, in particular of the war against the Athenians, during which Paches took their city. Timophanes, one of the well off, left behind two daughters; and when Dexander was treated high-handedly and failed to obtain them for his sons, he initiated factional conflict and stirred up the Athenians, as he was their agent.[26] (7) Among the Phocians a factional conflict also arose from an heiress, involving Mnaseas the father of Mnason and Euthycrates the father of Onomarchus; this factional conflict was the beginning of the Sacred War for the Phocians.[27] The regime in Epidamnus also underwent revolution in connection with a marriage: someone had betrothed his daughter to a person whose father, as one of the officials, imposed a fine on him; feeling himself insulted, he attached to himself those who were outside the regime.[28]

(8) Regimes also undergo revolution into oligarchy, rule of the people, or polity as a result of an official board or a part of the city acquiring reputation in some way or growing. The council of the Areopagus, for example, as a result of the reputation it acquired during the Persian Wars, was held to have made the [Athenian] regime more strict; but then the seafaring mass, through being the cause of the victory at Salamis and, as a result of this, of the

24 · The episode, of which nothing else is known, must have occurred between 479 BC and the absorption of Hestiaea by Athens in 446.

25 · More details are given by Plutarch, *Precepts for Governing a Republic* 32.

26 · For the revolt of Mytilene against Athens during the Peloponnesian War, see Thucydides 3.2.

27 · Nothing else is known of this conflict or its relationship to political events in Phocis or to the outbreak of the Sacred War between Phocis and the Amphictyonic League in 356 BC. Mnason is said to have been a friend of Aristotle's.

28 · It is not certain whether this is the same revolution referred to in 1.10–11.

leadership the Athenians exercised on account of their power at sea, made
25   the democracy stronger.[29] (9) In Argos too the notables acquired reputation in connection with the battle of Mantinea against the Spartans, and
undertook to overthrow the rule of the people.[30] In Syracuse, the people,
as the cause of victory in the war against the Athenians, made a revolution
30   from polity to democracy.[31] At Chalcis the tyrant Phoxus was removed by
the people together with the notables, and the former immediately got hold
of the regime.[32] At Ambracia, similarly, the people joined with those who attacked Periander to expel him and then brought the regime around to themselves.[33] (10) In general, therefore, this should not be overlooked: those who
35   come to be a cause of power's being acquired, whether private individuals, offices, tribes, or generally a part or multitude of any sort, give rise to factional
conflict. For either those who envy their being honored initiate factional
conflict or they themselves are unwilling to remain on an equal footing on
account of their preeminence.

(11) Regimes undergo change also when parts of the city that are held to
1304b   be in opposition become equal to one another—for example, the wealthy
and the people—and there is nothing or very little in the middle. For if either of the parts is greatly preeminent, the one that remains is unwilling to
put itself at risk against one that is manifestly superior. (12) Hence those who
5   are outstanding for virtue do not engage in factional conflict to speak of; for
they are few against many.

Concerning all regimes universally, then, the beginning points and causes
of factional conflicts and revolutions stand in this manner. Regimes are
sometimes changed through force, sometimes through deceit. Force may be
10   used right at the beginning, or they may resort to compulsion later on. Deceit is also twofold. (13) Sometimes they use deceit at first and make revolution in the regime with the others willing, and then later on keep hold of it by

29 · The lowest class of Athenians (the so-called Thetes) had been excluded from all
military pursuits prior to their enlistment as rowers in the fleet at the time of the battle
of Salamis in 480 BC. Cf. *Ath. Pol.* 23; Plutarch, *Themistocles* 10.

30 · For this oligarchic revolution at Argos (418 BC), which was short lived, see
Thucydides 5.72.3, Diodorus Siculus 12.75.79–80.

31 · The responsibility of the Syracusan people for the victory over Athens in 413 BC
does not emerge clearly from the account of Thucydides, but Aristotle may have in
mind particularly the showing of the Syracusan fleet (Thucydides 7.41, 55). The primary democratic development occurring at this time appears to have been the use of
the lot in the selection of officials; cf. Diodorus Siculus 13.34.6.

32 · Nothing is known of this event.

33 · This occurred around 580 BC (Plutarch, *Amatorius* 23); see further 10.16.

force when the others are unwilling (at the time of the four hundred, for example, they deceived the people by asserting that the king [of Persia] would provide funds for the war against the Spartans, and having put out this lie attempted to keep hold of the regime[34]); but sometimes they both persuade   15
at the beginning and maintain the persuasion later on, and rule over willing persons. In a simple sense, then, revolutions occur in the case of all regimes as a result of the things spoken of.

CHAPTER 5

(1) What derives from these things should be split up and studied in the case of each kind of regime.

Now democracies undergo revolution particularly on account of the wan-   20
ton behavior of the popular leaders. On the one hand, by harassing individually those owning property they get them to combine (for common fear brings together even the worst enemies); on the other hand, they egg on the multitude publicly against them. One may see many cases where this hap-   25
pened. (2) At Cos the democracy underwent revolution when vicious popular leaders arose there, for the notables revolted.[35] At Rhodes the popular leaders provided pay to the people and at the same time prevented the triarchs' getting what was owed them, while these, on account of the suits   30
brought against them, were compelled to stand together and overthrow the rule of the people.[36] (3) The rule of the people was also overthrown in Heracleia immediately after the colony was settled on account of the popular leaders: the notables were treated unjustly by them and went into exile, but the exiles later gathered together and returned to overthrow the rule of the people.[37] (4) The democracy in Megara was also overthrown in a similar way.   35
The popular leaders, in order to be in a position to confiscate their goods, expelled many of the notables, until they had created many exiles, who then returned, defeated the people in battle, and established an oligarchy.[38] The
same thing happened in the case of the democracy at Cyme which was over-   1305a

---

34 · The reference is to the oligarchic regime of 411 BC in Athens.
35 · Nothing is known of this event.
36 · Cf. 3.4. Apparently, the popular leaders used money that was to be used for ship construction or repair to provide subsidies to the people for attendance at the assembly or similar activities.
37 · The city is probably Heracleia on the Black Sea, colonized from Megara in the middle of the sixth century; nothing else is known of these events.
38 · Nothing is known of this event, which is evidently the same one referred to in 3.5.

thrown by Thrasymachus.[39] (5) And one would see in studying other cases as well that revolutions occur just about in this manner. Sometimes, in order to win favor with the people, popular leaders treat the notables unjustly and cause them to combine, making them yield up their properties for redivision, or their revenues as a result of public services; sometimes they slander the wealthy in order to be in a position to confiscate their goods.

(6) In ancient times, when the same person was both popular leader and general, democracies underwent revolution into tyranny; most of the ancient tyrants arose from popular leaders. (7) The reason this happened then but does not now is that the popular leaders then came from those who served as generals, and were not particularly skilled at speaking, whereas now with the growth of rhetoric those who are capable speakers act as popular leaders, but on account of their inexperience in military matters they do not attempt anything, though this may have happened somewhere in rare cases. (8) Tyrannies arose more frequently earlier than now also because great offices were in the hands of individuals—as in Miletus one arose from the presidency, for the president had authority over many and great matters.[40] This happened further because cities then were not large: the people lived in the fields and were occupied by their work, while those who were heads of the people, when they became expert in military matters, attempted to set up a tyranny. (9) All of them did this having won the people's trust; this trust was based on their hostility toward the wealthy. At Athens, for example, Pisistratus claimed to merit becoming tyrant as a result of engaging in factional conflict with those of the plain;[41] Theagenes did so at Megara by slaughtering the cattle of the well off when he caught them grazing by the river, (10) and Dionysius by accusing Daphnaeus and the wealthy[42]—all winning trust on account of this enmity as being of the popular sort.

Democracies undergo revolution as well from traditional democracy to the most recent sort. Wherever offices are chosen by election, and this is not

39 · Nothing is known of this event.

40 · Possibly the tyranny of Thrasyboulus (Herodotus 1.20), but the reference is uncertain.

41 · Pisistratus became tyrant of Athens in 560 BC after making himself champion of the popular faction ("those of the hill") against the oligarchic faction ("those of the plain"); see Herodotus 1.59–64, *Ath. Pol.* 13 ff.

42 · Nothing is known of the incident involving Theagenes, tyrant of Megara in the seventh century. For the events connected with the accession of Dionysius as tyrant of Syracuse in 405 BC, see Diodorus Siculus 13.85–96.

done on the basis of assessments, and the people elect, those seeking office establish the people as having authority even over the laws in order to make themselves popular. (11) A remedy so that this will not occur, or will occur less, is to have the tribes vote for officials, not the entire people. Nearly all the 35 revolutions in democracies occur, then, for these reasons.

CHAPTER 6

(1) Of the modes in which oligarchies undergo revolution, two in particular are the most evident. One is when they treat the multitude unjustly. Any leader is then adequate to make revolution, particularly when the leader 40 comes from the oligarchy itself, as happened in Naxos in the case of Lygdamis, who later became tyrant of the Naxians.[43] (2) Factional conflict that 1305b has its beginning point from others[44] also involves several varieties. Sometimes the overthrow of an oligarchy comes about through the well off themselves—those not in the group that holds the offices, when those who do enjoy prerogatives are very few. This has happened at Massilia, for example, at Istrus, at Heracleia, and in other cities. (3) Those who had no share in the 5 offices sought change, until first the elder brothers could take part, and later the younger as well. (In some places father and son may not hold offices at the same time, in others an elder and younger brother.) The result was that 10 the oligarchy in Massilia became more like a polity, at Istrus it ended in rule of the people, and at Heracleia it went from being a small number to six hundred.[45] (4) At Cnidos too the oligarchy underwent revolution when the notables fell into factional conflict against one another because few took part in the offices—as was said, if a father took part, the son could not, and if 15 there were several brothers, only the eldest. For as this factional conflict proceeded the people stepped in, picked one of the notables as their head, attacked them, and conquered—for any group engaged in factional conflict is weak.[46] (5) And at Erythrae during the oligarchy of the Basilids in ancient

---

43 · Lygdamis became tyrant of Naxos around 540 BC; see Herodotus 1.61 and 64, *Ath. Pol.* 15.

44 · That is, apparently, from persons or groups other than the oligarchs themselves.

45 · Little is known of the internal history of these cities. For Massilia (Marseilles) cf. 6.7. 4; the Heracleia in question is probably the one on the Black Sea (cf. 5.3), where Istrus was also located.

46 · Nothing else is known of these events; the occasion referred to in 6.16 would appear to be different.

20   times, even though matters were well superintended by those in charge of
the regime, the people chafed at being ruled by a few and made a revolution
in the regime.[47]

(6) Oligarchies undergo change from within in the first place through the
rivalry of those seeking popularity. Popular leadership is twofold. One sort
25   involves the few themselves; for a popular leader may arise even among a very
few, as for example the thirty at Athens. For Charicles and those around
him became strong by seeking popularity with the thirty, and Phrynichus
and those around him among the four hundred in the same manner.[48]
The other is when those in the oligarchy seek popularity with the mass, as at
30   Larisa, for example, where the regime guardians[49] sought popularity with
the mass on account of their being elected, and in all oligarchies where those
who elect to offices are not those from whom the officials are drawn, but the
offices are filled from those with large assessments or those of certain clubs,
and election is by those having heavy arms or by the people (which was the
case at Abydus).[50] (7) This also happens wherever the courts are not drawn
35   from the governing body; for in seeking popularity with a view to judicial
decisions they make a revolution in the regime, as occurred at Heracleia on
the Black Sea.[51] It happens further when some draw the oligarchy into fewer
hands, for those who seek equality are compelled to bring in the people to
assist them.

40   (8) Revolutions in oligarchies also occur when they expend their private
wealth in wanton living. For such persons attempt sedition, and either aim
1306a   at tyranny themselves or help institute it for someone else (as Hipparinus
did for Dionysius at Syracuse).[52] At Amphipolis, someone named Cleoti-
mus brought in Chalcidian settlers and, once they were there, aroused them
to factional conflict against the well off.[53] (9) At Aegina, this sort of thing

47 · Nothing is known of this event. The Basilid family was presumably descended
from the original kings of the city.
48 · The regime of the "thirty tyrants" ruled Athens in 404/3 BC, that of the four
hundred in 411. See *Ath. Pol.* 28–38.
49 · Nothing is known of the nature of these officials. For the term *politophylakes*, see
2.8. 9.
50 · Regimes based on oligarchic "clubs" (*hetairiai*) were set up by the Spartan admiral
Lysander after the battle of Aegospotami (Plutarch, *Lysander* 13). A regime of this sort
may have arisen at Abydus at the time of its revolt from Athens in 411 BC.
51 · Nothing is known of this event. Cf. 5.3, 6.2–3.
52 · See Diodorus Siculus 13.92–94.
53 · Nothing is known of these events. Amphipolis had been originally settled by
Athenians, who remained few in comparison with inhabitants drawn from the region.

was the reason for the one who struck the bargain with Chares to attempt 5
revolution in the regime.[54] Sometimes, then, such persons immediately attempt some change; sometimes too they steal common funds, with the result
that either they themselves or those who resist their stealing initiate factional
conflict against the oligarchs, as happened at Apollonia on the Black Sea.[55]

(10) An oligarchy marked by concord is not easily ruined from within. 10
The regime at Pharsalus is an indication of this: they are few, but they have
authority over many because they treat one another finely.[56] But oligarchies
are overthrown as well when they make another oligarchy within the oligarchy. (11) This is when, the governing body as a whole being few, not all of 15
these few partake in the greatest offices. This happened at one time in Elis.
For while their regime was in the hands of a few, very few became senators because there were ninety of them serving for life, and their election was characteristic of rule of the powerful, similar to that of the senators at Sparta.[57]

(12) A revolution in oligarchies can occur both in peace and in war. 20
They occur in war when oligarchs are compelled to use mercenaries on account of their distrust of the people: if these are handed to a single person
to command, he often becomes tyrant, as was the case with Timophanes at
Corinth;[58] if to several, these set up a regime of the powerful for themselves.
Sometimes out of fear of these things oligarchs give a part in the regime to 25
the multitude as a result of being compelled to make use of the people. (13) In
peacetime, on account of their distrust of one another, they hand over their
defense to mercenaries and to a neutral official—who sometimes gains authority over both groups. This happened at Larisa in the case of the rule of
Simus and his followers among the Aleuads, and at Abydus at the time of the 30
clubs, one of which was that of Iphiades.[59]

---

54 · Chares was an Athenian mercenary commander; the attempted subversion of the
Aeginetan government may have occurred while he was stationed in Corinth in 367 BC,
but nothing else is known of the incident.

55 · Nothing is known of this event.

56 · Nothing is known of the oligarchy of Pharsalus in Aristotle's time; the city had had
a recent history of factional conflict (cf. Xenophon, *Hellenica* 6.1. 2 ff.), and was a political dependency of Macedon after 350 BC.

57 · Little else is known of the internal politics of Elis.

58 · Timophanes made himself tyrant of Corinth during the war with Argos (350 BC);
he was subsequently killed by his brother Timoleon (Plutarch, *Timoleon* 4).

59 · The Aleuads were one of the great feudal clans of Thessaly; Simus is probably the
Simus of Larissa who helped bring Thessaly into subjection to Philip of Macedon in
342 BC (Demosthenes, *On the Crown* 48, *Philippics* 3.26). Nothing is known of the incident in Abydus.

(14) Factional conflicts also arise when some of those in the oligarchy are treated by others in high-handed fashion in connection with marriages or lawsuits and driven into factional conflict. Where the cause is a marriage

35 there are, for example, those spoken of earlier as well as the oligarchy of the cavalrymen at Eretria, which Diagoras overthrew when he was done an injustice concerning a marriage.[60] (15) Factional conflict arose from a judicial decision in Heraclea and at Thebes, where punishment for adultery (in

1306b Heracleia of Eurytion, in Thebes of Archias) was imposed in a way that was both just and factious: out of rivalry their enemies had them pilloried in the marketplace.[61] (16) Many regimes have been overthrown, too, when the oligarchies had too many of the features of rule by a master, by those in the re-

5 gime who were resentful; this was the case with the oligarchy in Cnidus and with that in Chios.[62]

Revolutions also occur as a result of accident, both in so-called polity and in oligarchies in which they deliberate, adjudicate, and rule in the other offices on the basis of an assessment. (17) For frequently the assessment is ar-

10 ranged at first with a view to existing circumstances, so that the few will share in the oligarchy or middling persons in the polity; and it then happens that the same properties come to merit an assessment many times as great, as a result of prosperity that arises from peace or some other sort of good fortune,

15 so that all citizens come to share in all offices. Sometimes the revolution happens gradually and is overlooked, but sometimes it happens quickly.

(18) Oligarchies undergo revolution and factional conflict, then, through causes of this sort. Democracies and oligarchies generally sometimes also undergo alteration not into opposing sorts of regimes, but into those of the

20 same type—for example, from democracies and oligarchies of the sort that are under law into the [sort where the ruling element is wholly] authoritative, and from the latter into the former.

CHAPTER 7

(1) In aristocracies factional conflicts arise on the one hand on account of there being few who partake of the prerogatives, which was said to be what effects change in oligarchies as well; this is because aristocracy too is in some

25 sense an oligarchy. In both, the rulers are few, and though it is not on account

60 · The earlier discussion is 4.5–7. Nothing else is known of the overthrow of the Eretrian oligarchy (cf. *Ath. Pol.* 15).

61 · Nothing is known of these events.

62 · Nothing is known of the revolution in Chios; for Cnidus cf. 6.4.

of the same thing that they are few, aristocracy too is at any rate held to be a sort of oligarchy on account of these things. (2) This necessarily results above all when there is a certain multitude of persons who presume themselves to be similar on the basis of virtue—as for example the so-called Partheniae   30 at Sparta, who came from the peers and, when discovered conspiring, were sent off by them to Tarentum as settlers.[63] Or it results when those who are great and inferior to no one in virtue are dishonored by persons held in greater honor, as Lysander was by the kings, for example; (3) or when some-one of a manly sort does not partake of the prerogatives, such as the Cina-   35 don who instigated the attack on the Spartiates in the time of Agesilaus.[64] Further, it results when some persons are very poor and others well off, as happens most particularly during wars. This was the result, for instance, in Sparta at the time of the war with Messene. (4) This is clear from the poem of Tyrtaeus called "Good Governance": persons who were hard-pressed on   1307a account of the war claimed to merit a redivision of the land.[65] Further, it re-sults if someone who is great and has the capacity to be yet greater instigates factional conflict in order to become sole ruler, as Pausanias—the one who was general during the Persian War—is held to have done in Sparta, for ex-   5 ample, or Hanno in Carthage.[66]

(5) But both polities and aristocracies are overturned above all through a deviation from justice in the regime itself. The beginning point in polity is when democracy and oligarchy have not been finely mixed, and in aristoc-racy these things and virtue as well, though above all the two—I mean rule   10 of the people and oligarchy; for these are what both polities and most of the so-called aristocracies attempt to mix. (6) Aristocracies differ in this from what are named polities, and it is on account of this that the latter are more lasting, the former less so. For those regimes that incline more toward oligar-   15 chy they term aristocracies, and those inclining more toward the multitude,

---

63 · The Partheniae are variously said to have been the illegitimate offspring of Spar-tan fathers or Spartan mothers or disenfranchised citizens at the time of the First Mes-senian War in the late eighth century BC. "Peers" (*homoioi*, literally "similars") was a term used of the Spartiates, the Spartan citizen class.

64 · Lysander was the outstanding Spartan admiral of the final stage of the Pelopon-nesian War; for these incidents, see Xenophon, *Hellenica* 2.4. 29, Plutarch, *Lysander* 23. For the conspiracy of Cinadon in 398 BC, see Xenophon, *Hellenica* 3.3. 4–11.

65 · The reference is to the Second Messenian War in the seventh century BC. Tyrtaeus's "Good Governance" (*Eunomia*) is extant (frs. 2–5 Diehl).

66 · For Pausanias cf. 1.10 and 7.14.20. Hanno is probably the Carthaginian general who fought in Sicily against the elder Dionysius of Syracuse around 400 BC (Justin 20.5. 11 ff., 22.7. 10), but this is not certain.

polities; it is on this account that those of the latter sort are more stable than the former sort. For the majority is superior, and they are more content, as they have equality; (7) but those who are well off, if the regime gives them
20   preeminence, seek to act arrogantly and aggrandize themselves. In general, to whichever group the regime inclines, it is in that direction that it is transformed when either is able to enhance its position—polity into rule of the people, that is, and aristocracy into oligarchy; or it is in an opposite direction, [when either preeminent group weakens itself by acting unjustly,][67]— that is, aristocracy into rule of the people, when those who are poorer pull the regime around to its opposite on the grounds that they are being treated
25   unjustly, and polities into oligarchy, [when those who are better off make revolution on the grounds that] the only lasting thing is equality based on merit and having one's due. (9) What was just spoken of happened at Thurii. Offices having originally been [tightly restricted] on the basis of a rather large assessment, there was a shift to a smaller one and a larger number of official
30   boards; but the notables were nevertheless able to acquire between them all the land, contrary to the law (for the regime was still oligarchic and allowed them to aggrandize themselves in this way). [This led to factional conflict and civil war, with the notables operating from garrisoned strong points in the country and the people holding the city]. But the people, who had been trained for war, proved superior to the garrisons, until those having more than their share of the land voluntarily gave it up.[68] (10) Further, as all aris-
35   tocratic regimes have an oligarchic character, the notables tend to aggrandize themselves—even in Sparta, for example, properties are always coming into the hands of fewer persons.[69] It is also open to the notables to a greater extent to do whatever they wish and connect themselves by marriage with whomever they wish. Hence the city of the Locrians suffered as a result of the marriage connection with Dionysius—something that would not have
40   happened in a democracy, or in an aristocracy that has been well mixed.[70]
1307b   (11) Revolutions in aristocracies are particularly apt to be overlooked

67 · A line appears to have dropped out of the text at this point; I have supplied what I take to be the sense.
68 · Nothing else is known of these events at Thurii (which are probably unrelated to those mentioned in 3.12). I follow Dreizehnter in assuming a lacuna, and supply what I take to be the sense.
69 · Cf. 2.9. 13 ff.
70 · The reference is to the tyranny exercised at Locri (in southern Italy) during the 350s by Dionysius the Younger, son of Dionysius the Elder of Syracuse and a Locrian woman. See Diodorus Siculus 14.44.6.

because they are overturned by small steps, a point made in the earlier discourses universally with respect to all regimes—that even a small thing can
be a cause of revolution.[71] For once they abandon anything of what pertains to the regime, after this it is easier to effect another and slightly greater   5
change, until they change the entire order. (12) This too happened in the case
of the regime of Thurii. There being a law that one could be general only at
five year intervals, some of the younger men who had become expert in war
and developed a reputation with the multitude of garrison troops, holding
in contempt those who were in charge of affairs and considering it an easy   10
matter to prevail over them, undertook first of all to overturn this law, so
that it would be open to the same persons to be general continuously, since
they saw that the people would eagerly vote them in. (13) Those of the officials who were charged with this—the so-called councillors—set out at first
to oppose this, but were then persuaded, as they supposed that once these   15
had changed this law they would leave the rest of the regime alone; yet later,
when they wanted to prevent other things from being changed, they were no
longer able to do anything more, and the entire arrangement of the regime
underwent a revolution, becoming rule of the powerful of those who had attempted subversion.[72]

(14) All regimes are overturned sometimes from within themselves and   20
sometimes from outside, when an opposite sort of regime is either nearby or
far away but powerful. This is what happened in the case of the Athenians
and the Spartans: the Athenians overthrew oligarchies everywhere, and the
Spartans democracies.[73] Where revolutions in regimes come from, then, and
factional conflicts, has for the most part been spoken of.   25

CHAPTER 8

(1) We have to speak next about the preservation of regimes, both in common and separately for each sort. Now in the first place it is clear that if
we have an understanding of the things that destroy them, we will also have
an understanding of the things that preserve them; for opposites are productive of opposite things, and destruction is the opposite of preservation.   30
(2) In well-blended regimes, then, one should watch out to ensure there are
no transgressions of the laws, and above all be on guard against small ones.
Transgression of the laws slips in unnoticed, just as small expenditures con-

71 · The last phrase is probably a later gloss. Cf. 3.10.
72 · Nothing else is known of these events. Cf. 7.9, 3.12.
73 · The reference is to the period of the Peloponnesian War. Cf. 4.11.18–19.

35

40

1308a

sume a person's property when frequently repeated. (3) The expenditure goes unnoticed because it does not happen all at once: the mind is led to reason fallaciously by this, as in the sophistical argument "if each is small, so are all." This is so in one sense, but in another sense not. The whole and all things[74] are not something small, but are composed of small things.

(4) One must be on guard in the first instance, then, against this sort of beginning point [of destruction]. Next, one should not trust to those things that have been devised against the multitude, for they are thoroughly refuted by the facts. (As to which sort of devices in regimes we mean, this was spoken of earlier.[75])

5

(5) Further, one should see that not only some aristocracies but even some oligarchies last, not because the regimes are stable, but because those occupying the offices treat well those outside the regime as well as those in the governing body—those who do not have a part, by not acting unjustly toward them and by bringing into the regime those among them who have the mark of leaders, not acting unjustly toward the ambitious by depriving them of prerogatives or toward the many with regard to profit; and themselves and those who do have a part, by treating one another in a popular spirit. (6) For the equality that those of the popular sort seek for the multitude is not only just but advantageous for persons who are similar. Hence where there are a number of persons in the governing body, many legislative measures of a popular sort are advantageous, such as having offices be for six months, so that all those who are similar may take part in them. For similar persons are already a people, as it were, and hence popular leaders often arise among them, as was said earlier.[76] (7) Oligarchies and aristocracies will then be less apt to decline into rule of the powerful, for it is not easy for rulers to act as badly in a short time as over a longer one. Indeed, it is on this account that tyrannies arise in oligarchies and democracies. For those who aim at tyranny in either regime are either the greatest persons—the popular leaders in the one, the powerful in the other—or those who hold the greatest offices, when they rule for a long time.

10

15

20

25

(8) Regimes are preserved not only on account of the things that destroy them being distant, but sometimes also through their being nearby; for when men are afraid, they get a better grip on the regime. Thus those who take

74 · These expressions were commonly used to refer to the world or the universe.

75 · Cf. 4.13.1–5. "Devices" here and elsewhere translates *sophismata*, "sophistical schemes."

76 · Cf. 6.5–6.

thought for the regime should promote fears—so that they will defend and
not overturn the regime, keeping watch on it like a nocturnal guard—and   30
make the far away near.

(9) Further, one should try to guard against the rivalries and factional
conflicts of the notables, both through laws and by guarding against those
who are outside the rivalry getting caught up in it themselves—for to recognize an ill as it arises in the beginning belongs not to an ordinary person but
rather to a man expert in politics.

(10) With regard to the revolution from oligarchy and polity that oc-   35
curs on account of assessments, when this happens while the assessments
remain the same but money becomes abundant, it is advantageous to investigate what the amount of the common assessment[77] is compared with
that of the past (in cities which assess every year, on the basis of that period;   40
in larger ones, every third or fifth year), and if the amount is many times   1308b
greater or less than before at the time when the assessment rates for the regime were established, to have a law that tightens or relaxes the assessments—
if the total current amount exceeds the old, tightening the assessments in   5
proportion to the increase, if it falls short, relaxing the rate of assessment and
making it less. (11) If this is not done in oligarchies and polities, the result
in the one case is that in the latter an oligarchy arises and in the former rule
of the powerful, while in the other case a democracy arises from polity, and
from oligarchy a polity or rule of the people.[78]

(12) It is a thing common to rule of the people and oligarchy and to monar-   10
chy[79] and every regime not to allow any person to grow overly great contrary
to proportion, but to attempt to give small prerogatives over a long period of
time rather than great ones quickly[80] (for they become corrupted—it does
not belong to every man to bear good fortune), or failing this, at least not to   15
give them all at the same time and then take them back all at the same time,

77 · Reading *koinou* ("common") with the MSS rather than *kainou* ("new") with
Coraes and Dreizehnter: the "common assessment" is clearly a valuation of the total
assets of the citizen body. What the passage as a whole argues primarily is the need to
adjust property qualifications to take account of inflation or deflation in the currency.

78 · The first case reflects a deflationary, the second an inflationary situation.

79 · The words *kai en monarchiai* are omitted in Π²; Dreizehnter brackets them as a
gloss, probably rightly.

80 · Or possibly "but rather to attempt to give small prerogatives over a long period
of time or great ones briefly," reading *brachy* instead of the odd *tachy* ("quickly") of the
MSS. It is also conceivable that something has dropped out of the text here.

but rather gradually. Above all, one should try to shape matters by means of the laws so that there arises no one especially preeminent by the power of his friends or riches, or failing this, that such persons have sojourns abroad.[81]

20   (13) Since men also attempt subversion on account of their private lives, one should create an office to oversee those who live in a manner that is disadvantageous relative to the regime—in a democracy, relative to democracy, in an oligarchy, relative to oligarchy, and similarly for each of the other re-

25 gimes. For the same reasons, the prospering of a part of the city should be guarded against. (14) A remedy for this is always to place actions and offices in the hands of the opposing parts (I speak of the respectable as opposed to the multitude, and the poor as opposed to the well off), and to try either to

30 mix together the multitude of the poor and that of the well off, or to increase the middling element, for this dispels the factional conflicts that result from inequality.

    (15) But a very great thing in every regime is to have the laws and management of the rest arranged in such a way that it is impossible to profit from the offices. This is something that must be looked after particularly in oli-

35 garchies. (16) The many do not chafe as much at being kept away from ruling—they are even glad if someone leaves them the leisure for their private affairs—as they do when they suppose that their rulers are stealing common funds; then it pains them both not to partake in the prerogatives and not to share in the profits. (17) Indeed, the only way it is possible for democracy

40 and aristocracy to exist together is if someone instituted this. For it would
1309a then be possible for both the notables and the multitude to have what they want. Having it open to all to rule is characteristic of democracy; having the notables in the offices is characteristic of aristocracy. (18) But this is what

5 will happen when it is impossible to profit from the offices. The poor will not want to rule on account of not profiting, but rather will want to attend to their private affairs; the well off will be able to rule because they will need nothing from the common funds. The result for the poor is that they will become well off through spending their time at work; for the well off, that

10 they will not be ruled by ordinary persons. (19) To prevent the stealing of common funds, then, let the transfer of funds occur in the presence of all the citizens, and let records of this be deposited with each clan, company,[82] and

81 · The meaning of the word *parastaseis* ("sojourns") is not entirely certain: though usually considered to involve some form of ostracism (cf. Plato, *Laws* 855c), it could perhaps refer merely to official missions such as embassies or military commands.
82 · The term *lochos* is usually found in military contexts; here it perhaps refers to an organization of the common messes (cf. 2.5.17).

tribe. But to ensure profitless rule, there should be legislation assigning honors to those of good reputation.

(20) In democracies, the well off should be spared, not only by not having their possessions redivided, but not even their incomes, which in some regimes happens unnoticed; it is better to prevent them from taking on expensive but useless public services, such as leading choruses, officiating at torch races, and other similar things, even if they are willing. In oligarchy, on the other hand, much care should be taken of the poor, and offices from which gains accrue distributed to them, and if one of the well off behaves arrogantly toward them, the penalty should be greater than if toward one of their own. Also, inheritances should be passed on not by bequest but on the basis of family, and the same person should not receive more than one inheritance. In this way, properties would be more on a level, and more of the poor could establish themselves among the well off. (21) And it is advantageous both in a democracy and in an oligarchy to assign equality or precedence to those who share least in the regime—in rule of the people, to the well off, in oligarchy, to the poor—in all respects other than the authoritative offices of the regime; these should be kept in the hands only or mainly of those from the regime.

CHAPTER 9

(1) Those who are going to rule in the authoritative offices ought to have three things: first, affection for the established regime; next, a very great capacity for the work involved in rule; third, virtue and justice—in each regime the sort that is relative to the regime (for if justice is not the same in all regimes, justice must also necessarily have varieties). (2) When all of these things do not occur in the same person, the question arises how one ought to make a choice.[83] If, for example, someone were an expert general, but a vicious person and not friendly to the regime, and another were just and friendly, how should one make the choice? It would seem that one should look to two things: which of these do all share in to a greater extent, and which to a lesser? (3) In the case of generalship, then, one should look to experience rather than virtue, as all partake in generalship to a lesser extent, in respectability to a greater extent. For a guardian of property or a treasurer, however, the opposite is the case: this requires more virtue than the many possess, but the knowledge is common to all. (4) One might also raise the

15

20

25

30

35

40

1309b

5

83 · Or simply "a question arises," if Dreizehnter is correct in bracketing *pōs chrē poieisthai tēn hairesin* as a gloss.

question why, if the capacity is present as well as affection for the regime,
10   there is a need for virtue; for even the two will provide what is advantageous.
Or is it because it is possible for those who possess these two things to lack
self-control, so that just as they do not serve themselves by knowing and being friendly to themselves, there is nothing to prevent some persons from
being in this condition with respect to the community?[84]

(5) Simply speaking, whatever things in the laws we say are advantageous
15   to the regimes, all these preserve the regimes, as does the great principle that
has often been mentioned—to keep watch to ensure that the multitude
wanting the regime is superior to those not wanting it.[85]

(6) Besides all these things, one should not neglect—what is neglected
20   now by the deviant regimes—the middling element; for many of the things
that are held to be characteristically popular overturn democracies, and
many of those held to be characteristically oligarchic overturn oligarchies.
(7) Those who suppose this to be the single virtue pull the regime to an extreme, ignorant that just as a nose that deviates from the straightness that is
25   most beautiful toward being hooked or snub can nevertheless still be beautiful and appealing to look at, yet if someone tightens it further in the direction of an extreme he will in the first place eliminate any moderateness in the
part and eventually will go so far as to make it not even appear to be a nose,
on account of the preeminence and the deficiency of the opposites (and it is
30   the same with the other parts of the body as well), (8) so this is what results
in the case of regimes too. For it is indeed possible for an oligarchy or a democracy to be in an adequate condition in spite of departing from the best
arrangement. But if someone tightens either of them further, he will make
the regime worse first of all, and eventually not even a regime.

35   (9) Hence the lawgiver and the expert in politics should not be ignorant
of which of the characteristically popular things preserve democracy and
which destroy it, and which of the characteristically oligarchic things preserve oligarchy and which destroy it. For neither of these regimes can exist
40   and last without the well off and the multitude, and when a leveling of prop-
1310a   erty occurs, such a regime necessarily becomes a different one, so that in destroying [differences in property] by laws reflecting the preeminence [of the

84 · The argument is that knowledge and the proper disposition do not guarantee the
proper action because men lacking in virtue will be unable to control their passions.
There is a further question, however, as to whether even an education to virtue can
guarantee control of the passions. For an extended treatment of "lack of self-control"
(*akrasia*) see *Eth. Nic.* 1145a15–52a36.
85 · Cf. 4.9. 10, 12.1.

people], they destroy the regime.[86] (10) Errors are made both in democracies and in oligarchies. Popular leaders err in democracies where the multitude has authority over the laws: by always fighting with the well off they make   5
the city two cities, yet they should do the opposite, and always be held to be spokesmen for the well off. And in oligarchies the oligarchic leaders should be held to be spokesmen for the people, and they should swear oaths just the opposite of those oligarchic leaders swear now. (11) For there are some cities now where they swear: "I will bear ill will toward the people and take counsel to plan whatever ill I can against them." But they ought both to have and to   10
act as if they had the opposite conception, and declare in their oaths: "I will not act unjustly toward the people."

But the greatest of all the things that have been mentioned with a view to making regimes lasting—though it is now slighted by all—is education relative to the regimes. (12) For there is no benefit in the most beneficial laws,   15
even when these have been approved by all those engaging in politics, if they are not going to be habituated and educated in the regime—if the laws are popular, in a popular spirit, if oligarchic, in an oligarchic spirit. If lack of self-control exists in the case of an individual, it exists also in the case of a city. (13) But to be educated relative to the regime is not to do the things that oli-   20
garchs or those who want democracy enjoy, but rather the things by which the former will be able to run an oligarchy and the latter to have a regime that is run democratically. At present, however, in oligarchies the sons of the rulers live luxuriously, while those of the poor undergo exercise and labor, so   25
that they are both more inclined to attempt subversion and more capable of it; (14) on the other hand, in those democracies which are held to be most particularly democratic, what has become established is the opposite of what is advantageous. The cause of this is that they define freedom badly. For there are two things by which democracy is held to be defined: the majority having authority, and freedom. (15) Justice is held to be something equal; equality   30
requires that whatever the multitude resolves is authoritative, and freedom and equality[87] involve doing whatever one wants. So in democracies of this

86 · This sentence has been variously understood. The awkward language may conceal textual corruption; an easy emendation (*tous* for *tois* in 1310a1) would provide some improvement: "in destroying by laws those who enjoy preeminence [*phtheirontes tous kath' hyperochēn nomois*] they destroy the regimes." The implicit argument would seem to be that the destruction of the well off in democracies invariably prepares the way for tyranny.
87 · Reading *kai ison* ("and equality") with the MSS rather than bracketing the phrase with Spengel and Dreizehnter.

sort everyone lives as he wants and "toward whatever [end he happens] to
35 crave," as Euripides says.[88] (16) But this is a poor thing. To live with a view
to the regime should not be supposed to be slavery, but preservation.

Such, then, simply speaking, are the things that cause regimes to undergo
revolution and destruction and those through which they are preserved and
made to last.

CHAPTER 10

40 (1) It remains to address monarchy, and the things that are naturally apt to
1310b cause its destruction and its preservation. What happens in the case of kingships and tyrannies is very close to what has been spoken of in connection
with [republican] regimes.[89] (2) Kingship accords with aristocracy, while
tyranny is composed of the ultimate sort of oligarchy and of democracy—
5 hence it is the most harmful to the ruled, inasmuch as it is composed of two
bad regimes and involves the deviations and errors of both of them. (3) The
origin of each of these sorts of monarchy lies in exactly opposite circumstances. Kingship arose with a view to providing assistance to the respect-
10 able against the people; kings are selected from the respectable on the basis
of preeminence in virtue or in the actions that come from virtue, or on the
basis of preeminence of a family of this sort. The tyrant, however, arises from
the people or the multitude against the notables, in order that the people
15 not be done injustice by them. (4) This is evident from events: most tyrants
arose from popular leaders who were trusted because of their slanders of the
notables. (5) Some tyrannies were established in this fashion when cities had
already grown in size; some arose prior to these through kings who deviated
from traditional ways and strove for the sort of rule characteristic of a master;
20 some from persons elected to the authoritative offices, as in ancient times the
people selected magistrates and ambassadors for long periods of time; and
some in oligarchies that elected a single person with authority over the greatest offices. (6) It was easy for all of them to achieve their aim in these situa-
25 tions if only they wanted to do so, on account of the power they already had,
whether through kingly office or the power of their prerogative. For example,

88 · Euripides, fr. 891 Nauck² (from an unknown play).
89 · Throughout this chapter, a distinction is implied between "monarchies"—personal
rule whether kingly or tyrannical—and "regimes" (*politeiai*) in the sense of republican
or constitutional political orders. This usage seems to be confined to this part of book
5 of the *Politics* (though cf. 3.15.11), but it may be found in Isocrates and other contemporary writers.

Pheidon of Argos and others established themselves as tyrants where a kingship already existed, those in Ionia and Phalaris as a result of their prerogatives, and Panaetius at Leontini, Cypselus at Corinth, Pisistratus at Athens,   30
and Dionysius at Syracuse and others in the same manner as a result of their
popular leadership.[90]

(7) Now as we said, kingship is an arrangement that accords with aristocracy. For it accords with merit, whether based on individual virtue, virtue of
family, benefactions, or these things together with capacity. (8) For all those   35
who obtained this prerogative had benefited or were capable of benefiting
their cities or nations. Some kept them from being enslaved in war, such as
Codrus; others, such as Cyrus, liberated them, or founded a city or acquired
territory, such as the kings of the Spartans, Macedonians, and Molossians.[91]   40
(9) A king tends to be a guardian, seeing to it that those possessing property   1311a
suffer no injustice, and that the people are not treated with arrogance. Tyranny, as has often been said, looks to nothing common, unless it is for the
sake of private benefit. The tyrant's goal is pleasure; the goal of a king is the   5
noble. (10) Hence, of the objects of aggrandizement, material goods are characteristic of tyranny, while what pertains to honor is characteristic of kingship. It is characteristic of kingship that its defense is carried out by citizens;
of tyranny, that it is carried out by foreigners.[92]

(11) That tyranny has the evils both of democracy and of oligarchy is
evident.Having wealth as its end comes from oligarchy (for of necessity it   10
is only in this way that it can both defend itself and provide luxury), as does
its distrust of the multitude. Hence the sequestration of heavy arms, and the
fact that common to both — to tyranny as well as oligarchy — is ill-treatment
of the mass and its expulsion from town and resettlement.[93] (12) From de-   15
mocracy comes their war on the notables — doing away with them secretly
and openly, and exiling them as rivals in the art of ruling and impediments

90 · Pheidon was tyrant of Argos in the middle of the seventh century. Thrasyboulus
of Miletus, one of the best known of the Ionian tyrants, had risen from general, as was
also the case with Phalaris of Agrigentum (cf. *Rhet.* 1393b10 ff.).
91 · According to legend, Codrus saved Athens from a Dorian invasion while already
king; whether some other event is referred to is uncertain. The elder Cyrus liberated
the Persians from the rule of the Medes and became the first king of the Persian Empire
in the middle of the sixth century. The territory acquired by Sparta to which reference
is made is most probably Messenia. For the origins of Macedonia see Herodotus 8.138;
for the Molossian kingdom, see Plutarch, *Pyrrhus* 1.
92 · One of the clearest indicators of a tyrannical regime was the presence of a bodyguard of foreign troops.
93 · This was done, for example, by the thirty at Athens (Xenophon, *Hellenica* 2.4. 1).

to their rule. For it is from these that conspiracies arise—both of those who
20   wish to rule themselves and those who do not want to be enslaved. (13) Hence
the piece of advice that Periander gave to Thrasyboulus, the lopping off of
the preeminent ears, the assumption being that it is necessary always to eliminate the preeminent among the citizens.[94]

As has in effect been said, one should consider the beginning points of
25   revolutions to be the same in monarchies as in [republican] regimes. For it is
on account of injustice, fear, and contempt that the ruled in many cases attack monarchies (with respect to injustice it is through arrogance above all,
but sometimes also through seizure of private possessions). (14) The ends
30   are also the same there as in connection with tyrannies and kingships; for
the wealth and honor belonging to monarchs are of such a magnitude that
all strive after them. Some attacks are carried out against the person of the
rulers, some against the office. Those owing to arrogance are against the person. (15) Though arrogance is of many sorts, each of them gives rise to anger,
35   and most of those who are angry attack for the sake of revenge rather than
preeminence. The attack on the Pisistratids, for example, took place because
of the abusive treatment of Harmodius's sister and the insult of Harmodius
(for Harmodius attacked because of his sister, and Aristogeiton because of
40   Harmodius).[95] (16) They also conspired against Periander, the tyrant in Am-
1311b   bracia, because when drinking with his favorite he asked whether he was yet
pregnant by himself. The attack on Philip by Pausanias was because Philip let
him be treated arrogantly by Attalus and those around him; that on Amyn-
5   tas the Little by Derdas because Amyntas made fun of his youth; that of
the eunuch against Euagoras of Cyprus on the grounds of arrogant treatment, because Euagoras's son had taken away his wife.[96] (17) Many attacks
have also occurred because of the disgraceful behavior of certain monarchs
toward the person of others. For example, the attack of Crataeus on Arche-
10   laus—he was always resentful of their relationship, so that even a lesser excuse would have been adequate, but he did it because Archelaus gave none
of his daughters to him although he had agreed to do so, but the eldest he
gave to the king of Elimeia when he was hard pressed in the war against Sir-

---

94 · Cf. 3.13.17.

95 · For the fall of the Pisistratid tyranny at Athens, see *Ath. Pol.* 18, Thucydides 6.54.

96 · For Periander cf. 4.9. Philip of Macedon was murdered by the youth Pausanias
in 336 BC (Diodorus Siculus 16.91–94); nothing is known of the incident involving
Derdas and Amyntas, who was almost certainly another Macedonian king; a fuller account of the murder of Euagoras of Cyprus in 374/3 BC is provided by Theopompus
(*FGH* 115F103.12).

ras and Arrabaeus, and the younger to his son Amyntas, supposing that this
would be likely to prevent him from quarreling with his son by Cleopatra;   15
but the beginning point of their estrangement was his resentment at the sexual favors [he provided Archelaus]. (18) Hellanocrates of Larisa joined him
in the attack for the same reason: because Archelaus made use of his youth
and yet kept refusing to restore him to his home although he had promised
to do so, he supposed the relationship had come about as a result of arrogance rather than erotic desire.[97] Python and Heracleides of Aenus did away   20
with Cotys to avenge their father, and Adamas revolted against Cotys on
the grounds of arrogant treatment, because he had been castrated by him
as a child.[98] (19) And many, in anger at physical outrages and feeling arro-   25
gantly treated, have killed, or attempted to, persons holding office or with
royal connections.[99] For example, when the Penthilids at Mytilene went
around and struck people with clubs, Megacles and his friends attacked and
eliminated them; and later, Smerdis killed Penthilus after being beaten and
dragged away from his wife.[100] (20) Decamnichus became leader of the at-   30
tack on Archelaus, having been the first to stir up the attackers; the reason
for his anger was that Archelaus had handed him over to the poet Euripides
for whipping—Euripides was enraged at something he had said about the
smell of his breath.

(21) And many others have been eliminated or conspired against for   35
reasons of this sort. And similarly through fear (for this was one of the
causes mentioned earlier, in monarchies as in case of [republican] regimes).
Artapanes, for example, [killed] Xerxes out of fear of being accused in connection with Darius, whom he had had hanged without orders from Xerxes,
but on the supposition that he would forgive him on account of his forget-   40
fulness when carousing.[101]

(22) Other attacks have been undertaken on account of contempt, as   1312a
when someone saw Sardanapalus carding wool with the women, if what the
retailers of stories say is true (though if not of him, this might well be true of

97 · For the murder of Archelaus of Macedon in 399 BC, see Diodorus Siculus 14.37.5,
Aelian 8.9, Plutarch, *Amatorius* 23.

98 · Cotys, king of the Thracians, was murdered in 359 BC.

99 · The phrase is *basilikai dynasteiai*. Cf. Plato, *Laws* 711d.

100 · The Penthilids were apparently the leading family in the oligarchy of Mytilene;
these events (which date from the seventh century) are alluded to in the poetry of
Alcaeus (fr. 22 ff. Diehl).

101 · For the murder of Xerxes, the Persian king, in 465 BC, see Diodorus Siculus
11.69, Justin 3.1, Ctesias, *FGH* 688F13.33.

5   another); (23) and Dion attacked Dionysius the Younger because of his contempt for him, when he saw the citizens in the same condition and Dionysius
himself always drunk.[102] Even certain of their friends attack them through
contempt, for they feel contempt because they are trusted and will escape
notice [when conspiring]. (24) Those who suppose they are capable of tak-
10   ing control of the office also in a manner attack on account of contempt:
they make the attempt easily, as they feel themselves capable and feel contempt for the danger on account of their capacity. Thus generals attack their
monarchs—as Cyrus attacked Astyages, for example, out of contempt both
for his way of life and his power, because his power had deteriorated while
he himself lived luxuriously, and the Thracian Seuthes attacked Amadocus
15   when he was his general.[103] (25) Some also attack for several of these reasons, for example, both out of contempt and through profit, as Mithridates
attacked Ariobarzanes.[104] The attempt is made for this reason above all by
those who are bold in their nature and hold a military prerogative from their
20   monarchs; courage coupled with power produces boldness, and it is on account of both of these that they attack, on the assumption that they will conquer easily.

Of those who attack through ambition the cause operates in a different
manner than in the case of those spoken of before. (26) Some make an attempt against tyrants because they see both great profits and great prerogatives in store for them, but this is not why each of those attacking through
25   ambition deliberately chooses to court danger: the former do it for the reason mentioned, the latter make an attempt against monarchs because they
30   want not a monarchy but reputation, just as in the case of any other extraordinary action from which men acquire a name and become notable in the eyes
of others. (27) Those who are impelled by this sort of reason are, to be sure,
very few in number, for underlying this there must be a lack of all thought

102 · The reference to "retailers of stories" (*hoi mythologountes*) would seem to be particularly to Ctesias, the historian of the Persian court (see *FGH* 688F1.23–27 for his
account of Sardanapalos). For the fall of Dionysius II of Syracuse in 357 BC, see Plutarch, *Dion* 22 ff.

103 · Aristotle appears to assume, contrary to most authorities, that Cyrus was not
also the grandson of Astyages, the king of the Medes; cf. Herodotus 1.107–30, Ctesias,
FGH 688F9. For Seuthes and Amadocus, king of the Odrysians, cf. Xenophon, *Hellenica* 4.8. 26.

104 · Probably a reference to the Ariobarzanes who was satrap of the Persian province
of Pontus in the mid-fourth century, but this is not certain. A lacuna or some dislocation in the text has been suspected here.

for preservation in the event the action is not successful. (28) Accompanying
them should always be the conception of Dion, though it is not easy for this
to arise in many persons: he set off on the campaign against Dionysius with   35
a few followers and asserting that matters stood with him in such a way that,
however far he was able to proceed, it was enough for him to have that much
of a part in the action—for example, if it should happen that he met his end
after just setting foot on land, that death would be a noble one for him.

(29) One mode in which tyranny is destroyed, just as in the case of each of   40
the other regimes, is from outside, if there is some regime opposite [in type]   1312b
that is stronger. (The wish to destroy it will be present on account of the opposition implied by the choice [of regime type]; and what men want to do,
all do who are capable of it). (30) But [republican] regimes are [necessarily]
opposed—rule of the people to tyranny in accordance with Hesiod's "potter   5
against potter,"[105] since the extreme sort of democracy is a tyranny; kingship
and aristocracy because of the opposition of the regime. Hence the Spartans
overthrew very many tyrannies, as did the Syracusans during the period they
were governed finely.

(31) Another mode in which tyranny is destroyed is from within itself,
when those sharing power fall into factional conflict, as in the tyranny of   10
Gelo and his family, and in that of Dionysius and his family today. The tyranny of Gelo was destroyed when Thrasyboulus, the brother of Hiero, sought
popularity with Gelo's son and impelled him toward pleasures, so that he
might rule himself; [though succeeding in this, Thrasyboulus aroused the
opposition of others in the family. When this conflict became evident to
the notables, some began to take up arms; the result was that] the kin combined together so that the tyranny would not be entirely overthrown, but
only Thrasyboulus, while those among [the notables] who had combined,   15
having the occasion, expelled all of them.[106] (32) Dion, who was connected

105 · A proverbial expression for the rivalry of like with like (*Works and Days* 22 ff.).
106 · This compressed and obscure account of the fall of the dynasty of Gelon in Syracuse (466 BC) almost certainly involves textual corruption: probably several lines have
been lost describing the intervention of other elements in the city in the quarrel between Thrasyboulus and the adherents of Gelon's son; I have tried to supply the sense.
It is stated in 12.6 that Thrasyboulus ruled as tyrant for ten months following the death
of Hiero; it would seem that he was able to eliminate Gelon's son from the succession,
but only at the price of fatally weakening the position of the entire family with respect
to the notables or some section of them, who rose up and instituted an aristocracy or
polity. Cf. Diodorus Siculus 11.66–67.

by marriage with Dionysius, campaigned against him and, getting the people on his side, expelled him, and was himself killed.

There are two reasons for which they attack tyrannies above all, hatred and contempt. The former of these, hatred, always exists for tyrants, and many have been overthrown as a result of contempt. An indication of this is that most of those who acquired their offices also defended them, while their successors all perished immediately, so to speak. For because they live a life of gratification they fall easily into contempt and provide many occasions for others to attack them. Anger too should be regarded as a part of hatred, for in a certain manner it acts as a cause of the same actions. (34) Often, indeed, it is more conducive to action than hatred: they attack in more determined fashion on account of the passion not using calculation (it particularly happens that they let themselves follow their spiritedness as a result of arrogance, which is the reason the tyranny of the Pisistratids was overthrown and many others), while hatred does this to a greater extent. (35) For anger is accompanied by pain, so that it is not easy to calculate, while enmity is without pain.

To speak summarily, whatever causes we spoke of in the case both of the unmixed and final sort of oligarchy and of the extreme sort of democracy are to be regarded as causes in the case of tyranny as well; for these regimes happen to be tyrannies divided [among many persons].

(36) Kingship is destroyed least of all by things outside itself, and hence is long-lasting; most of the sources of destruction are internal. It is destroyed in two modes: one when those sharing in the kingship fall into factional conflict, the other mode when they try to administer it in more tyrannical fashion, and claim to merit authority over more matters and contrary to the law. (37) Kingships no longer arise today; if monarchies do arise, they tend to be tyrannies. This is because kingship is a voluntary sort of rule, with authority over relatively great matters, but [today] there are many persons who are similar, with none of them so outstanding as to match the extent and the claim to merit of the office. So on this account men do not voluntarily endure it; and if someone should rule through deceit or force, this is already held to be a sort of tyranny. (38) In kingships based on family one should regard as a cause of destruction, in addition to the ones spoken of, the fact that many kings are easy to hold in contempt, and that they behave arrogantly in spite of possessing only a kingly prerogative and not tyrannical power. For their overthrow used to be easy: one ruling unwilling persons will immediately cease to be king, while the tyrant rules even over unwilling persons. Monarchies are destroyed, then, through these and other such causes.

CHAPTER 11

(1) It is clear that they are preserved, on the other hand, by opposite things simply speaking, and in the case of kingships in particular, by drawing them toward greater moderateness. For the fewer the things over which kings have   20
authority, the greater the period of time their rule as a whole will necessarily last: they themselves are less like masters and more equal in their characters, and are less envied by those they rule. (2) It is on this account that the kingship of the Molossians has lasted for a long time, and also that of the Spar-   25
tans, both because the office was divided from the beginning into two parts and because Theopompus moderated it, among other things by establishing in addition the office of the overseers. By taking away from its power, he increased the duration of the kingship, and so in a certain manner made it not less but greater. (3) This is just what he is supposed to have answered his wife   30
when she asked him whether he was not ashamed to hand over to his sons a kingship that was lesser than the one he had received from his father, and he said: "Not at all—I am handing over one that will be longer lasting."[107]

(4) Tyrannies are preserved in two modes that are quite opposite to one another. One is the mode that has been handed down, according to which   35
most tyrants administer their rule. Most of these [tyrannical methods] are said to have been established by Periander of Corinth; many such things may also be seen in the rule of the Persians. (5) These include both what was spoken of some time ago as relating to the preservation (so far as this is pos-
sible) of tyrannies—lopping off the preeminent and eliminating those with   40
high thoughts—and also not permitting common messes, clubs, education,   1313b
or anything else of this sort, but guarding against anything that customar-
ily gives rise to two things, high thoughts and trust. Leisured discussions are not allowed, or other meetings connected with leisure,[108] but everything is done to make all as ignorant of one another as possible, since knowledge   5

---

107 · Cf. 2.9. 29–30, 3.14.3–4. The attribution of the establishment of the overseers to Theopompus, king of Sparta in the late eighth century BC, is not found before Aris-totle; cf. Plato, *Laws* 692a. Little is known of the political institutions of the relatively primitive Molossians; cf. Plutarch, *Pyrrhus* 5.

108 · The term *scholai* ("leisured discussions") is probably meant to apply to gatherings for philosophical and literary discussion of the sort represented in many Platonic dia-logues, as well as to "schools" such as Aristotle's Lyceum; other "meetings connected with leisure" (*syllogoi scholastikoi*) probably include gatherings at gymnasia and social and religious functions.

tends to create trust of one another. (6) Also, residents of the city are made to be always in evidence and pass their time about the doors [of the tyrant's palace];[109] in this way their activities would escape notice least of all, and they would become habituated to having small thoughts through always acting like slaves. And there are other such features of tyranny, in Persia and among the barbarians, which have the same power. (7) Also, to attempt to let nothing that is done or said by any of those he rules escape his notice, but to have spies, like the women called "inducers" at Syracuse, and the "eavesdroppers" Hiero sent out whenever there was some meeting or gathering (for men speak less freely when they fear such persons, and if they do speak freely they are less likely to escape notice).[110] (8) Also a feature of tyranny is to slander them to one another, and set friends at odds with friends, the people with the notables, and the wealthy with themselves. It is also a feature of tyranny to make the ruled poor, so that they cannot sustain their own defense,[111] and are so occupied with their daily needs that they lack the leisure to conspire. (9) Examples of this are the pyramids in Egypt, the monuments of the Cypselids, the construction of the temple of Olympian Zeus by the Pisistratids, and the work done by Polycrates on the temples at Samos.[112] All of these things have the same effect—lack of leisure and poverty on the part of the ruled. (10) There is also the matter of taxes, as in Syracuse, where in the time of Dionysius it happened that they were taxed for their entire property over a period of five years. The tyrant is also a warmonger, so that they will always be kept lacking in leisure and in need of a leader. Kingship is preserved by friends of the king, but it is characteristic of the tyrant to distrust his friends, on the assumption that all wish to overthrow him, but these are particularly capable of it.

109 · A practice of Persian origin; see Xenophon, *Education of Cyrus* 8.1. 6–8, 16–20.

110 · This was also a well-known Persian practice (Xenophon, *Education of Cyrus* 8.2. 10–12). For its use by the tyrants of Syracuse, see Plutarch, *Dion* 28.

111 · The meaning of this phrase is uncertain; it seems to refer to the ability of the citizens to afford heavy arms, but the word *phylakē* has sometimes been interpreted as implying some sort of standing military force. Absence of heavy arms would seem to be the "incapacity" referred to in 16.

112 · The monuments of the Cypselids (the family of Periander of Corinth) were votive statues erected in the sanctuaries in Olympia and Delphi, the most noteworthy being a colossal golden statue of Zeus at Olympia (cf. Plato, *Phaedrus* 236b). The temple of Olympian Zeus at Athens was begun by Pisistratus (cf. Pausanias 1.18.6–9). The exact sense of the reference to Polycrates is uncertain; I take it to refer to statuary rather than temple structures (cf. Herodotus 3.60).

(11) Everything that happens in connection with democracy of the extreme sort is characteristic of tyranny—dominance of women in the household, so that they may report on their husbands, and laxness toward slaves 35 for the same reasons. Slaves and women do not conspire against tyrants, and as they prosper under such circumstances they necessarily have a benevolent view both of tyrannies and of democracies (for, indeed, the people wish to be a monarch). (12) Hence also the flatterer is held in honor by both—the pop- 40 ular leader by peoples, as the popular leader is a flatterer of the people, and by tyrants, persons approaching them in obsequious fashion, which is the work 1314a of flattery. On this account tyranny is friendly to the base, for they delight in being flattered, and no one would do this who had free thoughts: respectable persons may be friends, but they will certainly not flatter. (13) And the base are useful for base things: "nail [is driven out] by nail," as the proverb 5 has it. It is also a feature of tyranny not to delight in anyone who is dignified or free; for the tyrant alone claims to merit being such, and one who asserts a rival dignity and a spirit of freedom takes away the preeminence and the element of mastery of tyranny; hence these are hated as persons undermining the tyrant's rule. (14)It is also characteristic of the tyrant to have foreigners 10 rather than persons from the city as companions for dining and entertainment, the assumption being that the latter are enemies, while the former do not act as rivals.

Such things are, then, characteristic of tyrants and help preserve their rule—though in no respect do they fall short in depravity. All of these things are encompassed, so to speak, under three heads. (15) For tyranny aims at 15 three things: one, that the ruled have only modest thoughts (for a small-souled person will not conspire against anyone); second, that they distrust one another (for a tyranny will not be overthrown before some persons are able to trust each other—hence they make war on the respectable as being harmful to their rule not merely because they claim not to merit being ruled 20 in the fashion of a master, but also because they are trustworthy, both among themselves and with respect to others, and will not denounce one another or others); (16) and third, an incapacity for activity,[113] for no one will undertake something on behalf of those who are incapable, so that not even a tyranny will be overthrown where the capacity is lacking. The defining prin- 25 ciples to which the wishes of tyrants may be reduced are, then, these three.

113 · The meaning of the phrase "incapacity for activity" (*adynamia tōn pragmatōn*) is uncertain, but Aristotle seems to have in mind economic and military as well as political weakness.

For one might reduce all things characteristic of tyranny to these presuppositions—that they not trust one another, that they not be capable, that they have modest thoughts.

30   (17) The one mode of preservation for tyrannies, then, is of this sort; the other involves a sort of superintendence that is practically the opposite of what has been spoken of. (18) One may grasp this in connection with the destruction of kingships. For just as one mode of destruction for kingship

35   is to make the rule more tyrannical, so it is a source of preservation for tyranny to make it more kingly, provided one thing only is safeguarded—his power,[114] so that he may rule not only willing persons, but also those who are unwilling; for if this is thrown away, so is the tyranny. (19) This must remain as a presupposition, then, but in whatever else he does or is held to do

40   he should give a fine performance of the part of the kingly ruler. In the first
1314b place, he should be held to take thought for the common funds, not only by not making expenditures on gifts that enrage the multitude (when they take from persons working and exerting themselves in penury, and give lavishly

5   to prostitutes, foreigners, and artisans), but also by rendering an account of what has been taken in and what expended, as some tyrants have in fact done in the past. One administering matters in this way might be held a manager [of the city] rather than a tyrant. (20) There is no need to be afraid of running short of funds, since he has authority in the city; and, in any event, for

10   tyrants who are campaigning away from their own territory this is even more advantageous than leaving behind a great hoard, as in that case those safeguarding the city would be less likely to attack his position (such persons are more fearsome to tyrants when they are away from home than the citizens, for the latter are away with him, but the former remain behind). (21) Next,

15   he should make a show of collecting taxes and public services for the sake of management of the city, particularly if something should be needed for use in times of war, and he should generally present himself as guardian and treasurer of common rather than private funds.

He should appear not harsh but dignified, and further, of such a sort that
20   those encountering him feel awe rather than fear. (22) This is not easy to achieve, however, for one who is readily held in contempt. Hence, though he may concern himself with none of the other virtues, he must concern himself with military[115] virtue, and create a reputation of this sort for himself.

114 · The word *dynamis* ("power") can also refer to a military force, and it is possible that Aristotle thinks primarily or exclusively of the tyrant's bodyguard.

115 · Accepting Madvig's conjectural *polemikēs* for the *politikēs* ("political") of the MSS.

Further, not only should he himself avoid any appearance of arrogant behavior toward any of those he rules, including youths and girls, but so also   25
should those around him. (23) Their women, too, should stand in a similar
relation to other women, for many tyrannies have perished on account of the
arrogant behavior of women. In connection with bodily gratifications, they
should do the opposite of what certain tyrants now do: not only do they engage in this beginning at dawn and continuing for many days, but they wish   30
to be seen doing so by others, so that they will be admired as persons who are
happy and blessed. (24) On the contrary, he ought to be moderate in such
matters, or if not, at least he should avoid appearing so to others. It is the
drunkards, not the sober, the drowsy, not the wakeful, who are readily at-   35
tacked and held in contempt.

Indeed, what must be done is the opposite in nearly every case of the
things mentioned previously. He must furnish and adorn the city as if he
were a steward rather than a tyrant. (25) Further, he must always show himself to be seriously attentive to the things pertaining to the gods. For men are   49
less afraid of being treated in some respect contrary to the law by such persons, if they consider the ruler a god-fearing sort who takes thought for the   1315a
gods, and they are less ready to conspire against him as one who has the gods
too as allies. In showing himself of this sort, however, he must avoid silliness.
(26) He should also honor those who have proven themselves good in some
respect, and in such a way that they consider they would not have been hon-   5
ored more by citizens living under their own laws. He should distribute such
honors himself; but punishments should be administered through others—
through officials and courts.

(27) A precaution common to every sort of monarchy is to make no single
person great but where necessary to elevate several persons, as they will watch
one another. Or if it is necessary after all to make one person great, it should   10
at least not be someone who is of a bold character; such a character is most
ready for the attack in connection with every sort of action. And if it is held
necessary to remove someone from power, this should be done gradually—
his functions should not all be taken away at once. (28) Further, he should
refrain from every sort of arrogance, and from two above all the rest: that in-   15
volving bodily abuse, and that involving [taking sexual advantage of] youth.
This precaution is to be taken particularly in connection with ambitious persons. A slight affecting their material goods bears heavily on the greedy; a
slight involving dishonor bears heavily on the ambitious and the respectable among human beings. (29) Hence he must either not engage in such   20
things, or else be seen to administer punishments in a paternal spirit rather

than in order to slight, to engage in relations with the young for erotic reasons and not because of [a desire to flaunt] the license [he enjoys], and generally to compensate for any acts that are held to involve dishonor with greater honors.

(30) Of those who make attempts at assassination, the ones who are most to be feared and require the most precautions are those who deliberately choose not to try to save their lives once they have carried out the assassination. (31) Hence he must beware particularly of those who consider him to have behaved arrogantly either toward themselves or toward those they cherish; for those who undertake such a deed out of spiritedness are not sparing of themselves. As Heraclitus said, "it is hard to fight with spiritedness," as it "pays the price of soul."[116]

(32) Since cities are constituted out of two parts, human beings who are poor and others who are well off, both should conceive that they are being preserved and that neither is being treated unjustly by the other on account of the tyrant's rule. But whichever is stronger, these he should particularly attach to his rule, so that, his position being enhanced in this way, there will be no necessity for the tyrant to effect a freeing of slaves or a sequestration of heavy arms. For the addition of one of these parts to his power is enough to make them superior to any attackers.

(33) To speak of such matters in detail would be superfluous. The aim is evident: he should appear to the ruled not as a tyrannical sort but as a manager and a kingly sort, not as an appropriator of the things of others but as a steward. He should pursue moderateness in life, not the extremes; further, he should seek the company of the notables, but seek popularity with the many. (34) As a result of these things, not only will his rule necessarily be nobler and more enviable by the fact that he rules over persons who are better and have not been humbled and does so without being hated and feared, but his rule will also be longer lasting; further, in terms of character he will either be in a state that is fine in relation to virtue or he will be half-decent—not vicious but half-vicious.

CHAPTER 12

(1) Oligarchy and tyranny are, however, the most short-lived regimes. The tyranny of Orthagoras's sons and of Orthagoras himself at Sicyon existed

---

116 · That is, spiritedness seeks satisfaction even if the price is death. Heraclitus, fr. 85 DK.

for the longest period; it lasted a hundred years. The reason for this was that   15
they treated the ruled moderately and in many respects were slaves to the
laws; also, because Cleisthenes was a warlike sort he could not readily be held
in contempt, and in many respects they sought popularity by acts of concern.[117] (2) It is said of Cleisthenes, at any rate, that he gave a crown to the
person who denied him victory in a competition; some assert that the statue   20
of a seated person in the marketplace there is a representation of the one who
gave this judgment. They also assert that Pisistratus once put up with being
summoned as defendant in a suit before the Areopagus.[118]

(3) The second longest was that of the Cypselids at Corinth. This went on
for seventy-three years and six months. Cypselus was tyrant for thirty years,   25
Periander for forty and a half,[119] and Psammetichus the son of Gorgus for
three years. (4) The reasons are the same in this case: Cypselus was a popular
leader, and went without a bodyguard throughout his entire rule; Periander,
though a tyrannical sort, was at the same time warlike.[120]

(5) The third was that of the Pisistratids at Athens, though it was not con-   30
tinuous. Pisistratus twice went into exile when tyrant, so that in thirty-three
years he was tyrant for seventeen of these; his sons ruled for eighteen years,
so that altogether it existed for thirty-five years.[121]

(6) Of those remaining, the longest was that connected with Hiero and
Gelo at Syracuse. Yet not even this lasted long, only eighteen years altogether.   35
Gelo was tyrant for seven years and died in the eighth; Hiero for ten years;
Thrasyboulus went into exile after ten months. Most tyrannies have been
quite short-lived, however.[122]

(7) The things connected both with [republican] regimes and with mon-   40
archies that lead to their destruction and their preservation have nearly all   1316a
been spoken of. Now in the *Republic* there is a discussion of revolutions by
Socrates,[123] but he does not argue rightly. In the case of the regime that is best
and first he does not speak of a revolution proper to it. (8) He asserts the rea-

117 · The tyranny of Orthagoras at Sicyon was instituted in 670 BC; Cleisthenes was
his great-grandson. Cf. Herodotus 6.126.
118 · Cf. Ath. Pol.16, Plutarch, *Solon* 31.
119 · Accepting the conjectural *hemisy* ("half") in place of the *tettara* ("four") of
the MSS.
120 · The tyranny at Corinth was instituted in about 657 BC. Cf. Herodotus 5.92, Aristotle, fr. 611.20 Rose.
121 · Cf. *Ath. Pol.* 17 and 19.
122 · For the tyranny at Syracuse see 10.31. This entire passage (1–6) has often been
bracketed by editors as an interpolation.
123 · Plato, *Republic* 545c ff.

5   son is that nothing is lasting, but everything undergoes revolution over a certain cycle, and the beginning point lies in those things where "a basic ratio of
four to three, yoked to five, produced two modes," saying that this happens
when the number of this figure is cubed,[124] the assumption being that nature
10 sometimes brings into being persons who are mean and beyond education.
Now in saying this he is perhaps not wrong, for there may be persons who
are incapable of being educated and becoming excellent men. (9) But why
should this be a sort of revolution peculiar to the regime he calls the best,
rather than belonging to all the others and to all persons coming into exis-
15 tence? And is it because of time, through which he says all things undergo
revolution, that even things not beginning simultaneously should undergo
revolution simultaneously? If something came into being on the day before
the turning point, will it then undergo revolution simultaneously?

(10) In addition to these things, what is the reason for its undergoing revolution in the direction of the Spartan regime? All regimes undergo revolution more frequently into their opposite than into a regime of a neighbor-
20 ing sort. The same argument also applies to the other revolutions. He asserts
that from the Spartan regime there is a revolution in the direction of oligarchy, from this to democracy, and from democracy to tyranny. (11) Yet revolution may also go the other way—from rule of the people to oligarchy, for
example; and this is more likely to happen than revolution in the direction
25 of monarchy. Further, in the case of tyranny he does not say either if there
will be a revolution or, if there will not, what the reason is for this, or into
which sort of regime. The reason for this is that it would not have been easy
for him to say, as it is impossible to determine. According to him it should
be in the direction of the first and best, for in this way there would be a con-
30 tinuous circle. (12) But tyranny also undergoes revolution into tyranny, for
example the one at Sicyon, where the tyranny of Myron was replaced by that
of Cleisthenes; into oligarchy, like that of Antileon at Chalcis; into democracy, like that of Gelo and his family at Syracuse; and into aristocracy, like
35 that of Charilaus in Lacedaemon, and at Carthage.[125] (13) There can also be

---

124 · Plato, *Republic* 546c. The allusion is to the notorious riddle of the "nuptial number," which Socrates claims should define the periods for breeding in his best regime.
Interpretation of the mathematics involved is highly uncertain.

125 · Cleisthenes was apparently the brother of Myron (Nicolaus of Damascus, *FGH*
90F61); nothing is known of Antileon. In 10.30, Aristotle indicates that the regime succeeding Gelo's tyranny at Syracuse was an aristocracy or polity rather than a democracy. For Charilaus cf. 2.10.2 and Aristotle, fr. 611.10 Rose. That a tyranny once existed
at Carthage is often held to contradict 2.11.2; but there Aristotle seems to refer to ty-

a revolution from oligarchy to tyranny, as happened with most of the ancient oligarchies in Sicily—to the tyranny of Panaetius at Leontini, to that
of Cleander at Gela, to that of Anaxilaus at Rhegium, and similarly in many
other cities.[126]

(14) It is also odd to suppose that there is a revolution in the direction   40
of oligarchy because those holding the offices are greedy and involved in
money-making, and not because those who are very preeminent by the fact   1316b
of their property suppose it is not just for those possessing nothing to have
a share in the city equal to that of the possessors. In many oligarchies, to engage in money-making is not permitted, and there are laws preventing this;   5
on the other hand, at Carthage they engage in money-making although it is
run timocratically,[127] and have not yet undergone a revolution. (15) It is also
odd to assert[128] that an oligarchic city is really two cities, of the wealthy and
the poor. For why should it have this characteristic more than the Spartan or
any other sort of regime where all do not possess equal things or are not good   10
men in a similar way? (16) Without anyone's becoming poorer than before,
regimes can nonetheless undergo revolution from oligarchy to democracy,
if the poor become a majority, or from rule of the people to oligarchy, if the
well-off element is superior to the multitude and the latter neglect [politics]
while the former put their mind to it.

(17) Though there are many reasons for revolutions occurring from oli-   15
garchy to democracy, he only speaks of one—their becoming poor by extrav-
agant living and paying out interest on loans,[129] the assumption being that
all or most were wealthy from the beginning. But this is false. Rather, when
certain of the leaders have squandered their properties, these engage in sedition, but in the case of others nothing terrible happens, and even if it should,   20
revolutions would be no more likely to occur in the direction of rule of the
people than in that of any other sort of regime. (18) Further, men engage in

---

rants arising after the establishment of the republican regime. Loss of the name of the
Carthaginian tyrant in the present passage has often been suspected.

126 · Panaetius is also mentioned in 10.6. For Cleander, see Herodotus 7.154 ff.; for
Anaxilaus, Herodotus 6.23, 7.165, 170. Rhegium was actually on the Italian mainland
opposite Sicily.

127 · Accepting Newman's conjectural *timokratoumenēi* for the *dēmokratoumenēi*
("democratically run") of the MSS. Cf. 6.5. 9 as well as the thematic discussion of the
Carthaginian regime in 2.11. It would be natural for Aristotle to use the Platonic term
for (conventional) aristocracy in this context.

128 · Plato, *Republic* 551d ff.

129 · Plato, *Republic* 555c–d.

factional conflict and effect revolution in regimes if they have no part in the prerogatives or if they are treated unjustly or arrogantly, even where they have not consumed all their property on account of the license to do what-
25   ever they want, the cause of which he asserts is too much freedom. Although there are many sorts of oligarchies and democracies, Socrates speaks of the revolutions as if there were only one sort of each.[130]

130 · The text here is almost certainly corrupt. A lacuna is probably to be marked after *ousian* ("property") in 23, as is done by Susemihl, Immisch, and others, as the latter part of this sentence seems to refer not to the transition from oligarchy to democracy but to that from democracy to tyranny (cf. *Republic* 557b). The abrupt ending of the book has led to the suspicion that additional material may have been lost as well.

Book 6

(1) How many varieties there are, and which they are, both of the deliberative and authoritative element of the regime and of the arrangement connected with the offices; concerning courts, which sorts are organized with a view to which sort of regime; further, concerning the destruction and preservation of regimes, from what things these arise and through what causes—this was spoken of earlier.[1] (2) But since it turned out that there are several kinds of democracy as well as of the other regimes in similar fashion, it is not a bad thing to investigate anything that remains to be said about the former, and at the same time to identify the mode of organization that is proper and advantageous to each. (3) Further, combinations of all the modes that have been spoken of must also be investigated; for when these are conjoined, they make regimes overlap, so that there are oligarchic aristocracies and polities of a more democratic cast. (4) I mean that there are conjunctions that should be investigated, but at present have not been—for example, if the deliberative element and what is connected with the selection of officials is organized oligarchically, but matters connected with the courts aristocratically; or these and what is connected with the deliberative element oligarchically, and what is connected with the selection of officials aristocratically; or if in some other manner not all of what is combined is proper to the regime.[2]

35

40

1317a

5

1 · 4.14–5.12.
2 · Two themes appear to be announced here: the varieties of democracy and the (institutional) "modes" appropriate to them, and possible "combinations" of such modes forming hybrid "conjunctions" of a variety of different regimes. A discussion of democracy (and derivatively of oligarchy) occupies chapters 1–7. Chapter 8, which deals with the varieties and functions of offices, would appear to be preparatory to a discussion of the second theme, which is missing from book 6 and the *Politics* as we have it.

10   (5) What sort of democracy is suitable for what sort of city, and in the same way too what sort of oligarchy is suitable for what sort of multitude, and of the remaining regimes which is advantageous for which peoples, was spoken of earlier.[3] (6) Yet since it should be made clear not only which of
15   these sorts of regimes is best for cities, but also how one should institute both these and others, let us address this in succinct fashion. Let us speak first of democracy—for how one should do this will become evident also for the regime that corresponds to it, the one some call oligarchy.

(7) With a view to this inquiry, it is necessary to grasp all the things that
20   are characteristic of popular rule or that are held to accompany democracies. For it is as a result of the bringing together of these that the kinds of democracy arise, and that there are several sorts of democracy that differ, and not a single sort. (8) There are two reasons there are several sorts of democracy.
25   First, there is the one spoken of earlier, that peoples are different.[4] For one multitude is of the farming sort, another of the working and laboring sort; and if the first of these is added to the second, or again the third to both, these create a difference not only with respect to the democracy being better or worse, but even with respect to its being the same sort of democracy. The
30   second reason is the one we are speaking of now. (9) For the things that accompany democracies and are held to belong to this sort of regime make democracies different when they are brought together differently: one sort will be accompanied by fewer, another by more, another by all of them. It is useful to be familiar with each of these things both with a view to instituting whichever sort of democracy one happens to want and with a view to reforming
35   existing ones. (10) Those who establish regimes seek to combine everything that derives from the basic premise of the regime, but they err in so doing, as was said earlier in the discourses on the sources of destruction and preservation of regimes.[5] Let us now speak of the claim and character of the different types of democracy and what they strive for.

CHAPTER 2

40   (1) Now the basic premise of the democratic sort of regime is freedom. It is
1317b customarily said that only in this sort of regime do men partake of freedom, for, so it is asserted, every democracy aims at this. One aspect of freedom is

3 · 4.12.
4 · 4.4. 20–21.
5 · 5.9.

being ruled and ruling in turn. (2) The justice that is characteristically popular is to have equality on the basis of number and not on the basis of merit; where justice is of this sort, the multitude must necessarily have authority, and what is resolved by the majority must be final and must be justice, for, they assert, each of the citizens must have an equal share. The result is that in democracies the poor have more authority than the well off, for they are the majority, and what is resolved by the majority is authoritative. (3) This, then, is one mark of freedom, and it is regarded by those of the popular sort as the defining principle of the regime. Another is to live as one wants. For this is, they assert, the work of freedom, since not living as one wants is characteristic of a person who is enslaved. (4) This, then, is the second defining principle of democracy. From it has come [the claim to merit] not being ruled by anyone, or failing this, [to rule and be ruled] in turn. It contributes in this way to the freedom that is based on equality.

(5) These things being given and democratic rule being of this sort, the following are characteristically popular: election to all offices from among all the citizens; rule of all over each, and of each over all in turn; having all offices chosen by lot, or those not requiring experience and art; having offices not based on any assessment, or based on the smallest possible; the same person not holding any office more than once, or doing so rarely, or in few cases, apart from those relating to war; having all offices of short duration, or those where this is possible; having all adjudicate or persons chosen from all, and concerning all matters or most, and these the greatest and most authoritative (for example, concerning audits, or the regime, or private transactions); the assembly having authority over all matters or the greatest, and no office having authority over any, or having it over as few as possible (6) (of the offices the most popular is the council, when there is not a ready supply of pay for all—when there is, the power even of this office is eliminated, for if the people are well supplied with pay they have all decisions referred to themselves, as was said earlier in the inquiry preceding this[6]); (7) next, providing pay—particularly for all, for the assembly, courts, and offices, but failing this, for the offices, courts, council, and assemblies that are authoritative, or for those offices where it is necessary to have common messes with one another.[7] Further, since oligarchy is defined by family, wealth, and education, the opposites of these things are held to be characteristically popular—lack

6 · 4.15.12–13.
7 · This was an established practice in democratic Athens; see, for example, *Ath. Pol.* 43.3, 62.2.

of birth, poverty, and vulgarity.[8] (8) With regard to the offices, another pop-
1318a   ular characteristic is having none of them be for life, and if any such remain
out of a previous revolution, stripping them of their power and making the
holders chosen by lot rather than by election.[9]

(9) These things are common to democracies, then. But what is held to
be democracy or rule of the people above all is what results from the sort of
5   justice that is agreed to be democratic, which is all having an equal share on
the basis of number. For it is equality if the poor rule no more than the well
off and do not have authority alone, but all do equally on the basis of num-
10   ber. For in this way they might consider both equality and freedom as being
present in the regime.

CHAPTER 3

(1) The question that arises after this is how they will come to have equality.
Should assessments be distinguished [in such a way that the total property
of the poor and the well off is equal—for example, that][10] of five hundred
persons to a thousand, and the thousand given power equal to the five hundred? Or is equality on this basis not to be sought in this way, and should
15   one not rather make this distinction and then take an equal number of persons from the five hundred and from the thousand and give them authority
over elections and the courts? (2) Is this, then, the most just sort of regime
that accords with popular justice, or rather the one that is based on the multitude? Those of the popular sort assert that justice is whatever is resolved by
20   the majority, while those of the oligarchic sort assert it is whatever is resolved
by those with the greater property (for they assert that decisions ought to be
made on the basis of the amount of property). (3) Both involve inequality
and injustice. For if justice is whatever the few decide, it is [indistinguishable
from] tyranny, for if a single individual has more than others who are well
25   off, on the basis of oligarchic justice it is just for him alone to rule. But if it
is what the majority decides on the basis of number, they will act unjustly by
confiscating the property of the rich few, as was said earlier.[11] (4) What sort
of equality there might be that both sides will agree on must be investigated

8 · This sentence is bracketed by Dreizehnter as an interpolation, almost certainly
rightly. "Vulgarity" renders *banausia*.
9 · This was notably the case in regard to the institution of kingship, at Athens and
elsewhere; cf. 3.14.13.
10 · It seems necessary to assume a lacuna in the text at this point.
11 · 3.10.1–2.

in connection with the definition of justice given by both. For they both say that whatever is resolved by the majority of the citizens should be authoritative. This may be allowed to stand, though not entirely. Rather, since it happens that there are two parts of which the city is constituted, rich and poor, whatever is resolved by both or by a majority of both should stand as authoritative; and if each resolves on opposite things, whatever is resolved by a majority which also has the greater assessment. (5) For example, if there are ten of the former and twenty of the latter, and something was resolved differently by six of the wealthy and fifteen of the poorer, four of the wealthy had joined the poor and five of the poor the wealthy. Whichever group's assessment predominates when those of both on either side are counted up, then—this is authoritative. (6) If it falls out equally, this must be considered a problem common to the way things are done now, if the assembly or the court is split; in such a case there must be resort to lot, or something else of this sort must be done.

But concerning equality and justice, even though it is very difficult to find the truth about these matters, it is still easier to hit on it than it is to persuade those who are capable of aggrandizing themselves. The inferior always seek equality and justice; those who dominate them take no thought for it.

CHAPTER 4

(1) Of the four sorts of democracy, the best is the one that is first in the arrangement spoken of in the discourses preceding these; it is also the oldest of them all.[12] But I call it first in the sense that one might distinguish among peoples. The best people is the farming sort, so that it is possible also to create the best democracy wherever the multitude lives from farming or herding. (2) For on account of not having much property it is lacking in leisure, and so is unable to hold frequent assemblies. Because they do not[13] have the necessary things, they spend their time at work and do not desire the things of others; indeed, working is more pleasant to them than engaging in politics and ruling, where there are not great spoils to be gotten from office. (3) For the many strive more for profit than for honor. A sign of this is that they used to put up with the ancient tyrannies and still put up with oligarchies, if no

12 · 4.6. 1–6. Five varieties of democracy are listed in 4.4. 22–25; but one of these appears to be the democracy based on equality of rich and poor that is discussed in 6.2. 9–3.6.

13 · Reading mē ("not") with the MSS rather than bracketing the word with Bojesen and Dreizehnter.

20 one prevents them from working or takes away anything from them: before
long some of them become rich, while others cease to be poor. (4) Further, if
they have any element of ambition, having authority to elect and audit would
satisfy their need. Indeed, among some peoples it is sufficient for the many if
they have no share in election to the offices but certain persons are elected to
25 do this from all by turns, as at Mantinea, provided they have authority over
deliberation. (5) One should consider even this a certain form of democracy,
as it once existed at Mantinea.[14]

Hence it is both advantageous and customarily belongs to the sort of democracy spoken of earlier to have all elect to the offices and audit and adju-
30 dicate, but for persons elected on the basis of assessments to hold the offices,
and the greater from the greater assessments—or else to elect none on the
basis of assessments, but rather capable persons. (6) Those who govern themselves in this way must necessarily be finely governed. The offices will always
be in the hands of the best persons, the people being willing and not envi-
35 ous of the respectable, while the arrangement is satisfactory for the respectable and notable. These will not be ruled by others who are their inferiors,
and they will rule justly by the fact that others have authority over the audits.
(7) For to be under constraint and unable to do everything one might resolve
40 to do is advantageous. The license to do whatever one wishes cannot defend
1319a against the mean element in every human being. So it necessarily results that
the respectable rule without falling into error, while the multitude does not
get less than its due—something that is most beneficial for regimes.
5 (8) That this is the best sort of democracy, then, is evident, and the reason for this—that it is because the people are of a certain quality. With a
view to instituting a farming people, certain of the laws that existed among
many in ancient times are entirely useful—laws either generally forbidding
the possession of land beyond a certain measure or forbidding it between
10 a certain location and the town or city. (9) In ancient times there also used
to be legislation forbidding the sale of the original allotments; there is also
the law they say derives from Oxylus, which has the same sort of power, forbidding borrowing against any part of the land belonging to an individual.
Given things as they are at present, one should attempt reform through the
15 law of the Aphytaeans as well, for it is useful in relation to what we are speaking of. (10) Though there are many of them and they possess little land, the
Aphytaeans nevertheless all engage in farming. For they are not assessed on
the basis of whole estates [as originally allotted], but they divide these into

14 · Nothing further is known of this arrangement at Mantinea.

parts of such a size that even the poor have enough to enable them to exceed the assessment [that is required for citizenship].[15]

(11) After the farming multitude, the best sort of people exists where they are herdsmen and live from livestock. These are in a condition very similar to farmers, and in what relates to military activities they are particulary well exercised with respect to their dispositions as well as useful with respect to their bodies and capable of living in the open. (12) The other sorts of multitude out of which the remaining sorts of democracy are constituted are almost all much meaner than these: their way of life is a mean one, with no task involving virtue among the things that occupy the multitude of human beings who are workers and merchants or the multitude of laborers. (13) Further, on account of their always frequenting the marketplace and the town, nearly all persons of this type can easily attend the assembly, while those engaged in farming, on account of their being scattered in the country, do not come together in this way and have no need of doing so. (14) But where it happens that the position of the territory is such that the country is far removed from the city, it is easy to create a decent democracy or a polity. For the multitude is compelled to have its dwelling places in the fields; so that even where there is a mass of merchants, one should not hold assemblies in democracies without the multitude from the country.

(15) How the best and first sort of democracy should be instituted, then, has been spoken of; how the others should be instituted is also evident. They should deviate progressively, always separating out a worse multitude [for citizenship]. The final sort, on account of all participating in it, is one that not every city can support, nor is it easy for it to last, as it is not well composed with respect to its laws and customs. (As to what results in the destruction both of this and of the other regimes, this was for the most part spoken of earlier.) (16) With a view to establishing this sort of democracy, those at the head of affairs customarily make the people stronger by adding as many persons as possible, admitting as citizens not only those who are legitimate but even bastards and those descended from a citizen either way, I mean either from the father or the mother; for this whole element is proper to this sort of people. (17) Popular leaders customarily institute it in this way, then.

15 · Oxylus was an ancient legislator of Elis. Nothing else is known of the legislation of Aphytis, and the meaning of the text is somewhat uncertain: the town, like its neighbor Potideia, had probably been settled as a colony, with citizenship restricted to those owning the equivalent of an original allotment of land; later, as a result of an increasing population, the assessment was evidently reduced to ownership of some small fraction of this allotment.

In fact, however, one should add citizens up to the point where the multitude predominates over the notables and the middling elements and not proceed beyond this. For if [the lower elements] are in excess, they introduce disorder into the regime, and goad the notables into looking harshly on the democracy and not putting up with it—something which turned out to be a cause of the factional conflict at Cyrene.[16] A base element is tolerated if it is few, but as it becomes more numerous it is more in front of one's eyes. (18) Also useful with a view to a democracy of this sort are the sort of institutions that Cleisthenes used at Athens when he wanted to enhance the democracy, or those at Cyrene who established rule of the people.[17] (19) Other and more numerous tribes and clans are to be created, private rites incorporated into a few common rites, and everything devised so that all are mixed together to the greatest possible extent, and their previous familiar [associations] broken up. (20) Further, tyrannical institutions too are held to be characteristic of popular rule—I mean, for example, lack of rule over slaves (which might be advantageous [to a democracy] up to a certain point) as well as over women and children, and tolerating everyone living as he wants. For the element assisting a regime of this sort will be considerable; living in a disorderly way is more pleasant to the many than living with moderation.

CHAPTER 5

(1) But instituting it is not the greatest or the only task of the legislator or of those wanting to constitute some regime of this sort, but rather to see that it is preserved; for it is not difficult to be governed in one fashion or another for one, two, or three days. (2) Hence one should take what was studied earlier, the sources of preservation and destruction of regimes, and try to institute stability, avoiding what destroys regimes and enacting laws—both written and unwritten—of a sort that will encompass above all what preserves regimes; and one should not consider as characteristic of popular rule or of oligarchy something that will make the city democratically or oligarchically run to the greatest extent possible, but something that will do so for the longest period of time. (3) The popular leaders of the present, seeking to win the favor of the people, undertake many confiscations through the courts. Those

16 · The reference is perhaps to civil disturbances at Cyrene in 401 BC (Diodorus Siculus 14.34).

17 · For the reforms of Cleisthenes, see *Ath. Pol.* 21. The reference to Cyrene is probably to the establishment of democracy there around 462 BC.

who cherish the regime should take action against this, legislating that nothing that is confiscated in a case affecting common matters should become public property, but rather sacred property. Those acting unjustly will be no less cautious, for they will be fined in the same way, but the mass will less frequently vote against those who are being tried, as they are not going to get anything out of it. (4) Further, public suits should always be kept as few as possible, those prosecuting in a frivolous way being curbed by large penalties. For they customarily bring these against the notables rather than the popular sort; but all the citizens should feel benevolent toward the regime, or failing this, they should at least not consider those in authority as their enemies.

(5) Since the ultimate sorts of democracy have a considerable population and it is difficult for them to attend the assembly without pay, this state of affairs—where there do not happen to be [external sources of] revenues—is inimical to the notables; for it must necessarily be got from taxes and confiscations and corruption of the courts, things which have before now brought down many democracies. Where there do not happen to be revenues, then, one should hold few assemblies, and the courts should have many members but meet only for a few days. (6) This contributes to the wealthy not fearing the expenditure, if the well off do not receive pay for attending court but the poor do; and it contributes to a much better judgment of suits, for the well off are unwilling to be away from their private affairs for many days, but are willing for a brief period of time. (7) Where there are revenues, however, one should not do what popular leaders do at present. They distribute any surplus; the people take it and at the same time ask for more of the same. This sort of assistance to the poor is the [proverbial] "punctured jar."[18] But one who is genuinely of the popular sort should see to it that the multitude is not overly poor; (8) for this is the reason for democracy being depraved. Measures must therefore be devised so that there will be abundance over time. Since this is advantageous also for the well off, what ought to be done is to accumulate what is left over of the revenues and distribute accumulated sums to the poor. This should particularly be done if one could accumulate enough for the acquisition of a plot of land, or failing this, for a start in trade or farming. (9) If this is not possible for all, it should be distributed on the basis of tribes or some other part of the city by turns; and in the meantime the well off should be taxed to provide pay for necessary meetings, while at

10

15

20

25

30

35

1320b

---

18 · The allusion is to the myth of the daughters of Danaus, who were punished in Hades for murdering their husbands by having to pour water into a leaking jar.

the same time being released from pointless sorts of public service. It is by
5   governing in such a manner that the Carthaginians have acquired the friendship of the people: they are constantly sending out some of the people to
the subject cities and making them well off.[19] (10) Also, notables who are refined and sensible will divide the poor among themselves and provide them
with a start in pursuing some work. It is also right to imitate what the Tar-
10 entines do. By making their possessions common for use by the poor, they
maintain the benevolence of the multitude.[20] (11) Further, they also created
all the offices in a double form, the ones chosen by election, the others by
lot—those chosen by lot so that the people could take part in them, those
chosen by election so that they would be better governed. (This same thing
15 can be done by splitting the same office between different persons chosen by
lot and by election.[21])

How democracies should be instituted, then, has been spoken of.

CHAPTER 6

(1) How one should do this in connection with oligarchies is very nearly evident from these things as well. Each sort of oligarchy should be combined
20 out of the opposite elements, reasoning in relation to the sort of democracy
opposite to it. The first and most well blended of the sorts of oligarchy [is
related to the first sort of democracy]; this is the one that is very close to so-
called polity. (2) In this there should be a distinction among assessments,
some being lesser and others greater: on the basis of the lesser they will take
25 part in the necessary offices, on the basis of the greater, in the more authoritative; it should be open to anyone possessing the assessment to take part in
the regime—bringing in through the assessment as many of the people as

19 · Cf. 2.11.15.
20 · Nothing is known of this arrangement. As Tarentum was a colony of Sparta, however, it is likely that the practice of common use of property there was similar to the
Spartan practice (2.5. 7–8).
21 · The meaning is somewhat uncertain. Aristotle is generally taken to argue that
the offices at Tarentum were of two kinds, those chosen by election and those chosen
by lot; yet such an arrangement would not have been particularly distinctive. The precise language used would seem to suggest instead that each office had both an elective
component and one chosen by lot—presumably, a popular "overseer" on the Spartan
model. If this interpretation is correct, Aristotle's parenthetical remark would also have
to be understood as referring to rotation in office rather than to a simultaneous sharing
of office by officials chosen by election and by lot.

will allow them to be superior to those not taking part; (3) and they should always take from the better part of the people those who are to be sharers in the regime.

The next sort of oligarchy should be instituted in a similar way, with a   30
slight tightening [of the qualifications for citizenship]. As regards the sort that corresponds to the extreme sort of democracy, the most powerful and tyrannical of the sorts of oligarchy, to the degree that it is the worst, it re-quires the greater defense. (4) For just as bodies that are in a good state with respect to health, or ships that are in a fine condition for a voyage with re-   35
spect to their crews, admit of more errors without being destroyed by them, while bodies that are in a diseased condition and ships with loosened timbers and a poor crew cannot bear up even under small errors, so too in the case of regimes the worse need the most defense.

(5) Democracies generally are preserved by their considerable popula-   1321a
tions; this is the antithesis of the sort of justice that is based on merit. But it is clear that oligarchy must, on the contrary, obtain its preservation by being well arranged.

CHAPTER 7

(1) Since there are four parts of the multitude, the farming, the working, the   5
merchant, and the laboring elements, and four parts of the city that are useful with a view to war, the horse-rearing, the heavy-armed, the light-armed, and the seafaring elements, wherever it happens that the country is suitable for horses, conditions are naturally apt for instituting a strong oligarchy (for the   10
preservation of the inhabitants derives from a force of this sort, and horse-rearing is done by those possessing large properties); where it is suitable for heavy arms, the next sort of oligarchy (for the heavy-armed element is made up of the well off more than the poor). (2) Light-armed and naval forces, on the other hand, are wholly popular. At present, therefore, wherever this sort   15
of multitude is numerous and there is a factional split, [the oligarchs] often get the worst of the contest. A remedy for this should be sought from those generals who are expert in war, who join to the cavalry and the heavy-armed force an appropriate light-armed force. (3) This is the way the people prevail over the well off in factional splits: being light-armed, they can easily con-   20
tend against a force of cavalry and heavy-armed troops. To establish such a force from these, therefore, is to establish one against themselves. Rather, there being a distinction of age, the older on one side and the young on the

25 other, they should teach their sons the working of auxiliary and light arms when still young, and some should be picked out from among the boys to be themselves practitioners of these tasks.[22]

(4) Giving a share in the governing body to the multitude can occur either in the way spoken of earlier, to those possessing the assessment, or as among the Thebans, to those abstaining for a certain period of time from workers'
30 tasks, or as at Massilia, where they make a judgment as to who merits office, whether those within the governing body or those outside it.[23]

(5) Further, with respect to the most authoritative offices, which should be retained by those in the regime, public services should be attached to them, so that the people may be willing to forego taking part in them, and
35 may feel indulgence for their rulers as having paid heavily for the office. (6) It is also appropriate for them both to offer magnificent sacrifices when they enter office and to institute something common,[24] so that the people, in sharing in what is connected with these festivities and seeing the city adorned with votive statues and buildings, are glad to see the regime endure; and it
40 will also result that the notables have a memorial of their expenditure. (7) At present, however, those connected with oligarchies do not do this, but rather the opposite: they are in search of spoils no less than honor. Hence it is well
1321b to speak of them as small democracies.[25]

As to how one ought to establish democracies and oligarchies, then, let our discussion stand in this manner.

CHAPTER 8

(1) It follows on what has been said to distinguish finely among the matters
5 connected with offices, how many and which there are and over which matters, as was said earlier.[26] Without the necessary offices it is impossible for a

22 · Particularly in the hands of skilled mercenary commanders, "light-armed" (*psiloi*) troops had become of increasing military significance during the fourth century; most commonly their armament consisted of a javelin and a small shield, but specialized forces of archers and slingers also existed in certain areas. Aristotle appears to counsel training in such specialties (which may be the "auxiliary" (*koupha*) arms referred to here; cf. 8.15) for all of the oligarchic youth, and the establishment of a select force drawn from the oligarchs themselves.

23 · For Thebes cf. 3.5. 6–7. Nothing else is known of the arrangement at Massilia.

24 · That is, apparently, to erect a public building or monument.

25 · In other words, the oligarchs lower themselves to the level of the people in their pursuit of profit.

26 · 4.15.22.

city to exist; without those that relate to its good arrangement and order, it
is impossible for it to be finely administered. (2) Further, in small cities there
must of necessity be fewer offices, and in large cities more, as was said ear-   10
lier.[27] Which offices can suitably be combined, then, and which separated,
should not be overlooked.

(3) First, then, of the necessary offices there is the superintendence connected with the market, for which there should be an office that has oversight
in the matter both of agreements and of orderliness. For very nearly all cities   15
must of necessity buy and sell certain things with a view to each other's necessary requirements, and this is the readiest way to self-sufficiency, on account
of which men are held to join together in one regime.

(4) Another sort of superintendence, connected with this sort and close
to it, is that over public and private property in town, to ensure orderliness,
and over the preservation and repair of decaying buildings and roads, and to   20
ensure that accusations do not arise concerning the boundaries between the
properties of the citizens themselves, and whatever else belonging to this sort
of superintendence is similar to these things. (5) Most call this sort of office
"town management"; it has a number of parts, and in more populous states
different officials are established for the different parts—for example, wall   25
builders, superintendents of wells, and harbor guards.

(6) Another office is necessary and quite similar to this. It is concerned
with the same things, but is connected with the country and matters outside
the town; they call these officials "field managers" in some places, in others   30
"foresters."

There are three sorts of superintendence over these matters, then. Another office is that by which revenues from common things are received,
guarded, and split up among each administrative element. They call these
"receivers" and "treasurers."

(7) Another office is that with which one registers both private agree-   35
ments and judgments from the courts. Before these same officials should also
come indictments and initiations of suits. In some places they split this office
too among several persons, but a single office has authority over all these matters.[28] They call them "sacred recorders," "supervisors," "recorders," and other
terms that resemble these.

(8) Next after this is one which is very nearly the most necessary as well   40
as the most difficult of the offices, that connected with actions taken against

27 · 4.15.7–8.
28 · Reading *estin de* with the MSS rather than *estin d' hou* with Thurot and Dreizehnter ("while in others a single office has authority").

1322a   persons found guilty or those whose names have been posted in notices,[29]
and with the guarding of prisoners. (9) It is difficult by the fact that it involves much odium, so that unless it is possible to make great profits, men
will either not put up with being officials of this sort or, if they do, they will
5   be unwilling to act in accordance with the laws; but it is necessary, because
there is no benefit in having suits about matters of justice if these do not
achieve their end, so that if it is impossible for men to be partners where there
are no suits, so also is it where there are no actions taken against those found
guilty. (10) Hence it is better for this not to be a single office, but rather for
it to be carried out by persons drawn from different courts, and in connec-
10   tion with the posting of notices to try to distinguish in the same way; and
further, to have some actions taken by officials [rather than by functionaries of the courts], and in particular to have incoming officials take action in
suits decided by outgoing ones, or in the case of serving officials to have one
determine guilt and another take the action—for example, the town managers would take action in cases coming from the field managers, and the latter
15   in cases from the former. (11) The less the odium that attaches to the actions
taken, the more will the actions achieve their end. To have the same persons
determining guilt and taking action involves a double odium, and to have
the same [taking action] in all cases [makes them] inimical to everyone.[30] In
many places the office that guards prisoners is distinguished from that which
20   takes actions, as at Athens in the case of the so-called eleven.[31] (12) Hence it
is better to make this separate too, and to seek the same device here as well.
This office is no less necessary than the one spoken of, but it happens that
the respectable avoid it above all, while it is not safe to give authority over it
25   to the depraved, as these are more in need of being guarded themselves than
capable of guarding others. (13) Hence there should not be a single office assigned to them, nor should the same one do it continuously, but they should
be superintended by different persons in turn—by the young, where there is
a body of cadets or garrison troops, and by [other] officials.

29 · That is, with the collection of fines and of public debts. The official chiefly concerned with these matters at Athens was called an "actioner" (*praktōr*).
30 · Accepting the reading of the MSS rather than the emendation of Dreizehnter;
but something may have dropped out of the text here.
31 · Reading *diēirētai* ("distinguished from") with the MSS rather than the conjecture
of Niemeyer and Dreizehnter. It is true that the Eleven at Athens (the officials in charge
of prisons) do appear to have had some role in the collection of public debts, but the
"actioners" nevertheless constituted a separate magistracy.

These offices must be set first, then, as being the most necessary. After   30
these are others which are no less necessary, but higher in rank arrangement,
as they require much experience and trust. (14) These would be the ones
connected with the defense of the city, and any that are arranged with a view
to military requirements. Both in peace and in war alike there should be su-   35
perintendents of the defense of gates and walls, and of the scrutiny and organization of the citizens. In some places there are more offices for all of these
things, in others fewer—in small cities, for example, there might be a single
one concerned with all. (15) They call such persons "generals" and "war officials." Further, if there are cavalry, light-armed troops, archers, or a naval el-   1322b
ement, an official is sometimes established for each of these, which they call
"admirals," "cavalry commanders," and "regimental commanders," and for the
parts under them, "warship commanders," "leaders of companies," and "tribal
commanders," and [others are appointed to command] any parts belonging
to these. The entirety of these things makes up a single kind of office, super-   5
intendence of military matters.

(16) In connection with this office, then, things stand in this manner. Now
since some of the offices, if not all of them, handle substantial quantities of
common funds, it is necessary for there to be a different office to receive the
accounts and to do an additional audit, one which does not itself handle any   10
other matter. Some call these "auditors," others "accountants," others "scruti-
nizers," and others "advisers."

(17) Besides all these offices, there is the one that is most particularly authoritative in all matters. For the same office often has authority over the final disposition as well as the introduction of all measures, or else it presides
over the multitude, wherever the people have authority; for there should be   15
something which convenes the authoritative element in the regime. In some
places it is called "preliminary councillors," because it engages in preliminary
deliberation; where there is a ruling multitude, it is called a "council" instead.

(18) Those of the offices that are political are very nearly this many. Another kind of superintendence is that connected with the gods—for example, priests and superintendents of matters connected with sacred things,   20
including the preservation of existing buildings and the restoration of those
that are in decay, and whatever other arrangements there are related to the
gods. (19) Sometimes it happens, as for example in small cities, that there is
a single superintendence for this; sometimes there are many officials who are
separate from the priesthood—for example, sacrificers, temple guardians,   25
and treasurers of sacred funds. (20) Next after this is the office that special-

izes in all the common sacrifices which the law does not assign to the priests, but which they have the prerogative of celebrating from the city's common hearth. These officials are called "kings" by some, "presidents" by others.

30   (21) The necessary sorts of superintendence are, then, to speak in summary fashion, the following. They are those connected with divine matters, military matters, revenues, expenditures, the market, the town, harbors, and the country; and further, those connected with courts, the registration of
35 agreements, actions against offenders, guarding of prisoners, receiving accounts, and the scrutinizing and auditing of officials; and finally, those connected with the element that deliberates about common matters. (22) Peculiar to those cities which enjoy greater leisure and are more prosperous, and which in addition take thought for orderliness, are the offices of manager of
1323a women, law guardian, manager of children, and exercise official, and in addition to these the superintendence connected with gymnastic and Dionysiac contests, as well as any other spectacles of this sort there may happen to be. (23) Some of these offices are evidently not of a popular sort—for example,
5 management of women and management of children: the poor must necessarily treat both their women and children as attendants on account of their lack of slaves.

    (24) There are three sorts of offices under the direction of which election to the authoritative offices is made—law guardians, preliminary councillors, and council; law guardians are aristocratic, preliminary councillors oligarchic, and a council popular.
10   Concerning offices, then, almost all of them have been spoken of in outline....[32]

---

32 · This sentence is clearly incomplete in the original.

Book 7

(1) Concerning the best regime, one who is going to undertake the investiga-   15
tion appropriate to it must necessarily discuss first what the most choiceworthy way of life is. As long as this is unclear, the best regime must necessarily
be unclear as well; for it is appropriate for those who govern themselves best
on the basis of what is available to them to act in the best manner, provided
nothing occurs contrary to reasonable expectation. (2) Hence there should   20
first be agreement on which is the most choiceworthy way of life for all, so
to speak, and after this, whether the same or a different way of life is choiceworthy for men in common and separately as individuals. Considering as adequate, then, much of what is said in the external discourses concerning the
best way of life,[1] we must use that here as well.

(3) For in truth no one would dispute that, there being a distinction
among three groups of good things, those that are external, those of the body,   25
and those of the soul, all these things ought to be available[2] to the blessed.
(4) No one would assert that a person is blessed who has no part of courage,
moderation, justice, or prudence, but is afraid of the flies buzzing around
him, abstains from none of the extremes when he desires to eat or drink, kills   30
his dearest friends for a trifle, and similarly regarding the things connected
with the mind, is as senseless and as thoroughly deceived [by a false percep-

1 · It is not known to what work Aristotle refers. For the general problem of the "external discourses," see Introduction, pp. xvii–xix above. For an analysis of the tortuous
but critically important argument of the first three chapters of book 7, see Lord 1982,
180–202.
2 · Reading *hyparchein* with the MSS and *chrē* with Π[1] ("ought to be available") following Ross rather than bracketing *chrē* on the basis of its omission in Π[2] and reading
hyparchei ("are available") with Dreizehnter.

tion of things] as a child or a madman. (5) Yet while all would admit what
35   has been said, they differ in regard to how much of each type of good is desirable and their relative degree of preeminence. For men consider any amount
of virtue to be adequate, but wealth, goods, power, reputation, and all such
things they seek to excess without limit. (6) We shall say to them that it is
40   easy to convince oneself concerning these matters through the facts as well,
when one sees that men do not acquire and safeguard the virtues by means
1323b   of external things, but the latter by means of the former, and that living happily—whether human beings find it in enjoyment or in virtue or in both—is
available to those who have to excess the adornments of character and mind
but behave moderately in respect to the external acquisition of good things,
5   rather than to those who possess more of the latter than what is useful but are
deficient in the former. Yet this can also be readily seen by those investigating
on the basis of argument.

(7) External things, like any instrument, have a limit: everything useful
belongs among[3] those things an excess of which must necessarily be either
10   harmful or not beneficial to those who have them. In the case of each of the
good things connected with the soul, however, the more it is in excess, the
more useful it must necessarily be—if indeed one should attribute to these
things not only what is fine but what is useful as well. (8) In general, it is clear,
we shall assert, that the best state of each thing in relation to other things cor-
15   responds with respect to its preeminence to the distance between the things
of which we assert that these are states. So if the soul is more honorable than
both property and the body, both simply and for us, the best state of each
must necessarily stand in the same relation as these things among themselves.
(9) Further, it is for the sake of the soul that these things are naturally choice-
20   worthy and that all sensible persons should choose them, and not the soul
for the sake of them.

(10) That the same amount of happiness falls to each person as of virtue and prudence and action in accordance with these, therefore, may stand
as agreed by us. We may use the god as testimony to this: he is happy and
25   blessed, yet not through any of the external good things but rather through
himself and by being of a certain quality in his nature. And it is on this account that good fortune necessarily differs from happiness. Of the good
things that are external to the soul the cause is chance and fortune; but no
one is just or sound by fortune or through fortune.

3 · Reading *estin hōn* with the MSS ("belongs among those things an excess of
which") rather than *eis ti hon* ("is for some purpose; of these an excess") with Immisch
and Dreizehnter.

(11) Next, and requiring the same arguments, is the assertion that the best   30
city is happy and acts finely.[4] It is impossible to act finely without acting to
achieve fine things; but there is no fine deed either of a man or of a city that
is separate from virtue and prudence. (12) The courage, justice, and prudence
of a city have the same power and form as those things human beings share   35
in individually who are called just, prudent, and sound.

(13) These things, so far as they go, may stand as a preface to our discourse.
For it is not possible either not to touch on them or to exhaust all of the arguments pertaining to them (these things are a task for an inquiry belonging
to another occasion[5]). For the present let us presuppose this much, that the   40
best way of life both separately for each individual and in common for cities
is that accompanied by virtue—virtue that is equipped to such an extent as   1324a
to allow them to take part in the actions that accord with virtue. (14) With
regard to those who dispute such an argument, we must pass over them for
the purposes of the present inquiry, but shall make a thorough investigation
later, if anyone happens not to be persuaded by what has been said.[6]

CHAPTER 2

(1) Whether happiness must be asserted to be the same both for a single in-   5
dividual human being and for a city or not the same, however, remains to be
spoken of. But this too is evident: all would agree it is the same. (2) For those
who ascribe living well to wealth in the case of a single person also call the
city as a whole blessed if it is wealthy; those who honor the tyrannical way of   10
life above all would also assert that the city is happiest which rules the greatest number of persons; and if anyone accepts that the individual is happy on
account of virtue, he will also assert that the more excellent city is the one
that is happier.

(3) But the following two things are in need of investigation: one, which
is the more choiceworthy way of life, that which involves engaging jointly in   15
politics and sharing in a city, or rather that characteristic of the foreigner and
divorced from the political community; and further, which regime and which
state of the city are to be regarded as best (regardless of whether sharing in a
city is choiceworthy for all or only for most and not for certain persons).

4 · Here and throughout this discussion, the phrases "act finely" (*kalōs prattein*) and
"act well" (*eu prattein*) bear their idiomatic meaning "do well" or "prosper." *Kalos* will
also regularly be rendered "noble" throughout this discussion.

5 · Literally, "another sort of leisure (*scholē*)."

6 · The reference would appear to be to 7.13, but this is not certain.

20   (4) Since this—but not what is choiceworthy for the individual—is a
task for political thought and study, and since at present we have intentionally chosen [to limit ourselves to] this sort of investigation, the former is in-
cidental to, the latter a task for, this inquiry.

(5) Now that the best regime must necessarily be that arrangement un-
25   der which anyone might act in the best manner and live blessedly[7] is evident. Yet there is a dispute among those who agree that the most choiceworthy way of life is that accompanied by virtue as to whether the political
and active way of life is choiceworthy, or rather that which is divorced from
all external things—that involving some sort of study, for example—which
some assert is the only philosophic way of life.[8] (6) For it is evident that
30   these two ways of life are the ones intentionally chosen by those human beings who are most ambitious with a view to virtue, both in former times
and at the present; the two I mean are the political and the philosophic. It
makes no small difference on which side the truth lies, for a sensible person, at any rate, must necessarily organize matters with a view to the bet-
35   ter aim both in the case of human beings individually and for the regime
in common. (7) There are some who consider rule over one's neighbors,
if undertaken after the fashion of a master, to be accompanied by injustice
of the greatest sort, and if in political fashion, not to involve injustice but
to be an impediment to one's own well-being. Others hold opinions that
40   are virtually the opposite of these. They believe that the active and political way of life is the only one for a man,[9] and that in the case of each sort
of virtue there is no more room for action on the part of private individu-
1324b   als than on the part of those who are active with respect to common matters and engage in politics. (8) This is the conception some of them have;
but others assert that the mode of regime involving mastery and tyranny is
the only happy one. Indeed, with some cities this is the defining principle
5   of the regime and the laws—that they exercise mastery over their neighbors. (9) Hence while most of the usages existing among most cities are,
so to speak, a mere jumble, nevertheless if the laws anywhere look to one
thing, it is domination that all of them aim at. In Sparta and Crete, for ex-

7 · Aristotle appears to use "blessed" (*makarios*) as a synonym for "happy" (*eudaimōn*);
the former, however, carries a stronger religious connotation. Heroes were said to go to
the "Islands of the Blessed" after death.

8 · For the debate between proponents of the political and philosophical ways of life
see, for example, Plato, *Gorgias* 484c–86d.

9 · That is, a "real man:" *Anēr* carries a strong connotation of maleness or manliness.

ample, it is with a view to wars[10] that education and the greatest part of the
laws are organized. (10) Further, among all nations that are capable of ag-   10
grandizing themselves, power of this sort is honored—for example, among
the Scythians, the Persians, the Thracians, and the Celts. Among some of
them there are also certain laws stimulating men to this sort of virtue; for
example at Carthage, so it is asserted, they receive armlets to adorn themselves for each campaign they go on. (11) There was once a law in Macedonia   15
as well that any man who had not killed an enemy had to wear a tether for a
belt; among the Scythians one who had not killed an enemy was not permitted to drink from the cup passed around at a banquet; among the Iberians,
a warlike nation, they fix in the ground around a tomb as many spits as the   20
number of enemies [the deceased] has killed; (12) and there are many other
things of this sort among other nations, some of them prescribed by laws,
others by customs.

Yet it may perhaps seem absurd to those wishing to investigate the matter
that this should be the function of one expert in politics—to be able to discern how to exercise [imperial] rule and mastery over those nearby, whether   25
they wish it or not. (13) How could this be characteristic of political or legislative expertise when it is not even lawful? It is not lawful to rule a city in
this fashion justly, let alone unjustly; and it is possible to conquer others unjustly.[11] Yet not even in the other sciences do we see this: it is not a function   30
of the doctor or the pilot to either persuade or compel persons to submit to
their rule—patients in the one case, voyagers in the case of the other. (14) But
most people seem to suppose that expertise in mastery and in political rule
are the same thing, and they are not ashamed to practice in relation to others what they deny is just or advantageous for themselves. For among them-   35
selves they seek just rule, but they care nothing about justice toward others.
(15) It would be odd if there did not exist by nature that which exercises mastery and that which does not exercise mastery,[12] so that if matters stand in
this manner, one should not try to exercise mastery over all things but only
over those that are to be mastered, just as one should not hunt human beings
for a feast or sacrifice, but rather that which is to be hunted for this purpose   40
(namely, any edible wild animal). (16) But even a single city in isolation could   1325a

10 · Π[1] has *tous polemious* ("enemies") instead of *tous polemous* ("wars"), perhaps
rightly.
11 · Contrary to those who equate might with right; cf. 1.6.
12 · Reading *despozon* (twice) with the MSS rather than *desposton* ("that which is to
be mastered and that which is not to be mastered") with Schneider and Dreizehnter.

be happy—which is to say, obviously, engage in politics in a fine manner, if indeed it is possible for a city to be settled in isolation somewhere using excellent laws—and the organization of its regime will not be with a view to
5   war and the conquest of enemies; for this is assumed not to exist.

(17) It is clear, therefore, that all the pursuits that have to do with war are to be regarded as fine, though not as the highest end of all, but rather as being for the sake of that. It belongs to the excellent legislator to see how a city, a stock of human beings,[13] and every other sort of community will share in the
10 good life and in the happiness that is possible for them. (18) Some of the prescribed customs will vary, however; and where neighboring peoples are present, it belongs to the legislator's expertise to see what sorts of training are to be undertaken with a view to what sorts of neighbors, and how the measures
15 appropriate in each case are to be applied. But this —toward what end the best regime should be directed—may be appropriately investigated later.[14]

CHAPTER 3

(1) In regard to those who agree that the most choiceworthy way of life is the one accompanied by virtue but differ about the practice of it—on the one
20 side they reject the holding of political offices, since they consider the way of life of the free person to be different from that of the political ruler and the most choiceworthy of all; on the other, they consider the latter the best, arguing that it is impossible for one who acts in nothing to act well, and that acting well and happiness are the same thing—we must say to both that they argue correctly in some respects and incorrectly in others. (2) The one side is correct in saying that the way of life of the free person is better than that
25 involving mastery. This is true: there is nothing dignified about using a slave as a slave; giving commands concerning necessary things has nothing noble about it. But to consider every sort of rule as mastery is not correct. There is no less distance between rule over free persons and rule over slaves than be-
30 tween what is by nature free and what is by nature slavish. But these things were discussed adequately in the initial discourses.[15]

(3) To praise inactivity more than activity is also not true. Happiness is a sort of action, and the actions of just and moderate persons bring to completion many noble things. Now when such matters are discussed in this way,
35 one might perhaps conceive that having authority over all persons is best, for

13 · *Genos anthrōpōn*, that is, a "nation" (*ethnos*).
14 · 7.13–15.
15 · 1.4–7.

in this way one would have authority over the greatest number and the noblest of actions. (4) So [on this understanding] one who is capable of doing so should not leave those nearby to rule themselves but should deprive them of it—and a father should take no account of his children nor children of their father nor a friend for his friend nor take any thought for it; for the best is what is most choiceworthy, and acting well is best. Perhaps they argue truly in this if the most choiceworthy of existing things will belong to those who plunder and use force. (5) But perhaps it is impossible that it belong to them, and this presupposition of theirs is false. For actions can no longer be noble for one who does not differ as much from those he rules as husband differs from wife, father from children, or master from slaves. So the transgressor could never make up later for the deviation from virtue he has already committed. Among similar persons nobility and justice are found in ruling and being ruled in turn, for this is something equal and similar: (6) to assign what is not equal to equal persons and what is not similar to similar persons is contrary to nature, and nothing contrary to nature is noble. Hence when another person is superior on the basis of virtue and of the capacity that acts to achieve the best things, it is noble to follow this person and just to obey him. (7) (Not only virtue should belong to him but also capacity, on the basis of which he will act.)[16] But if these things are argued finely and happiness is to be regarded as the same as acting well, the best way of life both in common for every city and for the individual would be the active one.

(8) Yet the active way of life is not necessarily in relation to others, as some suppose, nor those thoughts alone active that arise from activity for the sake of what results, but rather much more those that are complete in themselves, and the sorts of studies and thoughts that are for their own sake. Acting well is the end, so it too is a certain action; and even in the case of external actions we speak of master craftsmen—whose activity consists in thoughts—as acting in the authoritative sense. (9) Indeed, not even cities that are situated by themselves and intentionally choose to live in this way are necessarily inactive. For activity can come about relative to a city's parts: there are many sorts of shared activities[17] undertaken by the parts of the city in relation to one another. (10) This is possible in a similar way for any individual human being as well. For otherwise the god and the entire universe could hardly be in a fine condition, since they have no external actions beyond those that are proper to themselves. That the same way of life must necessarily be the best

16 · Cf. 5.9.1309a33-39.
17 · Literally, "communities" (*koinōniai*).

both for each human being individually and for cities and human beings in common, then, is evident.

(1) Since this has been said by way of preface about these things, and since
35 the other sorts of regimes were studied earlier,[18] the beginning point of what remains is to speak in the first instance of the sorts of presuppositions there should be concerning the city that is to be constituted on the basis of what one would pray for. (2) For it is impossible for the best regime to come into being without equipment to match. Hence there are many things that we should presuppose for ourselves in advance, like persons offering prayer; yet
40 none of these things should be impossible. I mean, for example, concerning the number of citizens and the amount of territory. (3) For just as in the case of the other craftsmen—the weaver, for example, or the shipbuilder—
1326a material must be available that is suitable to work on (for to the extent that this has been better prepared, what is brought into being by the art is necessarily finer), so too in the case of the political expert and the legislator the
5 proper material should be available in a suitable condition. (4) To the equipment proper to the city belongs in the first instance both the multitude of human beings—how many should be available and of what quality by nature—and the territory in the same way—how much there should be and of what quality. Now most persons suppose that it is appropriate for the happy
10 city to be great. If this is true, they are ignorant of what sort of city is great and what sort small. (5) They judge one to be great on the basis of the number of the multitude of inhabitants, but one should look not to their number but to their capacity. For there exists a certain function of a city too, so that the city most capable of bringing this to completion is the one that must be
15 supposed the greatest—just as one might assert that Hippocrates is greater not as a human being but as a doctor than someone excelling him in bodily size. (6) Yet even if one should judge by looking to number, this must not be done on the basis of any chance multitude (for perhaps of necessity there is
20 present in cities a large number of slaves as well as aliens and foreigners), but only those who are a part of the city—of those proper parts out of which a city is constituted. It is preeminence in the multitude of these people that is an indication of a great city. One that can send out a large number of work-

18 · The reference would seem to be to the discussion of candidate best regimes in book 2.

ers but few heavy-armed troops cannot possibly be great. To be a great city
and a populous one is not the same thing.   25

(7) This too, at any rate, is evident from the facts: that it is difficult—
perhaps impossible—for a city that is too populous to be well managed. Of
those that are held to be finely governed, at any rate, we see none that is
lax in regard to [restricting the] number [of inhabitants]. This is clear also
through the proof afforded by arguments. (8) For law is a certain sort of   30
order, and good governance must of necessity involve good order.[19] But an
overly excessive number is incapable of partaking in order. This is, indeed, a
task requiring divine power, which is what holds together the whole itself.
[At the same time, too small a number is also inadequate for a good or beautiful arrangement,[20]] since the beautiful, at any rate, we are accustomed to
perceive in [things substantial in] number and size. (9) Hence that city too
must necessarily be the finest where, together with size, the defining principle mentioned is present. But there is a certain measure of size in a city as   35
well, just as in all other things—animals, plants, instruments: none of these
things will have its own capacity if it is either overly small or excessive with
respect to size, but it will sometimes be wholly robbed of its nature, and at
other times in a poor condition. A ship that is a foot long, for example, will   40
not be a ship at all, nor one of twelve hundred feet, and as it approaches a certain size it will make for a bad voyage, in the one case because of smallness, in   1326b
the other because of excess. (11) Similarly with the city as well, the one that
is made up of too few persons is not self-sufficient, though the city is a self-
sufficient thing, while the one that is made up of too many persons is with
respect to the necessary things self-sufficient like a nation, but is not a city;
for it is not easy for a regime to be present. Who will be general of an overly   5
excessive number, or who will be herald, unless he has the voice of Stentor?[21]

Hence the first city must necessarily be that made up of a multitude so
large as to be the first multitude that is self-sufficient with a view to living well
in the context of the political community. (12) It is possible for one that ex-   10
ceeds this on the basis of number to be a greater city, but this is not possible,
as we said, indefinitely. As to what the defining principle of the excess is, it is
easy to see from the facts. The actions of the city belong on the one hand to

19 · The term "good governance" (eunomia) is etymologically related to the term
"law" (nomos), but is suggestive of a condition of orderliness going beyond the obser-
vance of legal norms as such.
20 · A line appears to have dropped out of the text at this point; I have supplied what
I take to be the sense.
21 · The proverbial Stentor was one of Homer's warriors (Iliad 5.785–86).

the rulers, on the other to the ruled. The task of a ruler is command and judg-
15   ment. (13) With a view both to judgment concerning the just things and distributing offices on the basis of merit, the citizens must necessarily be familiar with one another's qualities; where this does not happen to come about,
what is connected with the offices and with judging is necessarily carried on
20   poorly. For in either case it is not just to act haphazardly—the very thing that
manifestly happens in an overly populous city. (14) Further, in such cities it
is easy for aliens and foreigners to assume a part in the regime: it is not difficult for them to escape notice on account of the excess of number. It is clear,
therefore, that the best defining principle for a city is this: the greatest excess
of number with a view to self-sufficiency of life that is readily surveyable.[22]
25   Concerning the size of a city, then, let the discussion stand in this manner.

CHAPTER 5

(1) Something very similar holds as well in what concerns the territory. As far
as its being of a certain quality, it is clear that everyone would praise the territory that is the most self-sufficient. That which bears every sort of thing is
of necessity such, for self-sufficiency is having everything available and being
30   in extent[23] and size the territory should be large enough
so that the inhabitants are able to live at leisure in the fashion of free men
and at the same time with moderation. (2) Whether regarding this defining
principle we are arguing finely or not must be investigated with greater precision later, when there will be an opportunity to give an account of [acquir-
ing] property and what is involved in being well off in terms of possessing
35   it—how and in what manner this should relate to the use of it.[24] For there
are many disputes in connection with this investigation on account of those
who invite us toward either sort of excess in our way of life—the ones toward
penury, the others toward luxury.[25]

22 · The term is *eusynoptos*: easy to take in at a glance.
23 · Aristotle is perhaps thinking of the size of individual land holdings as well as the
overall size of the territory. The awkwardness of the transition here and the fact that
the question of the quality of the territory is not clearly exhausted (it appears to be returned to in 3–4) suggest that something may have been omitted from the text.
24 · Reading *autēs* for the *autēn* of the MSS, with Ross and Kraut. There is no discussion of this kind in the remainder of the *Politics* as we have it, and the meaning is
somewhat uncertain.
25 · The reference is probably to different systems of laws and customs concerning
property (the Spartan and the Carthaginian?); but Aristotle may also have in mind dif-

(3) It is not difficult to speak of the kind of territory (regarding certain   40
matters one should also be persuaded by those who are experienced in generalship)—that it ought to be difficult for enemies to enter, but readily ex-
ited by the citizens themselves, and further, just as we asserted that the mul-   1327a
titude of human beings should be readily surveyable, that the territory too
ought to be: being readily surveyable, the territory is readily defended. If the
position of the city is to be fixed according to what one would pray for, it is
appropriate for it to lie finely in relation to both sea and land. (4) One defin-   5
ing principle is that mentioned—the city should have access to all localities
with a view to defensive sallies. The remaining one is that it should be accessible with a view to the conveyance of crops, and further of materials for lum-
ber, and any other product of this sort the territory might happen to possess.   10

CHAPTER 6

(1) Concerning access to the sea, there is much dispute as to whether it is beneficial or harmful for well-governed cities. For, some assert, to let in certain
foreigners who have been raised under other laws is disadvantageous with
respect to good governance, as is overpopulation; for as a result of their use   15
of the sea for exporting and importing, a multitude of traders comes into existence, and this is contrary[26] to their engaging in politics in a fine manner.
(2) Now it is not unclear that, if these things do not result, it is better, both
with a view to safety and with a view to having a ready supply of necessary
things, for the city and the territory to be close to the sea. (3) With a view to   20
bearing up under enemies more easily, they should be capable of a ready defense in both elements—land and sea—if they are to preserve themselves.
And with a view to injuring the attackers, if this is not possible in both elements, to do so in one will still be easier for those who have access to both.   25
(4) It is also necessary for cities both to import the things that happen not to
be available at home and to export what exists in surplus. But the city should
be involved in trade for itself, not for others: those who set themselves up as a
market for all do so for the sake of revenue; a city that should not be party to   30

---

fering philosophical views—in particular those of the Cynics and Cyrenaics (consider,
for example, Diogenes Laertius 2.68–69, 6.8). Cf. 1.9.

26 · Reading *hypenantion* with a few MSS rather than *hypenantian* with the other
MSS and with Dreizehnter and most editors. I take *emporōn plēthos* as the subject of this
clause rather than *tēn polyanthrōpian*, as is commonly done. If *hypenantian* is retained,
the meaning would be: "which arises as a result of a multitude of traders using the sea
for exporting and importing, and which is contrary to their being finely governed."

this sort of aggrandizement should not possess a trading center of this sort. (5) Since we see at present many territories and cities having ports and harbors that are naturally well positioned in relation to the city, so that they nei-
35   ther form part of the same town nor are overly far away, but are dominated by walls and other fortifications of this sort,[27] it is evident that if any good thing results from such access, this will be available to the city, while anything harmful can be guarded against easily by means of laws that stipulate and define which sorts of persons should and which should not have dealings with one another.

40   (6) Concerning naval power, it is not unclear that it is best to have a cer-
1327b tain amount of it. They should be formidable and capable of putting up a defense by sea as well as by land not only for themselves but also for certain of their neighbors. (7) Concerning the extent and size of this force, one must
5   look to the way of life of the city. If it is going to have a way of life that involves leadership and is political, it must necessarily have this sort of power available as well to match its actions. Cities will not necessarily have the overpopulation that occurs in connection with the seafaring mass: these should
10   be no part of the city. (8) The marine element[28] is free and belongs to the infantry; this is in authority and dominates the crew. And if there is available a multitude of subjects[29] who farm the territory, there will necessarily be an abundance of sailors too. We see this too in certain cities at present, as for ex-
15   ample the city of the Heracleots, which sends out many warships in spite of being more modest in size than other cities.[30]

Concerning territory, harbors, cities, and the sea, and concerning naval power, then, let our discussion stand in this manner.

CHAPTER 7

(1) Concerning the political multitude, we spoke earlier of what its defin-
20   ing principle ought to be; let us speak now of what quality of persons they

---

27 · Piraeus, the port of Athens, stood some five miles from the city, but was connected to it by long walls, and its harbors were fortified against attack by sea. Megara, Corinth, and other cities with important maritime interests had similar arrangements.
28 · That is, heavy-armed troops embarked on ships as "marines."
29 · That is, agricultural serfs (as in Sparta, Crete or Thessaly).
30 · This argument is meant to answer a possible objection to the possession of naval power deriving from the experience of Athens, where the manpower requirements of the fleet had greatly increased the political strength of the lower classes (cf. 4.4. 21, 5.4. 8).

should be in their nature. Now one may ascertain this merely by looking both at those cities among the Greeks that are held in repute and at the entire inhabited world as divided among nations.[31] (2) The nations in cold locations, particularly in Europe, are filled with spiritedness,[32] but relatively lacking in thought and art; hence they remain freer, but lack political governance[33] and are incapable of ruling their neighbors. Those in Asia, on the other hand, have souls endowed with thought and art, but are lacking in spiritedness; hence they remain ruled and enslaved. (3) But the stock of the Greeks shares in both—just as it holds the middle in terms of location. For it is both spirited and endowed with thought, and hence both remains free and governs itself in the best manner and at the same time is capable of ruling all, should it obtain a single regime. (4) The nations of Greeks also display the same difference in relation to one another. Some have a nature that is one-sided, while others are well blended in relation to both of these capacities. It is evident, therefore, that those who are to be readily guided to virtue by the legislator should be both endowed with thought and spirited in their nature. (5) For as to what some assert should be present in guardians,[34] to be affectionate toward familiar persons but savage toward those who are unknown, it is spiritedness that creates affectionateness; for this is the capacity of soul by which we feel affection. An indication of this is that spiritedness is more aroused against intimates and friends than against unknown persons when it considers itself slighted. (6) Hence Archilochus, when complaining of his friends, appropriately addressed his spiritedness: "Yes, it is among friends you are choked with rage."[35] Both the element of ruling and the element of freedom stem from this capacity for everyone: spiritedness is a thing expert at ruling and indomitable. (7) But it is not right to say that they are harsh toward those who are unknown. One ought not to be of this sort toward anyone, nor are magnanimous persons[36] savage in their nature, except toward those behaving unjustly. And, further, they will feel this rather toward their intimates, as was said earlier, if they consider themselves treated

31 · For what follows, see book 1, n. 31.
32 · "Spiritedness" (*thymos*) plays a major role in the psychology developed in Plato's *Republic*, but is not otherwise prominent in Aristotle's writings. Consider, however, Lord 1982, 159–73.
33 · The word is *apoliteuta*.
34 · An allusion to the warrior class of Plato's *Republic* (375b–c).
35 · Archilochus, fr. 67b Diehl.
36 · This seems to allude to the discussion of "magnanimity" or "greatness of soul" (*megalopsychia*) in *Eth. Nic.* 4.3.

unjustly. (8) Moreover, it is reasonable that this should happen. For when it is among those they suppose should be under obligation to return a benefaction, in addition to the injury they consider themselves deprived of this as
15   well. Thus it has been said: "harsh are the wars of brothers," and "those who have loved extravagantly will hate extravagantly too."[37]

(9) Concerning those engaging in politics, then, how many there should be and of what quality in their nature, and further with respect to the territory, how much and of what quality it should be, there has been enough discussion. The same precision should not be sought through arguments as through what depends on perception.

CHAPTER 8

(1) Just as in other things constituted according to nature those things without which the whole could not exist are not parts of the constitution of the thing as a whole, it is clear that those things must not be regarded as parts of
25   a city that belong to cities of necessity, nor of any other community out of which there is constituted something single in type. (2) For there should be one single thing that is both common and the same for all sharers, whether they have an equal or an unequal portion—in sustenance, for example, or an amount of territory, or anything else of this sort. (3) When one thing is [something] for the sake of which [other things exist][38] and another thing is
30   for the sake of this, there is nothing common to these things except that one acts and the other receives. I mean, for example, as between any instrument or the craftsmen and the work produced: there is nothing in common between a house and a house-builder, but the house-builders' art is for the sake of the house. (4) Hence while cities need property, property is no part of the
35   city. Many animate things are part of property. But the city is a community of similar persons, for the sake of a life that is the best possible. (5) Since happiness is the best thing, and this is the actualization of virtue and a certain complete practice of it,[39] and since it happens that some persons are able to partake of it while others are able to do so only to a small degree or not at
40   all, it is clear that this is the cause of there being several kinds and varieties of
1328b city and several sorts of regime. For it is through hunting for this in a differ-

37 · The quotations are from tragedies by Euripides (fr. 975 Nauck²) and an unknown author (fr. 78 Nauck²).
38 · "The for the sake of which" (*to hou heneka*) is a technical Aristotelian term synonymous with "end" or "final cause."
39 · See *Eth. Nic.* 1.7–8.

ent manner and by means of different things that individuals create ways of life and regimes that differ.

(6) We must also investigate how many things there are without which a city could not exist; what we speak of as being parts of a city would also be among those things which must necessarily be present.[40] We must therefore have a grasp of the number of tasks the city needs performed; it will be clear 5 from these things. (7) First, then, sustenance must be available; next, arts, for living requires many instruments; third, arms, for those who are sharers must necessarily also have arms among themselves, both with a view to ruling in the case of those who disobey and with a view to outsiders who attempt to do 10 them injustice; further, a ready supply of funds, so that they may have what suffices with a view both to their needs among themselves and to military needs; fifth, and first, the superintendence connected with the divine, which they call priestcraft; sixth in number, and the most necessary thing of all, decision concerning things advantageous and just in relation to one another. (8) These, then, are the tasks that virtually every city needs. For the city is not 15 any chance multitude, but one self-sufficient with a view to life, as we assert; and if any of these things happens to be omitted, it is impossible for this community to be simply self-sufficient. (9) A city must necessarily be constituted, therefore, on the basis of these tasks. Accordingly, there must be a multitude 20 of farmers who will provide sustenance, artisans, a fighting element, the well-off, priests, and those who decide regarding things just[41] and advantageous.

CHAPTER 9

(1) These things having been discussed, it remains to investigate whether all are to share in all of these things (for it is possible that the same persons 25 should all be farmers, artisans, and those who deliberate and adjudicate), or different persons are to be presupposed for each of the functions mentioned, or some of these are of necessity special and others common. It is not the same in every regime. (2) For, as we said, it is possible both for all to participate in everything and for all not to participate in everything, but some in 30 some things. These things too make regimes different: in democracies all

40 · Reading *en toutois an eiē ha* with Newman. The text of Π[1] has *en toutois an eiē dio* ("would be among these things, hence"), which does not seem satisfactory. Newman's conjectural *ha* (presupposing the omission of *dio* in Π[2]) is much preferable to Dreizehnter's bracketing of *an eiē dio*.

41 · Accepting (with Kraut) Lambinus's conjecture *dikaiōn* ("just") in place of the *anankaiōn* ("necessary") of the MSS.

take part in everything, while in oligarchies it is the opposite. (3) Since we
happen to be investigating concerning the best regime, and this is the one in
accordance with which the city would be happy above all, and since it was
said earlier[42] that happiness cannot be present apart from virtue, it is evident
from these things that in the city that is most finely governed—one possessing men who are just unqualifiedly and not relative to a presupposition—the
citizens should not live a worker's or a merchant's way of life, for this sort of
way of life is ignoble and contrary to virtue. (4) Nor, indeed, should those
who are going to be citizens in such a regime be farmers; for there is a need
for leisure both with a view to the creation of virtue and with a view to political activities. But since both the military element and the element that
deliberates concerning the advantageous things and judges concerning the
just things inhere in the city and are evidently parts of it above all, must these
too be regarded as different, or are both to be assigned to the same persons?
(5) This too is evident: in a manner it should be to the same persons, and in a
manner to different persons. Insofar as each of these tasks belongs to a different prime of life, the one requiring prudence, the other power, it should be to
different persons; but insofar as it is impossible that those who are capable of
using compulsion and preventing its being used against them will always put
up with being ruled, to this extent they should be the same persons. For those
who have authority over arms also have authority over whether the regime
will last or not. (6) What remains is for this regime to assign both things to
the same persons,[43] though not at the same time, but as it is natural for power
to be found among younger persons and prudence among older persons, it
is advantageous and just to distribute them to both, for this division reflects
what accords with merit.

(7) Possessions too should [be assigned] in connection with these persons.[44] For a ready supply must necessarily be available to the citizens, and
these are the citizens. For the worker element does not share in the city, nor
any other type that is not a "craftsman of virtue."[45] This is clear from the presupposition: happiness must necessarily be present together with virtue, and
one should call a city happy by looking not at a certain part of it, but rather

42 · 7.1.
43 · Reading *amphotera* with Ross and Kraut rather than *amphoterois* with the MSS,
and taking *tēn politeian tautēn* as the subject of *apodidonai*. The text of the MSS is usually translated, "What remains is to assign these political rights to both groups of persons."
44 · At least one word appears to have dropped out of the text at this point.
45 · Apparently an allusion to Plato, *Republic* 500d.

at all the citizens. (8) It is also evident that possessions must belong to these   25
persons if the farmers must necessarily be slaves or barbarian subjects.[46]

Of the things enumerated there remains the category of priests. (9) The
arrangement of these too is evident. No farmer or worker is to be appointed
priest, for it is proper for the gods to be honored by citizens. Since the politi-   30
cal element is divided into two parts—these being the armed element and
the deliberative element—and since it is proper that those worn out with age
should both render worship to the gods and find rest for themselves, it is to
these that priesthoods are to be assigned.

(10) We have spoken of the things without which a city cannot be consti-   35
tuted and of how many parts of a city there are. Farmers, artisans, and the entire laboring element must necessarily be present in cities; the armed element
and the deliberative element are parts of the city; and each of these is separate
from the others, some permanently, the others by turns.

CHAPTER 10

(1) That the city should be divided among separate types of persons, and that   40
the fighting and farming elements should be different, seems to be something   1329b
familiar to those philosophizing about the regime not only at present or in
recent times. Things stand in this manner in Egypt still today, and also in
Crete, Sesostris having legislated in this fashion for Egypt, so it is asserted,[47]
and Minos for Crete. (2) The arrangement of common messes also seems to   5
be ancient, those at Crete having arisen in connection with the kingship of
Minos, while those in Italy are much older than these. (3) For the chroniclers
who live there assert that a certain Italus became king of Oenotria, and that
on account of him they changed their name and were called Italians instead   10
of Oenotrians, and the name of Italy was acquired by that promontory of
Europe which is within the gulfs of Scylletium and Lametius, these being a
half-day's journey apart.[48] (4) Now they say that this Italus made farmers of
the nomadic Oenotrians and enacted laws for them, in particular institut-   15
ing—for the first time—common messes. Hence even now some of those
who are descended from him still use common messes and some of the laws.
(5) In the direction of Tyrrhenia there lived the Opicans, who were then
(and are at present) called by the surname Ausonians; and in the direction   20

46 · Bracketing the ē of the MSS ("barbarians or subjects") with Dreizehnter; cf. 10.13.
47 · See Herodotus 2.164.
48 · The modern gulfs of Squillace and S. Eufemia. The material referred to may derive from the chronicler Antiochus of Syracuse.

of Iapygia and the Ionian Gulf, in the so-called Siritis, lived the Chonians—the Chonians too being Oenotrians by stock.[49] (6) It was there, then, that the arrangement of common messes first arose, while the separation of the political multitude according to type originated in Egypt (for the kingship of Sesostris long precedes that of Minos). (7) One should therefore consider that practically everything has been discovered on many occasions—or rather an infinity of occasions—in the course of time. For it is likely that the necessary discoveries are taught by need, while those relating to elegance and superfluity may be reasonably expected to begin increasing once these are already present; and one should suppose that the things connected with regimes stand in the same manner. (8) That all such things are ancient is indicated by those connected with Egypt. For the Egyptians are held to be the most ancient of peoples, yet they have obtained laws and a political arrangement. Hence one should use what has been adequately discovered[50] while attempting to seek out what has been passed over.[51]

(9) That the territory should belong to those who possess heavy arms and those who share in the regime, then, was said earlier, and why the farmers should be different from these and how much and of what sort the territory ought to be was also discussed. We must now speak first about the distribution of land and, with regard to the farmers, who and of what sort they ought to be, since we assert both that property should not be common, as some have said, but rather should become common in use after the fashion of friends, and that none of the citizens should be in want of sustenance.[52] (10) Regarding common messes, all hold that it is useful for them to be present in well-instituted cities; the reason for our holding the same opinion will be spoken of later.[53] All the citizens should share in these, but it is not easy for the poor to contribute the required amount from their private funds and administer the rest of their household. Further, expenditures relating to the gods should be common to the entire city.

(11) It is necessary, therefore, to divide the territory into two parts, one being common and the other for private individuals, and to divide each of these

49 · Tyrrhenia corresponds roughly to modern Tuscany; Iapygia is modern Puglia, the southeastern extremity of the Italian peninsula.

50 · Reading *heurēmenois* with Lambinus and Dreizehnter instead of the *eirēmenois* ("what has been mentioned") of the MSS.

51 · Many editors consider part or all of this passage (1329a40–b25) to be a later interpolation.

52 · Cf. 2.5. 6–7.

53 · There is no discussion of this sort in the remainder of the *Politics* as we have it.

in two again. One part of the common territory should be for public service relating to the gods, the other for the expense of the common messes. Of the territory that belongs to private individuals, one part should be toward the frontiers, the other toward the city, so that, with two allotments assigned   15
to each individual, all partake in both locations. This provides equality and justice, as well as greater concord with a view to wars with their neighbors. (12) For wherever things do not stand in this manner, some make light of an enmity toward those on the border, while others are concerned with it overly   20
much and contrary to what is noble. Hence among some peoples there is a law that those who are neighbors of a bordering people may not share jointly in deliberation concerning wars against them, the assumption being that they are not capable of deliberating finely on account of their private interest.

(13) It is necessary to divide the territory in this manner, then, for the reasons just spoken of. As for the farmers, it is necessary above all—if one   25
should speak according to what one would pray for—that they be slaves who are neither all of the same stock nor of spirited ones, as in that way they would be useful with a view to the work and safe as regards their undertaking subversive activity; or, second, they should be barbarian subjects resembling in their nature those just mentioned. (14) Of these, the ones in private   30
hands should belong privately to those possessing the estates, while those on the common land should be common. In what manner slaves should be treated, and why it is better to hold out freedom as a reward for all slaves, we will speak of later.[54]

CHAPTER 11

(1) That the city should have access to the mainland and the sea as well as to   35
the territory as a whole, so far as circumstances allow, was said earlier.[55] As for its position relative to itself, one should pray to obtain this looking to four things.[56] The first, as being something necessary, is health. (2) Those cities are healthier which slope toward the east and toward the winds that blow   40
from the direction of the rising sun; second are those sloping in the direction the north wind blows, as these have better winters. Of the remaining things, one should look to see that the city is in a fine condition with a view to political and military activities. (3) With a view to military activities, it ought to be   1330b

54 · There is no discussion of this sort in the remainder of the *Politics* as we have it.
55 · Cf. 7.5.
56 · Text and meaning are somewhat uncertain. I read *katatynchanein* with the MSS rather than Dreizehnter's conjectural *kata tychēn*.

ready of exit for the citizens themselves but difficult for their adversaries to
approach and besiege. It should have available above all a multitude of pools
5   and springs of its own; but failing this, a way has been discovered to construct
great and ample receptacles for rain water, so that they will never run short
when they are cut off from their territory by war. (4) Since one should take
thought for the health of the inhabitants, this consists in the location being
10   finely situated on ground of this sort and toward an exposure of this sort,
and second, in using healthy sorts of water, and making this more than an in-
cidental concern; for the things we use most of and most often for the body
are what contribute most to health, and the capacity of waters and wind has
15   such a nature. (5) Hence in all sensible cities, if all the springs are not similar
or those of such a sort are not ample, a distinction should be made between
those for sustenance and those for other needs.

With regard to fortified places, what is advantageous is not the same for
all regimes. For example, a fortified height[57] is characteristic of oligarchy
20   and monarchy; levelness is characteristic of democracy; neither of these is
characteristic of aristocracy, but rather a number of strong places. (6) The
disposition of private dwellings is considered more pleasant and more useful for other activities if it involves straight rows in the newer manner of
25   Hippodamus,[58] but for safety in war the opposite manner that prevailed in
ancient times; for this made it difficult of entrance[59] for foreign troops and
difficult for attackers to find their way around. (7) Hence it should share in
both of these. If one institutes the sort of arrangement that among farmers
30   some call "clumps" of vines, it is possible to avoid having the city as a whole
disposed in straight rows, but for certain parts and places to be; in this way
it will be in a fine condition with a view to safety as well as ordered beauty.[60]

(8) As regards walls, those who deny that cities laying claim to virtue should have them have overly old-fashioned conceptions—especially
when they see the cities that have pretensions of that sort refuted by fact.[61]

57 · Many cities—notably Athens—had grown up around a "fortified height" (*akropo-
lis*) where citizens could take refuge during an invasion.
58 · For Hippodamus, see 2.8.
59 · Accepting Richards's conjecture *dyseisodos* for the *dysexodos* ("difficult of exit") of
the MSS with Ross and Kraut.
60 · A "clump" (*systas*, literally, a "close standing") of vine plants consisted of five plants
arranged like the five spots of a die. Aristotle appears to suggest that houses could be
grouped more or less irregularly in this fashion in the city's outlying parts, while large
boulevards and public areas would be reserved for the protected center.
61 · The allusion is to Sparta and its humiliation by Thebes during the invasion of
Epaminondas.

(9) Possibly it is not a noble thing to seek preservation from attackers who 35
are similar and not much greater in numbers by means of the fortification of
walls. But since it happens—and is [always] possible—that the preeminence
of the attackers is greater than virtue that is [only] human and resident in a
few [who make up the citizen body], the safest fortification of walls must 40
be supposed to be what most accords with military expertise, if the city is
to be preserved and not suffer any ills or be arrogantly treated, particularly 1331A
given the inventions of the present connected with missiles and machines
for improved proficiency in sieges.[62] (10) To claim that cities do not merit
having walls around them is like seeking to have the territory ready of access and mountainous places removed—it is like not having walls for private 5
houses on the grounds that the inhabitants will become unmanly. (11) This
too should not be overlooked, that it is open to those who have walls around
the city to treat their cities in either fashion, as having walls and as not hav- 10
ing them, while this is not open to those who do not possess them. If things
stand in this manner, not only must there be walls around a city, but they
should be taken care of in such a way that they should be in an appropriate
condition both with a view to order and beauty and with a view to military
requirements, in particular those that have arisen only recently. (12) For just
as the attackers pay attention to the ways they can gain the upper hand, so 15
in the case of the defenders some things have been discovered already, while
others should be sought out and investigated[63] by them. For men will not
even attempt an attack in the first place against those who are well prepared.

CHAPTER 12

(1) Since the multitude of the citizens should be distributed in common 20
messes, and since the walls should have guardhouses and towers at intervals
in convenient places, these things clearly suggest setting up some of the common messes in these guardhouses. (2) One might order these things, then,
in this manner. As for the buildings assigned to divine matters and the com- 25
mon messes for the most authoritative official boards, it is fitting for them to
be located together in a proper place, at least in the case of those temples that
the law or some prophecy of the Delphic oracle does not require to be separate. (3) This would be the sort of place whose position is adequate for mak-

62 · Catapults, battering rams, and movable towers were introduced into Greek warfare by the Carthaginians in the course of their struggle with Dionysius I of Syracuse;
Philip of Macedon used them extensively (cf. Demosthenes, *Philippics* 3.50).
63 · Literally, "philosophized about."

ing their virtue manifest[64] and at the same time better fortified in relation to
30   the neighboring parts of the city. Below this place it is proper to institute a
market of the sort they have in Thessaly—the one they call "free"; (4) this
is one that is kept clear of wares and where no worker or farmer or anyone
35   else of this sort can enter unless summoned by the officials. The place would
have added appeal if there was an arrangement there for the exercises of the
older men. (5) For it is proper to distinguish this order as well on the basis of
age, and to have some of the officials spend time with the younger men, and
40   the older with the officials; for being before the eyes of officials most of all
engenders a genuine sense of shame and the fear that belongs to free persons.
1331b   (6) The market for wares should be different from this and have a separate
location, one that is convenient for bringing together both the things that are
sent in from the sea and all the things from the country.

5   Since the multitude of the city is divided into priests, officials, [and soldiers, and since common messes have been provided on sacred ground for
officials,] it is proper that there should be an arrangement to have common
messes for the priests too in the vicinity of the sacred buildings.[65] (7) Those
of the official boards that superintend agreements, suits of indictment, sum-
monses, and other administration of this sort, and further, management of
10   the market and so-called town management, should be stationed near the
market or some accessible meeting place, this being one that is located near
the necessary market. For the upper market we regard as the one for being
at leisure, and this one as being with a view to necessary activities. (8) The
arrangement just spoken of ought to be imitated in matters pertaining to
15   the country. For there too with a view to guarding there must necessarily be
guardhouses and common messes for those officials some call "foresters" and
others "field managers," and further, temples must be distributed throughout
the country, some for gods and others for heroes.

    (9) But it is pointless to spend time at present giving a detailed account
20   and speaking of such things. It is not difficult to understand such things, but
more so to do them: speaking about them is a work of prayer, having them
come about, a work of chance. Hence anything further concerning such
things may be dismissed at present.

64 · Reading *thesin te echei pros tēn tēs aretēs epiphaneian* with Thomas instead of *epiphaneian te echei pros tēn tēs aretēs thesin* ("has conspicuousness in respect to the position of virtue") with the MSS and Dreizehnter.
65 · Text and meaning are uncertain. I assume a lacuna after *archontas* rather than
bracketing the word with Dreizehnter, or reading *proestos* ("the directing element") instead of the *plēthos* ("the multitude") of the MSS with a number of editors.

CHAPTER 13

(1) Concerning the regime itself, and out of which and what sort of persons the city that is going to be blessed and finely governed should be constituted, we must now speak. (2) There are two things that living well consists in for all: one of these is in correct positing of the aim and end of actions; the other, discovering the actions that bear on the end. These things can be consonant with one another or dissonant, for sometimes the aim is finely posited but in acting they miss achieving it, and sometimes they achieve everything with a view to the end, but the end they posited was bad. And sometimes they miss both. In connection with medicine, for example, doctors sometimes neither judge rightly what the quality of a healthy body should be nor achieve what is productive in relation to the object they set for themselves. But in all arts and sciences both of these should be kept in hand, the end and the actions directed to the end.

(3) Now that everyone strives for living well and for happiness is evident. It is open to some to achieve these things, but to others not, on account of some sort of fortune or nature; for living nobly requires a certain equipment too—less of it for those in a better state, more for those in a worse one. (4) Some, on the other hand, seek happiness incorrectly from the outset although it is open to them to achieve it. Since our object is to see the best regime, and this is one in accordance with which a city would be best governed, and it would be best governed in accordance with one that would make it possible for the city to be happy most of all, it is clear that one should not overlook what happiness is.

(5) We assert—and we have defined it thus in the discourses on ethics, if there is anything of benefit in those[66]—that happiness is the actualization and complete practice of virtue, and this not on the basis of a presupposition but unqualifiedly. (6) By "not on the basis of a presupposition" I mean necessary things, by "unqualifiedly," nobly. In the case of just actions, for example, just retributions and punishments derive from virtue, but they are necessary, and have the element of nobility only in a necessary way (for it would be more choiceworthy if no man or city required anything of the sort); but actions directed to honors and to what makes one well off are very noble in an unqualified sense. (7) For the one is in a sense the choice[67] of an evil, but ac-

25

30

35

40

1332a

5

10

15

---

66 · The reference appears to be to *Eth. Eud.* 1219a38, b2; cf. *Eth. Nic.* 1098b29–31, 1099b26, 1129b31.

67 · Reading *hairesis* with the MSS rather than *anairesis* ("removal") with Dreizehnter and many editors; cf. Newman ad loc.

tions of this latter sort are the opposite; they are providers and generators of
good things. An excellent man would deal in noble fashion with poverty, dis-
20   ease, and other sorts of bad fortune, but blessedness is in their opposites. Indeed, it was defined thus in the ethical discourses[68]—that the excellent person is one of a sort for whom on account of his virtue the things that are good
unqualifiedly are good; (8) and it is clear that his uses of these good things
25   must necessarily also be excellent and noble in an unqualified sense. Hence
human beings consider the causes of happiness to be those good things that
are external—as if the lyre rather than the art were to be held the cause of
brilliant and beautiful lyre playing.
Necessarily, therefore, some of the things mentioned must be present,
30   while others must be supplied by the legislator. (9) Hence we pray for the city
to be constituted on the basis of obtaining[69] those matters over which fortune has authority (we regard it as having authority [over the external things
we regard as being desirable for the best city to have present[70]]); but the city's
being excellent is no longer the work of fortune, but of knowledge and intentional choice. But a city is excellent, at any rate, through its citizens'—those
taking part in the regime—being excellent; and in our case all the citizens
35   take part in the regime. (10) This, then, must be investigated—how a man
becomes excellent. Now even if it is possible for all to be excellent but not
each of the citizens individually, the latter is more choiceworthy; for all being excellent follows from all individually being excellent.
40   Now men become good and excellent through three things. (11) These
three are nature, habit, and reason. For one must first develop naturally as
a human being and not some one of the other animals, and so also be of a
1332b   certain quality in body and soul. But there is no benefit in certain qualities
developing naturally, since habits make them alter: certain qualities are ambiguous in their nature, and through habits develop in the direction of worse
or better. (12) The other animals live by nature above all, but in some slight
5   respects by habit as well, while man lives also by reason (for he alone has reason); so these things should be consonant with one another. For men act in
many ways contrary to their habituation and their nature through reason, if
they are persuaded that some other condition is better. (13) Now as to the
sort of nature those should have who are going to be readily taken in hand

68 · The reference appears to be to *Eth. Eud.* 1248b26 ff.
69 · Reading *katatynchanein* with Kraut rather than *kat' euchēn* ("according to prayer")
with the MSS or *kata tychēn* ("according to fortune") with Dreizehnter.
70 · The text is somewhat uncertain; I assume a lacuna following *gar* in a30.

by the legislator, we discussed this earlier.[71] What remains at this point is the   10
work of education. For men learn some things by being habituated, others
by listening.

CHAPTER 14

(1) Since every political community is constituted of rulers and ruled, this
must then be investigated—if the rulers and the ruled should be different
or the same throughout life; for it is clear that education too will have to fol-   15
low in accordance with this distinction. (2) Now if the ones were as different
from the others as we believe gods and heroes differ from human beings—
much exceeding them in the first place in body, and then in soul, so that the   20
preeminence of the rulers is indisputable and evident to the ruled—it is clear
that it would always be better for the same persons to rule and the same to
be ruled once and for all. (3) But since this is not easy to assume, there being
none so different from the ruled as Scylax says the kings in India are,[72] it is   25
evident that for many reasons it is necessary for all in similar fashion to share
in ruling and being ruled in turn. For equality is the same thing [as justice[73]]
for persons who are similar, and it is difficult for a regime to last if its constitution is contrary to justice. (4) For the ruled [citizens] will have with them   30
all those [serfs] in the countryside who want to subvert it, and it is impossible
that those in the governing body will be numerous enough to be stronger
than all of these. Nevertheless, that the rulers should differ from the ruled is
indisputable. How this will be the case and how they will take part in ruling
and being ruled, then, should be investigated by the legislator.

(5) This was spoken of earlier. Nature has provided the distinction by   35
making that which is the same by type have a younger and an older element,
of which it is proper for the former to be ruled and the latter to rule. No one
chafes at being ruled on the basis of age or considers himself superior, particularly when he is going to recover his contribution[74] when he attains the age   40
to come. (6) In one sense, therefore, it must be asserted that the same persons
rule and are ruled, but in another sense different persons. So education too   1333a
must necessarily be the same in a sense, and in another sense different. For,

71 · 7.7.
72 · Scylax of Caryianda was a geographical writer of the late sixth century.
73 · Accepting Thurot's supplement *tōi dikaiōi*.
74 · A "contribution" (*eranos*) is a gift or loan for which repayment in some form is
anticipated.

so it is asserted, one who is going to rule finely should first have been ruled.[75] Now rule, as was said in our first discourses,[76] is on the one hand for the sake of the ruler, and on the other for the sake of the ruled. Of these sorts of rule we assert the former to be characteristic of a master, and the latter to belong to free persons.[77] (7) Now certain commands differ not by the tasks involved but by the end for the sake of which they are carried out. Hence it is noble for the free among the young to serve in many of the tasks that are held to be characteristic of servants; for, with a view to what is noble and what not noble, actions do not differ so much in themselves as in their end and that for the sake of which they are performed.

(8) Since we assert that the virtue of citizen and ruler is the same as that of the good man,[78] and the same person must be ruled first and ruler later, the legislator would have to make it his affair to determine how men can become good and through what pursuits, and what the end of the best life is.

(9) The soul is divided into two parts, of which the one has reason itself, while the other does not have it in itself, but is capable of obeying reason. To these belong, we assert, the virtues in accordance with which a man is spoken of as in some sense good.[79] As to which of these the end is more to be found in, what must be said is not unclear to those who distinguish in the way we assert should be done. (10) The worse is always for the sake of the better—this is evident in a similar way both in what accords with art and in what accords with nature; and the element having reason is better. This is divided in two in the manner we are accustomed to distinguish: there is reason of the active sort on the one hand and reason of the studying sort on the other.[80] (11) It is clear, therefore, that this part of the soul must also be divided in the same fashion. And we shall say that actions stand in a comparable relationship: those belonging to that part which is better by nature are more choiceworthy for those who are capable of achieving either all of them or [those belonging

75 · Both the structure of this sentence (*te* is unanswered) and the abrupt abandonment of the just introduced subject of education suggest that a substantial passage may have dropped out of the text at this point.

76 · 3.4. 10–13.

77 · A lacuna at this point in the text has been suspected by Immisch and others, perhaps rightly.

78 · 3.4–5.

79 · Compare particularly *Eth. Nic.* 1102a23–3a10.

80 · For the difference between "practical" and "theoretical" reason, see *Eth. Nic.* 1138b35–39b13 and the discussion that follows.

to] the two [lower parts]. For this is what is most choiceworthy for each in- 30
dividual always—to attain the highest thing possible for him.

(12) Life as a whole is divided, too, into occupation and leisure and war
and peace, and of matters involving action some are directed toward necessary and useful things, others toward noble things. (13) Concerning these
things there must of necessity be the same choice as in the case of the parts of
the soul and their actions: war must be for the sake of peace, occupation for 35
the sake of leisure, necessary and useful things for the sake of noble things.
The political ruler must legislate, therefore, looking to all these things in the
case both of the parts of the soul and of their actions, but particularly to the
things that are better and ends. (14) And he must do so in the same manner 40
in connection with the ways of life and the divisions[81] among activities; for
one should be capable of being occupied and going to war, but should rather 1333b
remain at peace and be at leisure, and one should act to achieve necessary and
useful things, but noble things more so. So it is with a view to these aims that
they must be educated when still children as well as during the other ages
that require education.

(15) Those of the Greeks who are at present held to be the best governed 5
and the legislators who established these regimes evidently did not organize
the things pertaining to the regime with a view to the best end, or the laws
and education with a view to all the virtues, but inclined in crude fashion
toward those which are held to be useful and of a more aggrandizing sort. 10
(16) Certain persons writing later in a spirit similar to this have expressed the
same opinion: in praising the regime of the Spartans they admire the aim of
the legislator, because he legislated everything with a view to domination and
war—views which are readily refutable on the basis of reason, and have now 15
been refuted by the facts. (17) For just as most human beings envy mastery
over many persons because it provides much equipment in the things of fortune, so Thibron and each of the others who write about their regime[82] evi- 20
dently admire the Spartans' legislator because they ruled over many persons
as a result of having trained themselves with a view to dangers. (18) And yet
since now at least ruling [an empire] is no longer available to the Spartans,
it clearly follows that they are not happy, and that their legislator was not a

81 · Reading *diaireseis* with the MSS and Kraut instead of *haireseis* ("choices") with
Coraes and Dreizehnter.
82 · Apart from Thibron, about whom nothing is known, Aristotle may have in mind
Xenophon's extant treatise on the Spartan regime; but he appears to indicate that such
treatises were numerous.

25   good one. But[83] this is ridiculous—that they should have lost the chance
      for living nobly even while abiding by his laws, and in the absence of any im-
      pediment to putting the laws into practice. (19) Nor do they have a correct
      conception concerning the sort of rule that the legislator should be seen to
      honor: rule over free persons is nobler and accompanied to a greater extent
      by virtue than ruling in the spirit of a master. Further, it is not on this ac-
      count that one should consider the city happy and praise the legislator, that
30   he trained it to conquer for the purpose of ruling those nearby; these things
      involve great harm. (20) For it is clear that any citizen who is capable of doing
      so must attempt to pursue the capability to rule his own city—the very thing
35   the Spartans accuse their king Pausanias of, even though he held so great a
      prerogative.[84] There is, indeed, nothing in such arguments and laws that is
      either political, beneficial, or true. (20) The same things are best for men
      both privately and in common, and the legislator should implant these in
      the souls of human beings. Training in matters related to war should be prac-
40   ticed not for the sake of reducing to slavery those who do not merit it, but in
      the first place in order that they themselves will not become slaves to others;
1334a next, so that they may seek leadership[85] for the sake of benefiting the ruled,
      but not for the sake of mastery over everyone; and third, to be master over
      those who merit being slaves. (22) That the legislator should give serious at-
      tention instead to arranging that legislation, and particularly that connected
5   with matters related to war, is for the sake of being at leisure and of peace, is
      testified to by events as well as arguments. Most cities of this sort preserve
      themselves when at war, but once having acquired [imperial] rule they come
      to ruin; they lose their edge, like iron, when they remain at peace. The reason
      is that the legislator has not educated them to be capable of being at leisure.

CHAPTER 15

      (1) Since the end appears to be the same for human beings both in common
      and privately, and there must necessarily be the same defining principle for
      the best man and the best regime, it is evident that the virtues directed to lei-
15   sure should be present; for, as has been said repeatedly, peace is the end of

83 · Reading *esti de* with Congreve instead of *eti de* ("further") with the MSS and
Dreizehnter.
84 · Presumably the Pausanias who attempted to become tyrant of Sparta after the
Persian War, although he was never technically king; but some have identified him with
a Pausanias who was king during the Peloponnesian War. Cf. 5.1. 10, 7.4.
85 · The Greek term is *hēgemonia*, connoting "hegemony" over other cities.

war, and leisure of occupation.[86] (2) The virtues useful with a view to leisure and pastime are both those that have their function in leisure and those that have it in occupation. For many of the necessary things should be present for it to be open to them to be at leisure. Hence it is appropriate that the city have moderation, courage, and endurance, for as the proverb has it, "there is   20 no leisure for slaves," and those who are incapable of facing danger in a courageous spirit are slaves of whoever comes along to attack them. (3) Now courage and endurance are required with a view to occupation; philosophy,[87] with a view to leisure; moderation and justice, at both times, and particularly   25 when they remain at peace and are at leisure. For war compels them to be just and behave with moderation, while the enjoyment of good fortune and being at leisure in peacetime tend to make them arrogant. (4) There is, then, a need for much justice and much moderation on the part of those who are held to act in the best way and who have all the gratifications that are regarded as   30 blessings, like those—if there are such—whom the poets assert are "in the islands of the blessed."[88] For these will be most particularly in need of philosophy and moderation and justice to the extent that they are at leisure in the midst of an abundance of good things of this sort.

(5) Why a city that is going to exist happily and be excellent should par-   35 take of these virtues, then, is evident. For if it is disgraceful not to be capable of using good things, it is still more so to be incapable of using them in leisure, but to be seen to be good men while occupied and at war but servile when remaining at peace and being at leisure. (6) Hence one should not train   40 in virtue as the city of the Spartans does. For it is not in this way that they differ from others, by not considering the greatest of good things to be the same things others do, but by considering that these things are gotten through   1334b some sort of virtue. But since they consider these good things and the gratification deriving from them to be greater than that deriving from the virtues, [the sort of virtue in which they are trained is only that useful and necessary for the acquisition of good things. That the sort of virtue is rather to be cultivated that governs the use of these good things, that this is preeminently the sort of virtue that is cultivated in leisure, and that it is to be cultivated[89]] on

86 · "Occupation" (*ascholia*) is literally "lack of leisure."

87 · Newman takes *philosophia* here to refer to "intellectual virtue," but this is by no means evident. Compare 2.5.15 ("habits, philosophy, and laws") and context, with Lord 1982, 199–200.

88 · A dwelling place for the souls of dead heroes; cf. Hesiod, *Works and Days* 170 ff.

89 · A lacuna of indeterminate and possibly substantial length occurs in the text at this point; I supply what I take to be the basic sense.

5   its own account, is evident from these things. How and through what things
it will exist is what must be studied now.

(7) We made a distinction earlier to the effect that there is a need for nature, habit, and reason. Of these things, what quality the citizens ought to
be in their nature was discussed earlier; what remains is to study whether
10   they are to be educated first by means of reason or by means of habits. These
should be consonant with one another, and the consonance should be the
best; for it is possible for one or both to have missed the best presupposition
in respect of reason and to have been similarly guided by habits. (8) This,
then, is evident at any rate in the first instance, with men just as among other
things—that birth derives from a beginning point, and the end from some
15   beginning point that is an end of something else;[90] but reason and intellect
are the end of our nature, so that it is with a view to these that birth and the
concern with habits should be handled. (9) Next, just as soul and body are
two things, so also do we see two parts of the soul, the irrational and that
having reason, and the dispositions belonging to these are two in number,
20   one of which is appetite and the other intellect; and just as the body is prior
in birth to the soul, so is the irrational part to that having reason. (10) This
too is evident, for spiritedness and will, and furthermore desire, are present
in children immediately on their being born, while reasoning and intellect
develop naturally in them as they go along. Hence in the first instance the
25   superintendence of the body must necessarily precede that of the soul; next
comes that of appetite; but that of appetite is for the sake of intellect, and
that of the body for the sake of the soul.

CHAPTER 16

(1) If, therefore, the legislator should see to it from the beginning that the
30   bodies of those being reared are to become the best possible, care must be
taken in the first place in connection with the union of men and women, to
determine when and with what quality of persons marital relations ought
to be brought about. (2) One should legislate with respect to this community with a view to the partners themselves and the length of time of their
35   lives together, in order that they arrive together in terms of their ages at the

90 · The meaning is somewhat uncertain, and the text may be corrupt. The argument
appears to be that just as birth is not a beginning simply but derives from a prior beginning point in the act of generation, so the end or completion of a human being does
not derive from one simple beginning point but proceeds through a number of stages,
the end of one being the beginning point of the next.

same juncture and their capacities not be dissonant, the male still being capable of generation and the female not capable, or the female capable and the male not; for these things create conflicts and differences among them. Next, one should legislate with a view to the succession of the offspring, for   40
the offspring should neither fall too short of their fathers in terms of age—since older fathers get no benefit from the gratitude of offspring, nor their offspring from the assistance rendered by fathers—nor be too close; (4) this   1335a
involves many difficulties: less respect is present in those of this sort as being contemporaries of their fathers, and closeness gives rise to accusations in connection with management of the household. Further, to return to where we began digressing to this point, one should legislate so that the bodies of   5
offspring in the process of generation become available in a way that answers to the will of the legislator.

Now virtually all of these things result from a single sort of superintendence. (5) Since the age of seventy at the outside defines in most cases the end of generation for men, and the age of fifty for women, the beginning of their   10
union in terms of their ages should be such as to arrive at its conclusion at these times. (6) The mating of young persons is a poor thing with a view to procreation: among all animals the issue of the young is incomplete, likely to bear females, and small of figure, so this same thing must necessarily result in the case of human beings as well. A proof of it is that in those cities where   15
the union of young men and women is the local fashion, the citizens are incomplete and small of body. (7) Further, young women labor more in childbirth, and more of them die—hence some assert it was for such a reason that the oracular response was given to the Troezenians, that it was as a result of   20
always marrying off younger women that so many children were dying, not anything related to the harvesting of the crops.[91] (8) Further, it is advantageous with a view to moderation for women to be given in marriage when they are older, for they are held to be more licentious if they have practiced intercourse when young. Also, the bodies of males are held to be injured with   25
respect to growth if they have intercourse while the seed is still growing; for there is a definite length of time for this as well, after which it is no longer plentiful. (9) Hence it is fitting for women to unite in marriage around the age of eighteen, and for men at thirty-seven or a little before.[92] At such an   30
age, union will occur when their bodies are in their prime, and will arrive at

91 · The oracle was "do not plough the young furrow"—in its literal meaning, a prohibition against the ploughing of fallow land.
92 · Reading *ē mikron* with the MSS; one or more words appear to have dropped out of the text here.

its conclusion conveniently for both of them with respect to the cessation
of procreation. (10) Further, the succession of the offspring—if birth occurs
shortly after marriage, as can reasonably be expected—will be for them at
35 the beginning of their prime, while for the fathers it will be when their age
has already run its course toward the seventieth year. When a union should
take place, then, has been spoken of. As regards time with respect to the season, the practice of most people at present is a fine one, setting apart winter
as the time to begin cohabitation. (11) Married persons themselves should
40 study what is said by doctors and experts in natural science in relation to procreation. Doctors give an adequate account of the occasions [best suited to
1335b procreation with respect to the condition] of bodies, and experts in natural
science of winds, praising northerly rather than southerly ones.

(12) As regards the quality of body that would be of most benefit to offspring in the process of generation, we must stop to speak of it more at length
5 in the discourses concerning management of children; at present it is enough
to speak of it in outline.[93] The bodily disposition of athletes is not useful either with a view to the good condition required of the citizen or with a view
to health and procreation, and neither is one that is overly valetudinarian and
ill-suited for exertion, but a middling sort between these. (13) One should
have a disposition formed by exertion, but not by violent exertion, and not
10 with a view to one thing only, like the athletes' disposition, but with a view to
the actions belonging to liberal persons.[94] And these things should be present in similar fashion in men and women. (14) Even pregnant women ought
to take care of their bodies, not remaining idle or taking meager sustenance.
15 This is easy for the legislator to do by mandating that they make a trip every
day to worship the goddesses who have been granted the prerogative connected with birth.[95] (The mind, however, unlike their bodies, may fittingly
spend time in more idle fashion.) For offspring in the process of generation
evidently draw resources from the one bearing them, just as plants do from
the earth.

20 (15) Concerning exposure and rearing of offspring when they are born, let
there be a law that no deformed child should be raised, but that none should
be exposed after they are born on account of number of offspring, where
the arrangement of customs forbids procreation beyond a certain number.

93 · There is no discussion of this sort in the remainder of the *Politics* as we have it; no
other Aristotelian writing of this sort is attested.
94 · "Liberal" renders *eleutherioi*, as in the expression "the liberal arts"; it is closely related to "free" (*eleutheroi*).
95 · The goddesses Artemis and Eileithyia are particularly referred to.

A number should indeed be defined for procreation,[96] but in cases of births in consequence of intercourse contrary to these, abortion should be induced   25
before perception and life arises (what is holy and what is not will be defined by reference to perception and life).

(16) Since the beginning point of the age when a man and a woman ought to begin their union has been defined, let us define also for how much time it is fitting for them to do public service with respect to procreation. The is-   30
sue of older persons, like that of younger persons, is born incomplete both in body and mind, while that of persons in old age is weak; hence the time may be defined on the basis of the mind's prime. (17) In most persons this comes—as some of those poets have said who measure age in periods of seven years[97]—around the time of the fiftieth year. So within four or five   35
years after this age they should be released from generation for public pur-poses, and for the time remaining it should be evident that they are having relations for the sake of health or some other reason of this sort. (18) Con-cerning relations with another man or another woman, let it be considered simply not a fine thing to indulge in it at all in any way when one is or is re-   40
ferred to as spouse; if someone should be found doing some such thing dur-   1336a
ing the period of procreation, let the person be punished with a loss of honor appropriate to the errant behavior.

CHAPTER 17

(1) Once offspring are born, one should suppose that it makes a great differ-ence with a view to the power of the body what sort of sustenance they get. It is evident to those investigating the other animals as well as those nations   5
that are concerned to cultivate a military disposition that sustenance of a sort rich in milk is most particularly suited to their bodies—and one that is rela-tively free of wine, on account of the diseases it produces. (2) Further, it is advantageous to have them engage in whatever movements are possible for those of that age. With a view to preventing distortion of their limbs due to   10
their softness, however, some nations even now use certain instruments de-vised to make the bodies of such persons straight. It is also advantageous to habituate them to the cold immediately from the time they are small chil-dren: this is most useful with a view both to health and to military activi-ties. (3) Hence among many barbarians it is customary either to plunge the   15

96 · Text and meaning are somewhat uncertain. I read *hōristhai gar dē dei* rather than *hōristhō dē* with Dreizehnter.
97 · Solon, fr. 19 Diehl.

newly born into a cold river or to give them light clothing, as for example among the Celts. In all those matters where habituation is possible, it is better to habituate immediately from the beginning, not to habituate gradually.

20 And the disposition of children is naturally apt on account of its warmth for training to bear cold.

(4) In connection with the first age, then, it is advantageous to have a superintendence of this sort or nearly so. During the age following up to

25 five years, which one should not apply to any sort of learning or to necessary exertions, so that their growth is not impeded, they should engage in enough movement that they avoid bodily idleness. This should be provided them through play, as well as through other activities. (5) The sorts of play, too, should neither be illiberal nor involve too much exertion or laxness.

30 Concerning the quality of the stories and tales those of this age should hear, let this be a matter of concern to the officials who are called managers of children. For all such things should prepare the road for their later pursuits. Hence most sorts of play should be imitations of the things they give serious

35 attention to later. (6) Those who in the *Laws* forbid the screaming and crying of children[98] are not correct in this prohibition: these things are advantageous with a view to growth; in a certain manner they provide exercise for bodies, for holding the breath gives strength to those exerting themselves, and it is this very thing that results from children screaming.

40 (7) The managers of children must monitor their pastime, particularly so
1336b as to ensure that as little of it as possible will be with slaves. For this age, up to seven years, must necessarily have its rearing at home; it is therefore reasonable to expect that even at such an age they will acquire an element of illiberality from what they hear and see [on account of the proximity of slaves].
(8) Generally, then, the legislator should banish foul speech from the city

5 more than anything else (for by speaking readily about some foul matter one comes closer to doing it), and particularly from among the young, so that they neither say nor hear anything of this sort. (9) One who is found speaking or

10 doing something that is forbidden, if he is a free person who cannot yet claim to merit reclining at table, should be punished with dishonor and with a beating, and if older than this age, with dishonor of an illiberal sort, because of the slavishness he has shown. Since we are banishing speaking about anything of this sort, it is evident that looking at unseemly paintings or stories also must

15 be banished. (10) Let it be a concern of the officials, then, that no statue or painting be an imitation of such actions, except in the case of the temples

98 · Plato, *Laws* 791e–92a.

of certain gods—those to whom the law also assigns scurrilous mockery.[99] In addition to these things, the law permits those still of a suitable age[100] to do homage to the gods on behalf of themselves, their offspring, and their women. (11) And there must be legislation that younger persons not be spec-   20
tators either of lampoons[101] or of comedy, until they reach the age at which they will be able to participate in reclining at table and drinking,[102] and education will make them all immune to the harm that arises from such things.

(12) At present we have given an account of these things in passing. Later   25
we must stop to discuss it more at length, raising the question first of all whether one should or should not [exclude the young from such performances], and how it should be done; on this occasion we have made mention of it as far as is necessary.[103] (13) For the remark of the tragic actor Theodorus was not a bad one—that he never allowed anyone to come out on stage before him, not even a poor actor, because the spectators make their own what   30
they hear first.[104] This same thing results in regard both to relations with human beings and to those with objects; we are always fonder of the first things we encounter. (14) Hence everything mean should be made foreign to the young, particularly things of this sort that involve either depravity or malice.   35
Once they have passed through the first five years, during the two up to seven they should become onlookers of the sorts of learning that they themselves will be required to learn.

(15) There are two ages with a view to which it is necessary to distinguish education, that following the age from seven up to puberty, and again that following the age from puberty up to twenty-one. Those who distinguish   40
ages by periods of seven years argue for the most part not badly,[105] but one   1337a

99 · Dionysus seems to be particularly meant; "scurrilous mockery" (*tōthasmos*) was also characteristic of the rites of Demeter and Core.

100 · The text is somewhat uncertain. The phrase "those still of a suitable age" is omitted in Π² and is bracketed by Newman; *eti* ("still") is bracketed by Dreizehnter. *Pros toutous* ("in regard to these") should perhaps be read instead of the *pros toutois* ("in addition to these things") of the MSS.

101 · "Lampoons" (*iamboi*) were indecent and abusive verses recited by actors at festivals of Dionysus. Cf. *Poet.* 1448b24–49a15.

102 · The age of twenty-one is probably intended; it seems to have been at this age that a young Spartan became a member of one of the common messes.

103 · There is no further discussion of this sort in the *Politics* as we have it.

104 · Theodorus was a famous actor of the fourth century. What is meant is probably that he insisted on appearing in the first play of every tragic tetralogy.

105 · Reading *legousin ou kakōs* with Dreizehnter and most editors rather than *legousin ou kalōs* ("argue not rightly") with the MSS.

should follow the distinction of nature, for all art and education wish to supply the element that is lacking in nature. (16) First, then, we must investigate whether some arrangement is to be created in connection with children; next, whether it is advantageous for the superintendence of them to be in common or on a private basis, which is what happens even now in most cities; and third, what quality this should have.

Book 8

(1) That the legislator must, therefore, make the education of the young his object above all would be disputed by no one. Where this does not happen in cities it hurts the regimes. (2) One should educate with a view to each sort, for the character that is proper to each sort of regime both customarily safe-guards the regime and establishes it at the beginning—the democratic char-acter a democracy, for example, or the oligarchic an oligarchy; and the bet-ter[1] character is always a cause of a better regime. Further, in relation to all capacities and arts there are things with respect to which a preparatory edu-cation and habituation are required with a view to the tasks of each, so it is clear that this is so also with a view to the actions of virtue.

(3) Since there is a single end for the city as a whole, it is evident that edu-cation must necessarily be one and the same for all, and that the superinten-dence of it should be common and not on a private basis—the manner in which each at present superintends his own offspring privately and teaches them whatever private sort of learning he holds best. For common things the training too should be made common. (4) At the same time, one ought not even consider that a particular citizen belongs to himself, but rather that all belong to the city; for each is a part of the city. But the superintendence of each part naturally looks to the superintendence of the whole. One might well praise the Spartans for this: they most of all pay serious attention to their children, and do so in common.

1 · Reading *beltion* with Ross and Kraut rather than *beltiston* ("best") with the MSS and Dreizehnter.

CHAPTER 2

(1) That there must be legislation concerning education, then, and that this
must be made common, is evident. But what education is, and how one
ought to educate, should not be neglected. For at present there is a dispute
concerning its functions. Not everyone conceives that the young should
learn the same things either with a view to virtue or with a view to the best
way of life, nor is it evident whether it is more appropriate that it be with a
view to the mind or with a view to the character of the soul. (2) Investigation on the basis of the education that is current yields confusion, and it is
not at all clear whether one should have training in things useful for life,
things contributing to virtue, or extraordinary things;[2] for all of these have
obtained some willing to decide in their favor. Concerning the things relating to virtue, nothing is agreed. Indeed, to start with, not everyone honors
the same virtue, so it is reasonable to expect them to differ as well in regard
to the training in it.

(3) Now that those of the useful things that are necessary should be taught
is not unclear, and also that not all should be taught: liberal tasks being distinguished from illiberal ones, it is evident that they should share in those of
the useful things that will not make the one sharing in them vulgar.[3] (4) One
should consider a vulgar task, art, or sort of learning to be any that renders
the body, the soul,[4] or the mind of free persons useless with a view to the
practices and actions of virtue. (5) Hence we call vulgar both the sorts of
arts that bring the body into a worse state and wage-earning sorts of work,
for they make the mind a thing abject and lacking in leisure. But it is also the
case that, while it is not unfree to share in some of the liberal sciences up to a
certain point, to persevere overly much in them with a view to proficiency[5] is
liable to involve the sorts of injury just mentioned. (6) It makes a difference,
too, for the sake of what one does or learns something. What is for one's own
sake or for the sake of friends or on account of virtue is not unfree, while the
person who does the same thing on account of others would often be held to
do something characteristic of the laborer or the slave.

---

2 · Aristotle seems to associate "extraordinary things" (*ta peritta*) with philosophy
or the sciences in particular. Cf. 2.6.6, *Eth. Nic.* 1141b3–8.

3 · *Banauson*, used in this context as a virtual synonym of "illiberal" (*aneleutheron*).

4 · *Tēn psychēn* here is bracketed by Ross, followed by Kraut.

5 · Or "precision" (*akribeia*).

CHAPTER 3

(1) Now the accepted sorts of learning are, as was said earlier, ambiguous. Essentially, there are four things men customarily educate in: letters, gymnastic, music,[6] and fourth, some in drawing—expertise in letters and drawing as being useful for life and having many uses, gymnastic as contributing to courage. But about music one might already raise a question. (2) At present most people partake in it for the sake of pleasure; but those who arranged to have it in education at the beginning did so because nature itself seeks, as has been said repeatedly, not only to be occupied in correct fashion but also to be capable of being at leisure in noble fashion. For this is the beginning point of everything—if we may speak of this once again.[7] (3) If both are required, but being at leisure is more choiceworthy than occupation and more an end, what must be sought is the activity they should have in leisure. Surely it is not play:[8] play would then necessarily be the end of life for us. (4) But if this is impossible, and the sorts of play are rather to be practiced in occupation (for a person who exerts himself requires rest, and play is for the sake of rest, while occupation is accompanied by exertion and tension), on this account those introducing play should observe the occasions for its use, the assumption being that they are administering it as a remedy. For this sort of motion of the soul is a relaxation and rest effected by pleasure. Being at leisure, on the other hand, is held itself to involve pleasure, happiness, and living blessedly. (5) This is not available to those who are occupied, but rather to those at leisure, for the person who is occupied is occupied for the sake of some end that is assumed not to be present, while happiness is an end, and something all suppose to be accompanied not by pain but by pleasure. This pleasure, however, is not regarded as the same by all, but by each individual in accordance with themselves and their own disposition; but the best sort regards it as the best pleasure and that deriving from the noblest things.

(6) So it is evident that certain things should be learned and there should

25

30

35

40

1338a

5

10

---

6 · The Greek term (*mousikē*) had a wider bearing than the familiar English word. Most poetry had some musical accompaniment, and lyric poetry was typically sung; conventional aristocratic music education thus included at least a rudimentary literary education.

7 · Cf. 7.14–15.

8 · Or "amusement" (*paidia*). Significantly, both this term and "education" (*paideia*) derive from the word for "child" (*pais*).

be education with a view to the leisure that is spent in pastime[9] as well, and
that these subjects of education and these sorts of learning should be for their
own sake, those with a view to occupation being necessary and for the sake of
other things. (7) Hence those of earlier times arranged that music too would
be in education, not as being something necessary, for it involves nothing of
the sort, nor as being something useful, as letters are with a view to money-
making, management of the household, learning, and many political activities (and drawing too is held to be useful with a view to judging more finely
the works of artisans), nor again as gymnastic is with a view to health and
vigor, for we see neither of these arising from music. (8) What remains is that
it is with a view to the pastime that is in leisure; and it is evidently for just this
purpose that they bring it in. For they arrange to have it in what they suppose
to be the pastime of free persons. Hence Homer wrote thus: "but him alone
it is needful to invite to the rich banquet," and then goes on to say that there
are certain persons (9) "who invite a singer, that he may bring delight to all."[10]
And elsewhere Odysseus says that this is the best pastime, when human beings are enjoying good cheer and "the banqueters seated in order throughout
the hall listen to a singer."[11]

(10) That there is a certain sort of education, therefore, in which children
are to be educated, not as being useful or necessary but as being liberal and
noble, is evident. As to whether this is of one or several sorts, and which these
are and how they should be taught, we must speak of these things later.[12]
(11) At present we have come this far along the road, that from the ancients
too we have some testimony deriving from the subjects of education. Music
makes this clear. It is also clear, further, that children should be educated in
some of the useful things not only on account of the element of utility, as for
example in the learning of letters, but also because many other sorts of learning become possible through them. (12) Similarly, they should be educated in
drawing not so that they may not make errors in their private purchases and
avoid being deceived in the buying and selling of wares, but rather because
it makes them expert at studying the beauty connected with bodies. To seek

9 · Reading *tēn en tēi diagōgēi scholēn* with the MSS instead of *tēn en tēi scholēi
diagōgēn* ("the pastime that is in leisure") with Coraes and Dreizehnter. A distinction
seems intended between leisure for political and military activities and leisure for pastime.
10 · Homer, *Odyssey* 17.382–85. The first line quoted does not appear in our text of the
Odyssey, but seems to have followed line 382 in the version used by Aristotle.
11 · Homer, *Odyssey* 9.5–6.
12 · There is no further discussion of this question in the *Politics* as we have it.

everywhere the element of utility is least of all fitting for those who are magnanimous and free.[13]

(13) Since it is evident that education through habits must come earlier
than education through reason, and education connected with the body ear-   5
lier than education connected with the mind, it is clear from these things
that children must initially be given over to gymnastic and to sports training. The first of these makes the disposition of the body of a certain quality,
the other [gives instruction in particular] tasks.

CHAPTER 4

(1) At present, of those cities that are most particularly held to superintend   10
children, some inculcate an athletic disposition, thereby damaging the forms
and growth of their bodies, while the Spartans, although they have not made
this error, turn out children resembling beasts by imposing severe exertions,
the assumption being that this is the most advantageous thing with a view
to courage. (2) As has been said repeatedly, however, this superintendence   15
must not look to a single virtue, and particularly not to this one;[14] yet even
if it did, they have not discovered how to secure even this. For neither among
the other animals nor in the case of [barbarian] nations do we see courage accompanying the most savage, but rather those with tamer and lionlike characters. (3) There are many nations that are ready to engage in killing and   20
cannibalism, such as the Achaeans and Heniochi of the Black Sea and others among the nations of the continent, some of them in similar fashion and
others more so: these are expert at brigandage, but have no share in courage.
(4) Further, we know that the Spartans themselves, so long as they persevered   25
in their love of exertion, had preeminence over others, while at present they
fall short of others in both gymnastic and military contests.[15] For it was not
by exercising the young in this manner that they stood out, but merely by the
fact of their training against others who did not train. (5) The element of nobility, not what is beastlike, should have the leading role. For it is not the wolf   30
or any of the other beasts that would join the contest in any noble danger, but
rather a good man. (6) Those who are overly lax with their children in this
direction and leave them untutored in the necessary things turn out citizens

13 · Ross reads "liberal" (*eleutheriois*) with Susemihl rather than "free" (*eleutherois*)
with the MSS, perhaps rightly.
14 · Cf. 2.9. 34, 7.14.15–20, 15.6.
15 · The reference would seem to be particularly to Thebes (cf. Plutarch, *Pelopidas* 7),
but Aristotle may also have Macedon in mind.

35 who are in the true sense vulgar, making them useful for political rule with a
view to one task only—and with a view to this, as the argument asserts, worse
than others. (7) One should not judge on the basis of their earlier deeds, but
on the basis of those of the present; for now they have rivals in the contest of
education, whereas before they did not.

   That gymnastic is to be practiced and how it is to be practiced, then, has
40 been agreed. Up to puberty lighter exercises are to be employed; reduced
sustenance and compulsory exertions should be forbidden, in order that
1339a nothing should impede their growth. (8) No small indication that they are
capable of having this effect is that in the Olympic games one would only
find two or three persons who won victories both as men and boys, because
training in youth impairs their capacity through its compulsory exercises.
5   (9) When during the three years following puberty they have devoted themselves to other subjects of learning, then it is fitting that the next age be taken
up both with exertion and with compulsory dieting. For one should not exert oneself with the mind and the body at the same time. Each of these acts of
exertion is naturally apt to produce opposite things, the exertion of the body
10 impeding the mind, that of the mind the body.

CHAPTER 5

   (1) Concerning music, we raised certain questions earlier in the argument,
and it will be well to take these up again now and develop them, in order to
provide a sort of prelude to the arguments one might make in expressing
15 views about it. (2) For it is not easy to distinguish what its power is or for the
sake of what one should partake in it, whether for the sake of play and rest,
as in the case of sleep and drinking (for in themselves these do not belong
among excellent things, but are pleasant and at the same time "put a stop to
20 care," as Euripides has it;[16] (3) hence music too is assigned to these and all—
sleep, drinking, and music—are treated in similar fashion; and some place
dancing among them as well); or whether it is rather to be supposed that music contributes something to virtue, the assumption being that, just as gymnastic makes the body of a certain quality, so also is music capable of making
the character of a certain quality by habituating it to be capable of enjoying
25 in correct fashion; (4) or whether it contributes in some way to pastime and
prudence; for this is to be posited as the third of the things mentioned.

   Now that the young should not be educated for the sake of play is not un-

16 · Euripides, *Bacchae* 381.

clear. They do not play when they are learning, as learning is accompanied by pain. On the other hand, neither is it fitting to assign pastime to children or those of such ages; for the end is not suited to anything incomplete. (5) But perhaps it might be held that what children seriously attend to is for the sake of their play once they have become men and complete. But if something of this sort is the case, for the sake of what would they have to learn it them-selves, and not have a share in the learning and the pleasure through others performing it, like the kings of the Persians and the Medes? (6) Indeed, what results will necessarily be better if performed by those who have made this very thing their work and art than by those who are concerning themselves with it only for so much time as is required for learning. And if they should exert themselves personally in such matters, they would themselves have to take up the activity of cooking; but this would be absurd.

(7) The same question arises even if it is capable of making their charac-ters better. For why should they learn these things themselves, and not both enjoy correctly and be capable of judging by listening to others, like the Spar-tans? For these, although they do not learn themselves, nevertheless are ca-pable of judging correctly, so they assert, which tunes[17] are decent and which are not. (8) The same argument applies as well if it is to be practiced with a view to well-being and liberal pastime: why should they learn themselves, and not have the benefit of others practicing it? We may permit ourselves to investigate the conception we have about the gods: Zeus himself does not sing and play the lyre for our poets. But we even call persons of this sort vul-gar, and the activity one not belonging to a man,[18] unless one who is drunk or playing.

(9) But perhaps these things must be investigated later.[19] What we must first seek to answer is whether music is to be placed in education or not, and what power it has of the three we raised questions about—whether educa-tion, play, or pastime. It is reasonable to arrange it under all of them; it evi-dently partakes in all. (10) For play is for the sake of rest, and rest must neces-sarily be pleasant, as it is a sort of healing of the pain coming from exertions; and pastime, it is agreed, should involve not only the element of nobility but also pleasure, for being happy derives from both of these. (11) But all of us as-sert that music belongs among the most pleasant things, both by itself and with melody (Musaeus, at any rate, asserts that "singing is the pleasantest

30

35

1339b

5

10

15

20

---

17 · Melē often refers, as here, to the various types of musical modes or harmonies, rather than to songs with words.
18 · That is, a "real man" (anēr).
19 · 8.6.

thing for mortals"; hence it is reasonable to expect it to be brought into social gatherings and pastimes, as being capable of providing good cheer),[20] so that on this account as well one might conceive that younger persons should be educated in it. (12) For those pleasures that are harmless are fitting not only with a view to the end but also with a view to rest; and since it happens that human beings rarely attain the end, but frequently rest and make use of play not only for some purpose beyond but also on account of the pleasure, it would be a useful thing to have them rest on occasion in the midst of the pleasures that derive from this.

(13) But it has happened to human beings that they make play an end. For the end too perhaps involves a certain pleasure—though not any chance pleasure; and while seeking the former they take the latter for it, on account of its having a certain similarity to the end of actions. For the end is choiceworthy not for the sake of anything that will be, and pleasures of this sort are not for the sake of anything that will be, but of things that have been, such as exertions and pain. (14) One might plausibly conceive this to be the reason, then, for their seeking happiness through these pleasures, though as far as sharing in music is concerned, it is not on this account only, but also because music is useful with a view to rest, as it seems.

(15) Yet we must investigate whether this result is not accidental and its nature is not more honorable than what accords with the need mentioned, and one should not only partake of the common pleasure that derives from it, of which all have a perception—for music involves a natural pleasure, hence the practice of it is agreeable to all ages and characters—but see whether in some way it contributes to the character and the soul. (16) This would be clear if we become of a certain quality in our characters on account of it. But that we do become of a certain quality is evident through many things, and not least through the tunes of Olympus; for it is agreed that these make souls inspired, and inspiration is a passion of the character connected with

20 · Musaeus was a semilegendary figure to whom various archaic poems and sayings were ascribed. In the epic language of the quotation, "singing" (aeidein) almost certainly refers to the recitation of poetry (to a simple musical accompaniment) by a professional "bard" (aoidos), but Aristotle seems to use the quotation in support of the view that singing in the ordinary sense is most pleasant. The view he is implicitly correcting would seem to be the view that poetry as such—that is, music "by itself" (psilē ousa, literally "bare")—is the truly pleasant element of music generally. Most translations of this passage wrongly assume that the phrase "music by itself" refers to purely instrumental music. The term "melody" (melōidia, literally "tune singing") here appears to mean "musical setting"; it connotes primarily choral song—the sort of singing characteristic of social gatherings in classical Greek times. Cf. Lord 1982, 85–92.

the soul.[21] (17) Further, all who listen to imitations come to experience similar passions, even apart from rhythms and tunes themselves.[22] Since music
belongs accidentally among pleasant things, and virtue is connected with   15
enjoying in correct fashion and feeling affection and hatred, it is therefore
clear that one should learn and become habituated to nothing so much as
to judging in correct fashion of, and enjoying, respectable characters and
noble actions. (18) For in rhythms and tunes there are likenesses particularly
close to the genuine natures of anger and gentleness, and further of cour-   20
age and moderation and of all the things opposite to these and of the other
things pertaining to character. This is clear from the facts: we are altered in
soul when we listen to such things. (19) But habituation to feel pain and enjoyment in similar things is close to being in the same condition relative to
the truth. For example, if someone enjoys looking at the image of something   25
for no other reason than the form itself, then the very study of the thing the
image of which he studies must necessarily be pleasant. (20) It happens that
no likeness of characters is present in other perceptible things—in things   30
touched or tasted, for example, while in visible things it is present only to
a slight degree. For there are figures of this sort, though only to a small extent, and all participate in this sort of perception; and further, these things
are not likenesses of characters, but the figures and colors that exist of this
sort are rather indications of characters, (21) and these only as manifested by
the body when it is in the grip of the passions. But to the extent that there is 35
a difference in connection with the study of these things as well, the young
should not study the [paintings] of Pauson but those of Polygnotus or of any
other painter or sculptor who is expert with respect to character.[23] In tunes
by themselves, however, there are imitations of characters. (22) This is evident: the nature of the harmonies diverged at the outset, so that those listen-   40
ing are in a different state and not in the same condition in relation to each of
them. In relation to some—for example, the so-called Mixed Lydian—they
are in a state more of grief and apprehension; in relation to others—for ex-   1340b
ample, the relaxed harmonies—they are softer of mind; they are in a mid-

21 · Olympus was a semilegendary personage who is said to have lived in Phrygia in
the eighth century BC; the "tunes" ascribed to him were solo pieces for the flute, apparently in the Phrygian mode. Cf. 6.9, 7.4 and Plato, *Symposium* 215c. "Inspiration"
translates the Greek *enthousiasmos*.
22 · The text and meaning of this sentence have been disputed, but it seems most likely
that poetic imitations in the broadest sense are what is meant. Cf. *Poet.* 1447a8–16.
23 · Little is known of the paintings of Polygnotus or Pauson, who were active in the
fifth century. Cf. *Poet.* 1448a1–6, 1450a26–29.

dling and settled state in relation to one above all, this being what Dorian
5   alone among the harmonies is held to make them; and Phrygian makes them
inspired. (23) This is what those who have philosophized in connection with
this sort of education argue, and finely; they find proofs for their arguments
in the facts themselves.[24] Things stand in the same manner in connection
with rhythms as well: some of them have a character that is more steadfast,
10 others a character marked by movement, and of these some have movements
of a cruder, others of a more liberal sort.

(24) It is evident from these things, then, that music can render the character of the soul of a certain quality. If it is capable of doing this, clearly it
must be employed and the young must be educated in it. (25) The teaching
15 of music is fitting in relation to the nature of those of such an age, for on account of their age the young do not voluntarily put up with anything that is
not sweetened, but music by nature belongs among the sweetened things.
Moreover, there seems to be a certain affinity on their part for harmonies
and rhythms; hence many of the wise assert either that the soul is a harmony
or that it involves harmony.[25]

CHAPTER 6

20 (1) But whether they themselves should learn through singing and playing
instruments or not—the question we raised earlier—must now be spoken
of. It is not unclear that it does indeed make a great difference with a view to
becoming of a certain quality if one shares in the performance oneself; for
25 it is an impossible or a difficult thing for them to become excellent judges
without sharing in this way. (2) At the same time, children should also have

24 · Greek music in the classical period was based not on a uniform scale but on a
modal system deriving originally from the divergent characteristics of different sorts
of musical instruments. The word "harmony" (*harmonia*) originally meant the tuning
or scale of a particular sort of instrument; it was then applied derivatively to the musical style associated with particular instruments as used for particular occasions. A
"tune" (*melos*) is properly a melodic realization of a particular harmony (the common
translation "song" is misleading in its implication that a vocal element is necessarily
present). The notion that different harmonies affect the soul differently seems to have
originated among the Pythagoreans; it was further developed by Damon, the musical
authority for Plato, and Aristoxenus, a student of Aristotle. Little is otherwise known
of the characteristics of the various harmonies; perhaps the fullest ancient accounts are
Plato, *Republic* 398d–99c and [Aristotle,] *Problems* 19.48.
25 · The views of the Pythagoreans and of Plato's Simmias (*Phaedo* 92a–95a) respectively.

some pursuit: "the rattle of Archytas,"[26] which they give to children so they will use this and not break anything around the house, should be supposed a fine thing; anything young is incapable of keeping still. This, therefore, is fitting for children in infancy, while education is a rattle for the young when they are bigger.

(3) That there is to be education in music in such a way that they will share in the performance, therefore, is evident from such things. What is appropriate and inappropriate for different ages is not difficult to define and resolve, in response to those who assert that the concern is a vulgar one. (4) In the first place, since one should take part in performing them for the sake of judging, on this account they should engage in performing when they are young, and when they become older leave off it, and be able to judge the noble things and to enjoy in correct fashion through the learning that occurred in their youth. (5) Concerning the criticism of some that music makes people vulgar, it is not difficult to resolve by investigating up to what point those who are being educated to political virtue should share in performing and which sorts of tunes and rhythms they should share in, and further, on which sorts of instruments they are to learn, for it is likely that this too makes a difference. (6) The resolution of the criticism lies in these things, for nothing prevents certain modes of music from producing the effect mentioned. It is evident that the learning of it should neither be an impediment with a view to later activities, nor make the body vulgar and useless with a view to military and political training—with a view on the one hand to the uses now, and on the other to the sorts of learning [to be undertaken] later.

(7) This would result in connection with the learning of music if they did not exert themselves to learn either what contributes to contests involving professional expertise or those works that are difficult and extraordinary (which have now come into the contests, and from the contests into education), (8) but learned such things as well [as other works of music only] up to the point where they are capable of enjoying noble tunes and rhythms and not merely the common element of music, as is the case even for some of the other animals, and further for the multitude of slaves and children.

It is clear from these things also which instruments are to be used. (9) Flutes are not to be brought into education, nor any other instrument involving professional expertise, such as the lyre or any other that may be of

---

26 · The invention of the rattle was proverbially ascribed to Archytas of Tarentum, the Pythagorean philosopher.

20   this sort, but only those that will make them good listeners either of music
education or of the other sort of education. Further, the flute is an instrument involving not character but rather frenzy, and so is to be used with a
view to those occasions when looking on has the power of purification rather
25   than learning.[27] (10) Let us add that the fact that the flute prevents speech
also tells against its use in education. Hence those of earlier times rightly rejected the use of it by the young and free, although they had used it before.
(11) For when [Greeks] came to have more leisure through being better off
and were more magnanimous in regard to virtue, and further, being full of
30   high thoughts on account of their deeds both before and after the Persian
Wars, they put their hand to every sort of learning, making no discrimination between them but seeking to advance further in all. Hence expertise
in the flute was also brought in among the sorts of learning. (12) Indeed, in
Sparta a certain chorus leader himself played the flute for the chorus, and
35   at Athens it became so much the local fashion that most free persons had a
share in it (this is clear from the tablet that Thrasippus, the chorus leader, set
up for Ecphantides).[28] Later, it was rejected as a result of the experience of
it, when they were better able to judge what contributes to virtue and what
does not. (13) The same thing happened also with many of the ancient instru-
40   ments, such as the pectis, the barbitos, and those contributing to the plea-
1341b   sure of those who listen to their practitioners, the heptagon, the trigon, and
the sambuca,[29] and all those requiring professional knowledge. And the tale
told by the ancients about flutes is a reasonable one. They assert that Athena,
though she had invented the flute, threw it away. (14) Now it is not bad to as-
5   sert that the goddess did this out of annoyance at the distortion of her face;
but it is more likely that it was because education in flute playing has nothing
to do with intelligence, for we ascribe to Athena knowledge and art.

(15) Since we reject professional education both in instruments and in
10   performance—we regard as professional education that with a view to contests, for one who is active in this does not undertake it for the sake of his
own virtue but for the sake of the pleasure of his listeners, and this a crude

27 · The flute (aulos), actually more akin to our oboe, was thought to be an instrument
that "stirs up frenzy" (orgiastikon), like the "inspirational" songs of Olympus. For "purification" (catharsis), see further 8.7 below.
28 · The "chorus leader" (chorēgos)—the producer—of a dramatic performance
sometimes set up a votive tablet to Dionysus recording the victory of the poet whose
play had been produced. (Ecphantides was an early Athenian comic poet.) The tablet
in question presumably recorded the flute player as well.
29 · These were all types of stringed instruments.

pleasure; hence we judge the performance as not belonging to free persons but being more characteristic of the laborer; (16) and indeed the result is that they become vulgar, for the aim with a view to which they create the end for themselves is a base one; the spectator, being crude himself, customarily alters the music, so that he makes the artisans engaging in it with a view to him of a certain quality themselves and with respect to their bodies on account of the movements....

CHAPTER 7

(1) We must investigate further in connection with harmonies and rhythms, both [whether the same harmonies and rhythms are appropriate for citizens and noncitizens and] whether all harmonies and all rhythms are to be used with a view to education or a distinction is to be made, and next, whether we shall posit the same definition for those exerting themselves with a view to education or some other third definition is needed.[30] Since we see that music depends on tune composition and rhythms, one should not overlook the power that each of these has with a view to education, and whether one should intentionally choose music with good tune over music with good rhythm.[31] (2) Considering as right, then, much of what has been said about these things by some of the current experts in music and by those in philosophy who have experience with the education connected with music,[32] we shall refer to them anyone who seeks a detailed account of each particular, and for the present we shall make distinctions in legal fashion and speak about these things only in outline.

(3) Since we accept the distinction of tunes as they are distinguished by certain persons in philosophy,[33] regarding some as relating to character,

30 · Text and meaning of this sentence have been much disputed. I believe a line has dropped out containing reference to the noncitizen class of the best regime, and that the three "definitions" apply to the harmonies used by the citizens simply, the harmonies used by the citizens for education simply, and the harmonies used by the citizens for the education of the young in singing and the playing of instruments. Cf. Lord 1982, 107-08, and for different interpretations, Kraut 1997 and Simpson 1998.

31 · This remark may refer to the difference between lyric and epic poetry respectively.

32 · The musical experts referred to are probably persons associated with the school of Damon; to the latter category belong Aristoxenus and Plato.

33 · The distinction very probably derives from Aristoxenus; it appears to be presupposed in the discussion in [Aristotle,] Problems 19.48. What little evidence is available suggests that the tunes "relating to character" (ēthika) corresponded to the harmonies

35   some to action, and some to inspiration (and they regard the nature of harmonies as akin to each of these, one of them to one part[34]), and since we assert that music should be practiced not for the sake of a single sort of benefit but for the sake of several (for it is for the sake both of education and of
purification—as to what we mean by purification, we will speak of it simply
40   at present, but again and more elaborately in the discourses on the poetic
art[35]—and third, it is useful with a view to pastime, rest, and the relaxation of
1342a strain), it is evident that all the harmonies are to be used, but that all are not
to be used in the same manner, but with a view to education those most relating to character, and with a view to listening to others performing those re-
5   lating to action and those relating to inspiration as well.[36] (4) For the passion
that occurs strongly in connection with certain sorts of souls is present in all,
but differs by greater and less—for example, pity and fear, and further, inspiration. For there are certain persons who are possessed by this motion, but as
10   a result of the sacred tunes—when they use the tunes that put the soul in a
frenzy—we see them calming down as if obtaining a cure and purification.[37]
(5) This same thing, then, must necessarily be experienced also by the pitying
and the fearful as well as by the generally passionate, and by others insofar as
to each falls a share in such things, and there must occur for all a certain pu-

---

of the Lydian group as well as to Dorian, those "relating to action" (*praktika*) to the
Hypophrygian (Ionian) and Hypodorian (Aeolian) harmonies, and those "relating to
inspiration" (*enthousiastika*) to the Phrygian harmony.

34 · A plausible emendation would give "tune" (*melos*) for the "part" (*meros*) of the
MSS.

35 · This phrase is usually taken to be a reference to the treatment of "purification"
(*katharsis*) in Aristotle's *Poetics;* but the matter is only alluded to in the text of that work
as it stands (6.1449b26–28). A possible alternative is that it refers to a later discussion
in the *Politics* itself, which was subsequently lost.

36 · The Dorian harmony can be identified as that "most relating to character." Aristotle appears to accept implicitly the use of this and other harmonies in the same category—notably Mixed Lydian, which was the mode characteristic of tragic choruses—
for purposes of "listening to others perform." The Hypophrygian and Hypodorian
modes were associated particularly with the heroes of tragedy.

37 · Aristotle appears to refer to "melancholics"—persons susceptible to episodes of
inspired or "enthusiastic" madness because of a physiological condition involving an
excess of black bile (see [Aristotle,] *Problems* 30.1). He indicates that a "purification"
of such persons could occur through exposure to the "sacred tunes" (probably to be
identified with the "tunes of Olympus" mentioned in 5.16) in the context of Dionysian
ritual, where their normal effect was precisely to induce the experience of religious inspiration or frenzy.

rification and a feeling of relief accompanied by pleasure.[38] In a similar way   15
the purificatory[39] tunes as well provide harmless delight to human beings.

(6) Hence it is to be set down that contestants undertaking theatrical music [should use[40]] harmonies of this sort and tunes of this sort. But as the
spectator is twofold, the one free and educated, the other crude and com-   20
posed of workers and laborers and others of this sort, contests and spectacles
are to be assigned to such persons as well with a view to rest. (7) Just as their
souls are distorted from the disposition that accords with nature, so too there
are deviations among the harmonies, and tunes that are strained and highly
colored; and what is akin according to nature is what creates pleasure for   25
each sort of individual. Hence license is to be given to those contesting with
a view to this sort of spectator to use a certain sort of music of this type.[41]

(8) With a view to education, as was said, those of the tunes that relate
to character are to be used and harmonies of this sort. The Dorian is of this   30
sort, as we said before, and one should accept any other that is approved for
us by those sharing in the pursuit of philosophy and in the education connected with music. (9) The Socrates of the *Republic* is not correct in leaving
Phrygian alone [in education] together with Dorian, especially as he rejects
the flute among the instruments.[42] For Phrygian has the same power among   1342b
the harmonies as the flute among the instruments: both are characteristically frenzied and passionate. (10) Poetry makes this clear. For all excitement
and all motion of this sort belongs particularly to the flute among the instruments, while among the harmonies these things find what is appropriate to   5
them in Phrygian tunes. The dithyramb, for example, is held by agreement
to be Phrygian. (11) Many instances of this are mentioned by those who understand these matters, but particularly the fact that Philoxenus attempted   10
to compose a dithyramb in Dorian— *The Mysians*—but was unable to do it,
but because of its very nature he fell back on Phrygian again, the harmony

38 · This sentence is arguably intended to describe the effect of tragic performances
on their audience. See the detailed analysis in Lord 1982, 110–41.

39 · Reading *kathartika* here with the MSS rather than the conjectural *praktika*, accepted by Ross.

40 · One or more words appear to have dropped out of the text at this point; I translate the supplement of Dreizehnter.

41 · The deviant harmonies are probably the "relaxed" and the "strained" Lydian; the
former was associated with feasting and drinking, the latter with funeral celebrations.
The "strained and highly colored tunes" are probably Phrygian tunes of the chromatic
or "colored" variety associated with the dithyrambic poetry of the fourth-century poet
Philoxenus.

42 · Plato, *Republic* 399a–c.

appropriate to it. (12) Concerning Dorian, all agree that it is the most steadfast and has most of all a courageous character. Further, since we praise the
15   middle between extremes and assert it ought to be pursued, and since Dorian
has this nature relative to the other harmonies, it is evident that it is appropriate for younger persons to be educated particularly in Dorian tunes.

(13) There are two aims, the possible and the appropriate; individuals
20   should undertake things possible and appropriate for them. These things
too are defined by ages. It is not easy for those exhausted with age, for example, to sing the strained harmonies, but nature suggests the relaxed ones
instead for persons of such an age. (14) Hence some of those connected with
25   music rightly criticize Socrates for this as well, that he would reject for purposes of education the relaxed harmonies,[43] taking them to have an effect
related to drinking—not of drunkenness, as drunkenness gives rise rather
to excitement, but of exhaustion. So one should take up both harmonies of
this sort and tunes of this sort with a view to the age to come when they are
30   older. (15) Further, if there is among the harmonies one of a sort that is appropriate to the age of children on account of its capacity to involve simultaneously both order and play,[44] as appears to be the case most particularly
with Lydian among the harmonies, it is clear that these three are to be made
defining principles for purposes of education—the middle, the possible, and
the appropriate.[45]

43 · Plato, *Republic* 398e.

44 · Reading *paidia* ("play") with Schneider rather than *paideia* ("education") with
the MSS and Dreizehnter. The notion of "order" (*kosmos*) would seem to encompass
education of character.

45 · This paragraph is regarded by some scholars as an interpolation, I believe rightly
(Lord 1982, 215–19). The association of the (relaxed) Lydian mode with education is
contrary to Aristotle's earlier argument, as is the notion that old men should sing (cf.
6.4); both appear to have been characteristic of the Damonian school. Kraut 1997 defends the passage as Aristotelian.

GLOSSARY

A

ACTION (*praxis*): purposive human action or activity, particularly moral or political activity. The related term *praktikos*, "active," is frequently used by Aristotle with reference to the practical or political way of life (see particularly 7.2–3) as well as the form of reasoning associated with it. The verb *prattein* is generally rendered "to act." The expressions *eu prattein* ("to act well") and *kalōs prattein* ("to act finely") carry the idiomatic meaning "to do well" or "to prosper."

ADJUDICATION (*dikē*): the process of determining what is lawful or just. In its narrow sense *dikē* is rendered "trial" or "lawsuit"; in a larger sense, it refers to the system of adjudication which is characteristic of any civilized community (consider 1.2. 16). Of related terms, *dikazein* is rendered "to adjudicate," *dikastēs* as "juror," *dikastērion* as "court." See JUSTICE.

ADMINISTER (*oikein*): dwell in and govern after the fashion of a household (*oikos*). Also rendered simply "to settle" or "to inhabit." See MANAGER.

AFFECTION (*philia*): friendship, friendly feeling, or (nonsexual) love. The related word *philos* is translated "friend"; "affectionateness" renders *to philētikon*. See *Eth. Nic.* 8–9.

AGGRANDIZEMENT (*pleonexia*): taking more than one's share (literally, "having more"); greedy or unjust behavior.

AMBITION (*philotimia*): see HONOR.

ARISTOCRACY (*aristokratia*): any form of regime in which virtue is taken into account in the selection of officials; more properly, rule of the few who are best (*aristoi*) on the basis of virtue, or a regime centrally concerned with the cultivation and practice of virtue. Cf. 3.7. 3, 4.7, 8.7–9.

ARMS (*hopla*): arms or weapons generally; the armament of a "heavy-armed soldier" (*hoplitēs*), the mainstay of most Greek citizen armies.

ARRANGEMENT (*taxis*): order or an ordered arrangement; a measure, regulation, or institution. The related verb *tattein* is generally translated "to arrange"; the compound words *syntaxis* and *syntattein* are rendered "organization" and "to organize."

ARROGANCE (*hybris*): arrogant, insulting, or violent behavior, particularly if such behavior is unprovoked and in disregard or defiance of conventional restraints; as a term of law, unprovoked physical or sexual assault.

ART (*technē*): any practical or productive activity based on a body of communicable knowledge or expertise. The related term *technitēs* is rendered "artisan."

ASSEMBLY (*ekklēsia*): a gathering (literally, "calling out") of the citizenry; the popular assembly, the dominant political institution in a democracy.

ASSESSMENT (*timēma*): a property valuation serving to distinguish classes of citizens for various civic purposes. The phrase *apo timēmatōn* ("on the basis of assessments") denotes a political arrangement involving some form of property qualification.

AUTHORITATIVE (*kyrios*): dominant or controlling in a political sense (the more common translation "sovereign" misleadingly suggests a purely legal form of authority). Also used of the controlling or most proper sense of a term. It will occasionally be rendered "control."

B

BARBARIAN (*barbaros*): anyone of non-Greek stock, including relatively civilized peoples such as the Persians or the Phoenicians of Carthage.

BASIC PREMISE (*hypothesis*): a fundamental or defining characteristic of a thing; also translated "presupposition."

C

CHARACTER (*ēthos*): the character or customary behavior of a living being or group; the character, in particular the moral character, of an individual.

CHOICE (*hairesis*): choice or election, particularly in a political sense; also translated "election." The related verb *haireisthai* is rendered "to choose" or "to elect." The compound words *proairesis* and *proaireisthai* are rendered "intentional choice" (or "intention") and "to choose intentionally"; for this term, which has a technical meaning in Aristotle's thought, see *Eth. Nic.* 3.2.

CITIZEN (*politēs*): a free person who is entitled to participate in the political life of a city through the holding of deliberative and judicial office. Cf. 3.1–2.

CITY (*polis*): a political community characterized by social and economic differentiation, the rule of law, and republican government; the chief urban center of such a community. See especially 1.1. 1–2, 2.2. 3–7, 3.3. 3–5, 3.9. 6–14, 7.8. 6–9.

COMMON (*koinos*): accessible to or shared by all (this sense is sometimes rendered "accessible" or "attainable"); the public as opposed to the individual or private. The expression *ta koina*, translated "common funds," denotes the public treasury of a city; *to koinon*, "community," denotes the public in a general sense, or the central authority of a political organization.

COMMUNITY (*koinōnia*): an association or partnership generally; a relationship of sharing. See also SHARE.

COUNCIL (*boulē*): a body of restricted membership with primarily deliberative functions, which often shared supreme authority with a popular assembly. A "preliminary council" (*proboulē*) was a smaller body, characteristic of oligarchies. Cf. 4.15.11–12, 6.8.17.

CUSTOM (*ethos*): the custom of a city or the habit of an individual; also translated "habit." The related verb *ethizein* is rendered "to habituate."

D

DEFINING PRINCIPLE (*horos*): principle, standard, limit, characteristic feature. Of related terms, *horismos* is rendered "definition," *horizein* "to define," and *diorizein* "to discuss" or "to determine."

DEMOCRACY (*dēmokratia*): any regime in which the "people" (*dēmos*) rule or control the authoritative institutions of the city; more properly, rule of the poor or the majority in their own interest. See particularly 3.8, 4.4, 6, 6.2–4. *Dēmokrateisthai* is rendered "to be run democratically." See PEOPLE.

DOMINATE (*kratein*): to conquer through force, to master or control; also rendered "to conquer." The verb derives from the noun *kratos*, "bodily strength"; a related term is *kreittōn*, "superior" or "stronger."

E

EDUCATION (*paideia*): the education of children (*paides*); the education or culture of man in general.

END (*telos*): the character of a thing when fully formed, its completion or perfection. Of related terms, *teleios* is rendered "complete," *teleisthai* "to be completed."

EQUALITY (*to ison*): equality or fairness.

EQUIPMENT (*chorēgia*): the expenditure required of a chorus leader (*chorēgos*) or producer of dramas; material preconditions, supplies, equipment. Used by Aristotle as a quasi-technical term to denote the external requirements or preconditions of the virtuous life.

ERROR (*hamartia*): a failing generally involving a moral as well as intellectual dimension, but less than full moral culpability.

EXPERTISE (*-ikē*): proficiency or skill in any human activity, art, or science (the adjectival form is frequently used by itself as a substantive).

F

FACTIONAL CONFLICT (*stasis*): political unrest, agitation, or sedition aimed at overturning a regime or altering its character in various ways (cf. 5.1. 8–10); the factional conflict or state of civil disorder resulting from this. "To engage in factional conflict" renders *stasiazein*; *diastasis* is translated "factional split."

FAMILY (*genos*): an extended family or lineage; a noble house; race or stock; type. Also translated "stock" and "type."

FEW (*hoi oligoi*): the upper classes, particularly the wealthy, as distinct from the common people.

FINE (*kalos*): morally or physically beautiful, noble, fine, right; also translated "noble." The related term *kallos* is rendered "beauty" or "good looks." See ACTION.

G

GENTLEMAN (*kaloskagathos*): a person of good family and established position (literally, a "noble and good man"); a person distinguished by education, refinement, and virtue.

GETTING GOODS (*chrēmatismos*): the activity of making money; more generally and properly, the activity of acquiring "goods" (*chrēmata*) "to use" (*chrēsthai*) in support of the needs of the household (see 1.8–10). *Chrēmata* is an elastic term that can denote things or objects very generally as well as money in an abstract sense; it is translated "funds" as well as "goods." More frequent than *chrēmatismos* is *chrēmatistikē*, "the art of getting goods" or "the art of making money."

GOOD GOVERNANCE (*eunomia*): a condition of good political order and good laws, often implying an old-fashioned or restricted form of democracy.

GOVERN (*politeuesthai*): to govern oneself or to be governed as a free citizen (the verb generally appears in the middle voice; both reflexive and passive translations are used according to context); more generally, to live as a free citizen in a city and participate in public life (this sense is regularly rendered "to engage in politics").

GOVERNING BODY (*politeuma*): the group or class that holds effective political power in a city (cf. 3.6. 1–2). See REGIME.

H

HABIT (*ethos*): see CUSTOM.

HAPPINESS (*eudaimonia*): happiness as a settled condition and state of mind, well-being. See *Eth. Nic.* 1. "Blessed" (*makarios*) is a stronger term connoting an extraordinary degree of happiness comparable to that associated with the gods.

HELOTRY (*heilōteia*): the institution of agricultural serfdom at Sparta based on the distinct class of persons known as helots (*heilōtai*). See SUBJECTS.

HONOR (*timē*): honor, esteem, value; mark of honor, prerogative (this sense is rendered "prerogative"). *Atimos*, "deprived of prerogatives," is a technical term for loss of civic rights or disenfranchisement. "Ambition" renders *philotimia* (literally, "love of honor"). See ASSESSMENT.

HOUSEHOLD MANAGEMENT (*oikonomia*): governance of the household, including rule over women, children, and slaves, and the provision of material necessities. Occasionally, *oikonomia* is used (as the related verb *oikonomein* generally is) in a broader sense, rendered "management." See MANAGER.

J

JUDGE (*krinein*): to distinguish, judge, decide, usually but not exclusively in a judicial context; sometimes translated "to decide." Of related terms, *kritēs* is translated "judge," *krisis* as "judgment" or "trial."

JUSTICE (*to dikaion*): what is right, fair, or morally justifiable; a right or rightful claim (this sense is generally rendered "claim to justice"). Of related terms, the adjective *dikaios* is translated "just," the adverb *dikaiōs* "justly" or "justifiably": *dikaiosynē*, denoting the virtue of justice, is also generally rendered "justice." See ADJUDICATION.

K

KIND (*eidos*): distinctive appearance (this sense is translated "look" or "mark"); form, character, species.

KINGSHIP (*basileia*): rule of one man in the common interest. "Absolute kingship" (*pambasileia*) is a form of kingship resembling paternal rule in the household. Cf. 3.14 17.

L

LABORER (*thēs*): an unskilled worker or day laborer. Laborers or "the laboring element" (*to thētikon*) constituted the lowest social stratum among free persons; their participation in politics was generally limited at best, even in democratic regimes.

LAW (*nomos*): written or unwritten law, custom, or convention; also on occasion translated "convention." *Nomos* in the broad sense is frequently understood in opposition to *physis*, "nature." Related terms are *nomimos* ("lawful"), *ta nomima* ("usages" or "ordinances"), *nomisma* ("money"), and *nomizein* ("to consider").

LEADER (*hēgēmōn*): head of a largely voluntary alliance or association. The term is particularly used of cities maintaining hegemony (as distinct from imperial rule) over other cities.

LEISURE (*scholē*): freedom from the need of working for a living; free time, leisure. See OCCUPATION.

LIBERAL (*eleutherios*): pertaining to a free man (*eleutheros*) as distinct from a slave; free from the constraints of economic necessity, generous or liberal. Cf. *Eth. Nic.* 4.1.

M

MAN (*anēr*): the male of the species in general; a manly or spirited type of man. "Man" also renders *anthrōpos* in its generic sense; this term is otherwise translated "human being." *Anēr* is sometimes rendered "male"; in some contexts, the translation "husband" is often equally appropriate. A related term is *andreia*, "courage."

MANAGER (*-nomos*): governor, regulator, supervisor, manager. The term is found only in compound forms; it derives from the verb *nemein* (to dispense or distribute; to shepherd or lead to pasture), which is itself related to *nomos*, "law." Apart from "household manager" (*oikonomos*), the head of household as ruler and provider, terms ending in *-nomos* generally refer to city officials having supervisory duties of various sorts. The verb *oikonomein* is translated "to manage"; *oikonomia* is on occasion also used in this broader sense, and is rendered "management" simply. "Good governance" renders *eunomia*, a word connoting social order and competent government.

MANY (*hoi polloi*): most people in a generic sense; the common people as distinct from the educated or wealthy "few."

MASS (*ochlos*): an unruly crowd of people; the lower classes.

MASTER (*despotēs*): the head of household in his capacity as master of slaves.

MEAN (*phaulos*): mean, contemptible, base, bad (also rendered "bad" and "poor"); as a social term, a person of the lower classes.

MERIT (*axia*): worth, desert, merit; also rendered "worth." The verb *axioun* is translated "to merit," "to claim to merit," or "to claim"; *axiōma* is rendered "claim."

MODE (*tropos*): manner, mode, style, temper; also rendered "manner" and occasionally "approach."

MODERATION (*sōphrosynē*): the virtue that controls the desires, particularly bodily desires; its opposite is the vice of "licentiousness" (*akolasia*). See *Eth. Nic.* 3.10–12. The related adjective *sōphrōn* is translated "sound"; it connotes soundness of mind or good sense as well as self-control. "Moderate" and "moderateness" render *metrios* and *metriotēs* respectively, terms which connote a measured or balanced condition.

MONEY (*nomisma*): coined money, currency. The drachma, the mina (100 drachmas), and the talent (60 minas) were the basic units of Greek coinage; one talent was a substantial sum of money to be held by a private individual. See LAW.

MULTITUDE (*plēthos*): any aggregation of independent units; an association of similar persons; in a political context, the body of the citizens, and in particular the majority of the citizens, or the lower classes. Also translated "number," "amount," "aggregate," and "bulk."

N

NATION (*ethnos*): a tribal or ethnically based state, usually organized as a loose confederation of villages under a hereditary king, but also extending to substantial empires such as the Persian.

NATURE (*physis*): origin, growth, development (the related verb *phyein* is translated "to grow" or "to develop"); the character of a thing when fully developed, its nature; nature or the universe. For Aristotle and the Greeks generally, "nature" is a term of distinction (it is frequently found in opposition to "chance," "art," or "law"), implying a standard of value independent of human thought or action.

NECESSARY (*anankaios*): compulsory; related to economic or material needs. The related verb *anankazein* is rendered "to compel."

NOBLE (*kalos*): see FINE.

NOTABLES (*hoi gnorimoi*): well-known or distinguished persons; a common term for the upper classes, particularly the hereditary aristocracy.

O

OCCUPATION (*ascholia*): necessary activity, business, work, occupation; literally, "lack of leisure."

OLIGARCHY (*oligarchia*): rule of the rich who are few (*oligoi*) in their own interest. Cf. 3.8, 4.5–6, 6.6–7.

ORDER (*kosmos*): order, beauty, adornment (also rendered "ordered beauty"); the visible universe or cosmos (rendered "universe"). "Orderers" (*kosmoi*) was the term for a magistracy in Crete similar to the Spartan overseers. "Orderliness" renders *eukosmia*, a term connoting public order or decency. The verb *kosmein* is translated "to adorn."

OVERSEERS (*ephoroi*): a powerful magistracy at Sparta comparable to Roman tribunes.

P

PART (*meros*): part, section, group, class. The common expression *kata merē* is rendered "in turn," "by turns," or "by groups."

PASTIME (*diagōgē*): any voluntary pursuit or occupation; the serious or cultivated pursuits of leisure.

PEOPLE (*dēmos*): the body of the people, the public; the common people or lower classes of a city; the government of the common people, or democracy (this sense is translated "rule of the people"). *Dēmos* was also an administrative unit (rendered "quarter") of Athens. See POPULAR; PUBLIC.

PHILOSOPHY (*philosophia*): theoretical investigation or study (literally, "love of wisdom"); culture (for this sense consider particularly 2.5. 15).

POLITICAL (*politikos*): pertaining to or characteristic of the city, or of political life generally; also, pertaining to or characteristic of polity. As a substantive, *politikos* denotes a person actively engaged in politics, a politician or statesman; it is translated "expert in politics," "political man," or "political ruler." The substantive *politikē*, denoting the art or science of politics, is rendered "political expertise." See CITY.

POLITY (*politeia*): a form of popular rule involving oligarchic features and directed to the common interest; more properly, any regime combining oligarchy and democracy. See particularly 3.7, 4.8. See REGIME.

POOR (*aporos*): a person not materially well off (literally, "lacking a supply"), though not destitute; as a political category, the majority in most cities. "Poor" in a morally pejorative sense translates *phaulos* (see MEAN).

POPULAR (*dēmotikos*): characteristic of or pertaining to the people (*dēmos*). "Those of the popular sort" (*hoi dēmotikoi*) is an expression designating the active supporters of a democratic regime, or a democratic party in a loose sense of that term (which could and frequently did include persons not belonging to the people as a class). "Popular leader" translates *dēmagōgos*; the verb *dēmagōgein* is rendered "to seek popularity with."

POSSESSION (*ktēma*): what one has acquired and owns. The related verb *ktasthai* is rendered "to acquire" or "to possess"; *ktēsis* is rendered "property."

POWER (*dynamis*): the capacity or potential of a thing in a general sense (*dynamis* derives from the common verb *dynasthai*, "to be able"); the nature or character of a thing as expressed in its potential; power in a specifically political and military sense; a military force; also rendered "capacity." *Dynastoi*, a term referring to exceptionally wealthy and powerful men, is translated "the powerful"; cf. RULE OF THE POWERFUL.

PREEMINENCE (*hyperochē*): superiority, predominance; political power, position, or influence.

PREROGATIVE (*timē*): see HONOR.

PRESUPPOSITION (*hypothesis*): a qualifying condition or assumption.

PRIVATE (*idios*): proper or peculiar to a person or thing (this sense is generally translated "peculiar"); the private or individual as opposed to the public or "common" (*koinos*). The related term *idiōtēs* is translated either "private individual" or "nonprofessional."

PROPERTY (*ousia*): property in an abstract sense (the word derives from the verb *einai*, "to be," and is also used as a technical term in metaphysics; compare English

"substance"); a property or estate. "Property" is also used to translate *ktēsis*; see
POSSESSION.

PRUDENCE (*phronēsis*): good sense or soundness of mind; wisdom or intelligence;
prudence. In Aristotle's thought, *phronēsis* is the virtue associated with the active or
practical portion of the rational part of the soul, prudence or practical wisdom. See
Eth. Nic. 6.5, 8–13.

PUBLIC (*dēmosios*): pertaining to the people (*dēmos*) as a whole; official, public.
Dēmoseuein, "to confiscate," means literally "to make public." The phrase "public service" renders *leitourgia*, a term frequently applied to large expenditures by private individuals for public purposes such as the building of warships (a form of indirect tax-
ation), but used generally of any official function, including worship of the gods (cf.
7.10.11).

R

REFINED (*charieis*): graceful, elegant, appealing; a term used euphemistically of the
upper or educated classes.

REGIME (*politeia*): the organization of offices in a city, particularly the most authoritative; the effective government or governing body of a city; the way of life of a city as
reflected in the end pursued by the city as a whole and by those constituting its governing body (the common translation "constitution" is misleading insofar as it connotes a
formal legal order). Cf. 3.6. 1, 4.1. 10, 3.5, 11.3. Sometimes *politeia* bears the meaning of
a specifically constitutional or republican regime as distinct from personal monarchic
rule. See GOVERNING BODY; POLITY.

RESOLUTION (*dogma*): an official decision reflecting the general "opinion" (*doxa*) of
a deliberative body. The related verb *dokein* ("seem") is generally translated "to hold"
or "to resolve."

RESPECTABLE (*epieikēs*): decent, fair, reasonable, equitable; as a substantive, a person
of the upper or educated classes.

REVOLUTION (*metabolē*): change or alteration (this sense is sometimes rendered "alteration"); change—not necessarily sudden or violent—in the essential character of a
regime. The related verb *metaballein* is rendered "to be altered" or "to undergo revolution."

RIGHT (*orthos*): right or correct; also translated "correct."

RULE (*archē*): the activity or institutions of governance; in particular, the executive
magistracies of a city (this sense is generally rendered "office"). *Archē* in the sense of
governance of other cities is translated "[imperial] rule." A different sense of the term
is rendered "beginning point" or "ruling principle."

RULE OF THE POWERFUL (*dynasteia*): a form of oligarchy characterized by the dominance of a few "powerful men" (*dynastoi*) and their families and retainers. See 2.10.14–15.

S

SCIENCE (*epistēmē*): knowledge in a general sense; an organized body of knowledge, a science (generally used of theoretical sciences as distinct from applied sciences or "arts").

SEDITIOUS (*kainotomos*): innovative or novel (this sense is translated "original"—cf. particularly 2.6. 6); seeking innovation or revolution in a city or its institutions.

SENATE (*gerousia*): council of "senators" or elders (*gerontes*), an aristocratic deliberative body particularly associated with Sparta.

SPIRITEDNESS (*thymos*): anger; more generally, the part of the soul or complex of passions (extending to anger, ambition, arrogance, and affection) connected with man's sociality. Cf. 7.7.

STUDY (*theōrein*): to look at, study, or contemplate; also rendered "to look at" and (in the aorist) "to discern." Of related words, *theōria* is translated as "looking on," "study," or "spectacle," *theōros* as "onlooker," and *theatēs* as "spectator."

SUBJECTS (*perioikoi*): dependent peoples (literally, "dwellers around"); used of the class of agricultural serfs (similar to the Spartan helots) in Crete, and of non-Spartiate free Lacedaemonians.

SUPERINTENDENCE (*epimeleia*): supervision, care, concern, practice; also translated "care" and "concern."

SUSTENANCE (*trophē*): what is required to sustain physical life; food; support or maintenance; nurturing or rearing (this sense is translated "rearing").

T

TASK (*ergon*): function, work; characteristic activity or result; deed, fact; also rendered "work," "deed," "function," and "fact." The related word *energeia* (literally, "at work"), rendered "actualization," is a technical term in Aristotelian metaphysics denoting the realization or completion of a potential.

TRADITIONAL (*patrios*): deriving from one's forefathers, ancestral. The related term *patrikos* is translated "hereditary."

U

USE (*chrēsthai*): to use, employ, or practice; also translated "to treat." Of related words, *chrēsimos* is translated "useful," *chrēstos* (a term of moral approbation) "decent," *chrēsis* "use" or "usage." Cf. GETTING GOODS.

V

VICE (*kakia*): badness, baseness, viciousness, vice. The adjective *kakos* is rendered "bad" or "wrong," the substantive *kakon* as "ill."

VIRTUE (*aretē*): the goodness, excellence, or right operation of a person or thing; moral or ethical virtue. See *Eth. Nic.* 2.1–6.

VULGAR (*banausos*): characteristic of craftsmen engaged in manual work (as distinct from laborers, farmers, or merchants); more properly, characteristic of any work, art, or kind of learning incompatible with the education of free persons in virtue (cf. 8.2. 4–5). As a substantive, it will be translated "worker."

W

WELL OFF (*euporos*): a materially affluent person (literally, "having a ready supply"). While sometimes used as a synonym of "wealthy" (*plousios*), the term seems to have a wider application, probably extending to all citizens capable of affording heavy arms (cf. 3.17.4).

WORKER (*banausos*): see under VULGAR.

SELECT BIBLIOGRAPHY

Editions, Translations, and Commentaries

Aubonnet, Jean. 1960–89. *Aristote Politique*. 3 vols. Paris. [Text and translation]

Barker, Sir Ernest. 1946. *The Politics of Aristotle*. Oxford. [Translation]

Dreizehnter, Alois, 1970. *Aristoteles' Politik*. Munich. [Text]

Everson, Stephen. 1996. *Aristotle: The Politics and the Constitution of Athens*. Cambridge Texts in Political Thought. Cambridge. [Translation by Benjamin Jowett as revised by Jonathan Barnes]

Immisch, Otto. 1929. *Aristotelis Politica*. Leipzig. [Text]

Jowett, Benjamin. 1885. *The Politics of Aristotle*, 2 vols. Oxford. Revised edition by W. D. Ross, 2006. [Translation]

Keyt, David. 1999. *Aristotle: Politics Books V and VI*. Oxford. [Translation and commentary]

Kraut, Richard. 1997. *Aristotle: Politics Books VII and VIII*. Oxford. [Translation and commentary]

Lord, Carnes. 1984. *Aristotle, The Politics*. Chicago. [Translation]

Newman, William L. 1887–1902. *The Politics of Aristotle*, 4 vols. Oxford. [Text and commentary]

Rackham, H. 1972. *Aristotle, Politics*. Loeb Classical Library. Cambridge, MA. [Text and translation]

Robinson, Richard. 1962. *Aristotle: Politics Books III and IV*. Oxford. Reprinted with a supplementary essay by David Keyt, 1995. [Translation and commentary]

Ross, W. D. 1957. *Aristotelis Politica*. Oxford. [Text]

Saunders, Trevor. 1995. *Aristotle: Politics Books I and II*. Oxford. [Translation and commentary]

Schütrumpf, Eckart. 1991. *Aristoteles Politik*, 2 vols. (Books I-III). Berlin. [Translation, and commentary]

Schütrumpf, Eckart, and Hans-Joachim Gierke. 1996. *Aristoteles Politik* (Books IV-VI). Berlin. [Translation and commentary]

Schütrumpf, Eckart. 2005. *Aristoteles Politik* (Books VII-VIII). Berlin. [Translation and commentary]

Simpson, Peter L. Phillips. 1997. *The Politics of Aristotle*. Chapel Hill, NC. [Translation]

Simpson, Peter L. Phillips. 1998. *A Philosophical Commentary on the Politics of Aristotle*. Chapel Hill, NC. [Commentary]

Sinclair, Thomas A. 1962. *Aristotle: The Politics*. Harmondsworth, UK. Revised edition by Trevor Saunders, 1981, 1992. [Translation]

Susemihl, Franz, and Robert D. Hicks. 1894. *The Politics of Aristotle*. London. [Text and commentary on books I–III, VII–VIII]

Other Works of Aristotle

Ath. Pol. = Constitution of Athens. F. G. Kenyon, *Aristotelis Atheniensium Republica*. Oxford, 1920. [Text] Kurt von Fritz and Ernst Kapp, *Aristotle's Constitution of Athens and Related Texts*. New York, 1950. [Translation and commentary]. P. J. Rhodes, *A Commentary on the Aristotelian Athenaion Politeia*. Oxford, 1981. [Commentary]

Eth. Eud. = Eudemian Ethics. R. R. Walzer and J. M. Mingay, *Aristotelis Ethica Eudemia*. Oxford, 1991. [Text] Michael Woods, *Aristotle's Eudemian Ethics, Books I, II, and VIII*. Oxford, 1982. [Translation and commentary]

Eth. Nic. = Nicomachean Ethics. I. Bywater, *Aristotelis Ethica Nicomachea*. Oxford, 1894. [Text] Robert C. Bartlett and Susan D. Collins, *Aristotle's Nicomachean Ethics*. Chicago, 2011. [Translation].

Fr. = Aristotelis qui ferebantur Librorum Fragmenta. V. Rose. Leipzig, 1886.

Poet. = Poetics. Rudolf Kassel, *Aristotelis De Arte Poetica Liber*. Oxford, 1965. [Text] Richard Janko, *Poetics: With the Tractatus Coislinianus, Reconstruction of Poetics II, and the Fragments of the On Poets (Bk. I)*. Indianapolis, 1987. [Translation] Stephen Halliwell, *Aristotle's Poetics*. London, 1986. [Commentary]

Protr. = Protrepticus. Ingemar Düring, *Aristotle's Protrepticus: An Attempt at Reconstruction*. Göteborg, 1961. [Text, translation, and commentary]

Rhet. = Rhetoric. W. D. Ross, *Aristotelis Ars Rhetorica*. Oxford, 1959. [Text] George A. Kennedy, *On Rhetoric: A Theory of Civic Discourse*. Oxford, 1991. [Translation and commentary]

Other Classical Reference Works

DK = H. Diel and W. Kranz, *Die Fragmente der Vorsokratiker*, 2 vols. Berlin, 1964.

FGH = F. Jacoby, *Die Fragmente der griechischen Historiker*. Berlin, 1923.

Books

Aalders, G. J. D. 1968. *Die Theorie der Gemischten Verfassung im Altertum*. Amsterdam.

Aubenque, Pierre, ed. 1993. *Aristote Politique: Études sur la Politique d'Aristote*. Paris.

Barker, Sir Ernest. 1959. *The Political Thought of Plato and Aristotle*. New York.

Bien, Günther. 1973. *Die Grundlegung der politischen Philosophie bei Aristoteles*. Freiburg and Munich.

Bodéüs, Richard. 1982. *Le philosophe et la cité: Recherches sur les rapports entre morale et politique dans la pensée d'Aristote*. Paris. Translated as *The Political Dimension of Aristotle's Ethics*, by Jan Edward Garrett. 1993. Albany, NY.

Bodéüs, Richard. 1991. *Politique et philosophie chez Aristote*. Namur.

Chroust, Anton-Hermann. 1979. *Aristotle: New Light on His Life and on Some of His Lost Works*, 2 vols. Notre Dame and London.

Collins, Susan D. 2006. *Aristotle and the Rediscovery of Citizenship*. Cambridge.

Cooper, John M. 1975. *Reason and Human Good in Aristotle*. Cambridge, MA.

Davis, Michael. 1996. *The Politics of Philosophy: A Commentary on Aristotle's Politics*. Lanham, MD.

Düring, Ingemar. 1957. *Aristotle in the Ancient Biographical Tradition*. Göteborg.

Frank, Jill. 2005. *A Democracy of Distinction: Aristotle and the Work of Politics*. Chicago.

Hansen, M. H. 1991. *The Athenian Democracy in the Age of Demosthenes: Structure, Principles and Ideology*. Oxford.

Hansen, M. H. 1998. *Polis and City-State: An Ancient Concept and Its Modern Equivalent*. Copenhagen.

Hansen, M. H., ed. 1993. *The Ancient Greek City-State*. Copenhagen.

Irwin, Terence H. 1988. *Aristotle's First Principles*. Oxford.

Jaeger, Werner. 1948. *Aristotle: Fundamentals of the History of his Development*, trans. Richard Robinson, 2nd ed. London.

Johnson, Curtis N. 1990. *Aristotle's Theory of the State*. New York.

Kamp, Andreas. 1985. *Die politische Philosophie des Aristoteles und ihre metaphysischen Grundlagen*. Freiburg and Munich.

Kenny, Anthony. 1992. *Aristotle on the Perfect Life*. Oxford.

Keyt, David and Fred D. Miller, Jr., eds. 1991. *A Companion to Aristotle's Politics*. Oxford.

Kraut, Richard. 1989. *Aristotle on the Human Good*. Princeton.

Kraut, Richard. 2002. *Aristotle: Political Philosophy*. Oxford.

Kraut, Richard and Steven Skultety, eds. 2005. *Aristotle's Politics: Critical Essays*. Lanham, MD.

Lord, Carnes. 1982. *Education and Culture in the Political Thought of Aristotle*. Ithaca, NY.

Lord, Carnes and David K. O'Connor, eds. 1991. *Essays on the Foundations of Aristotelian Political Science*. Berkeley.

Meikle, Scott. 1994. *Aristotle's Economic Thought*. Oxford.

Miller, Fred D., Jr. 1995. *Nature, Justice, and Rights in Aristotle's Politics*. Oxford.

Mulgan, R. G. 1977. *Aristotle's Political Theory*. Oxford.

Nichols, Mary P. 1992. *Citizens and Statesmen: A Study of Aristotle's Politics*. Lanham, MD.

Nippel, Wilfried. 1980. *Mischverfassungstheorie und Verfassungsrealität in Antike und früher Neuzeit*. Stuttgart.

Ober, Josiah. 1989. *Mass and Elite in Democratic Athens: Rhetoric, Ideology, and the Power of the People*. Princeton.

Ober, Josiah. 1998. *Political Dissent in Democratic Athens: Intellectual Critics of Popular Rule*. Princeton.

Ober, Josiah, and Charles Hedrick, eds. 1996. *Demokratia: A Conversation on Democracy, Ancient and Modern*. Princeton.

Patzig, Günther, ed. 1990. *Aristoteles' "Politik."* Akten des XI. Symposium Aristotelicum. Göttingen.

Rowe, Christopher, and Malcolm Schofield, eds. 2000. *The Cambridge History of Greek and Roman Political Thought*. Cambridge.

Salkever, Stephen G. 1990. *Finding the Mean: Theory and Practice in Aristotelian Political Philosophy*. Princeton.

Strauss, Leo. 1953. *Natural Right and History*. Chicago.

Strauss, Leo. 1964. *The City and Man*. New York.

Swanson, Judith A. 1992. *The Public and the Private in Aristotle's Political Philosophy*. Ithaca, NY.

Swanson, Judith A. and C. David Corbin. 2009. *Aristotle's Politics: A Reader's Guide*. London and New York.

Tessitore, Aristide, ed. 2002. *Aristotle and Modern Politics: The Persistence of Political Philosophy*. Notre Dame, IN.

Weil, Raymond. 1960. *Aristote et l'histoire*. Paris.

Yack, Bernard. 1993. *The Problems of a Political Animal: Community, Justice, and Conflict in Aristotelian Political Thought*. Berkeley.

Articles

Ambler, Wayne H. 1985. "Aristotle's Understanding of the Naturalness of the City." *Review of Politics* 47:163–85.

Kahn, Charles H. 1990. "The Normative Structure of Aristotle's *Politics*." Patzig (1990), 369–84.

Kullmann, W. 1980. "Der Mensch als politisches Lebewesen bei Aristoteles." *Hermes* 108: 419–43. Revised and translated in Keyt and Miller, 94–117.

Lord, Carnes. 1981. "The Intention of Aristotle's *Rhetoric*." *Hermes* 109: 326–39.

Lord, Carnes. 1986. "On the Early History of the Aristotelian Corpus." *American Journal of Philology* 107: 137–61.

Lord, Carnes. 1991. "Aristotle's Anthropology." Lord and O'Connor (1991), 49–73.

Lord, Carnes. 1996. "Aristotle and the Idea of Liberal Education." Ober and Hedrick (1996), 271–88.

Mulgan, Richard. 1974. "Aristotle's Doctrine that Man is a Political Animal." *Hermes* 102: 438–45.

Rowe, Christopher J. 1977. "Aims and Methods in Aristotle's *Politics*." *Classical Quarterly* 27: 159–72. Revised version in Keyt and Miller, 57–74.

Salkever, Stephen G. 1991. "Women, Soldiers, Citizens: Plato and Aristotle on the Politics of Virility." Lord and O'Connor (1991), 165–90.

Salkever, Stephen G. 2007. "Teaching the Question: Aristotle's Philosophical Pedagogy in the *Nicomachean Ethics* and the *Politics*." *Review of Politics* 69: 192–214.

Touloumakos, Johannes. 1990–98. "Aristoteles' 'Politik' 1925–1985." Part 1. *Lustrum* 32 (1990): 177–282. Part 2. *Lustrum* 35 (1993): 181–289. Part 3. *Lustrum* 39 (1997): 8–305. Part 3 (concluded). *Lustrum* 40 (1998): 7–197.

Vander Waerdt, Paul A. 1985a. "The Plan and Intention of Aristotle's Ethical and Political Writings." *Illinois Classical Studies* 16:231–53.

Vander Waerdt, Paul. A. 1985b. "The Political Intention of Aristotle's Moral Philosophy." *Ancient Philosophy* 5: 77–89.

John R. Wallach. 1992. "Contemporary Aristotelianism," *Political Theory* 20:613–41.

INDEX OF PROPER NAMES

GENERAL INDEX

harmonies, 235–38
hatred, as reason for attacking tyran-
    nies, 160
health, cities and, 205
herdsmen, as best people for democ-
    racy, 177
honors, inequality of, 40
household management, 5–6, 72; at-
    tention to human beings and, 21–23;
    getting goods and, 12–13; parts of art
    of, 21
household rule, 21–24
households, 2–3

instruments, playing of, 232–35

judicial institutions, 127–28
just actions, 209
justice: equality and, 81–83; oligarchic
    and democratic views of, 75–77

kingship, 73–74, 99; absolute, 92–93;
    aptness for, 94–96; aristocracy and,
    154, 155; attacks on, 156–58; com-
    mon precaution of, 165–66; goal of,
    155; goals of, 166; as guardianship,
    155; moderation as source of preserva-
    tion of, 161; offspring and, 91–92; rule
    according to law and, 92–94; as rule
    of best man, 90–91; rules of law and,
    90–96; sources of destruction of, 160;
    Sparta and, 51, 51n92, 90; types of,
    87–89; tyranny and, 154–55; varieties
    of, 87–89

land, distribution of, farmers and, 204
law: Hippodamos and, 42–44; rule of,
    kingship and, 90–96
Laws (Plato), xxxi–xxxii, 52; regime of,
    35–38
legislation, xxx
legislators, regimes and, 58–61
leisure, 214–15; education and, 209–16
letters, 225

life, divisions of, 213
living well, 209
Lyceum, xvii–xix

man, 2; excellent citizen and good,
    67–69; methods of becoming good
    and excellent, 210; as political animal,
    4, 72
markets, cities and, 208
marriage, 216–18
masters, 6, 8; political rule and, 11–12
mastery, 72
men's messes, 54
Metaphysics (Aristotle), xxi
middling element, xiii–xiv
military activities, cities and, 205–6
monarchies: preservation of, 161–66;
    revolution in, 154–60
monarchy, 114. See also kingship
motion of illegality, 9, 9n28
multitude: democracy and, 177–78, 181–
    82; desirable qualities of persons in,
    198–200; parts of, 181
music, 225, 228–32; culture and, 235–38;
    playing instruments and, 232–35; pro-
    fessional education in, 234–35; sing-
    ing and, 232–35
music education, 228–35

nations, 3n10
natural ruling, 2
natural slavery, 11n31
nature, 210, 216; cities and, 4–5; impulse
    toward community and, 5; slavery
    and, 7–11
naval power, cities and, 198
Nicomachean Ethics (Aristotle), xix,
    xxix–xxx, xxxi, xxxii, xxxiii, xxxiv

offices, 118, 123–27; democracy and,
    182–86
officials: requirements for, 151–54; selec-
    tion of, 125–27
offspring. See children